ROTHMANS SNOOKER Y 1987-88

Editor: Janice Hale

ROTHMANS

Queen Anne Press

A Queen Anne Press BOOK

© **Rothmans Publications Ltd 1987**

First published in Great Britain in 1987 by
Queen Anne Press, a division of
Macdonald & Co (Publishers) Ltd
3rd Floor
Greater London House
Hampstead Road
London NW1 7QX

A BPCC plc Company

Front cover photograph: Jimmy White

Back cover photograph: Jimmy White and Rex Williams at the Rothmans Grand Prix 1986

All photographs: Eric Whitehead Picture Agency, Bolton

British Library Cataloguing in Publication Data

Rothmans snooker yearbook — Vol. 3
(1987–8).
1. Snooker — Periodicals
794.7'35'05   GV900.S6

ISBN 0-356-14690-1

Typeset by Acorn Bookwork, Salisbury, Wiltshire

Printed and bound in Great Britain by Hazell, Watson & Viney Ltd, Member of the BPCC Group, Aylesbury, Buckinghamshire

CONTENTS

ACKNOWLEDGEMENTS

The editor would like to thank the following for their assistance in compiling this book:
Clive Everton, editor of *Snooker Scene* magazine
Julie Kane, whose statistical research has been invaluable

FOREWORD
FROM ROTHMANS PUBLICATIONS LTD

The *Rothmans Snooker Yearbook* seems like an old favourite even though this is only the third edition.

In a short space of time 'the Rothmans' has established itself as the foremost reference book in the snooker world, valued by players and supporters alike as *the* book to settle all arguments.

During this publication's lifetime, Rothmans' involvement with snooker has continued to grow in other ways. Jimmy White won the third Rothmans Grand Prix, Steve Davis the first Rothmans Matchroom League, and a National Snooker Championship was launched for those players who are not members of the WPBSA.

The latter is a new competition, but you can be sure the winner will find his name in next year's Rothmans Snooker Yearbook, along with all the others that matter.

SNOOKER: THE STATE OF THE ART

Janice Hale, Editor, *Rothmans Snooker Yearbook*

Snooker is Britain's most popular television sport. Its viewing figures are consistently high and no one can question the quality of the presentation, skill and sportsmanship which actually appears on the screen. Promoters have perfected the art of creating a setting which provides the right ambience of intimacy, luxury and stillness while still generating the excitement which must accompany any sport.

What the viewing public does not see, however, is the amount of planning and organization which has to be done for the pre-televised stages of the six ranking tournaments.

The World Professional Billiards and Snooker Association (WPBSA) has 128 playing members who are eligible to compete in ranking tournaments. In addition it has non-tournament members who can compete only in the Embassy World Championship. In five ranking tournaments – the Fidelity Unit Trusts International, Rothmans Grand Prix, Tennents UK Open, Mercantile Credit Classic and Dulux British Open (the latter withdrew sponsorship in 1987) – the top 32 players in the world rankings are exempt until the last 64 stage of the tournament. In the Embassy World Championship, the top 16 players are exempt until the last 32 stage. To whittle the remaining membership down to the appropriate number to meet these exemptions, preliminaries are staged in surroundings far removed from the cockpit atmosphere of the later stages. In these preliminary rounds, play is on six or even eight tables, each partitioned from the others, with seating for comparatively few spectators. Often, there are just the two competitors, referee, marker and recorder. For the lowest-ranked players to proceed from the obscurity of the multi-table surroundings to being the cynosure of attention at centre stage means winning three rounds, the last against a player ranked in the top 32.

But the system does work. New faces are now beginning to appear on television and should do so in increasing numbers, now that the ranking list is based only on performances in the preceding two seasons as opposed to the three which was the case until two seasons ago.

With the introduction of new restrictions on televising tobacco-sponsored sport, fears were expressed that the tobacco companies might no longer be so interested in sponsoring snooker. These fears appear unfounded in the short term, but the issue could come to a head when the BBC contract expires in 1990.

Barry Hearn, the game's leading private sector promoter and manager, threw down the gauntlet at the end of last season by offering £5m for the television and promotional rights for the World Championship for the five years from 1991, with an option to purchase for

£7.5m for the five years after that. It is unlikely that this will be the final offer and, should a scheme of this sort be accepted, snooker may well enter an entirely different sphere of operation as the twenty-first century approaches. But if this were to transpire, snooker would enter the big league of genuine worldwide sports and its administration and political machinery will have to be of a similar calibre.

The usual tabloid run of snooker and sex stories can be shrugged off, but the latest issues are far more serious than this sort of trivia. The 1987 World Championship was dominated away from the table by the drugs issue. The WPBSA instituted drug testing for the 1985 World Championship, following rumours that a few players took illegal drugs. One subsequently admitted cocaine addiction for which he has now been treated.

The sport's administration, in an attempt to prevent the use of illegal drugs, had failed to realise the full implications of adopting the IOC/ Sports Council drug testing policy. Not only are illegal drugs, like cocaine, banned, but so too are those which tend to enhance performance. Very quickly, the WPBSA found itself in a quandary which has still not been resolved. Rex Williams, the WPBSA's chairman, has long been known to take beta blockers, a drug used to combat heart conditions and anxiety. Beta blockers are on the IOC banned list. The WPBSA decided that if the drug was prescribed by a doctor to treat a medical condition, they would permit its use. It emerged that John Spencer, Alex Higgins and Neal Foulds all took them. Controversy followed and, as we go to press, consultations between the Sports Council and the WPBSA are imminent.

Beta blockers are banned in other comparable sports. Sports medicine experts insist that there are alternative drugs which have the same medical effects without performance-enhancing capabilities. Other doctors remain sceptical of this.

Although the drugs issue has attracted most media attention, the game has been beset by other difficulties over the past year. Problems surrounded the WPBSA-instituted events in Belgium and Canada; the Belgian Classic fell into abeyance last season, and the future of the Canadian Masters is now in doubt after a sponsorship tangle. Furthermore, for the second year in succession, only a last-minute sponsor (Tuborg) could be found for the World Cup – and for only half the prize-money. The first ranking tournament of the season will therefore be enjoying its fourth sponsor in four years in September, as Fidelity Unit Trusts take over an event created by Jameson with Goya following in 1985 and BCE in 1986.

But while there have been problems with some WPBSA-promoted events, Barry Hearn, with his Matchroom team of Steve Davis, Jimmy White, Neal Foulds, Terry Griffiths, Dennis Taylor, Willie Thorne and Tony Meo, has been epitomising the virtues of private enterprise, spreading the game worldwide with prestigious sponsorships and shrewd public relations, whether in China or Brazil, Cleethorpes or Brighton.

The Hearn-initiated Straight Pool/Snooker/Nine Ball triathlon between Davis and the American Pool virtuoso Steve Mizerak enabled snooker to obtain prime-time American television coverage for the first time. The eight-man Rothmans Matchroom League, taking top-class snooker to places which rarely see it except on television, succeeded as spectacularly as a previous league venture failed under other management.

When the game was struggling, government by the players themselves seemed the ideal situation, but with growth came complexity. Players now – simply because they are players – do not have the independence, the specialist knowledge or width of thought and experience to cope with many of the problems which arise. As with any business which develops from sole proprietor to limited company to multi-national, it needs to acquire people with experience in specialised fields, and a chief executive who can cope with more or less anything that occurs with authority and the knowledge that the administration will back him.

Such changes can take a long time, but to secure the game's future they must come about. Encouragingly, there has been some modest progress and change of attitude.

Millions of people play, watch and enjoy the game. It has been around for 112 years. It was people who developed the sport, and it is to the public that snooker ultimately belongs. The game's administration has a duty to nurture it, cherish it, and keep it decent, honest and truthful.

CORONATION STREET WITH BALLS

Gordon Burn

Fifteen years ago I stayed at the same £5-a-night boarding house in Birmingham as Alex Higgins, and sat on a pile of beer crates in a working men's club for six nights to watch Higgins – who was then still only 22 – become the youngest-ever World Snooker Champion. 'The Hurricane', as he was already coming to be known, celebrated by cracking open the single bottle of sparkling wine that had been standing on the top of the wardrobe in his attic room back at 'The Pebbles' all week. He took home £480 for the week's work and estimated that, with his youth and flair – 'I'm a fiend for this game, it's an instinct, a natural gift, I'm . . . I'm phenomenal', he once boasted, scandalizing the snooker establishment – he stood to make as much as £20,000 in the coming year.

Two years ago I stayed at the Hong Kong Hilton with Steve Davis, Dennis Taylor and the other members of Barry Hearn's 'Matchroom' team, and travelled as part of a convoy of air-conditioned 'stretch-limos' to Kowloon, the New Territories and other parts of the Crown colony to watch Davis, Taylor and the rest perform their 'snooker cabaret' and open the giant new family-orientated snooker centres which have spread like a plague through Hong Kong in the last two years, replacing the old backstreet snooker parlours with their inevitable 'triad' and underworld connections.

In addition to what they were earning in the Far East from Riley Leisure (the snooker table and equipment manufacturers in which Steve Davis and his manager, Barry Hearn, have a substantial holding), Davis, Taylor, Terry Griffiths and Tony Meo (soon to have their ranks swollen by Jimmy White, Neal Foulds and Willie Thorne) were also being paid to endorse Goya 'Matchroom' men's toiletries, Cathay Pacific Airlines and Camus Cognac. By the end of the year, Hearn was to add Courage breweries, Ebel watches, Fabrex textiles, CDS computers, Just Wise luggage, Pirelli footwear – and a Top Ten record – to an endorsement portfolio which is the envy of British sport. It stands as a monument to the distance snooker has travelled since the night at Selly Park British Legion in 1972, when Alex Higgins sparked the revolution which saw snooker finally staggering like a hibernating rabbit into the bright lights of the second half of the twentieth century.

Less than a month before the beginning of the 1985 Far East summer tour, Higgins had been obliged to play his matches in the Australian Masters 25 miles away from where all the other competitors were playing theirs, because he was barred from entering the club where the tournament was being held. On his first visit, as the youngest-ever World Champion, he had been shown the door for calling a distinguished senior player 'an old no-hoper', and was evicted from his hotel for wrecking his room. Over the years this had become something of a signature activity: Higgins, who, like W. C. Fields, never tasted liquor before he was six, is probably more unwelcome at more hotels around the world than any other person in Britain.

Barry Hearn had only been in Hong Kong a few days when news of the latest Higgins 'outrage' reached him: 'Filthy Higgins groped me in front of my mother', was the story that had run in banner-headlines across the front page of that morning's *Daily Star*. The same story had also made page one of the *Sun*. 'How to ruin the image of snooker in one easy lesson!' Hearn groaned as the coach taking the officials and players to the Queen Elizabeth Stadium merged with commuter traffic splashing through the Central business district of Hong Kong.

According to Barry Hearn, it is the 'excitable youngsters' who identify with the Kirk Stevenses and the Higginses of the snooker world, and it's the grans who like Steve Davis. 'It's comfortable,' as Hearn says, 'it's nice, it's controlled, it doesn't frighten anybody. You can turn it off.' Not frightening anybody has been Barry Hearn's main aim in his campaign to turn snooker from a pastime associated almost exclusively with no-goods and no-hopers, into the most popular sport on British television and a multi-million-pound leisure industry.

Even as late as the mid-1970s, when most people thought of billiard halls they thought of somewhere like The Regal in Eric Street in the East End of London, the notorious hall owned throughout the fifties by Ronnie and Reggie Kray. When Barry Hearn decided to go into snooker seriously, which he did when he signed his one and only management contract with Steve Davis in 1978, he knew that his first task was to take a rag to the old public perception of snooker and wipe it clean. It is a tribute to his marketing abilities that he achieved what to many people appeared impossible in a period of a little over five years. In many ways, the story of snooker in the television age is the story of the 'Matchroom Professionals'.

The up-grading of the image of snooker and its consequent appeal to a mass audience has not been achieved without cost to the players. In the course of the season I spent travelling with the snooker 'circus' (researching my book *Pocket Money*), Kirk Stevens admitted that he was 'hopelessly addicted' to cocaine; Alex Higgins's marriage finally disintegrated in a welter of sensational headlines and messy public recrimination, and Tony Knowles, who had been accused by a former girlfriend of 'wearing ladies' undies for sex romps', was admitted to hospital when his whole body erupted in huge abscesses and boils. Higgins, of course, has since suffered a five-tournament ban for head-butting WPBSA tournament director, Paul Hatherell; and there have been further accusations of drug-taking involving leading players.

Even the £350,000-a-year-plus players associated with the Hearn camp are not immune to the tensions and pressures. In Hong Kong,

Terry Griffiths, alienated and turned in on himself, often seemed close to tears. 'I've changed a great deal over the last few years. And, being truthful, I don't really like the kind of person I've turned into. I used to be more of a giver in life,' Griffiths told me. He meditates before and during matches. So does Tony Meo. Willie Thorne at the time was attending a Harley Street specialist for hypnotherapy and positive motivational training. In the early stages of the 1987 World Championship, it was announced that Neal Foulds had been prescribed beta-blockers for an unusually rapid heartbeat which was attributable to stress.

Much of this, however, makes for the soap-opera element which is what Barry Hearn is convinced keeps the home audience tuning in in their millions, month after month, year after year. Some of the most familiar statistics in recent sporting history have attached themselves to the last frames of the final in which Dennis Taylor miraculously snatched the World Championship title out from under the nose of Steve Davis. Eighteen-and-a-half million people stayed up until the early hours of 29 April, 1985, smashing all viewing records – it was the highest-ever British television audience for a sporting event, the highest BBC2 audience ever recorded, and the highest-ever after-midnight audience in Britain.

Hearn is an unshakeable proponent of the 'Coronation Street with balls' theory of snooker. 'I've been waiting for Higgins to be destroyed for years,' he told me. 'He's looking worse and worse. There's nothing on him. Sores all over his face. . . . But the fact is: people *like* watching the process. I mean, you sit behind people that watch snooker, and they very rarely say: "Christ, that Steve Davis can't 'arf get some side on a ball!" They say: "Have you see that shirt? Have you seen Higgins's face? What d'you reckon he's got? Herpes?" This is what I think is one of the biggest things in our game.'

Among the other reasons frequently put forward to account for the phenomenal popularity of snooker, particularly among women (it is the only sport to have captured a bigger female than male audience in the history of sport on television) is the quiet delicacy and precision of the game, the simplicity of the formula and the cool, controlled demeanour of the players.

There is, of course, no one all-encompassing 'answer' to explain the hold snooker has come to have over the British television audience. But in an essay first published half a century ago, J. B. Priestley probably came as close as anybody has yet come to identifying the source of its appeal for the viewer. 'The voice in which he called out the scores was the most impersonal I have ever heard. It was a voice that belonged to solemn ritual, and it did as much as the four walls and the thickly-curtained windows to withdraw us from ordinary life,' Priestley wrote on an afternoon spent at Thurston's in Leicester Square, in the 1930s. 'After a few minutes, the world of daylight and buses and three o'clock winners receded, faded, vanished. I felt as if we were all sitting at ease somewhere at the bottom of the Pacific.'

Returning to the subject a couple of years later, Priestley seemed to come even closer to the heart of the matter. 'They hit the red and it vanishes into a pocket,' he wrote now. 'They have not to convince themselves that they have hit it and that it has probably gone into a pocket, as we have to do in our affairs. What can I do? What can you do? We think this, we imagine that, and we are never sure. These great cuemen are as sure as human beings can be . . . . What they can do, they can do, beyond any possible shadow of doubt.'

It is this more than anything, I am inclined to think, which sends half the country into work, the morning after a major televised snooker final, bleary-eyed.

THE 1986-87 SEASON: A REVIEW

Clive Everton, Editor, *Snooker Scene*

Through winning the Embassy World Championship for the fourth time, Steve Davis overtook John Spencer's total of three world titles and approaches Ray Reardon's tally of six. In an earlier age Fred Davis won eight; John Pulman won one on a tournament and successfully defended it five times on a challenge basis.

Joe Davis held the World title for the first 20 years it was in being, including the war years, so if his total of 14 titles is to be surpassed, the age of Steve Davis will have to last well into the 1990s.

Unlike snooker in any previous age, no one knows how long a player can last at or very near the top. In the age of Joe, there were very few professionals, even fewer of top class, and important matches lasted a week. There was no pressure from the media; many of the stresses and strains of modern life were not yet apparent.

The age of Steve is one in which TV coverage has given snooker new dimensions in terms of earning capacity and public interest. Long gone is the age of Joe when it was unthinkable that any championship match should be of fewer than the best of 73 frames. Now, even the World Final is only best of 35 and most matches in ranking tournaments are only best of nine – with all the intensity of preparation and effort that implies, not to mention the extremely fine margins that often separate winners and losers.

Steve Davis turned 30 just as he started the 1987–88 season. In the six ranking tournaments in 1986–87, he lost in one last 32, one last 16, and one quarter-final. He won the other three: the Tennents UK, the Mercantile Credit Classic and, of course, the Embassy World Championship. His 15-point lead at the top of the ranking list, at a point per round, is the equivalent of not turning up for $2\frac{1}{2}$ ranking tournaments.

As his career proceeds, the ongoing question will be how long can he maintain the love of the game and the intensity of desire to excel which fuels him. He has never done it for the money and with all the money he now has he is certainly not going to be doing it for the money in the future. But for all that he has won, the game will never become easier. Always he is there as a target, not only for his on-table rivals but for the public's and media's constant wish for new champions, new faces and new excitement.

Jimmy White improved from fifth to second in rankings, winning the Rothmans Grand Prix and the Dulux British Open. His game is better in the lower gears than it used to be; at 25 his nerve, his natural cuemanship is still in A1 condition. He lacks Davis's appetite for grinding out day to day excellence simply for his own satisfaction, but once the touchpaper of his inspiration is lit he is capable of anything.

Neal Foulds, who has improved dramatically in two seasons from twenty-third to thirteenth and now to third, accrued more ranking points last season (26) than anyone except Davis (29). Foulds is 24; he has both the game and the application to become World Champion; and with his sober lifestyle he is built to last.

For Cliff Thorburn, who dropped from second to fourth, the season has been a chapter of accidents. In the six ranking tournaments he was afflicted by tip trouble in two and, either 'flu or a throat virus prevented him from giving of his best in three of the other four. Even so, 123 other professionals would like to have done as well as he did.

Joe Johnson spent most of his year as the 1986 Champion overwhelmed by new pressures and expectations, but responded magnificently at the Crucible to get within one match of a successful title defence. This, and his fifth place in the ranking, forestalls anyone wanting to write him off as a one-performance wonder.

Terry Griffiths was consistent enough to improve from tenth to sixth and if he could sharpen his confidence to a slightly finer edge could start winning titles again.

Tony Knowles, number two to Davis only four seasons ago, slipped back from fourth to seventh, Dennis Taylor from third to eighth and Alex Higgins from sixth to ninth. Higgins, moreover, will have no ranking points to add from the first two ranking tournaments of the 1987–88 season, after having been suspended as punishment for a notorious head-butting incident during last season's Tennents UK Open and other assorted misdemeanours.

The most startling story of the season in many ways was that of Stephen Hendry, the 18-year-old Scottish Champion, who rose from fifty-first to twenty-third, reaching the quarter-finals of the Rothmans Grand Prix, the semi-finals of the Mercantile Credit Classic and the quarter-finals of the Embassy World Championship, losing 13-12 to Johnson after being four down with five to play. In flare, nerve, ability and confidence he has the stuff of which champions are made.

Jimmy White with the 1986 Rothmans Trophy

EDITOR'S NOTE

Because of the volume of statistics which modern snooker is constantly creating, the *Rothmans Snooker Yearbook* has had to limit to a certain extent which items are included under the various sections.

To qualify for inclusion in the 'Players' section, matches must have been played in a proper tournament and be of the best of nine frames or more.

The 'Circuit' section is more comprehensive, and here we have tried to record at least the result of the final in events where either the number of frames was insufficient, or where the early rounds were played on a 'round robin' basis.

RANKING LIST

As both the number of professionals and the number of tournaments have increased, the game's governing body, the World Professional Billiards and Snooker Association, have had to devise some form of ranking list, not only to quantify the standings of the players but also to enable them to seed tournaments.

The ranking list is drawn up at the end of each season and is based on performances over the past two seasons in events which are designated ranking tournaments.

To qualify for ranking status, a tournament must be open to all Snooker professionals. There are now six tournaments which qualify for world ranking points. These are: BCE International (1982–), Rothmans Grand Prix (1982–), Tennents UK Open (1984–), Mercantile Credit Classic (1984–), Dulux British Open (1985–) and the Embassy World Professional Championship (1976–).

When seedings are decided for each tournament, the defending titleholder is automatically seeded one with the world champion, if he is not the defending titleholder, two. The remaining seeds are then taken, in order, from the ranking list.

To separate players who tie on ranking points, merit points, 'A' points and 'frames won' in the first round have also been introduced to the system which also favours performances in the immediate preceding season.

Players seeded 1–16 are exempt until the last 32 of the World Championship but in the other five events, players seeded 1–32 are exempt only until the last 64.

The various points are awarded as follows. World Championship: winner – 10 ranking points; runner-up – 8 ranking points; losing semi-finalists – 6 ranking points; losing quarter-finalists – 4 ranking points; losers in last 16 – 2 ranking points; losers in last 32 – 1 ranking point (if qualifier), 2 merit points (if exempt); losers in last qualifying round – 2 merit points; losers in 2nd preliminary round – 1 merit point; losers in 3rd preliminary round – 1 'A' point; losers in 1st preliminary round: number of frames won. Other ranking events: winner – 6 ranking points; runner-up – 5 ranking points; losing semi-finalists – 4 ranking points; losing quarter-finalists – 3 ranking points; fifth round losers – 2 ranking points; fourth round losers – 1 ranking point; third round losers – 1 merit point; second round losers – 1 'A' point; first round losers: number of frames won.

WORLD RANKING LIST 1987

		1985–86						1986–87						Ranking Points	Merit Points	A Points	Frames
		Goya	Rothmans	Coral	Mercan-tile	Dulux	World	BCE	Rothmans	Tennents	Mercan-tile	Dulux	World				
1(1)	Steve Davis	3R	6R	6R	3R	6R	8R	3R	3R	6R	6R	1R	10R	61	0	0	0
2(5)	Jimmy White	5R	2R	4R	6R	1M	4R	1M	6R	2R	5R	6R	6R	46	2	0	0
3(13)	Neal Foulds	4R	1R	2R	3R	1R	1R	6R	4R	5R	1M	5R	6R	38	1	0	0
4(2)	Cliff Thorburn	6R	4R	2R	5R	2R	6R	5R	1M	3R	1R	4R	2M	38	3	0	0
5(8)	Joe Johnson	3R	2R	1R	3R	1R	10R	1R	1M	1R	1R	2R	8R	33	1	0	0
6(10)	Terry Griffiths	2R	3R	3R	1M	3R	4R	2R	2R	2R	3R	2R	4R	30	1	0	0
7(4)	Tony Knowles	1R	4R	3R	2R	1R	6R	2R	3R	3R	1M	4R	2M	29	3	0	0
8(3)	Dennis Taylor	4R	5R	4R	2R	1M	2M	2R	2R	1R	1M	3R	2R	25	4	0	0
9(6)	Alex Higgins	2R	2R	2R	3R	4R	2R	1R	2R	4R	1R	1M	2R	25	1	0	0
10(12)	Silvino Francisco	1M	3R	2R	1M	1R	2R	3R	4R	1R	3R	1R	2R	22	2	0	0
11(7)	Willie Thorne	2R	1M	5R	1M	5R	4R	1M	2R	2R	1M	2R	2M	22	6	0	0
12(16)	Rex Williams	1M	1R	2R	4R	2R	1R	2R	5R	1M	1R	2R	2M	20	4	0	0
13(17)	John Parrott	3R	1M	1R	1M	2R	2R	1M	1R	4R	3R	1M	2R	18	4	0	0
14(14)	Doug Mountjoy	1R	1R	1R	4R	1M	2R	1R	2R	1R	1M	2R	2R	17	2	0	0
15(29)	Dean Reynolds	2R	1M	1R	1R	1M	1R	3R	1M	2R	4R	1R	1R	16	3	0	0

16(27)	Mike Hallett	1M	1R	1R	1R	1R	2R	1M	2R	2R	1R	1R	4R	16	2	0	0
17(23)	Cliff Wilson	2R	3R	1M	1M	1R	1R	3R	1R	1M	3R	2R	2M	16	5	0	0
18(26)	Peter Francisco	1A	2R	1R	2R	2R	2M	4R	1R	1R	2R	1R	2M	16	4	1	0
19(19)	John Virgo	1R	1M	1R	1R	4R	1R	1R	1R	1R	1R	3R	1R	16	1	0	0
20(11)	Tony Meo	1R	2R	2R	2R	3R	2M	1M	3R	1R	2R	1M	2M	16	6	0	0
21(9)	Kirk Stevens	1M	3R	3R	1M	2R	4R	1M	1M	1M	1R	2R	2M	16	6	0	0
22(18)	John Campbell	2R	2R	1R	2R	2R	2R	1M	1R	1M	2R	1M	1R	15	3	0	0
23(51)	Stephen Hendry	1A	4F	2F	1R	1A	1R	1R	3R	1M	4R	1A	4R	14	1	3	6
24(20)	Eugene Hughes	1M	1R	1M	1M	1M	2R	4R	1M	2R	1M	1R	1R	13	5	0	0
25(21)	David Taylor	2R	1R	2R	1M	1M	2M	2R	1M	1R	1M	3R	1R	12	6	0	0
26(25)	Eddie Charlton	1M	1R	1M	1M	2R	2R	1R	1M	1R	2R	1R	2M	10	6	0	0
27(28)	Dave Martin	1R	1R	1R	1R	1R	1R	1M	1R	1R	1R	1R	2M	10	3	0	0
28(34)	John Spencer	1R	1M	1R	1M	1M	1R	1M	1M	2R	1R	3R	2M	9	7	0	0
29(30)	Barry West	4F	1M	1R	1R	1M	2M	1R	1M	1M	2R	1R	1R	9	6	0	4
30(22)	Murdo Macleod	2R	1M	2R	1R	2R	2M	1M	1M	1M	1M	1M	2R	9	8	0	0
31(31)	Steve Longworth	1M	2R	1M	1A	1R	2M	1M	1M	2R	1M	1M	2R	8	7	1	0
32(37)	Tony Drago	2F	2R	1R	4F	1M	1A	1R	1R	3R	1A	1M	1A	8	2	3	6
33(24)	Bill Werbeniuk	1R	1M	1M	2R	3R	1R	1M	1R	1M	1R	1M	2M	8	8	0	0
34(56)	Wayne Jones	1M	1R	1M	1A	1M	1M	1R	1R	3R	2R	1A	1M	7	6	2	0
35(39)	Dene O'Kane	1M	1M	1M	1R	1M	2M	1R	1A	1R	1A	1A	4R	7	6	3	0
36(32)	Jim Wych	1M	1A	1M	1M	3R	2M	1R	1M	1R	1M	1M	1R	7	7	1	0
37(35)	Steve Duggan	3R	1M	1A	1A	1M	1M	1R	1M	1A	2R	1R	1M	7	5	3	0

Rank	Player	1985–86						1986–87						Ranking Points	Merit Points	A Points	Frames
		Goya	Rothmans	Coral	Mercan-tile	Dulux	World	BCE	Rothmans	Tennents	Mercan-tile	Dulux	World				
38(15)	Ray Reardon	1M	1M	1R	1M	1M	2M	1R	1M	1R	1M	1R	2R	6	8	0	0
39(41)	Warren King	1R	1A	1M	1M	1A	2M	1R	1R	1M	1M	1R	1R	5	6	2	0
40(33)	Danny Fowler	1M	1R	1R	1M	1M	1R	1A	1A	1M	2R	1M	2M	5	7	2	0
41(53)	Robert Chaperon	1R	1A	1A	1M	1M	1M	2R	1R	1M	1M	1M	1M	4	7	2	0
42(38)	Marcel Gauvreau	1A	1A	1A	2R	1A	2M	2R	1A	1A	1M	1M	1M	4	5	6	0
43(48)	Paddy Browne	1A	1A	1M	1R	1R	1A	1A	2R	1A	1M	1A	1A	4	2	7	0
44(57)	Tommy Murphy	1R	1A	1M	1M	1A	2M	1M	1A	1M	1M	2R	2M	3	9	3	0
45(40)	Steve Newbury	1M	1M	1M	1A	1R	2M	1M	2R	1A	1M	1A	2M	3	9	3	0
46(55)	Tony Jones	1M	1M	1M	1R	1M	1M	1A	1M	1R	1M	1R	2M	3	9	1	0
47(43)	Mark Wildman	1M	1R	1M	1M	1R	2M	1M	1R	1A	1A	1M	1M	3	8	2	0
48(50)	Graham Cripsey	1M	1F	1R	1R	1A	4F	1A	1M	1M	1M	1R	2M	3	6	2	5
49(45)	Bob Harris	1R	1R	1A	1M	1M	1A	1A	1M	1M	1R	1M	1M	3	6	3	0
50(36)	Perrie Mans	1M	1M	1M	1R	1R	1R	–	–	–	1A	1A	–	3	3	2	0
51(71)	Jack McLaughlin	1A	1M	1M	1M	1M	1A	1M	1R	1M	1M	1R	1A	2	7	3	0
52(68)	Les Dodd	1M	1A	1M	1A	1M	2M	1M	1R	1A	1R	1A	1A	2	6	5	0
53(–)	Ken Owers	–	–	–	–	–	–	2R	2F	1M	1A	1M	1M	2	3	1	2
54(–)	Jon Wright	–	–	–	–	–	–	1A	1M	1M	1R	2F	1R	2	2	1	2

55(–) Mark Bennett	–	–	–	–	–	1M	1M	1M	8F	1M	1M	1M	1R	1R	2	2	0	12
56(65) Joe O'Boye	1A	1R	1M	1M	1M	1M	1M	1M	1M	1R	1R	1M	1M	1M	2	7	2	8
57(54) Malcolm Bradley	1R	1A	1M	1M	1M	1M	1A	1R	1A	1A	1A	1A	2M	2M	2	7	4	0
58(66) Roger Bales	1M	1M	2F	1A	2F	7F	1R	1A	1A	1A	1A	1A	1A	1A	2	2	6	9
59(49) Tony Chappel	1R	1M	1R	1A	1M	1M	1M	1A	1A	1A	1M	1A	2M	2M	2	7	4	0
60(46) Ray Edmonds	1A	1R	1M	1A	1M	1A	1A	1A	1A	1A	1A	1A	2M	2M	2	5	6	0
61(44) George Scott	1R	1R	1R	1A	1M	1A	1A	1A	1A	1A	1A	1M	1M	1M	2	5	5	0
62(47) Fred Davis	1A	1A	1R	1R	1A	1M	1A	1A	1A	1A	1A	1A	1A	1A	2	3	7	0
63(79) Geoff Foulds	1A	1M	1M	1A	1R	1M	1A	1A	1A	1M	1M	1A	1F	1A	1	5	5	1
64(112) Robby Grace	1A	–	–	1M	1A	1A	1A	1R	1A	1A	4F	1R	9F	–	1	1	2	13

65(91) Pat Houlihan 1-1-3-25; 66(101) Tony Kearney 1-0-8-15; 67(–) Steve James 1-0-3-7; 68(58) Paul Medati 1-9-4-0; 69(52) Graham Miles 1-8-3-0; 70(62) John Rea 1-7-4-0; 71(60) Matt Gibson 1-7-4-0; 72(59) Jimmy Van Rensberg 1-6-6-0; 73(63) Vic Harris 1-5-6-0; 74(61) Bernie Mikkelsen 1-5-6-0; 75(64) Ian Black 1-4-6-0; 76(42) Patsy Fagan 1-3-7-0; 77(70) Eddie Sinclair 0-8-4-0; 78(75) Mario Morra 0-6-6-0; 79(74) Colin Roscoe 0-6-5-3; 80(69) Robby Foldvari 0-6-7-0; 81(67) Ian Williamson 0-4-8-0; 82(77) Mike Watterson 0-4-2-8; 83(72) Dave Gilbert 0-4-5-17; 84(–) David Roe 0-3-3-0; 85(84) Bill Oliver 0-3-9-4; 86(86) Gino Rigitano 0-3-8-5; 87(82) Jim Bear 0-3-4-4; 88(73) Jim Donnelly 0-3-7-8; 89(76) Jack Fitzmaurice 0-3-5-8; 90(78) Mike Darrington 0-3-3-13; 91(–) Brian Rowswell 0-2-3-1; 92(85) Jim Meadowcroft 0-2-8-6; 93(87) Mick Fisher 0-2-7-8; 94(95) Greg Jenkins 0-2-5-8; 95(81) Dessie Sheehan 0-2-4-18; 96(98) Frank Jonik 0-1-7-12; 97(102) Glen Wilkinson 0-1-6-13; 98(104) Pascal Burke 0-1-5-23; 99(–) Paul Gibson 0-1-4-6; 100(–) Nigel Gilbert 0-1-4-1; 101(–) Ian Anderson 0-1-1-0; 102(110) Jim Rempe 0-1-1-2; 103(88) Bill Kelly 0-1-9-11; 104(83) John Dunning 0-1-5-3; 105(92) John Hargreaves 0-1-4-20; 106(93) Dennis Hughes 0-1-4-17; 107(90) Eddie McLaughlin 0-1-4-0; 108(94) Martin Smith 0-1-3-29; 109(96) Gerry Watson 0-1-0-8; 110(97) Paul Thornley 0-1-0-6; 111(99) Dave Chalmers 0-0-9-11; 112(103) Jack Rea 0-0-7-6; 113(100) Clive Everton 0-0-7-7; 114(106) Paul Watchorn 0-0-5-26; 115(108) Derek Mienie 0-0-3-29; 116(–) Terry Whitthread 0-0-2-12; 117(107) David Greaves 0-0-2-31; 118(–) François Ellis 0-0-2-10; 119(105) Joe Caggianello 0-0-2-7; 120(–) Mike Hines (NT) 0-0-1-6; 121(109) Bert Demarco (NT) 0-0-1-28; 122(111) Paddy Morgan (NT) 0-0-1-0; 123(113) Maurice Parkin (NT) 0-0-0-27; 124(114) Bernard Bennett (NT) 0-0-0-20; 125(117) James Giannaros (NT); 126(–) George Ganim (NT); 127(–) Lou Condo (NT); 128(–) Mannie Francisco (NT); 129(–) Steve Mizerak (NT); 130(–) Wayne Saunderson (NT)

Figure in brackets denotes previous year's ranking.

MONEY LIST 1986–87

		World	Ranking	Other	Breaks	Total £
1	Steve Davis	80,000	126,406	103,283	13,125	322,814
2	Jimmy White	24,000	150,265	29,993	21,500	225,759
3	Neal Foulds	24,000	124,593	17,500	6,000	172,093
4	Willie Thorne	3,375	15,084	128,430	5,950	152,839
5	Dennis Taylor	6,000	19,750	130,285	5,075	161,110
6	Cliff Thorburn	3,375	51,624	50,160	4,625	109,784
7	Tony Meo	3,375	16,984	77,733	4,000	102,092
8	Joe Johnson	48,000	12,826	40,327	–	101,153
9	Alex Higgins	6,000	27,554	65,271	1,000	99,825
10	Terry Griffiths	12,000	23,350	45,533	4,000	84,883
11	Tony Knowles	3,375	38,968	19,480	–	61,823
12	Stephen Hendry	12,000	26,257	21,000	500	59,757
13	Silvino Francisco	6,000	35,062	16,750	–	57,812
14	Rex Williams	3,375	43,959	10,125	–	57,459
15	John Parrott	6,000	30,242	9,500	–	45,742
16	Doug Mountjoy	6,000	14,420	24,208	1,000	45,628
17	Mike Hallett	12,000	14,718	15,750	–	42,468
18	Kirk Stevens	3,375	11,986	26,271	–	41,632
19	Eugene Hughes	3,375	20,203	16,271	–	39,849
20	Dean Reynolds	3,375	28,859	3,250	–	35,484
21	John Virgo	3,375	18,687	9,125	500	31,687
22	Peter Francisco	2,625	22,726	3,750	–	29,101
23	Ray Reardon	6,000	9,804	12,583	–	28,387
24	Cliff Wilson	2,625	21,326	1,437	–	25,388
25	David Taylor	3,375	16,808	3,500	–	23,683
26	John Spencer	2,625	17,890	1,687	875	23,077
27	Dene O'Kane	12,000	4,601	2,937	2,000	21,538
28	Eddie Charlton	2,625	12,460	5,099	–	20,184
29	Wayne Jones	1,375	16,179	2,375	–	19,929
30	Tony Drago	–	14,671	2,937	750	18,358
31	Les Dodd	–	5,851	12,500	–	18,351
32	John Campbell	3,375	9,804	4,800	–	17,979
33	Dave Martin	2,625	11,664	3,500	–	17,789
34	Bill Werbeniuk	2,625	7,015	7,604	500	17,744
35	Barry West	3,375	10,867	3,500	–	17,742
36	Steve Longworth	6,000	10,203	750	–	16,953
37	Warren King	3,375	7,035	5,998	–	16,408
38	Murdo Macleod	6,000	5,687	4,375	–	16,062
39	Tony Jones	2,625	8,109	4,500	–	15,234
40	Steve Newbury	2,625	5,984	5,937	–	14,546
41	Jim Wych	3,375	9,671	937	–	13,983

		World	Ranking	Other	Breaks	Total £
42	Steve Duggan	1,375	9,554	2,625	–	13,554
43	Joe O'Boye	1,375	7,148	5,000	–	13,523
44	Tommy Murphy	2,625	7,771	3,087	–	13,480
45	Danny Fowler	2,625	6,375	2,562	500	12,062
46	Tony Chappel	2,625	4,593	2,000	1,375	10,593
47	Robert Chaperon	1,375	7,695	937	–	10,007
48	Graham Cripsey	2,625	6,515	750	–	9,890
49	Ken Owers	1,375	5,250	2,562	–	9,187
50	Jack McLaughlin	–	8,742	150	–	8,892
51	Bob Harris	1,375	6,249	750	–	8,374
52	Jon Wright	3,375	4,937	–	–	8,312
53	Matt Gibson	1,375	3,281	3,437	–	8,093
54	Steve James	–	2,906	3,500	1,500	7,906
55	Mark Bennett	3,375	4,523	–	–	7,898
56	Malcolm Bradley	2,625	5,249	–	–	7,874
57	Mark Wildman	1,375	4,742	1,687	–	7,804
58	Paddy Browne	–	3,218	4,500	–	7,718
59	Marcel Gauvreau	1,375	5,031	937	–	7,343
60	Graham Miles	1,375	3,281	2,625	–	7,281
61	John Rea	–	5,687	1,250	–	6,937
62	Paul Medati	2,625	3,081	750	–	6,456
63	Ray Edmonds	2,625	2,078	1,687	–	6,390
64	Geoff Foulds	–	5,204	937	–	6,141
65	Eddie Sinclair	1,375	3,137	1,250	–	5,796
66	David Roe	–	3,828	1,875	–	5,703
67	Vic Harris	–	3,828	1,687	–	5,515
68 { Robbie Grace	–	4,218	937	–	5,155
68 { Colin Roscoe	–	3,718	1,437	–	5,155
70	George Scott	1,375	2,625	937	–	4,937
71	Patsy Fagan	–	1,203	3,087	–	4,290
72	Ian Williamson	–	2,406	1,687	–	4,093
73	Gino Rigitano	1,375	1,312	937	–	3,624
74	Mario Morra	–	3,609	–	–	3,609
75	Bill Oliver	2,625	–	937	–	3,562
76	Tony Kearney	–	2,421	1,000	–	3,421
77	Robbie Foldvari	–	2,078	1,224	–	3,302
78	Jimmy Van Rensberg	1,375	1,859	–	–	3,234
79	Billy Kelly	–	2,906	150	–	3,056
80	Jim Donnelly	–	–	2,937	–	2,937
81	Ian Black	1,375	765	500	–	2,640
82	Roger Bales	–	1,695	937	–	2,632

		World	Ranking	Other	Breaks	Total £
83	Brian Rowswell	–	2,625	–	–	2,625
84	Bernie Mikkelsen	–	2,406	–	–	2,406
85	Glen Wilkinson	–	1,312	816	–	2,128
86	Ian Anderson	–	1,203	816	–	2,019
87	Pascal Burke	–	765	1,000	–	1,765
88	Pat Houlihan	–	1,695	–	–	1,695
89	Greg Jenkins	–	1,093	408	–	1,501
90	Jim Rempe	1,375	–	–	–	1,375
91	Paul Gibson	–	1,312	–	–	1,312
	Nigel Gilbert	–	1,312	–	–	1,312
	Mike Watterson	–	1,312	–	–	1,312
94	Jim Bear	–	1,203	–	–	1,203
	Fred Davis	–	1,203	–	–	1,203
	Jim Meadowcroft	–	1,203	–	–	1,203
97	Mick Fisher	–	1,093	–	–	1,093
	Frank Jonik	–	1,093	–	–	1,093
	Dessie Sheehan	–	1,093	–	–	1,093
100	Dave Chalmers	–	–	937	–	937
	Mike Darrington	–	–	937	–	937
	Dave Gilbert	–	–	937	–	937
	Perrie Mans	–	–	937	–	937
104	Jack Fitzmaurice	–	–	750	–	750
105	Bert Demarco	–	–	500	–	500
106	James Giannaros	–	–	408	–	408
107	Jack Rea	–	–	150	–	150
	Paul Watchorn	–	–	150	–	150

Omprakesh Agrawal, Bernard Bennett, Joe Caggianello, John Dunning, François Ellis, Clive Everton, David Greaves, John Hargreaves, Mike Hines, Dennis Hughes, Eddie McLaughlin, Derek Mienie, Paddy Morgan, Maurice Parkin, Martin Smith, Paul Thornley, Gerry Watson and Terry Whitthread all failed to earn anything in prize money in major tournaments last season.

The 'Ranking' column takes into account the BCE International, Rothmans Grand Prix, Tennents UK Open, Mercantile Credit Classic and Dulux British Open.

The 'Other' column consists of Carlsberg Challenge, Langs Scottish Masters, Matchroom Trophy, Canadian Masters, Hofmeister World Doubles, Benson & Hedges Masters, Benson & Hedges Irish Masters, Tuborg World Cup, Camus Hong Kong Masters and national professional championships (except Canada – figures not available – and Ireland – not held at time of going to press).

THE PLAYERS

Figure in brackets denotes 1985–86 ranking.

IAN ANDERSON (Australia)

Born 2.4.46
Turned professional 1974
World ranking 101 (unranked)

1974	v Mans	1-8	1st round	World Championship
1975	v Condo	15-8	1st round	World Championship
	v Williams	4-15	2nd round	World Championship
1976	v Jack Rea	5-8	Qualifying	Embassy World Championship
1979	v S. Davis	1-9	Prelim	Embassy World Championship
1981	v Martin	3-9	Qualifying	Embassy World Championship
1982	v Houlihan	5-9	Qualifying	Embassy World Championship
	v Sinclair	2-5	Qualifying	Jameson International
	v David Taylor	1-5	1st round	Professional Players Tournament
1983	v King	6-10	Qualifying	Embassy World Championship
	v Oliver	9-1	Qualifying	Coral UK Championship
	v Dunning	2-9	Qualifying	Coral UK Championship
1984	v Watson	10-4	Qualifying	Embassy World Championship
	v Donnelly	6-10	Qualifying	Embassy World Championship
1985	v Kearney	10-8	Qualifying	Embassy World Championship
	v Browne	5-10	Qualifying	Embassy World Championship
	v King	2-8	Quarter-final	Australian Championship
1986	v Charlton	2-6	Quarter-final	Australian Championship
	v John Rea	1-5	2nd round	BCE International
	v Oliver	5-4	1st round	Rothmans Grand Prix
	v Murphy	5-4	2nd round	Rothmans Grand Prix

ROGER BALES (England)

Born 15.8.48
Turned professional 1984
World ranking 58 (66)
Best professional peformances Last 32 1986 Dulux British Open; last 32
BCE International.

1984	v Sheehan	5-2	Qualifying	Jameson International
	v Murphy	5-4	Qualifying	Jameson International
	v Fisher	5-3	Qualifying	Jameson International
	v Reynolds	4-5	Qualifying	Jameson International
	v Higgins	1-5	1st round	Rothmans Grand Prix
	v Chalmers	9-2	Qualifying	Coral UK Open

	v E. McLaughlin	9-4	Qualifying	Coral UK Open
	v Gauvreau	8-9	Qualifying	Coral UK Open
1985	v Bennett	5-1	Qualifying	Mercantile Credit Classic
	v Kelly	5-3	Qualifying	Mercantile Credit Classic
	v Virgo	1-5	Qualifying	Mercantile Credit Classic
	v Dodd	3-9	Qualifying	Tolly Cobbold English Championship
	v Black	6-4	Qualifying	Dulux British Open
	v Higgins	3-6	1st round	Dulux British Open
	v Chaperon	7-0	Qualifying	Embassy World Championship
	v Drago	5-2	1st round	Goya Matchroom Trophy
	v Edmonds	5-0	2nd round	Goya Matchroom Trophy
	v S. Davis	2-5	3rd round	Goya Matchroom Trophy
	v Smith	5-1	1st round	Rothmans Grand Prix
	v Fisher	5-3	2nd round	Rothmans Grand Prix
	v Wilson	1-5	3rd round	Rothmans Grand Prix
	v Simngam	2-9	1st round	Coral UK Open
1986	v Parkin	5-0	1st round	Mercantile Credit Classic
	v Fowler	4-5	2nd round	Mercantile Credit Classic
	v V. Harris	9-7	2nd round	Tolly Cobbold English Championship
	v Knowles	4-9	3rd round	Tolly Cobbold English Championship
	v Parkin	5-1	1st round	Dulux British Open
	v Dunning	*wo*	2nd round	Dulux British Open
	v Dennis Taylor	5-4	3rd round	Dulux British Open
	v Williams	4-5	4th round	Dulux British Open
	v Gilbert	7-10	Qualifying	Embassy World Championship
	v F. Davis	5-4	2nd round	BCE International
	v Stevens	5-3	3rd round	BCE International
	v Wilson	1-5	4th round	BCE International
	v F. Davis	4-5	2nd round	Rothmans Grand Prix
	v Cripsey	6-9	2nd round	Tennents UK Open
1987	v Murphy	2-5	2nd round	Mercantile Credit Classic
	v Owers	5-6	2nd round	Tolly Ales English Championship
	v Gauvreau	0-5	2nd round	Dulux British Open
	v Spencer	3-10	Qualifying	Embassy World Championship

JIM BEAR (Canada)

Born 8.8.50
Turned professional 1983
World ranking 87 (82)
Amateur career Runner-up 1982 World Amateur Championship.

1985	v Caggianello	4-5	1st round	Canadian Championship
	v Houlihan	5-2	1st round	Goya Matchroom Trophy
	v Donnelly	5-2	2nd round	Goya Matchroom Trophy
	v Johnson	1-5	3rd round	Goya Matchroom Trophy

v Kearney	3-5	1st round	Rothmans Grand Prix
v Demarco	9-1	1st round	Coral UK Open
v Watterson	9-0	2nd round	Coral UK Open
1986 v Kearney	0-5	1st round	Mercantile Credit Classic
v O'Boye	1-5	1st round	Dulux British Open
v Burke	10-8	Qualifying	Embassy World Championship
v Gauvreau	5-10	Qualifying	Embassy World Championship
v Chaperon	3-6	1st round	Canadian Championship
v Watchorn	5-1	1st round	BCE International
v Duggan	4-5	2nd round	BCE International
v B. Bennett	5-2	1st round	Rothmans Grand Prix
v Fowler	5-2	2nd round	Rothmans Grand Prix
v Williams	2-5	3rd round	Rothmans Grand Prix
v Everton	9-1	1st round	Tennents UK Open
v Edmonds	6-9	2nd round	Tennents UK Open
1987 v Jack Rea	10-5	Qualifying	Embassy World Championship
v Gauvreau	5-10	Qualifying	Embassy World Championship

MARK BENNETT (Wales)

Born 23.9.63
Turned professional 1986
World ranking 55
Amateur career 1985 Welsh champion.
Best professional performance Last 32 1987 Embassy World Championship, 1986 Rothmans Grand Prix.

1986 v Smith	5-4	1st round	BCE International
v Browne	5-1	2nd round	BCE International
v Virgo	1-5	3rd round	BCE International
v Watterson	5-1	1st round	Rothmans Grand Prix
v O'Kane	5-2	2nd round	Rothmans Grand Prix
v Macleod	5-1	3rd round	Rothmans Grand Prix
v Browne	0-5	4th round	Rothmans Grand Prix
v Sheehan	8-9	1st round	Tennents UK Open
1987 v Sheehan	5-3	1st round	Mercantile Credit Classic
v Black	5-3	2nd round	Mercantile Credit Classic
v Virgo	3-5	3rd round	Mercantile Credit Classic
v W. Jones	3-6	1st round	Matchroom Welsh Championship
v Morra	4-5	1st round	Dulux British Open
v Hargreaves	10-6	Qualifying	Embassy World Championship
v Mikkelsen	10-4	Qualifying	Embassy World Championship
v W. Jones	10-3	Qualifying	Embassy World Championship
v Werbeniuk	10-8	Qualifying	Embassy World Championship
v Dennis Taylor	4-10	1st round	Embassy World Championship

IAN BLACK (Scotland)

Born 11.12.54
Turned professional 1981
World ranking 75 (64)
Best professional performance 1981 Scottish champion.

1981	v Macleod	5-4	Quarter-final	Scottish Championship
	v E. McLaughlin	6-3	Semi-final	Scottish Championship
	v Gibson	**11-7**	**Final**	**Scottish Championship**
	v E. McLaughlin	5-3	Qualifying	Jameson International
	v Houlihan	4-9	Qualifying	Coral UK Championship
1982	v Parkin	9-6	Qualifying	Embassy World Championship
	v Williams	2-9	Qualifying	Embassy World Championship
	v Macleod	6-0	Quarter-final	Scottish Championship
	v Ross	6-4	Semi-final	Scottish Championship
	v Sinclair	7-11	Final	Scottish Championship
	v Fitzmaurice	3-5	Qualifying	Jameson International
	v Virgo	2-5	1st round	Professional Players Tournament
	v Fisher	3-9	Qualifying	Coral UK Championship
1983	v Morra	10-9	Qualifying	Embassy World Championship
	v Medati	10-4	Qualifying	Embassy World Championship
	v Mans	3-10	1st round	Embassy World Championship
	v E. McLaughlin	6-4	1st round	Scottsh Championship
	v Macleod	2-6	Semi-final	Scottish Championship
	v King	3-5	Qualifying	Jameson International
	v Spencer	2-5	1st round	Professional Players Tournament
	v Williamson	9-6	Qualifying	Coral UK Championship
	v White	1-9	1st round	Coral UK Championship
1984	v Hines	5-10	Qualifying	Embassy World Championship
	v Browne	5-4	Qualifying	Jameson International
	v Watterson	5-3	Qualifying	Jameson International
	v Macleod	3-5	Qualifying	Jameson International
	v P. Francisco	4-5	Qualifying	Rothmans Grand Prix
	v Chappel	3-9	Qualifying	Coral UK Open
1985	v J. McLaughlin	0-5	Qualifying	Mercantile Credit Classic
	v M. Gibson	2-6	1st round	Scottish Championship
	v Bales	4-6	Qualifying	Dulux British Open
	v Chalmers	4-10	Qualifying	Embassy World Championship
	v Rigitano	5-4	2nd round	Goya Matchroom Trophy
	v Mans	5-4	3rd round	Goya Matchroom Trophy
	v Duggan	1-5	4th round	Goya Matchroom Trophy
	v G. Foulds	3-5	2nd round	Rothmans Grand Prix
	v V. Harris	3-9	2nd round	Coral UK Open
1986	v G. Foulds	2-5	2nd round	Mercantile Credit Classic
	v Gibson	5-0	2nd round	Dulux British Open
	v S. Davis	2-5	3rd round	Dulux British Open
	v E. McLaughlin	6-4	Quarter-final	Canada Dry Scottish Championship
	v Hendry	2-6	Semi-final	Canada Dry Scottish Championship
	v B. Harris	10-8	Qualifying	Embassy World Championship

	v Newbury	2-10	Qualifying	Embassy World Championship
	v Wright	5-1	2nd round	BCE International
	v Charlton	0-5	3rd round	BCE International
	v Morra	4-5	2nd round	Rothmans Grand Prix
	v Watterson	3-9	2nd round	Tennents UK Open
1987	v M. Bennett	3-5	2nd round	Mercantile Credit Classic
	v John Rea	1-6	1st round	Scottish Championship
	v Roe	0-5	2nd round	Dulux British Open
	v Williamson	10-8	Qualifying	Embassy World Championship
	v O'Kane	2-10	Qualifying	Embassy World Championship

MALCOLM BRADLEY (England)

Born 8.7.48
Turned professional 1984
World ranking 57 (54)
Best professional performances Last 32 1985 Goya Matchroom Trophy,
1987 Mercantile Credit Classic.

1984	v Darrington	5-3	Qualifying	Jameson International
	v Jack Rea	5-2	Qualifying	Jameson International
	v Morra	3-5	Qualifying	Jameson International
	v Jonik	5-1	Qualifying	Rothmans Grand Prix
	v Virgo	0-5	1st round	Rothmans Grand Prix
	v V. Harris	9-8	Qualifying	Coral UK Open
	v Kelly	9-6	Qualifying	Coral UK Open
	v Meadowcroft	9-7	Qualifying	Coral UK Open
	v Hallett	8-9	Qualifying	Coral UK Open
1985	v Browne	3-5	Qualifying	Mercantile Credit Classic
	v Williamson	9-8	Qualifying	Tolly Cobbold English Championship
	v Knowles	8-9	Qualifying	Tolly Cobbold English Championship
	v Morra	6-2	Qualifying	Dulux British Open
	v David Taylor	6-3	1st round	Dulux British Open
	v Fowler	5-4	2nd round	Dulux British Open
	v S. Davis	2-5	3rd round	Dulux British Open
	v Mienie	10-4	Qualifying	Embassy World Championship
	v Mikkelsen	10-9	Qualifying	Embassy World Championship
	v Wych	7-10	Qualifying	Embassy World Championship
	v John Rea	5-1	2nd round	Goya Matchroom Trophy
	v Hallett	5-4	3rd round	Goya Matchroom Trophy
	v Johnson	2-5	4th round	Goya Matchroom Trophy
	v Gibson	4-5	2nd round	Rothmans Grand Prix
	v Jenkins	9-3	2nd round	Coral UK Open
	v White	4-9	1st round	Coral UK Open
1986	v Oliver	5-3	2nd round	Mercantile Credit Classic
	v N. Foulds	3-5	3rd round	Mercantile Credit Classic
	v Gilbert	9-5	2nd round	Tolly Cobbold English Championship
	v S. Davis	3-9	3rd round	Tolly Cobbold English Championship
	v Jack Rea	5-1	2nd round	Dulux British Open
	v Higgins	3-5	3rd round	Dulux British Open

	v Gilbert	7-10	Qualifying	Embassy World Championship
	v Wilkinson	5-4	2nd round	BCE International
	v Wych	2-5	3rd round	BCE International
	v Wright	0-5	2nd round	Rothmans Grand Prix
	v Meadowcroft	9-2	2nd round	Tennents UK Open
	v Parrott	4-9	3rd round	Tennents UK Open
1987	v Rowswell	5-4	2nd round	Mercantile Credit Classic
	v David Taylor	5-1	3rd round	Mercantile Credit Classic
	v White	0-5	4th round	Mercantile Credit Classic
	v D. Gilbert	6-3	2nd round	Tolly Ales English Championship
	v Fowler	3-6	3rd round	Tolly Ales English Championship
	v O'Boye	1-5	2nd round	Dulux British Open
	v Rowswell	10-6	Qualifying	Embassy World Championship
	v O'Boye	10-7	Qualifying	Embassy World Championship
	v Wych	7-10	Qualifying	Embassy World Championship

PADDY BROWNE (Republic of Ireland)

Born 1.3.65
Turned professional 1983
World ranking 43 (48)
Amateur career 1982 Irish champion.
Best professional performance Last 16 1986 Rothmans Grand Prix.

	v Murphy	2-5	Qualifying	Professional Players Tournament
1983	v Murphy	2-5	Qualifying	Professional Players Tournament
1984	v Duggan	10-9	Qualifying	Embassy World Championship
	v Roscoe	10-4	Qualifying	Embassy World Championship
	v Sinclair	1-10	Qualifying	Embassy World Championship
	v John Rea	5-2	Qualifying	Jameson International
	v Black	4-5	Qualifying	Jameson International
	v Duggan	2-5	Qualifying	Rothmans Grand Prix
	v G. Foulds	9-5	Qualifying	Coral UK Open
	v King	5-9	Qualifying	Coral UK Open
1985	v Bradley	5-3	Qualifying	Mercantile Credit Classic
	v Everton	5-0	Qualifying	Mercantile Credit Classic
	v Miles	5-3	Qualifying	Mercantile Credit Classic
	v White	2-5	1st round	Mercantile Credit Classic
	v Newbury	0-6	Qualifying	Dulux British Open
	v Murphy	3-6	Qualifying	Irish Championship
	v Anderson	10-5	Qualifying	Embassy World Championship
	v Morra	6-10	Qualifying	Embassy World Championship
	v B. Harris	3-5	2nd round	Goya Matchroom Trophy
	v B. Harris	3-5	2nd round	Rothmans Grand Prix
	v Chalmers	9-4	2nd round	Coral UK Open
	v Thorne	6-9	3rd round	Coral UK Open
1986	v Everton	5-0	2nd round	Mercantile Credit Classic
	v Wilson	5-3	3rd round	Mercantile Credit Classic
	v Gauvreau	3-5	4th round	Mercantile Credit Classic
	v Hendry	5-0	2nd round	Dulux British Open
	v Spencer	5-0	3rd round	Dulux British Open

	v Charlton	1-5	4th round	Dulux British Open
	v Hendry	9-10	Qualifying	Embassy World Championship
	v Burke	4-5	1st round	Strongbow Irish Championship
	v M. Bennett	1-5	2nd round	BCE International
	v Sheehan	5-4	2nd round	Rothmans Grand Prix
	v Johnson	5-2	3rd round	Rothmans Grand Prix
	v M. Bennett	5-0	4th round	Rothmans Grand Prix
	v Hendry	3-5	5th round	Rothmans Grand Prix
	v Williamson	4-9	2nd round	Tennents UK Open
1987	v Dunning	5-1	2nd round	Mercantile Credit Classic
	v Campbell	2-5	3rd round	Mercantile Credit Classic
	v Rigitano	4-5	2nd round	Dulux British Open
	v Wright	6-10	Qualifying	Embassy World Championship
	v Jack Rea	5-3	1st round	Matchroom Irish Championship
	v Burke	6-2	Quarter-final	Matchroom Irish Championship
	v Dennis Taylor	1-6	Semi-final	Matchroom Irish Championship

PASCAL BURKE (Republic of Ireland)

Born 19.6.32
Turned professional 1982
World ranking 98 (104)
Amateur career 1974 & 1976 Irish champion.

	v E. Hughes	2-6	Quarter-final	Irish Championship
1983	v E. Hughes	2-6	Quarter-final	Irish Championship
	v Meo	0-5	1st round	Benson & Hedges Irish Masters
	v Morgan	9-10	Qualifying	Embassy World Championship
	v G. Foulds	2-5	Qualifying	Jameson International
	v G. Foulds	5-4	Qualifying	Professional Players Tournament
	v Johnson	3-5	1st round	Professional Players Tournament
1984	v Kelly	10-7	Qualifying	Embassy World Championship
	v B. Harris	10-4	Qualifying	Embassy World Championship
	v Hallett	5-10	Qualifying	Embassy World Championship
	v Kearney	5-4	Qualifying	Jameson International
	v Newbury	0-5	Qualifying	Jameson International
	v Darrington	5-3	Qualifying	Rothmans Grand Prix
	v Meo	1-5	1st round	Rothmans Grand Prix
	v Longworth	4-9	Qualifying	Coral UK Open
1985	v Newbury	1-5	Qualifying	Mercantile Credit Classic
	v Chalmers	5-6	Qualifying	Dulux British Open
	v Kearney	6-4	Qualifying	Irish Championship
	v Higgins	0-6	Quarter-final	Irish Championship
	v Newbury	3-10	Qualifying	Embassy World Championship
	v Rempe	3-5	1st round	Goya Matchroom Trophy
	v Newbury	3-5	2nd round	Rothmans Grand Prix
	v Jenkins	5-9	1st round	Coral UK Open
1986	v D. Hughes	5-3	1st round	Mercantile Credit Classic
	v Chaperon	2-5	2nd round	Mercantile Credit Classic
	v Gilbert	1-5	1st round	Dulux British Open
	v Jim Bear	8-10	Qualifying	Embassy World Championship

	v Browne	5-4	1st round	Strongbow Irish Championship
	v E. Hughes	3-6	Quarter-final	Strongbow Irish Championship
	v Fitzmaurice	5-4	1st round	BCE International
	v T. Jones	5-4	2nd round	BCE International
	v Thorburn	0-5	3rd round	BCE International
	v Roscoe	5-3	1st round	Rothmans Grand Prix
	v Spencer	3-5	2nd round	Rothmans Grand Prix
	v Watterson	0-9	1st round	Tennents UK Open
1987	v King	0-5	2nd round	Mercantile Credit Classic
	v Scott	2-5	2nd round	Dulux British Open
	v Oliver	5-10	Qualifying	Embassy World Championship
	v Fagan	5-3	1st round	Matchroom Irish Championship
	v Browne	2-6	Quarter-final	Matchroom Irish Championship

JOE CAGGIANELLO (Canada)

Born 16.5.55
Turned professional 1983
World ranking 119 (105)

	v Darrington	10-7	Qualifying	Embassy World Championship
1984	v Darrington	10-7	Qualifying	Embassy World Championship
	v Oliver	7-10	Qualifying	Embassy World Championship
1985	v Jim Bear	5-4	1st round	Canadian Championship
	v Thorburn	2-6	Quarter-final	Canadian Championship
	v Hargreaves	5-2	1st round	Goya Matchroom Trophy
	v King	0-5	2nd round	Goya Matchroom Trophy
	v Watterson	1-5	2nd round	Rothmans Grand Prix
1986	v Watson	3-6	1st round	Canadian Championship
1987	v Dunning	7-10	Qualifying	Embassy World Championship

JOHN CAMPBELL (Australia)

Born 10.4.53
Turned professional 1982
World ranking 22 (18)
Amateur career 1979 Australian champion.
Best professional performances Last 16 1986 Embassy World Championship, 1985 Rothmans Grand Prix, 1985 Goya Matchroom Trophy, 1986 Mercantile Credit Classic, 1986 Dulux British Open, 1987 Mercantile Credit Classic; 1985 Australian champion.

	v Watterson	10-6	Qualifying	Embassy World Championship
1983	v Watterson	10-6	Qualifying	Embassy World Championship
	v Donnelly	10-2	Qualifying	Embassy World Championship
	v Thorburn	5-10	1st round	Embassy World Championship
	v E. McLaughlin	2-5	Qualifying	Jameson International
	v Mountjoy	5-3	1st round	Professional Players Tournament
	v Miles	5-2	2nd round	Professional Players Tournament

	v Martin	5-0	3rd round	Professional Players Tournament
	v Knowles	3-5	Quarter-final	Professional Players Tournament
1984	v White	1-5	Qualifying	Lada Classic
	v Gauvreau	7-10	Qualifying	Embassy World Championship
	v G. Foulds	5-3	Qualifying	Jameson International
	v S. Davis	1-5	1st round	Jameson International
	v W. Jones	5-4	1st round	Rothmans Grand Prix
	v Thorburn	1-5	2nd round	Rothmans Grand Prix
	v Donnelly	9-6	Qualifying	Coral UK Open
	v White	7-9	1st round	Coral UK Open
1985	v Scott	4-5	Qualifying	Mercantile Credit Classic
	v O'Kane	4-6	1st round	Dulux British Open
	v Morra	10-9	Qualifying	Embassy World Championship
	v Charlton	3-10	1st round	Embassy World Championship
	v Charlton	5-4	Quarter-final	Winfield Australian Masters
	v Parrott	6-4	Semi-finals	Winfield Australian Masters
	v Meo	2-7	Final	Winfield Australian Masters
	v Foldvari	8-5	Quarter-final	Australian Championship
	v King	9-6	Semi-final	Australian Championship
	v Charlton	**10-7**	**Final**	**Australian Championship**
	v Morra	5-2	3rd round	Goya Matchroom Trophy
	v Mountjoy	5-1	4th round	Goya Matchroom Trophy
	v Thorburn	0-5	5th round	Goya Matchroom Trophy
	v Van Rensberg	5-4	3rd round	Rothmans Grand Prix
	v Mountjoy	5-2	4th round	Rothmans Grand Prix
	v Knowles	2-5	5th round	Rothmans Grand Prix
	v Medati	9-7	3rd round	Coral UK Open
	v David Taylor	4-9	4th round	Coral UK Open
1986	v Donnelly	5-2	3rd round	Mercantile Credit Classic
	v Mikkelsen	5-2	4th round	Mercantile Credit Classic
	v N. Foulds	1-5	5th round	Mercantile Credit Classic
	v West	5-4	3rd round	Dulux British Open
	v Medati	5-4	4th round	Dulux British Open
	v S. Davis	0-5	5th round	Dulux British Open
	v Van Rensberg	10-6	Qualifying	Embassy World Championship
	v Reardon	10-8	1st round	Embassy World Championship
	v Thorne	9-13	2nd round	Embassy World Championship
	v Wilkinson	6-1	Quarter-final	Australian Championship
	v Foldvari	8-3	Semi-final	Australian Championship
	v King	3-10	Final	Australian Championship
	v Duggan	3-5	3rd round	BCE International
	v G. Foulds	5-0	3rd round	Rothmans Grand Prix
	v Griffiths	1-5	4th round	Rothmans Grand Prix
	v W. Jones	3-9	3rd round	Tennents UK Open
1987	v Browne	5-2	3rd round	Mercantile Credit Classic
	v Spencer	5-3	4th round	Mercantile Credit Classic
	v Griffiths	3-5	5th round	Mercantile Credit Classic
	v James	1-5	3rd round	Dulux British Open
	v Chappel	10-6	Qualifying	Embassy World Championship
	v S. Francisco	3-10	1st round	Embassy World Championship

DAVE CHALMERS (England)

Born 14.7.48
Turned professional 1984
World ranking 111 (99)
Amateur career 1982 English champion.

1984 v Oliver	5-4	Qualifying	Jameson International
v Meadowcroft	1-5	Qualifying	Jameson International
v Andrewartha	5-2	Qualifying	Rothmans Grand Prix
v Williams	0-5	1st round	Rothmans Grand Prix
v Bales	2-9	Qualifying	Coral UK Open
1985 v Mikkelsen	1-5	Prelim	Mercantile Credit Classic
v Meadowcroft	9-3	Qualifying	Tolly Cobbold English Championship
v White	5-9	Qualifying	Tolly Cobbold English Championship
v Burke	6-5	Qualifying	Dulux British Open
v Griffiths	0-6	1st round	Dulux British Open
v Greaves	10-3	Qualifying	Embassy World Championship
v E. McLaughlin	10-9	Qualifying	Embassy World Championship
v Black	10-4	Qualifying	Embassy World Championship
v Hallett	1-10	Qualifying	Embassy World Championship
v Chaperon	2-5	2nd round	Goya Matchroom Trophy
v Scott	2-5	2nd round	Rothmans Grand Prix
v Browne	4-9	2nd round	Coral UK Open
1986 v Donnelly	0-5	2nd round	Mercantile Credit Classic
v Fisher	9-2	2nd round	Tolly Cobbold English Championship
v Hallett	1-9	3rd round	Tolly Cobbold English Championship
v Scott	1-5	2nd round	Dulux British Open
v F. Davis	6-10	Qualifying	Embassy World Championship
v Houlihan	1-5	1st round	BCE International
v Agrawal	5-1	1st round	Rothmans Grand Prix
v Chaperon	2-5	2nd round	Rothmans Grand Prix
v Oliver	6-9	1st round	Tennents UK Open
1987 v G. Foulds	4-5	1st round	Mercantile Credit Classic
v Wright	5-6	1st round	Tolly Ales English Championship
v Wildman	0-5	2nd round	Dulux British Open
v T. Jones	1-10	Qualifying	Embassy World Championship

ROBERT CHAPERON (Canada)

Born 10.5.58
Turned professional 1983
World ranking 41 (53)
Best professional performance Last 16 1986 BCE International.

1984 v Fowler	0-5	Qualifying	Jameson International
v Kearney	5-1	Qualifying	Rothmans Grand Prix
v Gibson	5-4	Qualifying	Rothmans Grand Prix
v Martin	4-5	Qualifying	Rothmans Grand Prix

v T. Jones	1-9	Qualifying	Coral UK Open
1985 v G. Foulds	3-5	Qualifying	Mercantile Credit Classic
v Fagan	6-5	Qualifying	Dulux British Open
v Werbeniuk	6-1	1st round	Dulux British Open
v W. Jones	5-2	2nd round	Dulux British Open
v S. Francisco	2-5	3rd round	Dulux British Open
v Bales	10-7	Qualifying	Embassy World Championship
v Heywood	10-1	Qualifying	Embassy World Championship
v Morgan	10-3	Qualifying	Embassy World Championship
v F. Davis	9-10	Qualifying	Embassy World Championship
v Thornley	5-1	1st round	Canadian Championship
v Stevens	6-4	Quarter-final	Canadian Championship
v Jonik	6-3	Semi-final	Canadian Championship
v Thorburn	4-6	Final	Canadian Championship
v Chalmers	5-2	2nd round	Goya Matchroom Trophy
v S. Francisco	5-3	3rd round	Goya Matchroom Trophy
v Macleod	4-5	4th round	Goya Matchroom Trophy
v O'Boye	3-5	2nd round	Rothmans Grand Prix
v J. McLaughlin	5-9	2nd round	Coral UK Open
1986 v Burke	5-2	2nd round	Mercantile Credit Classic
v S. Davis	1-5	3rd round	Mercantile Credit Classic
v V. Harris	5-0	2nd round	Dulux British Open
v Wilson	3-5	3rd round	Dulux British Open
v Jonik	10-8	Qualifying	Embassy World Championship
v Gauvreau	8-10	Qualifying	Embassy World Championship
v Bear	6-3	1st round	Canadian Championship
v Jonik	3-6	2nd round	Canadian Championship
v N. Gilbert	5-3	2nd round	BCE International
v Martin	5-4	3rd round	BCE International
v Drago	5-1	4th round	BCE International
v E. Hughes	0-5	5th round	BCE International
v Chalmers	5-2	2nd round	Rothmans Grand Prix
v Reardon	5-3	3rd round	Rothmans Grand Prix
v Hendry	2-5	4th round	Rothmans Grand Prix
v Dodd	9-4	2nd round	Tennents UK Open
v David Taylor	8-9	3rd round	Tennents UK Open
1987 v Roe	5-4	2nd round	Mercantile Credit Classic
v Stevens	3-5	3rd round	Mercantile Credit Classic
v Fisher	5-2	2nd round	Dulux British Open
v Stevens	4-5	3rd round	Dulux British Open
v Fitzmaurice	10-2	Qualifying	Embassy World Championship
v Spencer	4-10	Qualifying	Embassy World Championship

TONY CHAPPEL (Wales)

Born 28.5.60
Turned professional 1984
World ranking 59 (49)
Best professional performance Last 32 1985 Goya Matchroom Trophy.

1984	v Mikkelsen	4-5	Qualifying	Jameson International
	v Scott	5-1	Qualifying	Rothmans Grand Prix
	v Stevens	3-5	1st round	Rothmans Grand Prix
	v Houlihan	9-3	Qualifying	Coral UK Open
	v Black	9-3	Qualifying	Coral UK Open
	v Reynolds	9-6	Qualifying	Coral UK Open
	v Stevens	7-9	1st round	Coral UK Open
	v Giannaros	2-5	Qualifying	Mercantile Credit Classic
	v Williamson	6-5	Qualifying	Dulux British Open
	v S. Davis	5-6	1st round	Dulux British Open
	v Hines	8-10	Qualifying	Embassy World Championship
	v M. Owen	6-0	1st round	BCE Welsh Championship
	v Griffiths	0-6	Quarter-final	BCE Welsh Championship
1985	v Meadowcroft	5-2	2nd round	Goya Matchroom Trophy
	v Stevens	5-3	3rd round	Goya Matchroom Trophy
	v Wilson	0-5	4th round	Goya Matchroom Trophy
	v Dodd	5-2	2nd round	Rothmans Grand Prix
	v Mountjoy	1-5	3rd round	Rothmans Grand Prix
	v O'Kane	9-5	1st round	Coral UK Open
	v White	5-9	2nd round	Coral UK Open
1986	v Murphy	4-5	2nd round	Mercantile Credit Classic
	v Griffiths	4-6	Quarter-final	Zetters Welsh Championship
	v Fowler	4-5	2nd round	Dulux British Open
	v Wych	6-10	Qualifying	Embassy World Championship
	v Roscoe	5-3	2nd round	BCE International
	v E. Hughes	4-5	3rd round	BCE International
	v Kearney	5-1	2nd round	Rothmans Grand Prix
	v Meo	1-5	3rd round	Rothmans Grand Prix
	v Wilkinson	9-2	2nd round	Tennents UK Open
	v S. Davis	7-9	3rd round	Tennents UK Open
1987	v Wright	4-5	2nd round	Mercantile Credit Classic
	v Reardon	6-4	Quarter-final	Matchroom Welsh Championship
	v Mountjoy	2-9	Semi-final	Matchroom Welsh Championship
	v Kearney	5-3	2nd round	Dulux British Open
	v White	1-5	3rd round	Dulux British Open
	v Morra	10-8	Qualifying	Embassy World Championship
	v Duggan	10-3	Qualifying	Embassy World Championship
	v Campbell	6-10	Qualifying	Embassy World Championship

EDDIE CHARLTON (Australia)

Born 31.10.29
Turned professional 1960
World ranking 26 (25)
Best professional performances Runner-up 1973 World Championship, 1975 World Championship; 1964–67, 1969–84 Australian champion.

1970	v Simpson	22-27	Semi-final	World Championship
1972	v David Taylor	31-25	Quarter-final	World Championship
	v Spencer	32-37	Semi-final	World Championship
1973	v Mans	16-8	2nd round	World Championship
	v Miles	16-6	Quarter-final	World Championship
	v Higgins	23-9	Semi-final	World Championship
	v Reardon	32-38	Final	World Championship
1974	v Dunning	13-15	2nd round	World Championship
1975	v F. Davis	5-3	Quarter-final	Benson & Hedges Masters
	v Spencer	2-5	Semi-final	Benson & Hedges Masters
	v Werbeniuk	15-11	2nd round	World Championship
	v Thorburn	19-12	Quarter-final	World Championship
	v Dennis Taylor	19-12	Semi-final	World Championship
	v Reardon	30-31	Final	World Championship
1976	v Williams	4-1	2nd round	Benson & Hedges Masters
	v Reardon	4-5	Semi-final	Benson & Hedges Masters
	v Pulman	15-9	1st round	Embassy World Championship
	v F. Davis	15-13	Quarter-final	Embassy World Championship
	v Higgins	18-20	Semi-final	Embassy World Championship
1977	v David Taylor	13-5	1st round	Embassy World Championship
	v Thorburn	12-13	Quarter-final	Embassy World Championship
1978	v Thorne	13-12	1st round	Embassy World Championship
	v Thorburn	13-12	Quarter-final	Embassy World Championship
	v Reardon	14-18	Semi-final	Embassy World Championship
1979	v Higgins	2-5	Quarter-final	Benson & Hedges Masters
	v Mountjoy	13-6	1st round	Embassy World Championship
	v F. Davis	13-4	Quarter-final	Embassy World Championship
	v Griffiths	17-19	Semi-final	Embassy World Championship
1980	v Spencer	2-5	Quarter-final	Benson & Hedges Masters
	v Virgo	13-12	2nd round	Embassy World Championship
	v Stevens	7-13	Quarter-final	Embassy World Championship
1981	v Mountjoy	0-5	1st round	Benson & Hedges Masters
	v Mountjoy	7-13	2nd round	Embassy World Championship
	v Martin	2-5	3rd round	Jameson International
1982	v White	5-4	1st round	Benson & Hedges Masters
	v Higgins	1-5	Quarter-final	Benson & Hedges Masters
	v Wilson	10-5	1st round	Embassy World Championship
	v Werbeniuk	13-5	2nd round	Embassy World Championship
	v Knowles	13-11	Quarter-final	Embassy World Championship
	v Reardon	11-16	Semi-final	Embassy World Championship
	v Virgo	4-5	1st round	Jameson International
	v D. Hughes	5-2	1st round	Professional Players Tournament
	v Williams	5-2	2nd round	Professional Players Tournament
	v Meo	5-3	3rd round	Professional Players Tournament
	v Reynolds	5-2	Quarter-final	Professional Players Tournament
	v Reardon	7-10	Semi-final	Professional Players Tournament
1983	v Virgo	5-2	1st round	Lada Classic
	v S. Davis	4-5	Quarter-final	Lada Classic
	v Meo	5-3	1st round	Benson & Hedges Masters
	v Werbeniuk	5-3	Quarter-final	Benson & Hedges Masters

	v Thorburn	5-6	Semi-final	Benson & Hedges Masters
	v David Taylor	5-4	1st round	Benson & Hedges Irish Masters
	v S. Davis	1-5	Quarter-final	Benson & Hedges Irish Masters
	v Dodd	10-7	1st round	Embassy World Championship
	v Spencer	13-11	2nd round	Embassy World Championship
	v S. Davis	5-13	Quarter-final	Embassy World Championship
	v Johnson	5-2	1st round	Jameson International
	v Morra	5-3	2nd round	Jameson International
	v Thorne	5-0	Quarter-final	Jameson International
	v S. Davis	2-9	Semi-final	Jameson International
	v E. McLaughlin	5-0	1st round	Professional Players Tournament
	v Fisher	5-4	2nd round	Professional Players Tournament
	v Johnson	0-5	3rd round	Professional Players Tournament
1984	v Wilson	5-0	Qualifying	Lada Classic
	v White	5-3	1st round	Lada Classic
	v Wildman	4-5	Quarter-final	Lada Classic
	v White	2-5	1st round	Benson & Hedges Masters
	v Higgins	2-5	1st round	Benson & Hedges Irish Masters
	v Stevens	3-5	1st round	Tolly Cobbold Classic
	v Andrewartha	10-4	1st round	Embassy World Championship
	v White	7-13	2nd round	Embassy World Championship
	v David Taylor	5-4	Quarter-final	Winfield Australian Masters
	v Knowles	0-6	Semi-final	Winfield Australian Masters
	v Johnson	1-5	1st round	Jameson International
	v Everton	5-1	1st round	Rothmans Grand Prix
	v Parrott	5-1	2nd round	Rothmans Grand Prix
	v Mountjoy	4-5	3rd round	Rothmans Grand Prix
	v S. Francisco	9-4	1st round	Coral UK Open
	v Thorne	7-9	2nd round	Coral UK Open
1985	v Macleod	1-5	1st round	Mercantile Credit Classic
	v Spencer	3-5	1st round	Benson & Hedges Masters
	v B. Harris	3-6	1st round	Dulux British Open
	v Dennis Taylor	5-4	1st round	Benson & Hedges Irish Masters
	v Knowles	3-5	Quarter-final	Benson & Hedges Irish Masters
	v Campbell	10-3	1st round	Embassy World Championship
	v Dennis Taylor	6-13	2nd round	Embassy World Championship
	v Campbell	4-5	Quarter-final	Winfield Australian Masters
	v Wilkinson	8-2	Quarter-final	Australian Championship
	v Morgan	9-3	Semi-final	Australian Championship
	v Campbell	7-10	Final	Australian Championship
	v Gibson	4-5	3rd round	Goya Matchroom Trophy
	v G. Foulds	5-1	3rd round	Rothmans Grand Prix
	v Drago	3-5	4th round	Rothmans Grand Prix
	v P. Francisco	5-9	3rd round	Coral UK Open
1986	v P. Francisco	1-5	3rd round	Mercantile Credit Classic
	v Stevens	5-4	1st round	Benson & Hedges Masters
	v Knowles	4-5	Quarter-final	Benson & Hedges Masters
	v Gilbert	5-2	3rd round	Dulux British Open
	v Browne	5-1	4th round	Dulux British Open
	v Virgo	4-5	5th round	Dulux British Open

	v Wilson	10-6	1st round	Embassy World Championship
	v Stevens	12-13	2nd round	Embassy World Championship
	v Anderson	6-2	Quarter-final	Australian Championship
	v King	6-8	Semi-final	Australian Championship
	v Black	5-0	3rd round	BCE International
	v Knowles	1-5	4th round	BCE International
	v Drago	4-5	3rd round	Rothmans Grand Prix
	v V. Harris	9-2	3rd round	Tennents UK Open
	v S. Davis	6-9	4th round	Tennents UK Open
1987	v Fisher	5-0	3rd round	Mercantile Credit Classic
	v Williams	5-4	4th round	Mercantile Credit Classic
	v Parrott	4-5	5th round	Mercantile Credit Classic
	v Medati	5-4	3rd round	Dulux British Open
	v Dennis Taylor	1-5	4th round	Dulux British Open
	v King	4-10	Qualifying	Embassy World Championship

GRAHAM CRIPSEY (England)

Born 8.12.54
Turned professional 1982
World ranking 48 (50)
Best professional performances Last 32 1985 Coral UK Open, 1986 Mercantile Credit Classic.

1982	v French	1-5	Qualifying	Jameson International
	v B. Harris	6-9	Qualifying	Coral UK Championship
1983	v D. Hughes	10-2	Qualifying	Embassy World Championship
	v Meadowcroft	6-10	Qualifying	Embassy World Championship
	v Ganim	4-5	Qualifying	Professional Players Tournament
	v Darrington	3-9	Qualifying	Coral UK Championship
1984	v Parkin	10-4	Qualifying	Embassy World Championship
	v Gauvreau	1-10	Qualifying	Embassy World Championship
	v Thornley	5-3	Qualifying	Jameson International
	v Dunning	3-5	Qualifying	Jameson International
	v Morra	3-5	Qualifying	Rothmans Grand Prix
	v Foldvari	9-7	Qualifying	Coral UK Open
	v Fitzmaurice	8-9	Qualifying	Coral UK Open
1985	v Medati	4-5	Qualifying	Mercantile Credit Classic
	v Bennett	9-0	Qualifying	Tolly Cobbold English Championship
	v David Taylor	5-9	1st round	Tolly Cobbold English Championship
	v O'Kane	4-6	Qualifying	Dulux British Open
	v Longworth	8-10	Qualifying	Embassy World Championship
	v Bennett	5-3	1st round	Goya Matchroom Trophy
	v Medati	5-2	2nd round	Goya Matchroom Trophy
	v Dennis Taylor	1-5	3rd round	Goya Matchroom Trophy
	v Hargreaves	1-5	1st round	Rothmans Grand Prix
	v Greaves	9-4	1st round	Coral UK Open

	v Dunning	*wo*	2nd round	Coral UK Open
	v Wilson	9-7	3rd round	Coral UK Open
	v Dennis Taylor	2-9	4th round	Coral UK Open
1986	v Drago	5-4	1st round	Mercantile Credit Classic
	v Newbury	5-4	2nd round	Mercantile Credit Classic
	v Spencer	5-1	3rd round	Mercantile Credit Classic
	v Higgins	2-5	4th round	Mercantile Credit Classic
	v Meadowcroft	9-1	2nd round	Tolly Cobbold English Championship
	v Wildman	5-9	3rd round	Tolly Cobbold English Championship
	v Darrington	5-4	1st round	Dulux British Open
	v Williamson	4-5	2nd round	Dulux British Open
	v Drago	4-10	Qualifying	Embassy World Championship
	v Houlihan	1-5	2nd round	BCE International
	v P. Gibson	5-3	2nd round	Rothmans Grand Prix
	v Parrott	4-5	3rd round	Rothmans Grand Prix
	v Bales	9-6	2nd round	Tennents UK Open
	v N. Foulds	7-9	3rd round	Tennents UK Open
1987	v Mienie	5-0	2nd round	Mercantile Credit Classic
	v Thorburn	0-5	3rd round	Mercantile Credit Classic
	v Dunning	6-1	2nd round	Tolly Ales English Championship
	v White	4-6	3rd round	Tolly Ales English Championship
	v Watchorn	5-4	2nd round	Dulux British Open
	v Werbeniuk	5-2	3rd round	Dulux British Open
	v Thorburn	2-5	4th round	Dulux British Open
	v Meadowcroft	10-9	Qualifying	Embassy World Championship
	v M. Gibson	10-4	Qualifying	Embassy World Championship
	v David Taylor	7-10	Qualifying	Embassy World Championship

MIKE DARRINGTON (England)

Born 13.9.31
Turned professional 1982
World ranking 90 (78)

1983	v Williams	0-10	Qualifying	Embassy World Championship
	v Williamson	5-3	Qualifying	Jameson International
	v S. Francisco	2-5	Qualifying	Jameson International
	v Duggan	4-5	Qualifying	Professional Players Tournament
	v Cripsey	9-3	Qualifying	Coral UK Championship
	v Hallett	1-9	Qualifying	Coral UK Championship
1984	v Caggianello	7-10	Qualifying	Embassy World Championship
	v Bradley	3-5	Qualifying	Jameson International
	v Burke	3-5	Qualifying	Rothmans Grand Prix
	v Longworth	5-9	Qualifying	Coral UK Open
1985	v Hargreaves	2-5	Qualifying	Mercantile Credit Classic
	v Virgo	0-9	1st round	Tolly Cobbold English Championship
	v Scott	3-6	Qualifying	Dulux British Open

	v T. Jones	2-10	Qualifying	Embassy World Championship
	v Gilbert	5-2	1st round	Goya Matchroom Trophy
	v Sinclair	0-5	2nd round	Goya Matchroom Trophy
	v Greaves	5-2	1st round	Rothmans Grand Prix
	v Foldvari	5-3	2nd round	Rothmans Grand Prix
	v N. Foulds	0-5	3rd round	Rothmans Grand Prix
	v Foldvari	9-6	2nd round	Coral UK Open
	v Martin	3-9	3rd round	Coral UK Open
1986	v O'Boye	0-5	1st round	Mercantile Credit Classic
	v Fowler	3-9	2nd round	Tolly Cobbold English Championship
	v Cripsey	4-5	1st round	Dulux British Open
	v Meadowcroft	10-6	Qualifying	Embassy World Championship
	v Edmonds	5-10	Qualifying	Embassy World Championship
	v Jack Rea	4-5	1st round	BCE International
	v Watchorn	2-5	1st round	Rothmans Grand Prix
	v Whitthread	9-8	1st round	Tennents UK Open
	v Fowler	6-9	2nd round	Tennents UK Open
1987	v Roe	0-5	1st round	Mercantile Credit Classic
	v V. Harris	3-6	2nd round	Tolly Ales English Championship
	v James	3-5	1st round	Dulux British Open
	v Demarco	10-6	Qualifying	Embassy World Championship
	v Hendry	7-10	2nd round	Embassy World Championship

FRED DAVIS (England)

Born 14.8.13
Turned professional 1930
World ranking 62 (47)
Best professional performances Winner World Championship 1948–49, 1951–56.

1969	v Reardon	25-24	Quarter-final	World Championship
	v G. Owen	28-45	Semi-final	World Championship
1970	v Reardon	26-31	Quarter-final	World Championship
1972	v Spencer	21-31	Quarter-final	World Championship
1973	v Greaves	16-1	2nd round	World Championship
	v Higgins	14-16	Quarter-final	World Championship
1974	v Werbeniuk	15-5	2nd round	World Championship
	v Higgins	15-14	Quarter-final	World Championship
	v Reardon	3-15	Semi-final	World Championship
1975	v Charlton	3-5	Quarter-final	Benson & Hedges Masters
	v Dennis Taylor	14-15	2nd round	World Championship
1976	v Thorburn	4-2	1st round	Benson & Hedges Masters
	v Spencer	0-4	2nd round	Benson & Hedges Masters
	v Werbeniuk	15-12	1st round	Embassy World Championship
	v Charlton	13-15	Quarter-final	Embassy World Championship
1977	v Mountjoy	2-4	Quarter-final	Benson & Hedges Masters
	v Pulman	12-13	1st round	Embassy World Championship

	v Fagan	0-5	2nd round	Super Crystalate UK Championship
1978	v Miles	3-4	1st round	Benson & Hedges Masters
	v Virgo	9-8	Qualifying	Embassy World Championship
	v Dennis Taylor	13-9	1st round	Embassy World Championship
	v Fagan	13-10	Quarter-final	Embassy World Championship
	v Mans	16-18	Semi-final	Embassy World Championship
	v Dunning	9-2	1st round	Coral UK Championship
	v Higgins	4-9	Quarter-final	Coral UK Championship
1979	v Mountjoy	2-5	1st round	Benson & Hedges Masters
	v Stevens	13-8	1st round	Embassy World Championship
	v Charlton	4-13	Quarter-final	Embassy World Championship
	v Edmonds	6-9	3rd round	Coral UK Championship
1980	v David Taylor	5-13	2nd round	Embassy World Championship
	v Wildman	9-6	2nd round	Coral UK Championship
	v Higgins	6-9	Quarter-final	Coral UK Championship
1981	v Stevens	5-4	1st round	Benson & Hedges Masters
	v Griffiths	2-5	Quarter-final	Benson & Hedges Masters
	v Edmonds	6-9	1st round	John Courage English
	v David Taylor	3-13	2nd round	Embassy World Championship
	v Williams	0-5	2nd round	Jameson International
	v Knowles	6-9	2nd round	Coral UK Championship
1982	v Reynolds	7-10	1st round	Embassy World Championship
	v Fisher	3-5	Qualifying	Jameson International
	v Sinclair	2-5	1st round	Professional Players Tournament
	v Hallett	7-9	1st round	Coral UK Open
1983	v Williams	1-10	Qualifying	Embassy World Championship
	v Kelly	5-1	Qualifying	Jameson International
	v Morgan	3-5	Qualifying	Jameson International
	v Fisher	4-5	1st round	Professional Players Tournament
	v Watterson	6-9	Qualifying	Coral UK Championship
	v Donnelly	10-5	Qualifying	Embassy World Championship
	v Werbeniuk	4-10	1st round	Embassy World Championship
1984	v Dunning	5-4	Qualifying	Jameson International
	v Virgo	3-5	Qualifying	Jameson International
	v V. Harris	1-5	Qualifying	Rothmans Grand Prix
	v Fowler	4-9	Qualifying	Coral UK Open
1985	v E. McLaughlin	1-5	Qualifying	Mercantile Credit Classic
	v G. Foulds	2-9	Qualifying	Tolly Cobbold English Championship
	v Longworth	1-6	Qualifying	Dulux British Open
	v Chaperon	10-9	Qualifying	Embassy World Championship
	v Williams	6-10	Qualifying	Embassy World Championship
	v Duggan	1-5	2nd round	Goya Matchroom Trophy
	v Simngam	2-5	2nd round	Rothmans Grand Prix
	v John Rea	9-8	2nd round	Coral UK Open
	v Werbeniuk	9-7	3rd round	Coral UK Open
	v Higgins	2-9	4th round	Coral UK Open
1986	v Kelly	5-3	2nd round	Mercantile Credit Classic
	v Stevens	5-2	3rd round	Mercantile Credit Classic
	v E. Hughes	3-5	4th round	Mercantile Credit Classic
	v D. Hughes	9-6	2nd round	Tolly Cobbold English Championship

v Martin	8-9	3rd round	Tolly Cobbold English Championship
v Kelly	5-4	2nd round	Dulux British Open
v Macleod	4-5	3rd round	Dulux British Open
v Chalmers	10-6	Qualifying	Embassy World Championship
v P. Francisco	1-10	Qualifying	Embassy World Championship
v Bales	4-5	2nd round	BCE International
v Bales	5-4	2nd round	Rothmans Grand Prix
v Higgins	0-5	3rd round	Rothmans Grand Prix
v Rowswell	4-9	2nd round	Tennents UK Open
1987 v Fisher	2-5	2nd round	Mercantile Credit Classic
v James	2-6	2nd round	Tolly Ales English Championship
v Owers	3-5	2nd round	Dulux British Open
v Owers	5-10	Qualifying	Embassy World Championship

STEVE DAVIS (England)

Born 22.8.57
Turned professional 1978
World ranking 1 (1)
Best professional performances Winner Embassy World Championship
1981, 1983, 1984, 1987, Coral UK Championship 1980, 1981, 1984, 1985,
Tennents UK Open 1986; winner of 6 ranking tournaments, 14 non-
ranking tournaments, 2 English Championships.

1979 v Anderson	9-1	Prelim	Embassy World Championship
v Fagan	9-2	Qualifying	Embassy World Championship
v Dennis Taylor	11-13	1st round	Embassy World Championship
v Dunning	9-3	2nd round	Coral UK Championship
v Mountjoy	9-5	3rd round	Coral UK Championship
v Virgo	7-9	Quarter-final	Coral UK Championship
1980 v Morgan	9-0	Qualifying	Embassy World Championship
v Fagan	10-6	1st round	Embassy World Championship
v Griffiths	13-10	2nd round	Embassy World Championship
v Higgins	9-13	Quarter-final	Embassy World Championship
v Hallett	9-1	1st round	Coral UK Championship
v Werbeniuk	9-3	2nd round	Coral UK Championship
v Meo	9-5	Quarter-final	Coral UK Championship
v Griffiths	9-0	Semi-final	Coral UK Championship
v Higgins	**16-6**	**Final**	**Coral UK Championship**
1981 v Mans	3-5	1st round	Benson & Hedges Masters
v Dennis Taylor	5-2	Semi-final	Yamaha International Masters
v David Taylor	**9-6**	**Final**	**Yamaha International Masters**
v Meadowcroft	9-2	1st round	John Courage English
v Spencer	9-7	2nd round	John Courage English
v Edmonds	9-0	Semi-final	John Courage English
v Meo	**9-3**	**Final**	**John Courage English**
v White	10-8	1st round	Embassy World Championship
v Higgins	13-8	2nd round	Embassy World Championship

	v Griffiths	13-9	Quarter-final	Embassy World Championship
	v Thorburn	16-10	Semi-final	Embassy World Championship
	v Mountjoy	**18-12**	**Final**	**Embassy World Championship**
	v Mountjoy	5-0	Quarter-final	Langs Scottish Masters
	v White	5-6	Semi-final	Langs Scottish Masters
	v Mans	5-3	3rd round	Jameson International
	v David Taylor	5-1	Quarter-final	Jameson International
	v Higgins	9-8	Semi-final	Jameson International
	v Dennis Taylor	**9-0**	**Final**	**Jameson International**
	v Higgins	5-2	1st round	Northern Ireland Classic
	v Griffiths	9-6	Semi-final	Northern Ireland Classic
	v White	9-11	Final	Northern Ireland Classic
	v Thorne	9-2	3rd round	Coral UK Championship
	v Werbeniuk	9-5	Quarter-final	Coral UK Championship
	v White	9-0	Semi-final	Coral UK Championship
	v Griffiths	**16-3**	**Final**	**Coral UK Championship**
1982	v Spencer	5-2	1st round	Lada Classic
	v Reardon	5-4	Semi-final	Lada Classic
	v Griffiths	8-9	Final	Lada Classic
	v Mountjoy	5-2	Quarter-final	Benson & Hedges Masters
	v Meo	6-4	Semi-final	Benson & Hedges Masters
	v Griffiths	**9-5**	**Final**	**Benson & Hedges Masters**
	v Griffiths	**9-7**	**Final**	**Yamaha International Masters**
	v Miles	5-2	Semi-final	Tolly Cobbold Classic
	v Dennis Taylor	**8-3**	**Final**	**Tolly Cobbold Classic**
	v Mountjoy	5-2	Quarter-final	Benson & Hedges Irish Masters
	v Higgins	6-2	Semi-final	Benson & Hedges Irish Masters
	v Griffiths	5-9	Final	Benson & Hedges Irish Masters
	v Knowles	1-10	1st round	Embassy World Championship
	v Knowles	5-4	1st round	Langs Scottish Masters
	v Dennis Taylor	6-1	Semi-final	Langs Scottish Masters
	v Higgins	**9-4**	**Final**	**Langs Scottish Masters**
	v Roscoe	5-0	1st round	Jameson International
	v Reynolds	5-0	2nd round	Jameson International
	v David Taylor	3-5	Quarter-final	Jameson International
	v Williams	9-6	1st round	Coral UK Open
	v Fagan	9-3	2nd round	Coral UK Open
	v Griffiths	6-9	Quarter-final	Coral UK Open
1983	v Dennis Taylor	5-2	1st round	Lada Classic
	v Charlton	5-4	Quarter-final	Lada Classic
	v Spencer	5-4	Semi-final	Lada Classic
	v Werbeniuk	**9-5**	**Final**	**Lada Classic**
	v Wildman	5-2	1st round	Benson & Hedges Masters
	v Mountjoy	4-5	Quarter-final	Benson & Hedges Masters
	v Dennis Taylor	5-1	Semi-final	Tolly Cobbold Classic
	v Griffiths	**7-5**	**Final**	**Tolly Cobbold Classic**
	v Charlton	5-1	Quarter-final	Benson & Hedges Irish Masters
	v Griffiths	6-2	Semi-final	Benson & Hedges Irish Masters
	v Reardon	**9-2**	**Final**	**Benson & Hedges Irish Masters**
	v Williams	10-4	1st round	Embassy World Championship

	v Dennis Taylor	13-11	2nd round	Embassy World Championship
	v Charlton	13-5	Quarter-final	Embassy World Championship
	v Higgins	16-5	Semi-final	Embassy World Championship
	v Thorburn	**18-6**	**Final**	**Embassy World Championship**
	v Macleod	5-1	1st round	Langs Scottish Masters
	v Higgins	6-2	Semi-final	Langs Scottish Masters
	v Knowles	**9-6**	**Final**	**Langs Scottish Masters**
	v E. Hughes	5-1	1st round	Jameson International
	v Watterson	5-0	2nd round	Jameson International
	v S. Francisco	5-1	Quarter-final	Jameson International
	v Charlton	9-2	Semi-final	Jameson International
	v Thorburn	**9-4**	**Final**	**Jameson International**
	v Donnelly	5-1	1st round	Professional Players Tournament
	v Hallett	2-5	2nd round	Professional Players Tournament
	v G. Foulds	9-1	1st round	Coral UK Championship
	v Thorne	9-3	2nd round	Coral UK Championship
	v Meo	9-4	Quarter-final	Coral UK Championship
	v White	9-4	Semi-final	Coral UK Championship
	v Higgins	15-16	Final	Coral UK Championship
1984	v Spencer	5-2	1st round	Lada Classic
	v Griffiths	5-4	Quarter-final	Lada Classic
	v Parrott	5-4	Semi-final	Lada Classic
	v Meo	**9-8**	**Final**	**Lada Classic**
	v Meo	5-0	1st round	Benson & Hedges Masters
	v Stevens	3-5	Quarter-final	Benson & Hedges Masters
	v Meo	5-4	Quarter-final	Benson & Hedges Irish Masters
	v Higgins	6-4	Semi-final	Benson & Hedges Irish Masters
	v Griffiths	**9-1**	**Final**	**Benson & Hedges Irish Masters**
	v Thorne	5-2	1st round	Tolly Cobbold Classic
	v Stevens	5-4	Semi-final	Tolly Cobbold Classic
	v Knowles	**8-2**	**Final**	**Tolly Cobbold Classic**
	v King	10-3	1st round	Embassy World Championship
	v Spencer	13-5	2nd round	Embassy World Championship
	v Griffiths	13-10	Quarter-final	Embassy World Championship
	v Dennis Taylor	16-9	Semi-final	Embassy World Championship
	v White	**18-16**	**Final**	**Embassy World Championship**
	v Thorburn	5-2	1st round	Langs Supreme Scottish Masters
	v Higgins	6-4	Semi-final	Langs Supreme Scottish Masters
	v White	**9-4**	**Final**	**Langs Supreme Scottish Masters**
	v Campbell	5-1	1st round	Jameson International
	v David Taylor	5-1	2nd round	Jameson International
	v Higgins	5-1	Quarter-final	Jameson International
	v E. Hughes	9-3	Semi-final	Jameson International
	v Knowles	**9-2**	**Final**	**Jameson International**
	v Morra	5-2	1st round	Rothmans Grand Prix
	v Miles	5-0	2nd round	Rothmans Grand Prix
	v David Taylor	5-1	3rd round	Rothmans Grand Prix
	v Reynolds	5-0	Quarter-final	Rothmans Grand Prix
	v Thorburn	7-9	Semi-final	Rothmans Grand Prix
	v Murphy	9-1	1st round	Coral UK Open

	v Meo	9-7	2nd round	Coral UK Open
	v White	9-4	Quarter-final	Coral UK Open
	v Stevens	9-2	Semi-final	Coral UK Open
	v Higgins	**16-8**	**Final**	**Coral UK Open**
1985	v S. Francisco	5-0	1st round	Mercantile Credit Classic
	v Higgins	5-2	2nd round	Mercantile Credit Classic
	v Reardon	5-1	Quarter-final	Mercantile Credit Classic
	v Thorne	8-9	Semi-final	Mercantile Credit Classic
	v Higgins	4-5	1st round	Benson & Hedges Masters
	v Fowler	9-3	1st round	Tolly Cobbold English Championship
	v Williams	9-2	2nd round	Tolly Cobbold English Championship
	v Virgo	9-2	Quarter-final	Tolly Cobbold English Championship
	v Meo	9-8	Semi-final	Tolly Cobbold English Championship
	v Knowles	**9-2**	**Final**	**Tolly Cobbold English Championship**
	v Chappel	6-5	1st round	Dulux British Open
	v Virgo	5-2	2nd round	Dulux British Open
	v Bradley	5-2	3rd round	Dulux British Open
	v O'Kane	5-1	Quarter-final	Dulux British Open
	v Stevens	7-9	Semi-final	Dulux British Open
	v E. Hughes	5-4	Quarter-final	Benson & Hedges Irish Masters
	v Higgins	2-6	Semi-final	Benson & Hedges Irish Masters
	v N. Foulds	10-8	1st round	Embassy World Championship
	v David Taylor	13-4	2nd round	Embassy World Championship
	v Griffiths	13-6	Quarter-final	Embassy World Championship
	v Reardon	16-5	Semi-final	Embassy World Championship
	v Dennis Taylor	17-18	Final	Embassy World Championship
	v Bales	5-2	3rd round	Goya Matchroom Trophy
	v Virgo	5-1	4th round	Goya Matchroom Trophy
	v Macleod	5-1	5th round	Goya Matchroom Trophy
	v White	3-5	Quarter-final	Goya Matchroom Trophy
	v Agrawal	5-0	3rd round	Rothmans Grand Prix
	v Fowler	5-1	4th round	Rothmans Grand Prix
	v Higgins	5-0	5th round	Rothmans Grand Prix
	v S. Francisco	5-2	Quarter-final	Rothmans Grand Prix
	v Thorburn	9-5	Semi-final	Rothmans Grand Prix
	v Dennis Taylor	**10-9**	**Final**	**Rothmans Grand Prix**
	v Griffiths	5-4	1st round	BCE Canadian Masters
	v Thorburn	8-1	Semi-final	BCE Canadian Masters
	v Dennis Taylor	5-9	Final	BCE Canadian Masters
	v Sheehan	9-1	3rd round	Coral UK Open
	v Drago	9-2	4th round	Coral UK Open
	v Meo	9-5	5th round	Coral UK Open
	v West	9-1	Quarter-final	Coral UK Open
	v White	9-5	Semi-final	Coral UK Open
	v Thorne	**16-14**	**Final**	**Coral UK Open**
	v Reardon	5-2	1st round	Kit Kat
	v Higgins	6-1	Semi-final	Kit Kat
	v Dennis Taylor	5-9	Final	Kit Kat
1986	v Chaperon	5-1	3rd round	Mercantile Credit Classic
	v Van Rensberg	5-1	4th round	Mercantile Credit Classic

Neal Foulds

Steve Davis

v P. Francisco	5-0	5th round	Mercantile Credit Classic
v White	2-5	Quarter-final	Mercantile Credit Classic
v Griffiths	2-5	1st round	BCE Belgian Classic
v David Taylor	5-4	1st round	Benson & Hedges Masters
v Thorne	5-4	Quarter-final	Benson & Hedges Masters
v White	3-6	Semi-final	Benson & Hedges Masters
v Bradley	9-3	3rd round	Tolly Cobbold English Championship
v Martin	9-4	4th round	Tolly Cobbold English Championship
v Virgo	9-2	Quarter-final	Tolly Cobbold English Championship
v Meo	7-9	Semi-final	Tolly Cobbold English Championship
v Black	5-2	3rd round	Dulux British Open
v Martin	5-1	4th round	Dulux British Open
v Campbell	5-0	5th round	Dulux British Open
v Wych	5-2	Quarter-final	Dulux British Open
v Higgins	9-3	Semi-final	Dulux British Open
v Thorne	**12-7**	**Final**	**Dulux British Open**
v Edmonds	10-4	1st round	Embassy World Championship
v Mountjoy	13-5	2nd round	Embassy World Championship
v White	13-5	Quarter-final	Embassy World Championship
v Thorburn	16-12	Semi-final	Embassy World Championship
v Johnson	12-18	Final	Embassy World Championship
v Thorne	2-5	Semi-final	Camus Hong Kong Masters
v Griffiths	6-2	Semi-final	Matchroom Trophy
v Thorne	9-10	Final	Matchroom Trophy
v John Rea	5-1	3rd round	BCE International
v King	5-4	4th round	BCE International
v Williams	5-4	5th round	BCE International
v E. Hughes	4-5	Quarter-final	BCE International
v M. Gibson	5-1	3rd round	Rothmans Grand Prix
v Drago	5-1	4th round	Rothmans Grand Prix
v Griffiths	5-2	5th round	Rothmans Grand Prix
v Williams	1-5	Quarter-final	Rothmans Grand Prix
v White	5-2	1st round	BCE Canadian Masters
v Higgins	8-2	Semi-final	BCE Canadian Masters
v Thorne	**9-3**	**Final**	**BCE Canadian Masters**
v Chappel	9-7	3rd round	Tennents UK Open
v Charlton	9-6	4th round	Tennents UK Open
v Reynolds	9-5	5th round	Tennents UK Open
v Drago	9-8	Quarter-final	Tennents UK Open
v Higgins	9-2	Semi-final	Tennents UK Open
v N. Foulds	**16-7**	**Final**	**Tennents UK Open**
1987 v Jenkins	5-0	3rd round	Mercantile Credit Classic
v Virgo	5-2	4th round	Mercantile Credit Classic
v Meo	5-2	5th round	Mercantile Credit Classic
v Parrott	5-4	Quarter-final	Mercantile Credit Classic
v Hendry	9-3	Semi-final	Mercantile Credit Classic
v White	**13-12**	**Final**	**Mercantile Credit Classic**
v Mountjoy	2-5	1st round	Benson & Hedges Masters
v Gauvreau	5-0	3rd round	Dulux British Open
v Virgo	4-5	4th round	Dulux British Open

v Meo	5-2	Quarter-final	Benson & Hedges Irish Masters
v Griffiths	6-2	Semi-final	Benson & Hedges Irish Masters
v Thorne	**9-1**	**Final**	**Benson & Hedges Irish Masters**
v King	10-7	1st round	Embassy World Championship
v Reardon	13-4	2nd round	Embassy World Championship
v Griffiths	13-5	Quarter-final	Embassy World Championship
v White	16-11	Semi-final	Embassy World Championship
v Johnson	**18-14**	**Final**	**Embassy World Championship**

LES DODD (England)

Born 11.2.54
Turned professional 1982
World ranking 52 (69)
Best professional performances Last 32 1983 Embassy World Championship, 1986 Rothmans Grand Prix, 1987 Mercantile Credit Classic; runner-up 1987 Tolly Ales English Championship.

1982	v Macleod	5-1	Qualifying	Jameson International
	v Fitzmaurice	5-3	Qualifying	Jameson International
	v Mans	3-5	1st round	Jameson International
	v Williamson	9-1	Qualifying	Coral UK Championship
	v French	9-7	Qualifying	Coral UK Championship
	v David Taylor	7-9	1st round	Coral UK Championship
1983	v Williamson	10-9	Qualifying	Embassy World Championship
	v Charlton	7-10	1st round	Embassy World Championship
	v Gibson	1-5	Qualifying	Jameson International
	v Griffiths	3-5	1st round	Professional Players Tournament
	v G. Foulds	7-9	Qualifying	Coral UK Championship
1984	v Giannaros	10-1	Qualifying	Embassy World Championship
	v N. Foulds	4-10	Qualifying	Embassy World Championship
	v Foldvari	5-3	Qualifying	Jameson International
	v Wilson	5-1	Qualifying	Jameson International
	v Reardon	4-5	1st round	Jameson International
	v Medati	4-5	Qualifying	Rothmans Grand Prix
	v Newbury	9-6	Qualifying	Coral UK Open
	v Wilson	8-9	Qualifying	Coral UK Open
1985	v T. Jones	1-5	Qualifying	Mercantile Credit Classic
	v Bales	9-5	Qualifying	Tolly Cobbold English Championship
	v Thorne	1-9	1st round	Tolly Cobbold English Championship
	v V. Harris	1-6	Qualifying	Dulux British Open
	v O'Kane	7-10	Qualifying	Embassy World Championship
	v Simngam	5-4	2nd round	Goya Matchroom Trophy
	v N. Foulds	3-5	3rd round	Goya Matchroom Trophy
	v Chappel	2-5	2nd round	Rothmans Grand Prix
	v Thorburn	4-9	3rd round	Coral UK Open
1986	v Rigitano	3-5	2nd round	Mercantile Credit Classic
	v Oliver	5-9	2nd round	Tolly Cobbold English Championship

	v Jonik	5-4	2nd round	Dulux British Open
	v Thorne	2-5	3rd round	Dulux British Open
	v Fitzmaurice	10-6	Qualifying	Embassy World Championship
	v Watterson	10-1	Qualifying	Embassy World Championship
	v Mans	7-10	Qualifying	Embassy World Championship
	v Reynolds	2-5	3rd round	BCE International
	v Scott	5-2	2nd round	Rothmans Grand Prix
	v Stevens	5-4	3rd round	Rothmans Grand Prix
	v Hallett	2-5	4th round	Rothmans Grand Prix
	v Chaperon	4-9	2nd round	Tennents UK Open
1987	v Medati	5-4	2nd round	Mercantile Credit Classic
	v Mountjoy	5-4	3rd round	Mercantile Credit Classic
	v Wilson	4-5	4th round	Mercantile Credit Classic
	v Smith	6-3	2nd round	Tolly Ales English Championship
	v Knowles	6-2	3rd round	Tolly Ales English Championship
	v West	6-3	4th round	Tolly Ales English Championship
	v Hallett	6-5	Quarter-final	Tolly Ales English Championship
	v Johnson	9-5	Semi-final	Tolly Ales English Championship
	v Meo	5-9	Final	Tolly Ales English Championship
	v Fowler	1-5	2nd round	Dulux British Open
	v Newbury	7-10	Qualifying	Embassy World Championship

JIM DONNELLY (Scotland)

Born 13.6.46
Turned professional 1981
World ranking 88 (73)
Amateur career 1978 Scottish champion.
Best professional performance Runner-up 1987 Scottish Championship.

1981	v Johnson	4-5	Qualifying	Jameson International
	v Sinclair	5-0	Quarter-final	Scottish Championship
	v Gibson	4-6	Semi-final	Scottish Championship
	v Medati	7-9	Qualifying	Coral UK Championship
1982	v Gibson	9-8	Qualifying	Embassy World Championship
	v Sinclair	9-8	Qualifying	Embassy World Championship
	v Reardon	5-10	1st round	Embassy World Championship
	v Macleod	5-6	1st round	Scottish Championship
	v Williamson	3-5	Qualifying	Jameson International
	v Watterson	4-5	1st round	Professional Players Tournament
	v Ross	9-5	Qualifying	Coral UK Championship
	v Knowles	6-9	1st round	Coral UK Championship
1983	v Sheehan	10-6	Qualifying	Embassy World Championship
	v Campbell	2-10	Qualifying	Embassy World Championship
	v Demarco	6-4	1st round	Scottish Championship
	v Sinclair	5-6	Semi-final	Scottish Championship
	v Bennett	5-1	Qualifying	Jameson International
	v Wilson	5-1	Qualifying	Jameson International
	v David Taylor	5-3	1st round	Jameson International

	v S. Francisco	1-5	2nd round	Jameson International
	v S. Davis	1-5	1st round	Professional Players Tournament
	v Murphy	4-9	Qualifying	Coral UK Championship
1984	v Watchorn	10-7	Qualifying	Embassy World Championship
	v Anderson	10-6	Qualifying	Embassy World Championship
	v F. Davis	5-10	Qualifying	Embassy World Championship
	v G. Foulds	3-5	Qualifying	Jameson International
	v Hargreaves	5-4	Qualifying	Rothmans Grand Prix
	v Wilson	2-5	1st round	Rothmans Grand Prix
	v Gibson	9-6	Qualifying	Coral UK Open
	v Campbell	6-9	Qualifying	Coral UK Open
1985	v Watchorn	5-1	Qualifying	Mercantile Credit Classic
	v Williams	3-5	Qualifying	Mercantile Credit Classic
	v John Rea	2-6	1st round	Scottish Championship
	v W. Jones	1-6	Qualifying	Dulux British Open
	v Fowler	0-10	Qualifying	Embassy World Championship
	v Jim Bear	2-5	2nd round	Goya Matchroom Trophy
	v Kelly	4-5	2nd round	Rothmans Grand Prix
	v Drago	8-9	1st round	Coral UK Open
1986	v Chalmers	5-0	2nd round	Mercantile Credit Classic
	v Campbell	2-5	3rd round	Mercantile Credit Classic
	v Wilkinson	5-4	2nd round	Dulux British Open
	v Meo	3-5	3rd round	Dulux British Open
	v John Rea	1-6	Quarter-final	Canada Dry Scottish Championship
	v Smith	10-6	Qualifying	Embassy World Championship
	v West	5-10	Qualifying	Embassy World Championship
	v Murphy	2-5	2nd round	BCE International
	v N. Gilbert	5-1	1st round	Rothmans Grand Prix
	v King	2-5	2nd round	Rothmans Grand Prix
	v N. Gilbert	8-9	1st round	Tennents UK Open
1987	v Watchorn	0-5	1st round	Mercantile Credit Classic
	v Macleod	6-2	1st round	Scottish Championship
	v Sinclair	6-4	Semi-final	Scottish Championship
	v Hendry	7-10	Final	Scottish Championship
	v T. Jones	2-5	2nd round	Dulux British Open
	v W. Jones	3-10	Qualifying	Embassy World Championship

TONY DRAGO (Malta)

Born 22.9.65
Turned professional 1985
World ranking 32 (37)
Amateur career 1984 Malta champion.
Best professional performance Quarter-finals 1986 Tennents UK Open.

1985	v Bales	2-5	1st round	Goya Matchroom Trophy
	v Watchorn	5-2	1st round	Rothmans Grand Prix
	v King	5-4	2nd round	Rothmans Grand Prix

	v Macleod	5-3	3rd round	Rothmans Grand Prix
	v Charlton	5-3	4th round	Rothmans Grand Prix
	v Wilson	2-5	5th round	Rothmans Grand Prix
	v Gilbert	9-5	1st round	Coral UK Open
	v Donnelly	9-8	2nd round	Coral UK Open
	v Wildman	9-5	3rd round	Coral UK Open
	v S. Davis	2-9	4th round	Coral UK Open
1986	v Cripsey	4-5	1st round	Mercantile Credit Classic
	v Gauvreau	5-3	2nd round	Dulux British Open
	v Williams	1-5	3rd round	Dulux British Open
	v Cripsey	10-4	Qualifying	Embassy World Championship
	v P. Francisco	4-10	Qualifying	Embassy World Championship
	v Morra	5-3	2nd round	BCE International
	v Thorne	5-2	3rd round	BCE International
	v Chaperon	1-5	4th round	BCE International
	v Watchorn	5-3	2nd round	Rothmans Grand Prix
	v Charlton	5-4	3rd round	Rothmans Grand Prix
	v S. Davis	1-5	4th round	Rothmans Grand Prix
	v Morra	9-6	2nd round	Tennents UK Open
	v Williams	9-7	3rd round	Tennents UK Open
	v Virgo	9-6	4th round	Tennents UK Open
	v Thorne	9-5	5th round	Tennents UK Open
	v S. Davis	8-9	Quarter-final	Tennents UK Open
1987	v Jonik	2-5	2nd round	Mercantile Credit Classic
	v Oliver	5-1	2nd round	Dulux British Open
	v Johnson	0-5	3rd round	Dulux British Open
	v Sinclair	9-10	Qualifying	Embassy World Championship

STEVE DUGGAN (England)

Born 10.4.58
Turned professional 1983
World ranking 37 (35)
Best professional performance Quarter-finals 1985 Goya Matchroom Trophy.

1983	v Darrington	5-4	Qualifying	Professional Players Tournament
	v Dunning	5-2	1st round	Professional Players Tournament
	v Reardon	2-5	2nd round	Professional Players Tournament
	v G. Foulds	8-9	Qualifying	Coral UK Championship
1984	v Browne	9-10	Qualifying	Embassy World Championship
	v T. Jones	5-2	Qualifying	Jameson International
	v Sinclair	0-5	Qualifying	Jameson International
	v Browne	5-2	Qualifying	Rothmans Grand Prix
	v S. Francisco	3-5	1st round	Rothmans Grand Prix
	v O'Kane	6-9	Qualifying	Coral UK Open
1985	v W. Jones	5-0	Qualifying	Mercantile Credit Classic
	v King	4-5	Qualifying	Mercantile Credit Classic

v B. Harris	9-8	Qualifying	Tolly Cobbold English Championship
v Hallett	4-9	1st round	Tolly Cobbold English Championship
v Foldvari	4-6	Qualifying	Dulux British Open
v T. Jones	8-10	Qualifying	Embassy World Championship
v F. Davis	5-1	2nd round	Goya Matchroom Trophy
v Reardon	5-3	3rd round	Goya Matchroom Trophy
v Black	5-1	4th round	Goya Matchroom Trophy
v Thorne	5-4	5th round	Goya Matchroom Trophy
v Thorburn	2-5	Quarter-final	Goya Matchroom Trophy
v Gauvreau	5-4	2nd round	Rothmans Grand Prix
v Wildman	4-5	3rd round	Rothmans Grand Prix
v Wych	5-9	2nd round	Coral UK Open
1986 v King	2-5	2nd round	Mercantile Credit Classic
v Longworth	4-9	2nd round	Tolly Cobbold English Championship
v Murphy	5-1	2nd round	Dulux British Open
v Hallett	3-5	3rd round	Dulux British Open
v Fisher	10-3	Qualifying	Embassy World Championship
v Wych	5-10	Qualifying	Embassy World Championship
v Bear	5-4	2nd round	BCE International
v Campbell	5-3	3rd round	BCE International
v Williams	4-5	4th round	BCE International
v Whitthread	5-1	2nd round	Rothmans Grand Prix
v Thorne	0-5	3rd round	Rothmans Grand Prix
v O'Boye	4-9	2nd round	Tennents UK Open
1987 v Watchorn	5-1	2nd round	Mercantile Credit Classic
v N. Foulds	5-3	3rd round	Mercantile Credit Classic
v Werbeniuk	5-0	4th round	Mercantile Credit Classic
v White	2-5	5th round	Mercantile Credit Classic
v Fisher	6-0	2nd round	Tolly Ales English Championship
v Meo	3-6	3rd round	Tolly Ales English Championship
v P. Gibson	5-3	2nd round	Dulux British Open
v Longworth	5-2	3rd round	Dulux British Open
v Thorne	2-5	4th round	Dulux British Open
v Roscoe	10-7	Qualifying	Embassy World Championship
v Chappel	3-10	Qualifying	Embassy World Championship

JOHN DUNNING (England)

Born 18.4.27
Turned professional 1970
World ranking 104 (83)
Best professional performance Quarter-finals 1974 World Championship, reached final 'round robin' group 1984 Yamaha International.

1972 v Houlihan	11-10	Qualifying	World Championship
v Miles	11-5	Qualifying	World Championship

	v Pulman	7-19	1st round	World Championship
1973	v David Taylor	4-9	1st round	World Championship
1974	v David Taylor	8-6	1st round	World Championship
	v Charlton	15-13	2nd round	World Championship
	v Miles	13-15	Quarter-final	World Championship
1975	v G. Owen	8-15	2nd round	World Championship
1976	v Reardon	7-15	1st round	Embassy World Championship
1977	v Virgo	6-11	Qualifying	Embassy World Championship
	v Parkin	5-4	1st round	Super Crystalate UK Championship
	v Higgins	0-5	Quarter-final	Super Crystalate UK Championship
1978	v Fagan	5-9	Qualifying	Embassy World Championship
	v Greaves	9-3	Qualifying	Coral UK Championship
	v F. Davis	2-9	1st round	Coral UK Championship
1979	v Jack Rea	9-5	Prelim	Embassy World Championship
	v David Taylor	8-9	Qualifying	Embassy World Championship
	v Greaves	9-8	1st round	Coral UK Championship
	v S. Davis	3-9	2nd round	Coral UK Championship
1980	v Johnson	6-9	Qualifying	Coral UK Championship
1981	v Greaves	9-4	Qualifying	John Courage English
	v David Taylor	9-8	1st round	John Courage English
	v Thorne	0-9	2nd round	John Courage English
	v Bennett	9-6	Qualifying	Embassy World Championship
	v Fagan	9-7	Qualifying	Embassy World Championship
	v Stevens	4-10	1st round	Embassy World Championship
	v Gibson	5-3	Qualifying	Jameson International
	v Martin	2-5	1st round	Jameson International
1982	v Macleod	9-4	Qualifying	Embassy World Championship
	v Spencer	4-10	1st round	Embassy World Championship
	v Roscoe	2-5	Qualifying	Jameson International
	v Wildman	4-5	1st round	Professional Players Tournament
1983	v B. Harris	3-5	Qualifying	Jameson International
	v Duggan	2-5	1st round	Professional Players Tournament
	v Andrewartha	9-2	Qualifying	Coral UK Championship
	v Spencer	7-9	1st round	Coral UK Championship
1984	v Oliver	3-10	Qualifying	Embassy World Championship
	v Cripsey	5-3	Qualifying	Jameson International
	v F. Davis	4-5	Qualifying	Jameson International
	v D. Hughes	5-0	Qualifying	Rothmans Grand Prix
	v Mans	5-4	1st round	Rothmans Grand Prix
	v Knowles	1-5	2nd round	Rothmans Grand Prix
	v John Rea	3-9	Qualifying	Coral UK Open
1985	v W. Jones	6-10	Qualifying	Embassy World Championship
	v Everton	5-2	2nd round	Goya Matchroom Trophy
	v Meo	0-5	3rd round	Goya Matchroom Trophy
	v Agrawal	0-5	2nd round	Rothmans Grand Prix
1986	v West	3-10	Qualifying	Embassy World Championship
	v Demarco	5-4	1st round	BCE International
	v Newbury	4-5	2nd round	BCE International
	v P. Gibson	1-5	1st round	Rothmans Grand Prix
	v Kearney	9-6	1st round	Tennents UK Open

	v M. Gibson	2-9	2nd round	Tennents UK Open
1987	v B. Bennett	5-2	1st round	Mercantile Credit Classic
	v Browne	1-5	2nd round	Mercantile Credit Classic
	v Cripsey	1-6	2nd round	Tolly Ales English Championship
	v Watchorn	2-5	1st round	Dulux British Open
	v Caggianello	10-7	Qualifying	Embassy World Championship
	v Scott	7-10	Qualifying	Embassy World Championship

RAY EDMONDS (England)

Born 28.5.36
Turned professional 1978
World ranking 60 (46)
Amateur career World champion 1972, 1974; English champion 1969, 1974.
Best professional performance Quarter-finals 1979 Coral UK Championship.

1978	v Virgo	4-9	Qualifying	Coral UK Championship
1979	v Meadowcroft	9-3	2nd round	Coral UK Championship
	v F. Davis	9-6	3rd round	Coral UK Championship
	v Werbeniuk	8-9	Quarter-final	Coral UK Championship
1980	v Hood	9-6	Qualifying	Embassy World Championship
	v David Taylor	3-10	1st round	Embassy World Championship
	v Hallett	8-9	Qualifying	Coral UK Championship
1981	v Hallett	9-3	Qualifying	John Courage English
	v F. Davis	9-6	1st round	John Courage English
	v Johnson	9-5	2nd round	John Courage English
	v S. Davis	0-9	Semi-final	John Courage English
	v Wildman	9-3	Qualifying	Embassy World Championship
	v Williams	9-7	Qualifying	Embassy World Championship
	v Spencer	9-10	1st round	Embassy World Championship
	v E. Hughes	5-4	1st round	Jameson International
	v Spencer	3-5	2nd round	Jameson International
	v Thorne	4-9	2nd round	Coral UK Championship
1982	v Reynolds	6-9	Qualifying	Embassy World Championship
	v D. Hughes	5-0	Qualifying	Jameson International
	v Miles	5-1	Qualifying	Jameson International
	v Spencer	2-5	1st round	Jameson International
	v Dennis Taylor	4-5	1st round	Professional Players Tournament
	v Fisher	8-9	Qualifying	Coral UK Championship
1983	v Jonik	10-4	Qualifying	Embassy World Championship
	v Reynolds	6-10	Qualifying	Embassy World Championship
	v Jack Rea	5-1	Qualifying	Jameson International
	v E. McLaughlin	5-1	Qualifying	Jameson International
	v Knowles	1-5	1st round	Jameson International
	v Stevens	1-5	1st round	Professional Players Tournament
	v Medati	7-9	Qualifying	Coral UK Championship
1984	v Greaves	10-0	Qualifying	Embassy World Championship
	v Van Rensberg	9-10	Qualifying	Embassy World Championship

v Foldvari	1-5	Qualifying	Jameson International
v Rigitano	3-5	Qualifying	Rothmans Grand Prix
v John Rea	6-9	Qualifying	Coral UK Open
1985 v Hargreaves	5-2	Qualifying	Mercantile Credit Classic
v Watterson	5-2	Qualifying	Mercantile Credit Classic
v Johnson	4-5	Qualifying	Mercantile Credit Classic
v Longworth	4-9	Qualifying	Tolly Cobbold English Championship
v Mienie	6-1	Qualifying	Dulux British Open
v Miles	1-6	1st round	Dulux British Open
v Foldvari	10-3	Qualifying	Embassy World Championship
v Wildman	10-7	Qualifying	Embassy World Championship
v Stevens	8-10	1st round	Embassy World Championship
v Bales	0-5	2nd round	Goya Matchroom Trophy
v Kearney	5-2	2nd round	Rothmans Grand Prix
v O'Kane	5-2	3rd round	Rothmans Grand Prix
v Knowles	3-5	4th round	Rothmans Grand Prix
v Van Rensberg	9-5	2nd round	Coral UK Open
v Higgins	8-9	3rd round	Coral UK Open
1986 v Smith	2-5	2nd round	Mercantile Credit Classic
v Smith	9-8	2nd round	Tolly Cobbold English Championship
v David Taylor	9-6	3rd round	Tolly Cobbold English Championship
v N. Foulds	4-9	4th round	Tolly Cobbold English Championship
v Hargreaves	3-5	2nd round	Dulux British Open
v Kelly	10-0	Qualifying	Embassy World Championship
v Darrington	10-5	Qualifying	Embassy World Championship
v Wildman	10-9	Qualifying	Embassy World Championship
v S. Davis	4-10	1st round	Embassy World Championship
v James	5-2	2nd round	BCE International
v David Taylor	4-5	3rd round	BCE International
v O'Boye	2-5	2nd round	Rothmans Grand Prix
v Bear	9-6	2nd round	Tennents UK Open
v White	4-9	3rd round	Tennents UK Open
1987 v Williamson	2-5	2nd round	Mercantile Credit Classic
v Bennett	6-1	2nd round	Tolly Ales English Championship
v Reynolds	3-6	3rd round	Tolly Ales English Championship
v G. Foulds	3-5	2nd round	Dulux British Open
v James	10-1	Qualifying	Embassy World Championship
v Sinclair	10-6	Qualifying	Embassy World Championship
v Macleod	7-10	Qualifying	Embassy World Championship

FRANÇOIS ELLIS (South Africa)

Born –
Turned professional 1983
World ranking 118 (unranked)
Amateur career South African champion 1979, 1980.

1986 v Mans	7-6	2nd round	South African Championship
v Van Rensberg	8-2	Semi-final	South African Championship

	v S. Francisco	1-9	Final	South African Championship
	v Morra	3-5	1st round	BCE International
	v Wildman	1-5	2nd round	Rothmans Grand Prix
	v D. Hughes	6-9	1st round	Tennents UK Open
1987	v Morra	1-5	1st round	Mercantile Credit Classic
	v Smith	5-2	1st round	Dulux British Open
	v Medati	0-5	2nd round	Dulux British Open

CLIVE EVERTON (Wales)

Born 7.9.37
Turned professional 1981
World ranking 113 (100)

	v Kennerley	5-4	Qualifying	Jameson International
1981	v Kennerley	5-4	Qualifying	Jameson International
	v Watterson	4-5	Qualifying	Jameson International
	v Gibson	9-7	Qualifying	Coral UK Championship
	v White	4-9	Qualifying	Coral UK Championship
1982	v Reardon	1-6	1st round	Woodpecker Welsh Championship
	v D. Hughes	4-9	Qualifying	Embassy World Championship
	v Watterson	1-5	Qualifying	Jameson International
	v Fagan	5-2	1st round	Professional Players Tournament
	v Thorburn	2-5	2nd round	Professional Players Tournament
	v Murphy	4-9	Qualifying	Coral UK Championship
1983	v Griffiths	1-6	Quarter-final	Woodpecker Welsh Championship
	v Wilson	1-10	Qualifying	Embassy World Championship
	v Andrewartha	1-5	Qualifying	Jameson International
	v Thorne	1-5	1st round	Professional Players Tournament
	v Watterson	6-9	Qualifying	Coral UK Championship
1984	v Mountjoy	1-6	1st round	Strongbow Welsh Championship
	v Parrott	2-10	Qualifying	Embassy World Championship
	v Mikkelsen	0-5	Qualifying	Jameson International
	v Houlihan	5-3	Qualifying	Rothmans Grand Prix
	v Charlton	1-5	1st round	Rothmans Grand Prix
	v Watchorn	6-9	Qualifying	Coral UK Open
1985	v Browne	0-5	Qualifying	Mercantile Credit Classic
	v Fowler	1-6	Qualifying	Dulux British Open
	v G. Foulds	2-10	Qualifying	Embassy World Championship
	v Reardon	2-6	Quarter-final	BCE Welsh Championship
	v Dunning	2-5	2nd round	Goya Matchroom Trophy
	v P. Francisco	0-5	2nd round	Rothmans Grand Prix
	v Murphy	4-9	2nd round	Coral UK Open
1986	v Browne	0-5	2nd round	Mercantile Credit Classic
	v W. Jones	2-6	1st round	Zetters Welsh Championship
	v Medati	1-5	2nd round	Dulux British Open
	v Miles	3-10	Qualifying	Embassy World Championship
	v Jenkins	3-5	1st round	BCE International
	v Rigitano	1-5	1st round	Rothmans Grand Prix
	v Bear	1-9	1st round	Tennents UK Open

1987	v W. Jones	0-5	2nd round	Mercantile Credit Classic
	v Roscoe	2-6	1st round	Matchroom Welsh Championship
	v Fitzmaurice	2-10	Qualifying	Embassy World Championship

PATSY FAGAN (Republic of Ireland)

Born 15.1.51
Turned professional 1976
World ranking 76 (42)
Best professional performance Winner 1977 Super Crystalate UK Championship.

1977	v Meadowcroft	11-9	Qualifying	Embassy World Championship
	v Reardon	7-13	1st round	Embassy World Championship
	v Jack Rea	5-1	1st round	Super Crystalate UK Championship
	v F. Davis	5-0	2nd round	Super Crystalate UK Championship
	v Meadowcroft	5-4	Quarter-final	Super Crystalate UK Championship
	v Virgo	9-8	Semi-final	Super Crystalate UK Championship
	v Mountjoy	**12-9**	**Final**	**Super Crystalate UK Championship**
1978	v Pulman	2-4	1st round	Benson & Hedges Masters
	v Dunning	9-5	Qualifying	Embassy World Championship
	v Higgins	13-12	1st round	Embassy World Championship
	v F. Davis	10-13	Quarter-final	Embassy World Championship
	v David Taylor	7-9	1st round	Coral UK Championship
1979	v S. Davis	2-9	Qualifying	Embassy World Championship
	v Hallett	9-4	2nd round	Coral UK Championship
	v Miles	9-5	3rd round	Coral UK Championship
	v Dennis Taylor	6-9	Quarter-final	Coral UK Championship
1980	v S. Davis	6-10	1st round	Embassy World Championship
	v Johnson	9-4	1st round	Coral UK Championship
	v Griffiths	8-9	2nd round	Coral UK Championship
1981	v Dunning	7-9	Qualifying	Embassy World Championship
	v Watterson	5-2	Qualifying	Jameson International
	v Higgins	3-5	2nd round	Jameson International
	v Hallett	5-9	Qualifying	Coral UK Championship
1982	v Murphy	2-6	Quarter-final	Irish Championship
	v French	9-6	Qualifying	Embassy World Championship
	v David Taylor	10-9	1st round	Embassy World Championship
	v Stevens	7-13	2nd round	Embassy World Championship
	v Watterson	1-5	Qualifying	Jameson International
	v Everton	2-5	1st round	Professional Players Tournament
	v B. Harris	9-6	1st round	Coral UK Championship
	v S. Davis	3-9	2nd round	Coral UK Championship
1983	v Murphy	6-4	Quarter-final	Irish Championship
	v Dennis Taylor	1-6	Semi-final	Irish Championship
	v Fisher	8-10	Qualifying	Embassy World Championship
	v Martin	0-5	Qualifying	Jameson International
	v Parrott	2-5	1st round	Professional Players Tournament

1984	v Higgins	3-5	Qualifying	Lada Classic
	v Wych	3-10	Qualifying	Embassy World Championship
	v Newbury	0-5	Qualifying	Jameson International
	v T. Jones	2-9	Qualifying	Coral UK Open
1985	v Williamson	5-1	Qualifying	Mercantile Credit Classic
	v Wildman	5-3	Qualifying	Mercantile Credit Classic
	v Griffiths	0-5	1st round	Mercantile Credit Classic
	v Murphy	6-2	Quarter-final	Irish Championship
	v Higgins	3-6	Semi-final	Irish Championship
	v Gibson	10-8	Qualifying	Embassy World Championship
	v Wilson	10-9	Qualifying	Embassy World Championship
	v Thorne	10-6	1st round	Embassy World Championship
	v Reardon	9-13	2nd round	Embassy World Championship
	v Mienie	5-4	2nd round	Goya Matchroom Trophy
	v White	2-5	3rd round	Goya Matchroom Trophy
	v Oliver	4-5	2nd round	Rothmans Grand Prix
	v B. Harris	9-2	2nd round	Coral UK Open
	v N. Foulds	5-9	3rd round	Coral UK Open
1986	v Fitzmaurice	3-5	2nd round	Mercantile Credit Classic
	v Fitzmaurice	5-4	2nd round	Dulux British Open
	v Mountjoy	5-1	3rd round	Dulux British Open
	v Parrott	0-5	4th round	Dulux British Open
	v Knowles	5-4	Quarter-final	Benson & Hedges Irish Masters
	v White	0-6	Semi-final	Benson & Hedges Irish Masters
	v Thornley	7-10	Qualifying	Embassy World Championship
	v Kearney	0-5	1st round	Strongbow Irish Championship
	v Sinclair	0-5	2nd round	BCE International
	v Grace	5-3	2nd round	Rothmans Grand Prix
	v Virgo	2-5	3rd round	Rothmans Grand Prix
	v Wright	0-9	2nd round	Tennents UK Open
1987	v Grace	3-5	2nd round	Dulux British Open
	v Oliver	2-10	Qualifying	Embassy World Championship
	v Burke	3-5	1st round	Matchroom Irish Championship

MICK FISHER (England)

Born 12.7.44
Turned professional 1982
World ranking 93 (87)

1982	v Murphy	5-1	Qualifying	Jameson International
	v F. Davis	5-3	Qualifying	Jameson International
	v David Taylor	1-5	1st round	Jameson International
	v Black	9-3	Qualifying	Coral UK Championship
	v Edmonds	9-8	Qualifying	Coral UK Championship
	v Reynolds	6-9	1st round	Coral UK Championship
1983	v Fagan	10-8	Qualifying	Embassy World Championship
	v E. McLaughlin	10-9	Qualifying	Embassy World Championship
	v Stevens	2-10	1st round	Embassy World Championship

	v E. Hughes	4-5	Qualifying	Jameson International
	v F. Davis	5-4	1st round	Professional Players Tournament
	v Charlton	4-5	2nd round	Professional Players Tournament
	v Parrott	0-9	Qualifying	Coral UK Championship
1984	v Thornley	10-8	Qualifying	Embassy World Championship
	v Gibson	7-10	Qualifying	Embassy World Championship
	v Bales	3-5	Qualifying	Jameson International
	v Newbury	0-5	Qualifying	Rothmans Grand Prix
	v Watchorn	9-5	Qualifying	Coral UK Open
	v Williams	8-9	Qualifying	Coral UK Open
1985	v Longworth	1-5	Qualifying	Mercantile Credit Classic
	v French	9-8	Qualifying	Tolly Cobbold English Championship
	v Meo	3-9	1st round	Tolly Cobbold English Championship
	v John Rea	0-6	Qualifying	Dulux British Open
	v Rigitano	2-10	Qualifying	Embassy World Championship
	v Mikkelsen	3-5	1st round	Goya Matchroom Trophy
	v Bales	3-5	2nd round	Rothmans Grand Prix
	v Simngam	4-9	2nd round	Coral UK Open
1986	v Jack Rea	5-3	2nd round	Mercantile Credit Classic
	v Higgins	0-5	3rd round	Mercantile Credit Classic
	v Chalmers	2-9	2nd round	Tolly Cobbold English Championship
	v J. McLaughlin	3-5	2nd round	Dulux British Open
	v Duggan	3-10	Qualifying	Embassy World Championship
	v Hines	2-5	1st round	BCE International
	v Wright	1-5	1st round	Rothmans Grand Prix
	v Greaves	9-4	1st round	Tennents UK Open
	v V. Harris	4-9	2nd round	Tennents UK Open
1987	v Demarco	5-0	1st round	Mercantile Credit Classic
	v F. Davis	5-2	2nd round	Mercantile Credit Classic
	v Charlton	0-5	3rd round	Mercantile Credit Classic
	v Whitthread	6-3	1st round	Tolly Ales English Championship
	v Duggan	0-6	2nd round	Tolly Ales English Championship
	v Chaperon	2-5	2nd round	Dulux British Open
	v Owers	5-10	Qualifying	Embassy World Championship

JACK FITZMAURICE (England)

Born 25.4.28
Turned professional 1981
World ranking 89 (76)
Best professional performance Last 32 1982 Embassy World Championship.

1981	v Bennett	5-1	Qualifying	Jameson International
	v E. Hughes	3-5	Qualifying	Jameson International
	v Gibson	6-9	Qualifying	Coral UK Championship
1982	v Morra	9-7	Qualifying	Embassy World Championship
	v Stevens	4-10	1st round	Embassy World Championship

	v Black	5-3	Qualifying	Jameson International
	v Dodd	3-5	Qualifying	Jameson International
	v Sheehan	5-1	1st round	Professional Players Tournament
	v Reynolds	0-5	2nd round	Professional Players Tournament
	v Kelly	0-8	Qualifying	Coral UK Championship
1983	v E. Hughes	7-10	Qualifying	Embassy World Championship
	v Morgan	4-5	Qualifying	Jameson International
	v Martin	0-5	1st round	Professional Players Tournament
	v B. Harris	3-9	Qualifying	Coral UK Championship
1984	v Murphy	8-10	Qualifying	Embassy World Championship
	v O'Kane	4-5	Qualifying	Jameson International
	v John Rea	2-5	Qualifying	Rothmans Grand Prix
	v Cripsey	9-8	Qualifying	Coral UK Open
	v Parrott	6-9	Qualifying	Coral UK Open
1985	v G. Foulds	1-5	Qualifying	Mercantile Credit Classic
	v Greaves	9-3	Qualifying	Tolly Cobbold English Championship
	v Reynolds	2-9	1st round	Tolly Cobbold English Championship
	v Watterson	1-6	Qualifying	Dulux British Open
	v T. Jones	4-10	Qualifying	Embassy World Championship
	v Watterson	5-2	2nd round	Goya Matchroom Trophy
	v Macleod	1-5	3rd round	Goya Matchroom Trophy
	v Sinclair	5-3	2nd round	Rothmans Grand Prix
	v White	0-5	3rd round	Rothmans Grand Prix
	v W. Jones	3-9	2nd round	Coral UK Open
1986	v Fagan	5-3	2nd round	Mercantile Credit Classic
	v Dennis Taylor	1-5	3rd round	Mercantile Credit Classic
	v Miles	5-9	2nd round	Tolly Cobbold English Championship
	v Fagan	4-5	2nd round	Dulux British Open
	v Dodd	6-10	Qualifying	Embassy World Championship
	v Burke	4-5	1st round	BCE International
	v Mienie	2-5	1st round	Rothmans Grand Prix
	v Hines	9-4	1st round	Tennents UK Open
	v T. Jones	0-9	2nd round	Tennents UK Open
1987	v Wilkinson	2-5	1st round	Mercantile Credit Classic
	v Scott	6-2	2nd round	Tolly Ales English Championship
	v David Taylor	1-6	3rd round	Tolly Ales English Championship
	v Wilkinson	0-5	1st round	Dulux British Open
	v Everton	10-2	Qualifying	Embassy World Championship
	v Chaperon	2-10	Qualifying	Embassy World Championship

ROBBIE FOLDVARI (Australia)

Born 2.6.60
Turned professional 1984
World ranking 80 (69)

	v Rigitano	5-2	Qualifying	Jameson International
1984	v Edmonds	5-1	Qualifying	Jameson International
	v Dodd	3-5	Qualifying	Jameson International

v Gauvreau	2-5	Qualifying	Rothmans Grand Prix
v Greaves	9-5	Qualifying	Coral UK Open
v Cripsey	7-9	Qualifying	Coral UK Open
1985 v Houlihan	5-1	Qualifying	Mercantile Credit Classic
v Jack Rea	5-4	Qualifying	Mercantile Credit Classic
v Martin	5-2	Qualifying	Mercantile Credit Classic
v Thorne	2-5	1st round	Mercantile Credit Classic
v Duggan	6-4	Qualifying	Dulux British Open
v Meo	0-6	1st round	Dulux British Open
v Oliver	10-3	Qualifying	Embassy World Championship
v Edmonds	3-10	Qualifying	Embassy World Championship
v Robinson	7-2	2nd round	Australian Championship
v Campbell	5-8	Quarter-final	Australian Championship
v V. Harris	5-4	2nd round	Goya Matchroom Trophy
v Spencer	4-5	3rd round	Goya Matchroom Trophy
v Darrington	3-5	2nd round	Rothmans Grand Prix
v Darrington	6-9	2nd round	Coral UK Open
1986 v Houlihan	4-5	2nd round	Mercantile Credit Classic
v Kearney	5-2	2nd round	Dulux British Open
v Werbeniuk	4-5	3rd round	Dulux British Open
v Rigitano	10-6	Qualifying	Embassy World Championship
v Miles	10-7	Qualifying	Embassy World Championship
v Parrott	6-10	Qualifying	Embassy World Championship
v Jenkins	6-3	2nd round	Australian Championship
v Morgan	6-2	Quarter-final	Australian Championship
v Campbell	3-8	Semi-final	Australian Championship
v B. Harris	5-0	2nd round	BCE International
v Dennis Taylor	1-5	3rd round	BCE International
v W. Jones	3-5	2nd round	Rothmans Grand Prix
v Spencer	6-9	2nd round	Tennents UK Open
1987 v Mikkelsen	1-5	2nd round	Mercantile Credit Classic
v Mikkelsen	5-3	2nd round	Dulux British Open
v Williams	4-5	3rd round	Dulux British Open
v Wildman	5-10	Qualifying	Embassy World Championship

GEOFF FOULDS (England)

Born 20.11.39
Turned professional 1981
World ranking 63 (79)
Best professional performance Last 32 1986 BCE International.

1981 v French	2-5	Qualifying	Jameson International
v Kelly	9-7	Qualifying	Coral UK Championship
v Knowles	1-9	Qualifying	Coral UK Championship
1982 v Wildman	8-9	Qualifying	Embassy World Championship
v Kelly	4-5	Qualifying	Jameson International
v Spencer	1-5	1st round	Professional Players Tournament
v Gibson	9-3	Qualifying	Coral UK Championship

	v Williams	7-9	Qualifying	Coral UK Championship
1983	v Gibson	10-6	Qualifying	Embassy World Championship
	v Meo	4-10	Qualifying	Embassy World Championship
	v Burke	5-2	Qualifying	Jameson International
	v E. Hughes	1-5	Qualifying	Jameson International
	v Burke	4-5	Qualifying	Professional Players Tournament
	v Duggan	9-8	Qualifying	Coral UK Championship
	v Dodd	9-7	Qualifying	Coral UK Championship
	v S. Davis	1-9	1st round	Coral UK Championship
1984	v Morra	2-10	Qualifying	Embassy World Championship
	v P. Francisco	5-4	Qualifying	Jameson International
	v Williamson	5-4	Qualifying	Jameson International
	v Donnelly	5-3	Qualifying	Jameson International
	v Campbell	3-5	Qualifying	Jameson International
	v Murphy	1-5	Qualifying	Rothmans Grand Prix
	v D. Hughes	9-7	Qualifying	Coral UK Open
	v Browne	5-9	Qualifying	Coral UK Open
1985	v Chaperon	5-3	Qualifying	Mercantile Credit Classic
	v Jonik	5-2	Qualifying	Mercantile Credit Classic
	v Fitzmaurice	5-1	Qualifying	Mercantile Credit Classic
	v Hallett	4-5	Qualifying	Mercantile Credit Classic
	v F. Davis	9-2	Qualifying	Tolly Cobbold English Championship
	v Parrott	4-9	1st round	Tolly Cobbold English Championship
	v T. Jones	0-6	Qualifying	Dulux British Open
	v Parkin	10-6	Qualifying	Embassy World Championship
	v Everton	10-2	Qualifying	Embassy World Championship
	v Roscoe	10-7	Qualifying	Embassy World Championship
	v Johnson	6-10	Qualifying	Embassy World Championship
	v Roscoe	3-5	2nd round	Goya Matchroom Trophy
	v Black	5-3	2nd round	Rothmans Grand Prix
	v Charlton	1-5	3rd round	Rothmans Grand Prix
	v Sinclair	4-9	2nd round	Coral UK Open
1986	v Black	5-2	2nd round	Mercantile Credit Classic
	v Werbeniuk	3-5	3rd round	Mercantile Credit Classic
	v Watterson	9-1	2nd round	Tolly Cobbold English Championship
	v N. Foulds	4-9	3rd round	Tolly Cobbold English Championship
	v P. Francisco	2-5	2nd round	Dulux British Open
	v Roscoe	3-10	Qualifying	Embassy World Championship
	v V. Harris	5-4	2nd round	BCE International
	v Werbeniuk	5-2	3rd round	BCE International
	v N. Foulds	0-5	4th round	BCE International
	v Wilkinson	5-3	1st round	Rothmans Grand Prix
	v Mikkelsen	5-1	2nd round	Rothmans Grand Prix
	v Campbell	0-5	3rd round	Rothmans Grand Prix
	v Roe	1-7 retd	1st round	Tennents UK Open
1987	v Chalmers	5-4	1st round	Mercantile Credit Classic
	v O'Kane	5-4	2nd round	Mercantile Credit Classic
	v Martin	4-5	3rd round	Mercantile Credit Classic
	v B. Harris	1-6	2nd round	Tolly Ales English Championship

v Edmonds	5-3	2nd round	Dulux British Open
v Wilson	3-5	3rd round	Dulux British Open
v Watchorn	10-6	Qualifying	Embassy World Championship
v Fowler	6-10	Qualifying	Embassy World Championship

NEAL FOULDS (England)

Born 13.7.63
Turned professional 1983
World ranking 3 (13)
Best professional performances Winner 1986 BCE International; runner-up 1986 Tennents UK Open, 1987 Dulux British Open; semi-finals 1987 Embassy World Championship.

1983	v French	2-5	Qualifying	Professional Players Tournament
	v Roscoe	9-2	Qualifying	Coral UK Championship
	v Meadowcroft	9-2	Qualifying	Coral UK Championship
	v David Taylor	4-9	1st round	Coral UK Championship
1984	v French	10-5	Qualifying	Embassy World Championship
	v Dodd	10-4	Qualifying	Embassy World Championship
	v Meadowcroft	10-2	Qualifying	Embassy World Championship
	v Higgins	10-9	1st round	Embassy World Championship
	v Mountjoy	6-13	2nd round	Embassy World Championship
	v Bennett	5-0	Qualifying	Jameson International
	v Griffiths	3-5	1st round	Jameson International
	v Demarco	5-2	1st round	Rothmans Grand Prix
	v T. Jones	5-0	2nd round	Rothmans Grand Prix
	v Thorne	5-1	3rd round	Rothmans Grand Prix
	v Knowles	5-2	Quarter-final	Rothmans Grand Prix
	v Dennis Taylor	3-9	Semi-final	Rothmans Grand Prix
	v Fowler	6-9	Qualifying	Coral UK Open
1985	v Longworth	3-5	Qualifying	Mercantile Credit Classic
	v D. Hughes	9-3	1st round	Tolly Cobbold English Championship
	v White	7-9	2nd round	Tolly Cobbold English Championship
	v Hargreaves	6-1	1st round	Dulux British Open
	v Higgins	1-5	2nd round	Dulux British Open
	v Rigitano	10-8	Qualifying	Embassy World Championship
	v S. Davis	8-10	1st round	Embassy World Championship
	v Dodd	5-3	3rd round	Goya Matchroom Trophy
	v Knowles	5-3	4th round	Goya Matchroom Trophy
	v David Taylor	5-4	5th round	Goya Matchroom Trophy
	v Johnson	5-2	Quarter-final	Goya Matchroom Trophy
	v White	5-9	Semi-final	Goya Matchroom Trophy
	v Darrington	5-0	3rd round	Rothmans Grand Prix
	v Higgins	3-5	4th round	Rothmans Grand Prix
	v Fagan	9-5	3rd round	Coral UK Open
	v Johnson	9-8	4th round	Coral UK Open
	v Dennis Taylor	5-9	5th round	Coral UK Open

1986	v Bradley	5-3	3rd round	Mercantile Credit Classic
	v Hendry	5-4	4th round	Mercantile Credit Classic
	v Campbell	5-1	5th round	Mercantile Credit Classic
	v Mountjoy	3-5	Quarter-final	Mercantile Credit Classic
	v G. Foulds	9-4	3rd round	Tolly Cobbold English Championship
	v Edmonds	9-4	4th round	Tolly Cobbold English Championship
	v White	9-4	Quarter-final	Tolly Cobbold English Championship
	v Hallett	9-8	Semi-final	Tolly Cobbold English Championship
	v Meo	7-9	Final	Tolly Cobbold English Championship
	v Hargreaves	5-4	3rd round	Dulux British Open
	v Griffiths	3-5	4th round	Dulux British Open
	v P. Francisco	10-9	Qualifying	Embassy World Championship
	v Knowles	9-10	1st round	Embassy World Championship
	v Thorne	3-6	1st round	Matchroom Trophy
	v Miles	5-2	3rd round	BCE International
	v G. Foulds	5-0	4th round	BCE International
	v Owers	5-1	5th round	BCE International
	v Reynolds	5-2	Quarter-final	BCE International
	v E. Hughes	9-8	Semi-final	BCE International
	v Thorburn	**12-9**	**Final**	**BCE International**
	v Miles	5-1	3rd round	Rothmans Grand Prix
	v Wilson	5-0	4th round	Rothmans Grand Prix
	v Thorne	5-3	5th round	Rothmans Grand Prix
	v Meo	5-3	Quarter-final	Rothmans Grand Prix
	v Williams	8-9	Semi-final	Rothmans Grand Prix
	v Cripsey	9-7	3rd round	Tennents UK Open
	v Wych	9-3	4th round	Tennents UK Open
	v White	9-7	5th round	Tennents UK Open
	v Thorburn	9-2	Quarter-final	Tennents UK Open
	v Parrott	9-2	Semi-final	Tennents UK Open
	v S. Davis	7-16	Final	Tennents UK Open
1987	v Duggan	3-5	3rd round	Mercantile Credit Classic
	v Dennis Taylor	2-5	1st round	Benson & Hedges Masters
	v Owers	3-6	3rd round	Tolly Ales English Championship
	v Roe	5-1	3rd round	Dulux British Open
	v King	5-4	4th round	Dulux British Open
	v Thorne	5-2	5th round	Dulux British Open
	v Virgo	5-3	Quarter-final	Dulux British Open
	v Knowles	9-2	Semi-final	Dulux British Open
	v White	9-13	Final	Dulux British Open
	v Virgo	10-4	1st round	Embassy World Championship
	v Dennis Taylor	13-10	2nd round	Embassy World Championship
	v Hallett	13-9	Quarter-final	Embassy World Championship
	v Johnson	9-16	Semi-final	Embassy World Championship

DANNY FOWLER (England)

Born 30.7.56
Turned professional 1984
World ranking 40 (33)
Best professional performance Last 16 Mercantile Credit Classic.

1984	v Chaperon	5-0	Qualifying	Jameson International
	v Andrewartha	5-0	Qualifying	Jameson International
	v Martin	5-0	Qualifying	Jameson International
	v Dennis Taylor	0-5	1st round	Jameson International
	v Reynolds	2-5	1st round	Rothmans Grand Prix
	v Demarco	9-3	Qualifying	Coral UK Open
	v Oliver	9-3	Qualifying	Coral UK Open
	v F. Davis	9-4	Qualifying	Coral UK Open
	v N. Foulds	9-6	Qualifying	Coral UK Open
	v Reardon	2-9	1st round	Coral UK Open
1985	v Rigitano	5-0	Qualifying	Mercantile Credit Classic
	v Murphy	5-0	Qualifying	Mercantile Credit Classic
	v Meadowcroft	5-2	Qualifying	Mercantile Credit Classic
	v Wilson	4-5	Qualifying	Mercantile Credit Classic
	v Oliver	9-7	Qualifying	Tolly Cobbold English Championship
	v S. Davis	3-9	1st round	Tolly Cobbold English Championship
	v Everton	6-1	Qualifying	Dulux British Open
	v Williams	6-4	1st round	Dulux British Open
	v Bradley	4-5	2nd round	Dulux British Open
	v Hargreaves	10-0	Qualifying	Embassy World Championship
	v Donnelly	10-0	Qualifying	Embassy World Championship
	v Parrott	2-10	Qualifying	Embassy World Championship
	v Agrawal	5-2	2nd round	Goya Matchroom Trophy
	v Thorne	1-5	3rd round	Goya Matchroom Trophy
	v Jonik	5-4	2nd round	Rothmans Grand Prix
	v Werbeniuk	5-1	3rd round	Rothmans Grand Prix
	v S. Davis	1-5	4th round	Rothmans Grand Prix
	v Wilkinson	9-6	2nd round	Coral UK Open
	v Mans	9-2	3rd round	Coral UK Open
	v Meo	2-9	4th round	Coral UK Open
1986	v Bales	5-4	2nd round	Mercantile Credit Classic
	v White	1-5	3rd round	Mercantile Credit Classic
	v Darrington	9-3	2nd round	Tolly Cobbold English Championship
	v Johnson	7-9	3rd round	Tolly Cobbold English Championship
	v Chappel	5-4	2nd round	Dulux British Open
	v Virgo	1-5	3rd round	Dulux British Open
	v Oliver	10-8	Qualifying	Embassy World Championship
	v Scott	10-7	Qualifying	Embassy World Championship
	v Macleod	10-6	Qualifying	Embassy World Championship
	v Griffiths	2-10	1st round	Embassy World Championship
	v J. McLaughlin	2-5	2nd round	BCE International
	v Bear	2-5	2nd round	Rothmans Grand Prix
	v Darrington	9-6	2nd round	Tennents UK Open

	v Thorburn	7-9	3rd round	Tennents UK Open
1987	v Wilkinson	5-1	2nd round	Mercantile Credit Classic
	v Knowles	5-4	3rd round	Mercantile Credit Classic
	v Hallett	5-4	4th round	Mercantile Credit Classic
	v Hendry	4-5	5th round	Mercantile Credit Classic
	v Bradley	6-3	3rd round	Tolly Ales English Championship
	v Meo	0-6	4th round	Tolly Ales English Championship
	v Dodd	5-1	2nd round	Dulux British Open
	v Knowles	4-5	3rd round	Dulux British Open
	v G. Foulds	10-6	Qualifying	Embassy World Championship
	v B. Harris	10-6	Qualifying	Embassy World Championship
	v Parrott	3-10	Qualifying	Embassy World Championship

PETER FRANCISCO (South Africa)

Born 14.2.62
Turned professional 1984
World ranking 18 (26)
Amateur career South African champion 1981–83.
Best professional performance Semi-finals 1986 BCE International.

	v G. Foulds	4-5	Qualifying	Jameson International
1984	v G. Foulds	4-5	Qualifying	Jameson International
	v Black	5-4	Qualifying	Rothmans Grand Prix
	v Spencer	5-2	1st round	Rothmans Grand Prix
	v Reynolds	4-5	2nd round	Rothmans Grand Prix
	v Sheehan	9-5	Qualifying	Coral UK Open
	v Williamson	9-2	Qualifying	Coral UK Open
	v Sinclair	8-9	Qualifying	Coral UK Open
1985	v Longworth	4-5	Qualifying	Mercantile Credit Classic
	v Kelly	6-3	Qualifying	Dulux British Open
	v Virgo	2-6	1st round	Dulux British Open
	v Demarco	10-4	Qualifying	Embassy World Championship
	v Murphy	10-4	Qualifying	Embassy World Championship
	v Meadowcroft	10-5	Qualifying	Embassy World Championship
	v Macleod	7-10	Qualifying	Embassy World Championship
	v Gibson	4-5	2nd round	Goya Matchroom Trophy
	v Everton	5-0	2nd round	Rothmans Grand Prix
	v Virgo	5-4	3rd round	Rothmans Grand Prix
	v W. Jones	5-3	4th round	Rothmans Grand Prix
	v Griffiths	2-5	5th round	Rothmans Grand Prix
	v Charlton	9-5	3rd round	Coral UK Open
	v Williams	7-9	4th round	Coral UK Open
1986	v Jonik	5-2	2nd round	Mercantile Credit Classic
	v Charlton	5-1	3rd round	Mercantile Credit Classic
	v Martin	5-2	4th round	Mercantile Credit Classic
	v S. Davis	0-5	5th round	Mercantile Credit Classic
	v G. Foulds	5-2	2nd round	Dulux British Open
	v White	5-4	3rd round	Dulux British Open
	v Longworth	5-2	4th round	Dulux British Open

Terry Griffiths

Silvino Francisco

v Higgins	2-5	5th round	Dulux British Open
v Drago	10-4	Qualifying	Embassy World Championship
v F. Davis	10-1	Qualifying	Embassy World Championship
v N. Foulds	9-10	Qualifying	Embassy World Championship
v Grace	7-1	2nd round	South African Championship
v S. Francisco	3-8	Semi-final	South African Championship
v Wildman	5-2	3rd round	BCE International
v Higgins	5-4	4th round	BCE International
v Gauvreau	5-2	5th round	BCE International
v S. Francisco	5-3	Quarter-final	BCE International
v Thorburn	7-9	Semi-final	BCE International
v Medati	5-1	3rd round	Rothmans Grand Prix
v Knowles	3-5	4th round	Rothmans Grand Prix
v Watterson	9-4	3rd round	Tennents UK Open
v White	5-9	4th round	Tennents UK Open
1987 v Gauvreau	5-3	3rd round	Mercantile Credit Classic
v Johnson	5-3	4th round	Mercantile Credit Classic
v S. Francisco	1-5	5th round	Mercantile Credit Classic
v Sinclair	5-3	3rd round	Dulux British Open
v Mountjoy	3-5	4th round	Dulux British Open
v O'Kane	5-10	Qualifying	Embassy World Championship

SILVINO FRANCISCO (South Africa)

Born 3.5.46
Turned professional 1978
World ranking 10 (12)
Amateur career South African champion 1968, 1969, 1974, 1977.
Best professional performances Winner 1985 Dulux British Open, 1986
South African Championship.

1982 v Ross	9-0	Qualifying	Embassy World Championship
v Morgan	9-1	Qualifying	Embassy World Championship
v Dennis Taylor	10-7	1st round	Embassy World Championship
v Reynolds	13-8	2nd round	Embassy World Championship
v Reardon	8-13	Quarter-final	Embassy World Championship
1983 v Kelly	10-5	Qualifying	Embassy World Championship
v Dennis Taylor	9-10	1st round	Embassy World Championship
v Darrington	5-2	Qualifying	Jameson International
v Donnelly	5-1	2nd round	Jameson International
v S. Davis	1-5	Quarter-final	Jameson International
v Morra	5-3	1st round	Professional Players Tournament
v Scott	5-1	2nd round	Professional Players Tournament
v Knowles	0-5	3rd round	Professional Players Tournament
1984 v Thorburn	5-1	Qualifying	Lada Classic
v Wildman	1-5	1st round	Lada Classic
v Van Rensberg	10-3	Qualifying	Embassy World Championship
v Meo	10-5	1st round	Embassy World Championship

	v Reardon	8-13	2nd round	Embassy World Championship
	v Kelly	5-3	Qualifying	Jameson International
	v Spencer	5-2	1st round	Jameson International
	v Virgo	5-2	2nd round	Jameson International
	v Knowles	6-9	Semi-final	Jameson International
	v Duggan	5-3	1st round	Rothmans Grand Prix
	v White	5-1	2nd round	Rothmans Grand Prix
	v Reynolds	1-5	3rd round	Rothmans Grand Prix
	v Sinclair	9-4	Qualifying	Coral UK Open
	v Charlton	4-9	1st round	Coral UK Open
1985	v T. Jones	5-1	Qualifying	Mercantile Credit Classic
	v S. Davis	0-5	1st round	Mercantile Credit Classic
	v Kearney	6-4	1st round	Dulux British Open
	v White	5-4	2nd round	Dulux British Open
	v Chaperon	5-2	3rd round	Dulux British Open
	v Meo	5-4	Quarter-final	Dulux British Open
	v Higgins	9-6	Semi-final	Dulux British Open
	v Stevens	**12-9**	**Final**	**Dulux British Open**
	v Medati	10-7	Qualifying	Embassy World Championship
	v Dennis Taylor	2-10	1st round	Embassy World Championship
	v Parrott	3-4	1st round	Winfield Australian Masters
	v Knowles	5-4	1st round	Langs Scottish Masters
	v Thorburn	0-6	Semi-final	Langs Scottish Masters
	v Chaperon	3-5	3rd round	Goya Matchroom Trophy
	v Kelly	5-2	3rd round	Rothmans Grand Prix
	v Martin	5-3	4th round	Rothmans Grand Prix
	v White	5-4	5th round	Rothmans Grand Prix
	v S. Davis	2-5	Quarter-final	Rothmans Grand Prix
	v Wych	9-8	3rd round	Coral UK Open
	v Martin	9-6	4th round	Coral UK Open
	v Griffiths	5-9	5th round	Coral UK Open
1986	v Hendry	4-5	3rd round	Mercantile Credit Classic
	v Knowles	1-5	1st round	Benson & Hedges Masters
	v T. Jones	5-2	3rd round	Dulux British Open
	v Macleod	1-5	4th round	Dulux British Open
	v Williams	10-4	1st round	Embassy World Championship
	v Knowles	10-13	2nd round	Embassy World Championship
	v P. Francisco	8-3	Semi-final	South African Championship
	v Ellis	**9-1**	**Final**	**South African Championship**
	v Newbury	5-4	3rd round	BCE International
	v Virgo	5-0	4th round	BCE International
	v Dennis Taylor	5-0	5th round	BCE International
	v P. Francisco	3-5	Quarter-final	BCE International
	v Spencer	5-4	3rd round	Rothmans Grand Prix
	v W. Jones	5-4	4th round	Rothmans Grand Prix
	v Newbury	5-2	5th round	Rothmans Grand Prix
	v Knowles	5-2	Quarter-final	Rothmans Grand Prix
	v White	6-9	Semi-final	Rothmans Grand Prix
	v Owers	9-3	3rd round	Tennents UK Open
	v Reynolds	8-9	4th round	Tennents UK Open

1987	v Van Rensberg	5-4	3rd round	Mercantile Credit Classic
	v B. Harris	5-3	4th round	Mercantile Credit Classic
	v P. Francisco	5-1	5th round	Mercantile Credit Classic
	v Hendry	0-5	Quarter-final	Mercantile Credit Classic
	v Knowles	5-2	1st round	Benson & Hedges Masters
	v Dennis Taylor	3-5	Quarter-final	Benson & Hedges Masters
	v Rowswell	5-0	3rd round	Dulux British Open
	v Wilson	4-5	4th round	Dulux British Open
	v Campbell	10-3	1st round	Embassy World Championship
	v Hallett	9-13	2nd round	Embassy World Championship

MARCEL GAUVREAU (Canada)

Born 9.1.55
Turned professional 1983
World ranking 42 (38)
Best professional performances Last 16 1986 Mercantile Credit Classic,
1986 BCE International.

1983	v Miles	3-5	1st round	Professional Players Tournament
1984	v Campbell	10-7	Qualifying	Embassy World Championship
	v Cripsey	10-1	Qualifying	Embassy World Championship
	v Macleod	10-6	Qualifying	Embassy World Championship
	v David Taylor	5-10	1st round	Embassy World Championship
	v Jonik	5-1	Qualifying	Jameson International
	v Parrott	5-4	Qualifying	Jameson International
	v Stevens	5-1	1st round	Jameson International
	v Thorne	3-5	2nd round	Jameson International
	v Foldvari	5-2	Qualifying	Rothmans Grand Prix
	v Parrott	3-5	1st round	Rothmans Grand Prix
	v Bales	9-8	Qualifying	Coral UK Open
	v Mans	9-6	Qualifying	Coral UK Open
	v Knowles	5-9	1st round	Coral UK Open
1985	v Giannaros	5-3	Qualifying	Mercantile Credit Classic
	v Sinclair	5-1	Qualifying	Mercantile Credit Classic
	v Higgins	3-5	1st round	Mercantile Credit Classic
	v Greaves	6-3	Qualifying	Dulux British Open
	v Stevens	3-6	1st round	Dulux British Open
	v Van Rensberg	10-9	Qualifying	Embassy World Championship
	v Reynolds	1-10	Qualifying	Embassy World Championship
	v D. Hughes	4-5	2nd round	Goya Matchroom Trophy
	v Duggan	4-5	2nd round	Rothmans Grand Prix
	v O'Boye	5-9	2nd round	Coral UK Open
1986	v Simngam	5-1	2nd round	Mercantile Credit Classic
	v David Taylor	5-3	3rd round	Mercantile Credit Classic
	v Browne	5-3	4th round	Mercantile Credit Classic
	v White	2-5	5th round	Mercantile Credit Classic
	v Drago	3-5	2nd round	Dulux British Open

	v Jim Bear	10-5	Qualifying	Embassy World Championship
	v Chaperon	10-8	Qualifying	Embassy World Championship
	v Williams	3-10	Qualifying	Embassy World Championship
	v Jenkins	5-1	2nd round	BCE International
	v Macleod	5-4	3rd round	BCE International
	v Reardon	5-2	4th round	BCE International
	v P. Francisco	2-5	5th round	BCE International
	v J. McLaughlin	3-5	2nd round	Rothmans Grand Prix
	v J. McLaughlin	8-9	2nd round	Tennents UK Open
1987	v Rigitano	5-0	2nd round	Mercantile Credit Classic
	v P. Francisco	3-5	3rd round	Mercantile Credit Classic
	v Bales	5-0	2nd round	Dulux British Open
	v S. Davis	0-5	3rd round	Dulux British Open
	v Bear	10-3	Qualifying	Embassy World Championship
	v Medati	3-10	Qualifying	Embassy World Championship

MATT GIBSON (Scotland)

Born 7.5.53
Turned professional 1981
World ranking 71 (60)
Amateur career 1980 Scottish champion.
Best professional performance Last 32 1985 Goya Matchroom Trophy.

1981	v Hood	5-3	Qualifying	Jameson International
	v Parkin	5-3	Qualifying	Jameson International
	v Dunning	3-5	Qualifying	Jameson International
	v Demarco	5-3	Quarter-final	Scottish Championship
	v Donnelly	6-4	Semi-final	Scottish Championship
	v Black	7-11	Final	Scottish Championship
	v Fitzmaurice	9-6	Qualifying	Coral UK Championship
	v Everton	7-9	Qualifying	Coral UK Championship
1982	v Donnelly	8-9	Qualifying	Embassy World Championship
	v E. McLaughlin	6-3	Quarter-final	Scottish Championship
	v Sinclair	2-6	Semi-final	Scottish Championship
	v Wildman	1-5	Qualifying	Jameson International
	v Martin	2-5	1st round	Professional Players Tournament
	v G. Foulds	3-9	Qualifying	Coral UK Championship
1983	v G. Foulds	6-10	Qualifying	Embassy World Championship
	v Macleod	5-6	1st round	Scottish Championship
	v Dodd	5-1	Qualifying	Jameson International
	v Scott	3-5	Qualifying	Jameson International
	v Morgan	4-5	Qualifying	Professional Players Tournament
	v Johnson	6-9	Qualifying	Coral UK Championship
1984	v Rigitano	10-7	Qualifying	Embassy World Championship
	v Fisher	10-7	Qualifying	Embassy World Championship
	v Johnson	3-10	Qualifying	Embassy World Championship
	v Medati	5-3	Qualifying	Jameson International
	v W. Jones	2-5	Qualifying	Jameson International

	v Chaperon	4-5	Qualifying	Rothmans Grand Prix
	v Hargreaves	9-8	Qualifying	Coral UK Open
	v Donnelly	6-9	Qualifying	Coral UK Open
1985	v T. Jones	0-5	Qualifying	Mercantile Credit Classic
	v Black	6-2	1st round	Scottish Championship
	v Macleod	4-6	Semi-final	Scottish Championship
	v Demarco	6-1	Qualifying	Dulux British Open
	v Wildman	1-6	1st round	Dulux British Open
	v Hines	10-7	Qualifying	Embassy World Championship
	v Fagan	8-10	Qualifying	Embassy World Championship
	v P. Francisco	5-4	2nd round	Goya Matchroom Trophy
	v Charlton	5-4	3rd round	Goya Matchroom Trophy
	v Reynolds	0-5	4th round	Goya Matchroom Trophy
	v Bradley	5-4	2nd round	Rothmans Grand Prix
	v Knowles	1-5	3rd round	Rothmans Grand Prix
	v Longworth	2-9	2nd round	Coral UK Open
1986	v Virgo	3-5	3rd round	Mercantile Credit Classic
	v Black	0-5	2nd round	Dulux British Open
	v Sinclair	6-4	Quarter-final	Canada Dry Scottish Championship
	v John Rea	6-0	Semi-final	Canada Dry Scottish Championship
	v Hendry	5-10	Final	Canada Dry Scottish Championship
	v Jenkins	10-4	Qualifying	Embassy World Championship
	v Morra	10-9	Qualifying	Embassy World Championship
	v Medati	6-10	Qualifying	Embassy World Championship
	v Hines	5-1	2nd round	BCE International
	v Mountjoy	3-5	3rd round	BCE International
	v Mienie	5-4	2nd round	Rothmans Grand Prix
	v S. Davis	1-5	3rd round	Rothmans Grand Prix
	v Dunning	9-2	2nd round	Tennents UK Open
	v Reardon	6-9	3rd round	Tennents UK Open
1987	v J. McLaughlin	3-5	2nd round	Mercantile Credit Classic
	v Sinclair	2-6	1st round	Scottish Championship
	v J. McLaughlin	1-5	2nd round	Dulux British Open
	v Kelly	10-9	Qualifying	Embassy World Championship
	v Cripsey	4-10	Qualifying	Embassy World Championship

PAUL GIBSON (England)

Born 9.3.63
Turned professional 1986
World ranking 99 (–)

1986	v Meadowcroft	5-2	1st round	BCE International
	v Hendry	2-5	2nd round	BCE International
	v Dunning	5-1	1st round	Rothmans Grand Prix
	v Cripsey	3-5	2nd round	Rothmans Grand Prix
	v Agrawal	9-6	1st round	Tennents UK Open
	v Mans	*wo*	2nd round	Tennents UK Open
	v Griffiths	3-9	3rd round	Tennents UK Open

1987	v B. Harris	3-5	2nd round	Mercantile Credit Classic
	v D. Hughes	6-3	1st round	Tolly Ales English Championship
	v Medati	2-6	2nd round	Tolly Ales English Championship
	v Agrawal	5-0	1st round	Dulux British Open
	v Duggan	3-5	2nd round	Dulux British Open
	v Morra	6-10	Qualifying	Embassy World Championship

DAVE GILBERT (England)
Born 15.8.61
Turned professional 1985
World ranking 83 (72)

1985	v Darrington	2-5	1st round	Goya Matchroom Trophy
	v Wilkinson	5-4	1st round	Rothmans Grand Prix
	v Williamson	5-4	2nd round	Rothmans Grand Prix
	v Johnson	2-5	3rd round	Rothmans Grand Prix
	v Drago	5-9	1st round	Coral UK Open
1986	v Watson	5-4	1st round	Mercantile Credit Classic
	v T. Jones	3-5	2nd round	Mercantile Credit Classic
	v West	9-8	1st round	Tolly Cobbold English Championship
	v Bradley	5-9	2nd round	Tolly Cobbold English Championship
	v Burke	5-1	1st round	Dulux British Open
	v Morra	5-4	2nd round	Dulux British Open
	v Charlton	2-5	3rd round	Dulux British Open
	v Bales	10-7	Qualifying	Embassy World Championship
	v Bradley	10-7	Qualifying	Embassy World Championship
	v T. Jones	10-7	Qualifying	Embassy World Championship
	v Martin	5-10	Qualifying	Embassy World Championship
	v James	2-5	1st round	BCE International
	v Rowswell	5-1	1st round	Rothmans Grand Prix
	v Newbury	1-5	2nd round	Rothmans Grand Prix
	v Owers	8-9	1st round	Tennents UK Open
1987	v Spencer	4-5	2nd round	Mercantile Credit Classic
	v Bradley	3-6	2nd round	Tolly Ales English Championship
	v Murphy	4-5	2nd round	Dulux British Open
	v O'Kane	2-10	Qualifying	Embassy World Championship

NIGEL GILBERT (England)
Born 20.3.59
Turned professional 1986
World ranking 100 (–)

1986	v Agrawal	5-0	1st round	BCE International
	v Chaperon	3-5	2nd round	BCE International
	v Donnelly	1-5	1st round	Rothmans Grand Prix
	v Donnelly	8-9	1st round	Tennents UK Open

1987	v Smith	5-0	1st round	Mercantile Credit Classic
	v Van Rensberg	3-5	2nd round	Mercantile Credit Classic
	v B. Bennett	5-6	1st round	Tolly Ales English Championship
	v Houlihan	5-4	1st round	Dulux British Open
	v W. Jones	5-3	2nd round	Dulux British Open
	v Reynolds	2-5	3rd round	Dulux British Open
	v Sheehan	10-6	Qualifying	Embassy World Championship
	v O'Boye	5-10	Qualifying	Embassy World Championship

ROBBIE GRACE (South Africa)

Born –
Turned professional 1985
World ranking 64 (112)
Best professional performance Last 32 1986 Tennents UK Open.

1986	v Parkin	10-8	Qualifying	Embassy World Championship
	v W. Jones	3-10	Qualifying	Embassy World Championship
	v P. Francisco	1-7	2nd round	South African Championship
	v Houlihan	5-1	1st round	Rothmans Grand Prix
	v Fagan	3-5	2nd round	Rothmans Grand Prix
	v Houlihan	9-6	1st round	Tennents UK Open
	v Medati	9-5	2nd round	Tennents UK Open
	v Macleod	9-6	3rd round	Tennents UK Open
	v Thorne	1-9	4th round	Tennents UK Open
1987	v Rigitano	4-5	1st round	Mercantile Credit Classic
	v Meadowcroft	5-4	1st round	Dulux British Open
	v Fagan	5-3	2nd round	Dulux British Open
	v West	2-5	3rd round	Dulux British Open
	v Jenkins	9-10	Qualifying	Embassy World Championship

DAVID GREAVES (England)

Born 1.9.46
Turned professional 1973
World ranking 117 (107)

1973	v Bennett	9-8	1st round	World Championship
	v F. Davis	1-16	2nd round	World Championship
1975	v G. Owen	3-15	1st round	World Championship
1976	v Charlton	8-5	Qualifying	Embassy World Championship
	v David Taylor	1-8	Qualifying	Embassy World Championship
1977	v David Taylor	0-11	Qualifying	Embassy World Championship
	v David Taylor	4-5	1st round	Super Crystalate UK Championship
1978	v Barrie	3-9	Prelim	Embassy World Championship
	v Dunning	3-9	Qualifying	Coral UK Championship
1979	v Williams	2-9	Prelim	Embassy World Championship
	v Dunning	8-9	1st round	Coral UK Championship

1980	v Meadowcroft	1-9	Qualifying	Coral UK Championship
1981	v Dunning	4-9	Qualifying	John Courage English
	v Parkin	9-5	Qualifying	Embassy World Championship
	v Thorne	3-9	Qualifying	Embassy World Championship
	v E. McLaughlin	1-5	Qualifying	Jameson International
1982	v Morgan	2-9	Qualifying	Embassy World Championship
1983	v E. McLaughlin	7-10	Qualifying	Embassy World Championship
	v Martin	1-5	Qualifying	Jameson International
	v Andrewartha	5-2	Qualifying	Professional Players Tournament
	v Reynolds	1-5	1st round	Professional Players Tournament
	v Wildman	5-9	Qualifying	Coral UK Championship
1984	v Edmonds	0-10	Qualifying	Embassy World Championship
	v J. McLaughlin	3-5	Qualifying	Jameson International
	v King	0-5	Qualifying	Rothmans Grand Prix
	v Foldvari	5-9	Qualifying	Coral UK Open
1985	v T. Jones	2-5	Qualifying	Mercantile Credit Classic
	v Fitzmaurice	3-9	Qualifying	Tolly Cobbold English Championship
	v Gauvreau	3-6	Qualifying	Dulux British Open
	v Chalmers	3-10	Qualifying	Embassy World Championship
	v Simngam	2-5	1st round	Goya Matchroom Trophy
	v Darrington	2-5	1st round	Rothmans Grand Prix
	v Cripsey	4-9	1st round	Coral UK Open
1986	v Watchorn	5-4	1st round	Mercantile Credit Classic
	v Sinclair	1-5	2nd round	Mercantile Credit Classic
	v Medati	4-9	2nd round	Tolly Cobbold English Championship
	v Agrawal	3-5	1st round	Dulux British Open
	v Smith	4-10	Qualifying	Embassy World Championship
	v Rigitano	3-5	1st round	BCE International
	v Meadowcroft	2-5	1st round	Rothmans Grand Prix
	v Fisher	4-9	1st round	Tennents UK Open
1987	v Oliver	4-5	1st round	Mercantile Credit Classic
	v Roe	1-6	1st round	Tolly Ales English Championship
	v G. Foulds	3-5	1st round	Dulux British Open
	v Thornley	10-6	1st round	Embassy World Championship
	v Miles	7-10	2nd round	Embassy World Championship

TERRY GRIFFITHS (Wales)

Born 16.10.47
Turned professional 1978
World ranking 6 (10)
Amateur career 1977 & 1978 English champion.
Best professional performances Winner 1979 Embassy World Championship, 1982 Coral UK Championship, 1985 & 1986 Welsh Championship, 1982 Lada Classic, 1980 Benson & Hedges Masters, 1980–82 Benson & Hedges Irish Masters, 1986 BCE Belgian Classic.

1978	v Williams	8-9	Qualifying	Coral UK Championship
1979	v Bennett	9-2	Prelim	Embassy World Championship
	v Meadowcroft	9-6	Qualifying	Embassy World Championship
	v Mans	13-8	1st round	Embassy World Championship
	v Higgins	13-12	Quarter-final	Embassy World Championship
	v Charlton	19-17	Semi-final	Embassy World Championship
	v Dennis Taylor	**24-16**	**Final**	**Embassy World Championship**
	v Wilson	9-4	3rd round	Coral UK Championship
	v Higgins	9-7	Quarter-final	Coral UK Championship
	v Werbeniuk	9-3	Semi-final	Coral UK Championship
	v Virgo	13-14	Final	Coral UK Championship
1980	v Thorburn	5-3	Quarter-final	Benson & Hedges Masters
	v Spencer	5-0	Semi-final	Benson & Hedges Masters
	v Higgins	**9-5**	**Final**	**Benson & Hedges Masters**
	v Mountjoy	6-9	1st round	Woodpecker Welsh Championship
	v Mountjoy	**9-8**	**Final**	**Benson & Hedges Irish Masters**
	v S. Davis	10-13	2nd round	Embassy World Championship
	v Fagan	9-8	2nd round	Coral UK Championship
	v Dennis Taylor	9-7	Quarter-final	Coral UK Championship
	v S. Davis	0-9	Semi-final	Coral UK Championship
1981	v F. Davis	5-2	Quarter-final	Benson & Hedges Masters
	v Spencer	6-5	Semi-final	Benson & Hedges Masters
	v Higgins	6-9	Final	Benson & Hedges Masters
	v Reardon	6-9	Semi-final	Woodpecker Welsh Championship
	v Thorburn	6-5	Semi-final	Benson & Hedges Irish Masters
	v Reardon	**9-7**	**Final**	**Benson & Hedges Irish Masters**
	v Meo	13-6	2nd round	Embassy World Championship
	v S. Davis	9-13	Quarter-final	Embassy World Championship
	v Spencer	5-2	3rd round	Jameson International
	v Higgins	2-5	Quarter-final	Jameson International
	v Stevens	5-0	1st round	Northern Ireland Classic
	v S. Davis	6-9	Semi-final	Northern Ireland Classic
	v Miles	9-4	3rd round	Coral UK Championship
	v Knowles	9-5	Quarter-final	Coral UK Championship
	v Meo	9-3	Semi-final	Coral UK Championship
	v S. Davis	3-16	Final	Coral UK Championship
1982	v Thorburn	5-1	1st round	Lada Classic
	v Higgins	5-1	Semi-final	Lada Classic
	v S. Davis	**9-8**	**Final**	**Lada Classic**
	v Reardon	5-3	Quarter-final	Benson & Hedges Masters
	v Higgins	6-4	Semi-final	Benson & Hedges Masters
	v S. Davis	5-9	Final	Benson & Hedges Masters
	v S. Davis	7-9	Final	Yamaha International Masters
	v Roscoe	6-2	1st round	Woodpecker Welsh Championship
	v Wilson	9-6	Semi-final	Woodpecker Welsh Championship
	v Mountjoy	8-9	Final	Woodpecker Welsh Championship
	v Meo	5-3	Quarter-final	Benson & Hedges Irish Masters
	v Reardon	6-3	Semi-final	Benson & Hedges Irish Masters
	v S. Davis	**9-5**	**Final**	**Benson & Hedges Irish Masters**
	v Thorne	6-10	1st round	Embassy World Championship

v Reardon	5-3	1st round	Langs Scottish Masters
v Higgins	5-6	Semi-final	Langs Scottish Masters
v Williams	5-2	1st round	Jameson International
v Higgins	5-2	2nd round	Jameson International
v Stevens	3-5	Quarter-final	Jameson International
v Roscoe	5-1	1st round	Professional Players Tournament
v Watterson	5-2	2nd round	Professional Players Tournament
v Sinclair	5-3	3rd round	Professional Players Tournament
v White	2-5	Quarter-final	Professional Players Tournament
v Johnson	9-1	1st round	Coral UK Championship
v Dennis Taylor	9-7	2nd round	Coral UK Championship
v S. Davis	9-6	Quarter-final	Coral UK Championship
v Meo	9-7	Semi-final	Coral UK Championship
v Higgins	**16-15**	**Final**	**Coral UK Championship**
1983 v Mountjoy	1-5	1st round	Lada Classic
v Stevens	5-3	1st round	Benson & Hedges Masters
v Thorburn	3-5	Quarter-final	Benson & Hedges Masters
v Everton	6-1	Quarter-final	Woodpecker Welsh Championship
v Reardon	4-9	Semi-final	Woodpecker Welsh Championship
v Werbeniuk	5-3	Semi-final	Tolly Cobbold Classic
v S. Davis	5-7	Final	Tolly Cobbold Classic
v Mountjoy	5-4	Quarter-final	Benson & Hedges Irish Masters
v S. Davis	2-6	Semi-final	Benson & Hedges Irish Masters
v Wildman	10-8	1st round	Embassy World Championship
v Thorburn	12-13	2nd round	Embassy World Championship
v Thorburn	1-5	1st round	Langs Scottish Masters
v Miles	5-2	1st round	Jameson International
v Scott	5-0	2nd round	Jameson International
v Spencer	5-4	Quarter-final	Jameson International
v Thorburn	8-9	Semi-final	Jameson International
v Dodd	5-3	1st round	Professional Players Tournament
v Parrott	5-1	2nd round	Professional Players Tournament
v E. Hughes	2-5	3rd round	Professional Players Tournament
v Martin	9-4	1st round	Coral UK Championship
v Hallett	9-5	2nd round	Coral UK Championship
v Johnson	9-2	Quarter-final	Coral UK Championship
v Higgins	4-9	Semi-final	Coral UK Championship
1984 v Reynolds	5-2	Qualifying	Lada Classic
v Roscoe	5-2	1st round	Lada Classic
v S. Davis	4-5	Quarter-final	Lada Classic
v Werbeniuk	5-1	1st round	Benson & Hedges Masters
v Spencer	5-4	Quarter-final	Benson & Hedges Masters
v Knowles	6-4	Semi-final	Benson & Hedges Masters
v White	5-9	Final	Benson & Hedges Masters
v Andrewartha	6-1	1st round	Strongbow Welsh Championship
v Mountjoy	5-9	Semi-final	Strongbow Welsh Championship
v Werbeniuk	5-2	1st round	Benson & Hedges Irish Masters
v Knowles	5-0	Quarter-final	Benson & Hedges Irish Masters
v Dennis Taylor	5-4	Semi-final	Benson & Hedges Irish Masters
v S. Davis	1-9	Final	Benson & Hedges Irish Masters

	v Mifsud	10-2	1st round	Embassy World Championship
	v Werbeniuk	10-5	2nd round	Embassy World Championship
	v S. Davis	10-13	Quarter-final	Embassy World Championship
	v Knowles	3-5	1st round	Langs Scottish Masters
	v N. Foulds	5-3	1st round	Jameson International
	v Higgins	4-5	2nd round	Jameson International
	v T. Jones	3-5	1st round	Rothmans Grand Prix
	v Wilson	6-9	1st round	Coral UK Open
1985	v Fagan	5-0	1st round	Mercantile Credit Classic
	v Williams	5-3	2nd round	Mercantile Credit Classic
	v Thorburn	4-5	Quarter-final	Mercantile Credit Classic
	v Werbeniuk	5-2	1st round	Benson & Hedges Masters
	v Higgins	5-1	Quarter-final	Benson & Hedges Masters
	v Mountjoy	2-6	Semi-final	Benson & Hedges Masters
	v Chalmers	6-0	1st round	Dulux British Open
	v Newbury	3-5	2nd round	Dulux British Open
	v Higgins	2-5	1st round	Benson & Hedges Irish Masters
	v Williams	10-3	1st round	Embassy World Championship
	v Higgins	13-7	2nd round	Embassy World Championship
	v S. Davis	6-13	Quarter-final	Embassy World Championship
	v Chappel	6-0	Quarter-final	BCE Welsh Championship
	v Reardon	9-3	Semi-final	BCE Welsh Championship
	v Mountjoy	**9-4**	**Final**	**BCE Welsh Championship**
	v Newbury	5-2	3rd round	Goya Matchroom Trophy
	v Spencer	5-1	4th round	Goya Matchroom Trophy
	v Parrott	1-5	5th round	Goya Matchroom Trophy
	v J. McLaughlin	5-4	3rd round	Rothmans Grand Prix
	v Harris	5-3	4th round	Rothmans Grand Prix
	v P. Francisco	5-2	5th round	Rothmans Grand Prix
	v Thorburn	1-5	Quarter-final	Rothmans Grand Prix
	v S. Davis	4-5	1st round	BCE Canadian Masters
	v T. Jones	9-5	3rd round	Coral UK Open
	v Reynolds	9-7	4th round	Coral UK Open
	v S. Francisco	9-5	5th round	Coral UK Open
	v Thorne	7-9	Quarter-final	Coral UK Open
	v Reardon	5-2	1st round	Kit Kat
	v Dennis Taylor	4-6	Semi-final	Kit Kat
1986	v V. Harris	3-5	3rd round	Mercantile Credit Classic
	v S. Davis	5-2	1st round	BCE Belgian Classic
	v Knowles	5-2	Semi-final	BCE Belgian Classic
	v Stevens	**9-7**	**Final**	**BCE Belgian Classic**
	v Higgins	5-4	1st round	Benson & Hedges Masters
	v Thorburn	2-5	Quarter-final	Benson & Hedges Masters
	v Chappel	6-4	Quarter-final	Zetters Welsh Championship
	v Wilson	9-1	Semi-final	Zetters Welsh Championship
	v Mountjoy	**9-3**	**Final**	**Zetters Welsh Championship**
	v Scott	5-3	3rd round	Dulux British Open
	v N. Foulds	5-3	4th round	Dulux British Open
	v Macleod	5-2	5th round	Dulux British Open
	v Thorne	4-5	Quarter-final	Dulux British Open

	v Thorne	2-5	1st round	Benson & Hedges Irish Masters
	v Fowler	10-2	1st round	Embassy World Championship
	v Higgins	13-12	2nd round	Embassy World Championship
	v Johnson	12-13	Quarter-final	Embassy World Championship
	v Dennis Taylor	4-5	Semi-final	Camus Hong Kong Masters
	v Meo	6-3	1st round	Matchroom Trophy
	v S. Davis	2-6	Semi-final	Matchroom Trophy
	v Medati	5-3	3rd round	BCE International
	v West	5-1	4th round	BCE International
	v Thorburn	4-5	5th round	BCE International
	v Morra	5-3	3rd round	Rothmans Grand Prix
	v Campbell	5-1	4th round	Rothmans Grand Prix
	v S. Davis	2-5	5th round	Rothmans Grand Prix
	v P. Gibson	9-3	3rd round	Tennents UK Open
	v O'Kane	9-0	4th round	Tennents UK Open
	v Knowles	6-9	5th round	Tennents UK Open
1987	v O'Boye	5-1	3rd round	Mercantile Credit Classic
	v Martin	5-4	4th round	Mercantile Credit Classic
	v Campbell	5-3	5th round	Mercantile Credit Classic
	v White	3-5	Quarter-final	Mercantile Credit Classic
	v Higgins	4-5	1st round	Benson & Hedges Masters
	v W. Jones	6-2	Quarter-final	Matchroom Welsh Championship
	v Newbury	6-9	Semi-final	Matchroom Welsh Championship
	v John Rea	5-2	3rd round	Dulux British Open
	v T. Jones	5-3	4th round	Dulux British Open
	v Dennis Taylor	4-5	5th round	Dulux British Open
	v Higgins	5-1	1st round	Benson & Hedges Irish Masters
	v Johnson	5-0	Quarter-final	Benson & Hedges Irish Masters
	v S. Davis	2-6	Semi-final	Benson & Hedges Irish Masters
	v Wych	10-4	1st round	Embassy World Championship
	v Higgins	13-10	2nd round	Embassy World Championship
	v S. Davis	5-13	Quarter-final	Embassy World Championship

MIKE HALLETT

Born 6.7.59
Turned professional 1979
World ranking 16 (27)
Best professional performances Last 16 1986 Rothmans Grand Prix,
1986 Tennents UK Open; quarter-finals 1987 Embassy World Championship.

	v Parkin	9-1	1st round	Coral UK Championship
1979	v Fagan	4-9	2nd round	Coral UK Championship
1980	v Stevens	3-9	Qualifying	Embassy World Championship
	v Bennett	9-4	Qualifying	Coral UK Championship
	v Edmonds	9-8	Qualifying	Coral UK Championship
	v S. Davis	1-9	1st round	Coral UK Championship

1981	v Edmonds	3-9	Qualifying	John Courage English
	v Jonik	9-1	Qualifying	Embassy World Championship
	v Meo	4-9	Qualifying	Embassy World Championship
	v Demarco	5-4	Qualifying	Jameson International
	v Knowles	2-5	1st round	Jameson International
	v V. Harris	9-4	Qualifying	Coral UK Championship
	v D. Hughes	9-6	Qualifying	Coral UK Championship
	v Fagan	9-5	Qualifying	Coral UK Championship
	v Stevens	4-9	2nd round	Coral UK Championship
1982	v Johnson	9-8	Qualifying	Embassy World Championship
	v Virgo	4-10	1st round	Embassy World Championship
	v Jonik	5-2	Qualifying	Jameson International
	v Wildman	2-5	Qualifying	Jameson International
	v V. Harris	5-3	1st round	Professional Players Tournament
	v Virgo	2-5	2nd round	Professional Players Tournament
	v Demarco	9-1	Qualifying	Coral UK Championship
	v F. Davis	9-7	1st round	Coral UK Championship
	v Reardon	8-9	2nd round	Coral UK Championship
1983	v Andrewartha	10-7	Qualifying	Embassy World Championship
	v King	10-6	Qualifying	Embassy World Championship
	v Spencer	7-10	1st round	Embassy World Championship
	v Roscoe	5-2	Qualifying	Jameson International
	v Morra	3-5	Qualifying	Jameson International
	v Kelly	5-0	1st round	Professional Players Tournament
	v S. Davis	5-2	2nd round	Professional Players Tournament
	v Meo	3-5	3rd round	Professional Players Tournament
	v Darrington	9-1	Qualifying	Coral UK Championship
	v Miles	9-4	1st round	Coral UK Championship
	v Griffiths	5-9	2nd round	Coral UK Championship
1984	v Dennis Taylor	5-4	Qualifying	Lada Classic
	v Knowles	3-5	1st round	Lada Classic
	v Burke	10-5	Qualifying	Embassy World Championship
	v Mountjoy	4-10	1st round	Embassy World Championship
	v O'Kane	4-5	Qualifying	Jameson International
	v Sheehan	5-1	1st round	Rothmans Grand Prix
	v Higgins	5-3	2nd round	Rothmans Grand Prix
	v Stevens	3-5	3rd round	Rothmans Grand Prix
	v Bradley	9-8	Qualifying	Coral UK Open
	v Mountjoy	2-9	1st round	Coral UK Open
1985	v G. Foulds	5-4	Qualifying	Mercantile Credit Classic
	v Reardon	3-5	1st round	Mercantile Credit Classic
	v Duggan	9-4	1st round	Tolly Cobbold English Championship
	v Meo	4-9	2nd round	Tolly Cobbold English Championship
	v Meo	4-5	2nd round	Dulux British Open
	v Chalmers	10-1	Qualifying	Embassy World Championship
	v Thorburn	8-10	1st round	Embassy World Championship
	v Bradley	4-5	3rd round	Goya Matchroom Trophy
	v Mikkelsen	5-3	3rd round	Rothmans Grand Prix
	v Johnson	4-5	4th round	Rothmans Grand Prix
	v Meadowcroft	9-1	3rd round	Coral UK Open

	v Stevens	5-9	4th round	Coral UK Open
1986	v John Rea	5-2	3rd round	Mercantile Credit Classic
	v Thorburn	3-5	4th round	Mercantile Credit Classic
	v Chalmers	9-1	3rd round	Tolly Cobbold English Championship
	v Knowles	9-5	4th round	Tolly Cobbold English Championship
	v Johnson	9-6	Quarter-final	Tolly Cobbold English Championship
	v N. Foulds	8-9	Semi-final	Tolly Cobbold English Championship
	v Duggan	5-3	3rd round	Dulux British Open
	v Higgins	1-5	4th round	Dulux British Open
	v Wych	10-7	Qualifying	Embassy World Championship
	v Dennis Taylor	10-6	1st round	Embassy World Championship
	v Johnson	6-13	2nd round	Embassy World Championship
	v O'Kane	1-5	3rd round	BCE International
	v V. Harris	5-2	3rd round	Rothmans Grand Prix
	v Dodd	5-2	4th round	Rothmans Grand Prix
	v White	3-5	5th round	Rothmans Grand Prix
	v King	9-5	3rd round	Tennents UK Open
	v Meo	9-4	4th round	Tennents UK Open
	v Higgins	7-9	5th round	Tennents UK Open
1987	v Mikkelsen	5-3	3rd round	Mercantile Credit Classic
	v Fowler	4-5	4th round	Mercantile Credit Classic
	v Williamson	2-6	3rd round	Tolly Ales English Championship
	v Owers	6-2	4th round	Tolly Ales English Championship
	v Dodd	5-6	Quarter-final	Tolly Ales English Championship
	v Rigitano	5-0	3rd round	Dulux British Open
	v White	2-5	4th round	Dulux British Open
	v Newbury	10-4	Qualifying	Embassy World Championship
	v Knowles	10-6	1st round	Embassy World Championship
	v S. Francisco	13-9	2nd round	Embassy World Championship
	v N. Foulds	9-13	Quarter-final	Embassy World Championship

JOHN HARGREAVES (England)

Born 2.12.45
Turned professional 1983
World ranking 105 (92)

1983	v Morra	0-5	Qualifying	Professional Players Tournament
	v Williamson	4-9	Qualifying	Coral UK Championship
1984	v E. McLaughlin	5-10	Qualifying	Embassy World Championship
	v Houlihan	5-2	Qualifying	Jameson International
	v Kelly	2-5	Qualifying	Jameson International
	v Donnelly	4-5	Qualifying	Rothmans Grand Prix
	v Medati	9-6	Qualifying	Coral UK Open
	v Gibson	8-9	Qualifying	Coral UK Open
1985	v Darrington	5-2	Qualifying	Mercantile Credit Classic
	v Edmonds	2-5	Qualifying	Mercantile Credit Classic
	v Medati	8-9	Qualifying	Tolly Cobbold English Championship
	v N. Foulds	1-6	1st round	Dulux British Open

	v Fowler	0-10	Qualifying	Embassy World Championship
	v Caggianello	2-5	1st round	Goya Matchroom Trophy
	v Cripsey	5-1	1st round	Rothmans Grand Prix
	v Longworth	2-5	2nd round	Rothmans Grand Prix
	v Mienie	9-7	1st round	Coral UK Open
	v Meadowcroft	8-9	2nd round	Coral UK Open
1986	v Cripsey	5-1	1st round	Mercantile Credit Classic
	v Longworth	2-5	2nd round	Mercantile Credit Classic
	v Houlihan	5-9	1st round	Tolly Cobbold English Championship
	v Edmonds	5-3	2nd round	Dulux British Open
	v N. Foulds	4-5	3rd round	Dulux British Open
	v Mikkelsen	7-10	Qualifying	Embassy World Championship
	v Owers	3-5	1st round	BCE International
	v Roe	1-5	1st round	Rothmans Grand Prix
	v W. Jones	0-9	2nd round	Tennents UK Open
1987	v James	5-6	1st round	Tolly Ales English Championship
	v Parkin	5-4	1st round	Dulux British Open
	v John Rea	3-5	2nd round	Dulux British Open
	v M. Bennett	6-10	Qualifying	Embassy World Championship

BOB HARRIS (England)

Born 12.3.56
Turned professional 1982
World ranking 49 (45)
Best professional performances Last 32 1985 Goya Matchroom Trophy,
1985 Rothmans Grand Prix, 1987 Mercantile Credit Classic.

	v Scott	4-5	Qualifying	Jameson International
1982	v Scott	4-5	Qualifying	Jameson International
	v Cripsey	9-6	Qualifying	Coral UK Championship
	v Watterson	9-3	Qualifying	Coral UK Championship
	v Fagan	6-9	1st round	Coral UK Championship
1983	v Wildman	7-10	Qualifying	Embassy World Championship
	v Dunning	5-3	Qualifying	Jameson International
	v Wildman	2-5	Qualifying	Jameson International
	v King	3-5	Qualifying	Professional Players Tournament
	v E. McLaughlin	9-8	Qualifying	Coral UK Championship
	v Fitzmaurice	9-3	Qualifying	Coral UK Championship
	v Reardon	7-9	1st round	Coral UK Championship
1984	v Sheehan	10-3	Qualifying	Embassy World Championship
	v Burke	4-10	Qualifying	Embassy World Championship
	v Watchorn	7-9	Qualifying	Coral UK Open
1985	v Duggan	8-9	Qualifying	Tolly Cobbold English Championship
	v Meadowcroft	6-1	Qualifying	Dulux British Open
	v Charlton	6-3	1st round	Dulux British Open
	v E. Hughes	4-5	2nd round	Dulux British Open
	v Rigitano	4-10	Qualifying	Embassy World Championship
	v Browne	5-3	2nd round	Goya Matchroom Trophy

	v O'Kane	5-3	3rd round	Goya Matchroom Trophy
	v Dennis Taylor	3-5	4th round	Goya Matchroom Trophy
	v Browne	5-3	2nd round	Rothmans Grand Prix
	v Spencer	5-2	3rd round	Rothmans Grand Prix
	v Griffiths	3-5	4th round	Rothmans Grand Prix
	v Fagan	2-9	2nd round	Coral UK Open
1986	v Morra	5-3	2nd round	Mercantile Credit Classic
	v Johnson	4-5	3rd round	Mercantile Credit Classic
	v T. Jones	5-9	2nd round	Tolly Cobbold English Championship
	v Sinclair	5-3	2nd round	Dulux British Open
	v Martin	1-5	3rd round	Dulux British Open
	v Black	8-10	Qualifying	Embassy World Championship
	v Foldvari	0-5	2nd round	BCE International
	v Jack Rea	5-0	2nd round	Rothmans Grand Prix
	v Mountjoy	2-5	3rd round	Rothmans Grand Prix
	v Jack Rea	9-5	2nd round	Tennents UK Open
	v Wych	6-9	3rd round	Tennents UK Open
1987	v P. Gibson	5-3	2nd round	Mercantile Credit Classic
	v Wych	5-3	3rd round	Mercantile Credit Classic
	v S. Francisco	3-5	4th round	Mercantile Credit Classic
	v G. Foulds	6-1	2nd round	Tolly Ales English Championship
	v Thorne	2-6	3rd round	Tolly Ales English Championship
	v Kelly	5-2	2nd round	Dulux British Open
	v Thorne	1-5	3rd round	Dulux British Open
	v D. Hughes	10-2	Qualifying	Embassy World Championship
	v Fowler	6-10	Qualifying	Embassy World Championship

VIC HARRIS (England)

Born 16.8.45
Turned professional 1981
World ranking 73 (63)
Amateur career 1981 English champion.
Best professional performance Last 32 1986 Mercantile Credit Classic.

1981	v Sheehan	1-5	Qualifying	Jameson International
	v Higgins	3-5	Quarter-final	Langs Scottish Masters
	v Hallett	4-9	Qualifying	Coral UK Championship
	v Johnson	4-9	Qualifying	Embassy World Championship
1982	v Hallett	3-5	1st round	Professional Players Tournament
	v M. Owen	9-4	Qualifying	Coral UK Championship
	v Johnson	8-9	Qualifying	Coral UK Championship
	v Sheehan	5-3	Qualifying	Jameson International
	v Virgo	2-5	Qualifying	Jameson International
1983	v Meo	0-10	Qualifying	Embassy World Championship
	v Medati	0-5	Qualifying	Jameson International
	v Thorburn	1-5	1st round	Professional Players Tournament
	v Houlihan	9-6	Qualifying	Coral UK Championship
	v Williams	6-9	Qualifying	Coral UK Championship

1984	v Van Rensberg	7-10	Qualifying	Embassy World Championship
	v Williamson	0-5	Qualifying	Jameson International
	v F. Davis	5-1	Qualifying	Rothmans Grand Prix
	v Knowles	1-5	1st round	Rothmans Grand Prix
	v Bradley	8-9	Qualifying	Coral UK Open
1985	v Newbury	3-5	Qualifying	Mercantile Credit Classic
	v Scott	7-9	Qualifying	Tolly Cobbold English Championship
	v Dodd	6-1	Qualifying	Dulux British Open
	v Mountjoy	6-5	1st round	Dulux British Open
	v O'Kane	3-5	2nd round	Dulux British Open
	v O'Kane	5-10	Qualifying	Embassy World Championship
	v Foldvari	4-5	2nd round	Goya Matchroom Trophy
	v Wych	5-3	2nd round	Rothmans Grand Prix
	v Higgins	1-5	3rd round	Rothmans Grand Prix
	v Black	9-3	2nd round	Coral UK Open
	v Spencer	5-9	3rd round	Coral UK Open
1986	v Roscoe	5-1	2nd round	Mercantile Credit Classic
	v Griffiths	5-3	3rd round	Mercantile Credit Classic
	v Williams	1-5	4th round	Mercantile Credit Classic
	v Bales	7-9	2nd round	Tolly Cobbold English Championship
	v Chaperon	0-5	2nd round	Dulux British Open
	v T. Jones	7-10	Qualifying	Embassy World Championship
	v G. Foulds	4-5	2nd round	BCE International
	v Kelly	5-3	2nd round	Rothmans Grand Prix
	v Hallett	2-5	3rd round	Rothmans Grand Prix
	v Fisher	9-4	2nd round	Tennents UK Open
	v Charlton	2-9	3rd round	Tennents UK Open
1987	v O'Boye	1-5	2nd round	Mercantile Credit Classic
	v Darrington	6-3	2nd round	Tolly Ales English Championship
	v West	3-6	3rd round	Tolly Ales English Championship
	v Sheehan	5-4	2nd round	Dulux British Open
	v E. Hughes	1-5	3rd round	Dulux British Open
	v Rigitano	6-10	Qualifying	Embassy World Championship

STEPHEN HENDRY (Scotland)

Born 13.1.69
Turned professional 1985
World ranking 23 (51)
Amateur career Scottish champion 1984, 1985.
Best professional performances Quarter-finals 1987 Embassy World Championship; semi-finals 1987 Mercantile Credit Classic; 1986 Scottish champion.

1985	v West	5-4	1st round	Goya Matchroom Trophy
	v E. McLaughlin	3-5	2nd round	Goya Matchroom Trophy
	v O'Boye	4-5	1st round	Rothmans Grand Prix
	v Agrawal	2-9	Qualifying	Coral UK Open

1986 v Sheehan	5-2	1st round	Mercantile Credit Classic
v Miles	5-1	2nd round	Mercantile Credit Classic
v S. Francisco	5-4	3rd round	Mercantile Credit Classic
v N. Foulds	4-5	4th round	Mercantile Credit Classic
v D. Hughes	5-1	1st round	Dulux British Open
v Browne	0-5	2nd round	Dulux British Open
v Demarco	6-1	1st round	Canada Dry Scottish Championship
v Macleod	6-5	Quarter-final	Canada Dry Scottish Championship
v Black	6-2	Semi-final	Canada Dry Scottish Championship
v Gibson	**10-5**	**Final**	**Canada Dry Scottish Championship**
v Demarco	10-7	Qualifying	Embassy World Championship
v Browne	10-9	Qualifying	Embassy World Championship
v W. Jones	10-8	Qualifying	Embassy World Championship
v O'Kane	10-9	Qualifying	Embassy World Championship
v Thorne	8-10	1st round	Embassy World Championship
v White	1-5	1st round	Langs Scottish Masters
v P. Gibson	5-2	2nd round	BCE International
v Parrott	5-3	3rd round	BCE International
v Dennis Taylor	3-5	4th round	BCE International
v Williamson	5-1	2nd round	Rothmans Grand Prix
v E. Hughes	5-1	3rd round	Rothmans Grand Prix
v Chaperon	5-2	4th round	Rothmans Grand Prix
v M. Bennett	5-3	5th round	Rothmans Grand Prix
v White	4-5	Quarter-final	Rothmans Grand Prix
v Oliver	9-1	2nd round	Tennents UK Open
v Higgins	8-9	3rd round	Tennents UK Open
1987 v Jack Rea	5-1	2nd round	Mercantile Credit Classic
v Reardon	5-3	3rd round	Mercantile Credit Classic
v Wright	5-1	4th round	Mercantile Credit Classic
v Fowler	5-4	5th round	Mercantile Credit Classic
v S. Francisco	5-0	Quarter-final	Mercantile Credit Classic
v S. Davis	3-9	Semi-final	Mercantile Credit Classic
v Demarco	6-2	1st round	Scottish Championship
v John Rea	6-0	Semi-final	Scottish Championship
v Donnelly	**10-7**	**Final**	**Scottish Championship**
v Sinclair	2-5	2nd round	Dulux British Open
v Darrington	10-7	Qualifying	Embassy World Championship
v Rempe	10-4	Qualifying	Embassy World Championship
v Martin	10-7	Qualifying	Embassy World Championship
v Thorne	10-7	1st round	Embassy World Championship
v Longworth	13-7	2nd round	Embassy World Championship
v Johnson	12-13	Quarter-final	Embassy World Championship

Alex Higgins

Mike Hallett

ALEX HIGGINS (Northern Ireland)

Born 18.3.49
Turned professional 1971
World ranking 9 (6)
Amateur career 1968 Northern Ireland champion.
Best professional performances Winner 1972 World Championship, 1982 Embassy World Championship, 1983 Coral UK Championship, 1978 & 1981 Benson & Hedges Masters, 1980 British Gold Cup; 1983 Irish champion.

1972	v Gross	15-6	Qualifying	World Championship
	v Parkin	11-3	Qualifying	World Championship
	v Jack Rea	19-11	1st round	World Championship
	v Pulman	31-23	Quarter-final	World Championship
	v Williams	31-30	Semi-final	World Championship
	v Spencer	**37-32**	**Final**	**World Championship**
1973	v Houlihan	16-3	2nd round	World Championship
	v Davis	16-14	Quarter-final	World Championship
	v Charlton	9-23	Semi-final	World Championship
	v Spencer	2-8	Semi-final	Norwich Union Open
1974	v Bennett	15-4	2nd round	World Championship
	v F. Davis	14-15	Quarter-final	World Championship
	v Dennis Taylor	5-1	1st round	Norwich Union Open
	v Werbeniuk	5-4	Quarter-final	Norwich Union Open
	v Reardon	8-9	Semi-final	Norwich Union Open
1975	v Werbeniuk	5-0	1st round	Benson & Hedges Masters
	v Williams	3-5	Quarter-final	Benson & Hedges Masters
	v David Taylor	15-2	2nd round	World Championship
	v Williams	19-12	Quarter-final	World Championship
	v Reardon	14-19	Semi-final	World Championship
1976	v Miles	1-4	2nd round	Benson & Hedges Masters
	v Thorburn	15-14	1st round	Embassy World Championship
	v Spencer	15-14	Quarter-final	Embassy World Championship
	v Charlton	20-18	Semi-final	Embassy World Championship
	v Reardon	16-27	Final	Embassy World Championship
1977	v Mans	4-2	Quarter-final	Benson & Hedges Masters
	v Mountjoy	3-5	Semi-final	Benson & Hedges Masters
	v Mountjoy	12-13	1st round	Embassy World Championship
	v David Taylor	5-4	2nd round	Super Crystalate UK Championship
	v Dunning	5-0	Quarter-final	Super Crystalate UK Championship
	v Mountjoy	2-9	Semi-final	Super Crystalate UK Championship
1978	v Dennis Taylor	4-3	Quarter-final	Benson & Hedges Masters
	v Reardon	5-1	Semi-final	Benson & Hedges Masters
	v Thorburn	**7-5**	**Final**	**Benson & Hedges Masters**
	v Fagan	12-13	1st round	Embassy World Championship
	v Meadowcroft	9-6	1st round	Coral UK Championship
	v F. Davis	9-4	Quarter-final	Coral UK Championship
	v David Taylor	5-9	Semi-final	Coral UK Championship

1979 v Miles	3-6	Semi-final	Holsten Lager International
v Charlton	5-2	Quarter-final	Benson & Hedges Masters
v Mountjoy	5-1	Semi-final	Benson & Hedges Masters
v Mans	4-8	Final	Benson & Hedges Masters
v David Taylor	13-5	1st round	Embassy World Championship
v Griffiths	12-13	Quarter-final	Embassy World Championship
v Houlihan	9-3	3rd round	Coral UK Championship
v Griffiths	7-9	Quarter-final	Coral UK Championship
1980 v F. Davis	5-1	1st round	Benson & Hedges Masters
v Mans	5-1	Quarter-final	Benson & Hedges Masters
v Reardon	5-2	Semi-final	Benson & Hedges Masters
v Griffiths	5-9	Final	Benson & Hedges Masters
v Reardon	**5-1**	**Final**	**British Gold Cup**
v Meo	10-9	1st round	Embassy World Championship
v Mans	13-6	2nd round	Embassy World Championship
v S. Davis	13-9	Quarter-final	Embassy World Championship
v Stevens	16-13	Semi-final	Embassy World Championship
v Thorburn	16-18	Final	Embassy World Championship
v Thorne	9-7	2nd round	Coral UK Championship
v F. Davis	9-6	Quarter-final	Coral UK Championship
v Reardon	9-7	Semi-final	Coral UK Championship
v S. Davis	6-16	Final	Coral UK Championship
1981 v Mountjoy	5-1	Quarter-final	Benson & Hedges Masters
v Thorburn	6-5	Semi-final	Benson & Hedges Masters
v Griffiths	**9-6**	**Final**	**Benson & Hedges Masters**
v Reardon	5-6	Semi-final	Benson & Hedges Irish Masters
v S. Davis	8-13	2nd round	Embassy World Championship
v V. Harris	5-3	Quarter-final	Langs Scottish Masters
v Thorburn	2-6	Semi-final	Langs Scottish Masters
v Fagan	5-3	2nd round	Jameson International
v Mountjoy	5-1	3rd round	Jameson International
v Griffiths	5-2	Quarter-final	Jameson International
v S. Davis	8-9	Semi-final	Jameson International
v S. Davis	2-5	1st round	Northern Ireland Classic
v Martin	9-7	2nd round	Coral UK Championship
v David Taylor	9-5	3rd round	Coral UK Championship
v Meo	4-9	Quarter-final	Coral UK Championship
1982 v Dennis Taylor	5-1	1st round	Lada Classic
v Griffiths	1-5	Semi-final	Lada Classic
v Charlton	5-1	Quarter-final	Benson & Hedges Masters
v Griffiths	4-6	Semi-final	Benson & Hedges Masters
v D. Hughes	6-2	Semi-final	Irish Championship
v Dennis Taylor	13-16	Final	Irish Championship
v Wych	5-3	1st round	Benson & Hedges Irish Masters
v Thorburn	5-4	Quarter-final	Benson & Hedges Irish Masters
v S. Davis	2-6	Semi-final	Benson & Hedges Irish Masters
v Meadowcroft	10-5	1st round	Embassy World Championship
v Mountjoy	13-12	2nd round	Embassy World Championship
v Thorne	13-10	Quarter-final	Embassy World Championship
v White	16-15	Semi-final	Embassy World Championship

v **Reardon**	**18-15**	**Final**	**Embassy World Championship**
v Sinclair	5-1	1st round	Langs Scottish Masters
v Griffiths	6-5	Semi-final	Langs Scottish Masters
v S. Davis	4-9	Final	Langs Scottish Masters
v Kelly	5-3	1st round	Jameson International
v Griffiths	2-5	2nd round	Jameson International
v French	5-3	1st round	Professional Players Tournament
v Reardon	2-5	2nd round	Professional Players Tournament
v Martin	9-7	1st round	Coral UK Championship
v Reynolds	9-8	2nd round	Coral UK Championship
v Spencer	9-5	Quarter-final	Coral UK Championship
v Reardon	9-6	Semi-final	Coral UK Championship
v Griffiths	15-16	Final	Coral UK Championship
1983 v Werbeniuk	4-5	1st round	Lada Classic
v Werbeniuk	4-5	1st round	Benson & Hedges Masters
v Jack Rea	6-3	Quarter-final	Irish Championship
v E. Hughes	6-2	Semi-final	Irish Championship
v **Dennis Taylor**	**16-11**	**Final**	**Irish Championship**
v White	5-2	Quarter-final	Benson & Hedges Irish Masters
v Reardon	3-6	Semi-final	Benson & Hedges Irish Masters
v Reynolds	10-4	1st round	Embassy World Championship
v Thorne	13-8	2nd round	Embassy World Championship
v Werbeniuk	13-11	Quarter-final	Embassy World Championship
v S. Davis	5-16	Semi-final	Embassy World Championship
v White	5-3	1st round	Langs Supreme Scottish Masters
v S. Davis	2-6	Semi-final	Langs Supreme Scottish Masters
v Martin	2-5	1st round	Jameson International
v Watterson	2-5	1st round	Professional Players Tournament
v Macleod	9-6	1st round	Coral UK Championship
v Medati	9-1	2nd round	Coral UK Championship
v Knowles	9-5	Quarter-final	Coral UK Championship
v Griffiths	9-4	Semi-final	Coral UK Championship
v **S. Davis**	**16-15**	**Final**	**Coral UK Championship**
1984 v Fagan	5-3	Qualifying	Lada Classic
v Parrott	2-5	1st round	Lada Classic
v Mountjoy	5-2	1st round	Benson & Hedges Masters
v Knowles	1-5	Quarter-final	Benson & Hedges Masters
v Charlton	5-2	1st round	Benson & Hedges Irish Masters
v Reardon	5-2	Quarter-final	Benson & Hedges Irish Masters
v S. Davis	4-6	Semi-final	Benson & Hedges Irish Masters
v N. Foulds	9-10	1st round	Embassy World Championship
v Stevens	5-2	1st round	Langs Supreme Scottish Masters
v S. Davis	4-6	Semi-final	Langs Supreme Scottish Masters
v Knowles	3-5	1st round	Carlsberg Challenge
v Sinclair	5-1	1st round	Jameson International
v Griffiths	5-4	2nd round	Jameson International
v S. Davis	1-5	Quarter-final	Jameson International
v Bales	5-1	1st round	Rothmans Grand Prix
v Hallett	3-5	2nd round	Rothmans Grand Prix
v T. Jones	9-7	1st round	Coral UK Open

	v Williams	9-7	2nd round	Coral UK Open
	v Thorne	9-5	Quarter-final	Coral UK Open
	v Thorburn	9-7	Semi-finals	Coral UK Open
	v S. Davis	8-16	Final	Coral UK Open
1985	v Gauvreau	5-3	1st round	Mercantile Credit Classic
	v S. Davis	2-5	2nd round	Mercantile Credit Classic
	v S. Davis	5-4	1st round	Benson & Hedges Masters
	v Griffiths	1-5	Quarter-final	Benson & Hedges Masters
	v Bales	6-3	1st round	Dulux British Open
	v N. Foulds	5-1	2nd round	Dulux British Open
	v Thorburn	5-2	3rd round	Dulux British Open
	v E. Hughes	5-2	Quarter-final	Dulux British Open
	v S. Francisco	6-9	Semi-final	Dulux British Open
	v Griffiths	5-2	1st round	Benson & Hedges Irish Masters
	v Stevens	5-3	Quarter-final	Benson & Hedges Irish Masters
	v S. Davis	6-2	Semi-final	Benson & Hedges Irish Masters
	v White	5-9	Final	Benson & Hedges Irish Masters
	v Burke	6-0	Quarter-final	Irish Championship
	v Fagan	6-3	Semi-final	Irish Championship
	v Dennis Taylor	5-10	Final	Irish Championship
	v Reynolds	10-4	1st round	Embassy World Championship
	v Griffiths	7-13	2nd round	Embassy World Championship
	v Thorburn	5-4	Semi-final	Carlsberg Challenge
	v White	3-8	Final	Carlsberg Challenge
	v White	0-5	1st round	Langs Scottish Masters
	v D. Hughes	5-1	Third round	Goya Matchroom Trophy
	v Murphy	5-2	Fourth round	Goya Matchroom Trophy
	v Dennis Taylor	1-5	Fifth round	Goya Matchroom Trophy
	v V. Harris	5-1	3rd round	Rothmans Grand Prix
	v N. Foulds	5-3	4th round	Rothmans Grand Prix
	v S. Davis	0-5	5th round	Rothmans Grand Prix
	v Edmonds	9-8	3rd round	Coral UK Open
	v F. Davis	9-2	4th round	Coral UK Open
	v White	6-9	5th round	Coral UK Open
	v Thorburn	5-4	1st round	Kit Kat
	v S. Davis	6-1	Semi-final	Kit Kat
1986	v Fisher	5-0	3rd round	Mercantile Credit Classic
	v Cripsey	5-2	4th round	Mercantile Credit Classic
	v Dennis Taylor	5-4	5th round	Mercantile Credit Classic
	v Williams	2-5	Quarter-final	Mercantile Credit Classic
	v Dennis Taylor	5-1	1st round	BCE Belgian Classic
	v Stevens	4-5	Semi-final	BCE Belgian Classic
	v Griffiths	4-5	1st round	Benson & Hedges Masters
	v Bradley	5-3	3rd round	Dulux British Open
	v Hallett	5-1	4th round	Dulux British Open
	v P. Francisco	5-2	5th round	Dulux British Open
	v Werbeniuk	5-1	Quarter-final	Dulux British Open
	v S. Davis	3-9	Semi-final	Dulux British Open
	v Meo	4-5	1st round	Benson & Hedges Irish Masters
	v Spencer	10-7	1st round	Embassy World Championship

v Griffiths	12-13	2nd round	Embassy World Championship
v J. McLaughlin	6-2	Quarter-final	Strongbow Irish Championship
v E. Hughes	6-2	Semi-final	Strongbow Irish Championship
v Dennis Taylor	7-10	Final	Strongbow Irish Championship
v White	1-5	1st round	Carlsberg Challenge
v Johnson	5-2	1st round	Langs Scottish Masters
v Stevens	6-2	Semi-final	Langs Scottish Masters
v Thorburn	8-9	Final	Langs Scottish Masters
v Sinclair	5-3	3rd round	BCE International
v P. Francisco	4-5	4th round	BCE International
v F. Davis	5-0	3rd round	Rothmans Grand Prix
v Martin	5-2	4th round	Rothmans Grand Prix
v Williams	1-5	5th round	Rothmans Grand Prix
v Johnson	5-3	1st round	BCE Canadian Masters
v S. Davis	2-8	Semi-final	BCE Canadian Masters
v Hendry	9-8	3rd round	Tennents UK Open
v Martin	9-6	4th round	Tennents UK Open
v Hallett	9-7	5th round	Tennents UK Open
v W. Jones	9-5	Quarter-final	Tennents UK Open
v S. Davis	3-9	Semi-final	Tennents UK Open
1987 v Roscoe	5-2	3rd round	Mercantile Credit Classic
v Parrott	2-5	4th round	Mercantile Credit Classic
v Griffiths	5-4	1st round	Benson & Hedges Masters
v Johnson	5-1	Quarter-final	Benson & Hedges Masters
v Meo	6-2	Semi-final	Benson & Hedges Masters
v Dennis Taylor	8-9	Final	Benson & Hedges Masters
v J. McLaughlin	4-5	3rd round	Dulux British Open
v Griffiths	1-5	1st round	Benson & Hedges Irish Masters
v Wright	10-6	1st round	Embassy World Championship
v Griffiths	10-13	2nd round	Embassy World Championship

PAT HOULIHAN (England)

Born 7.11.29
Turned professional 1969
World ranking 65 (91)
Amateur career 1965 English champion.

1972 v Dunning	10-11	Qualifying	World Championship
1973 v Jack Rea	9-2	1st round	World Championship
v Higgins	3-16	2nd round	World Championship
1977 v Meadowcroft	1-5	1st round	Super Crystalate UK
1978 v Ross	9-1	Prelim	Embassy World Championship
v Meadowcroft	9-6	Qualifying	Embassy World Championship
v Thorburn	8-13	1st round	Embassy World Championship
v Andrewartha	3-9	Qualifying	Coral UK Championship
1979 v Barrie	9-5	Prelim	Embassy World Championship
v Mountjoy	6-9	Qualifying	Embassy World Championship
v Jack Rea	9-3	2nd round	Coral UK Championship

v Higgins	3-9	3rd round	Coral UK Championship
1980 v Meo	1-9	Qualifying	Embassy World Championship
v Meo	1-9	1st round	Coral UK Championship
1981 v Spencer	1-9	1st round	John Courage English
v French	3-5	Qualifying	Jameson International
v Kennerley	9-1	Qualifying	Coral UK Championship
v Black	9-4	Qualifying	Coral UK Championship
v Meadowcroft	9-4	Qualifying	Coral UK Championship
v Miles	3-9	2nd round	Coral UK Championship
1982 v Anderson	9-5	Qualifying	Embassy World Championship
v Martin	3-9	Qualifying	Embassy World Championship
v E. McLaughlin	2-5	Qualifying	Jameson International
v Knowles	4-5	1st round	Professional Players Tournament
v Mountjoy	3-9	1st round	Coral UK Championship
1983 v Murphy	9-10	Qualifying	Embassy World Championship
v Scott	0-5	Qualifying	Jameson International
v Sheehan	2-5	Qualifying	Professional Players Tournament
v V. Harris	6-9	Qualifying	Coral UK Championship
1984 v Williamson	5-10	Qualifying	Embassy World Championship
v Hargreaves	2-5	Qualifying	Jameson International
v Everton	3-5	Qualifying	Rothmans Grand Prix
v Chappel	3-9	Qualifying	Coral UK Open
1985 v Foldvari	1-5	Qualifying	Mercantile Credit Classic
v T. Jones	1-9	Qualifying	Tolly Cobbold English Championship
v Jim Bear	2-5	1st round	Goya Matchroom Trophy
v Robinson	5-0	1st round	Rothmans Grand Prix
v T. Jones	4-5	2nd round	Rothmans Grand Prix
v Watson	9-4	1st round	Coral UK Open
v Newbury	3-9	2nd round	Coral UK Open
1986 v Bennett	5-0	1st round	Mercantile Credit Classic
v Foldvari	5-4	2nd round	Mercantile Credit Classic
v Reynolds	1-5	3rd round	Mercantile Credit Classic
v Hargreaves	9-5	1st round	Tolly Cobbold English Championship
Houlihan *wo*			
Dunning *scr*		2nd round	Tolly Cobbold English Championship
v Spencer	5-9	3rd round	Tolly Cobbold English Championship
v Longworth	3-5	2nd round	Dulux British Open
v Sheehan	7-10	Qualifying	Embassy World Championship
v Chalmers	5-1	1st round	BCE International
v Cripsey	5-1	2nd round	BCE International
v Meo	5-4	3rd round	BCE International
v E. Hughes	1-5	4th round	BCE International
v Grace	1-5	1st round	Rothmans Grand Prix
1987 v Owers	1-5	1st round	Mercantile Credit Classic
v N. Gilbert	4-5	1st round	Dulux British Open
v Wright	4-10	Qualifying	Embassy World Championship

DENNIS HUGHES (England)

Born 30.1.37
Turned professional 1981
World ranking 106 (93)

1981	v Jack Rea	5-4	Qualifying	Jameson International
	v Demarco	1-5	Qualifying	Jameson International
	v Hallett	6-9	Qualifying	Coral UK Championship
1982	v Higgins	2-6	Semi-final	Irish Championship
	v Everton	9-4	Qualifying	Embassy World Championship
	v Meo	4-9	Qualifying	Embassy World Championship
	v Edmonds	0-5	Qualifying	Jameson International
	v Charlton	2-5	1st round	Professional Players Tournament
	v Meadowcroft	8-9	Qualifying	Coral UK Championship
1983	v Parkin	5-0	Qualifying	Jameson International
	v Johnson	1-5	Qualifying	Jameson International
	v Medati	1-5	Qualifying	Professional Players Tournament
	v Medati	2-9	Qualifying	Coral UK Championship
1984	v Parrott	3-10	Qualifying	Embassy World Championship
	v Oliver	4-5	Qualifying	Jameson International
	v Dunning	0-5	Qualifying	Rothmans Grand Prix
	v G. Foulds	7-9	Qualifying	Coral UK Open
1985	v Watchorn	0-5	Prelim	Mercantile Credit Classic
	v Watterson	9-5	Qualifying	Tolly Cobbold English Championship
	v N. Foulds	3-9	1st round	Tolly Cobbold English Championship
	v Mikkelsen	0-6	Qualifying	Dulux British Open
	v French	10-5	Qualifying	Embassy World Championship
	v Newbury	9-10	Qualifying	Embassy World Championship
	v Kearney	5-1	1st round	Goya Matchroom Trophy
	v Gauvreau	5-4	2nd round	Goya Matchroom Trophy
	v Higgins	1-5	3rd round	Goya Matchroom Trophy
	v Bennett	5-4	1st round	Rothmans Grand Prix
	v Morra	2-5	2nd round	Rothmans Grand Prix
	v Kearney	9-8	1st round	Coral UK Open
	v King	0-9	2nd round	Coral UK Open
1986	v Burke	3-5	1st round	Mercantile Credit Classic
	v F. Davis	6-9	2nd round	Tolly Cobbold English Championship
	v Hendry	1-5	1st round	Dulux British Open
	v Agrawal	6-10	Qualifying	Embassy World Championship
	v Roe	2-5	1st round	BCE International
	v Jack Rea	2-5	1st round	Rothmans Grand Prix
	v Ellis	9-6	1st round	Tennents UK Open
	v Murphy	0-9	2nd round	Tennents UK Open
1987	v Wright	2-5	1st round	Mercantile Credit Classic
	v P. Gibson	3-6	1st round	Tolly Ales English Championship
	v Whitthread	1-5	1st round	Dulux British Open
	v Parkin	10-5	Qualifying	Embassy World Championship
	v B. Harris	2-10	Qualifying	Embassy World Championship

EUGENE HUGHES (Republic of Ireland)

Born 4.11.55
Turned professional 1981
World ranking 24 (20)
Amateur career Republic of Ireland champion 1978, 1979.
Best professional performances Semi-finals 1984 Jameson International, 1986 BCE International.

1981	v M. Owen	5-1	Qualifying	Jameson International
	v Fitzmaurice	5-3	Qualifying	Jameson International
	v Sinclair	5-2	Qualifying	Jameson International
	v Edmonds	4-5	1st round	Jameson International
1982	v Mountjoy	4-5	1st round	Benson & Hedges Irish Masters
	v Jack Rea	6-1	Quarter-final	Irish Championship
	v Higgins	2-6	Semi-final	Irish Championship
	v Knowles	7-9	Qualifying	Embassy World Championship
	v Parkin	5-2	Qualifying	Jameson International
	v Martin	5-4	Qualifying	Jameson International
	v Reardon	3-5	1st round	Jameson International
	v Stevens	2-5	1st round	Professional Players Tournament
1983	v Burke	6-2	Quarter-final	Irish Championship
	v Higgins	2-6	Semi-final	Irish Championship
	v Fitzmaurice	10-7	Qualifying	Embassy World Championship
	v Sinclair	10-8	Qualifying	Embassy World Championship
	v Reardon	7-10	1st round	Embassy World Championship
	v Fisher	5-4	Qualifying	Jameson International
	v G. Foulds	5-1	Qualifying	Jameson International
	v S. Davis	1-5	1st round	Jameson International
	v Sinclair	5-4	1st round	Professional Players Tournament
	v Werbeniuk	5-0	2nd round	Professional Players Tournament
	v Griffiths	5-2	3rd round	Professional Players Tournament
	v Thorne	1-5	Quarter-final	Professional Players Tournament
1984	v Knowles	1-5	Qualifying	Lada Classic
	v Dennis Taylor	1-5	1st round	Benson & Hedges Irish Masters
	v Mifsud	5-10	Qualifying	Embassy World Championship
	v Roscoe	5-1	Qualifying	Jameson International
	v Mountjoy	5-1	1st round	Jameson International
	v Reardon	5-1	2nd round	Jameson International
	v Thorne	5-2	Quarter-final	Jameson International
	v S. Davis	3-9	Semi-final	Jameson International
	v John Rea	4-5	1st round	Rothmans Grand Prix
	v Morra	9-8	Qualifying	Coral UK Open
	v Meo	4-9	1st round	Coral UK Open
1985	v Newbury	5-3	Qualifying	Mercantile Credit Classic
	v Meo	5-4	1st round	Mercantile Credit Classic
	v Reardon	1-5	2nd round	Mercantile Credit Classic
	v Watchorn	6-4	1st round	Dulux British Open
	v B. Harris	5-4	2nd round	Dulux British Open

	v Macleod	5-2	3rd round	Dulux British Open
	v Higgins	2-5	Quarter-final	Dulux British Open
	v Reardon	5-0	1st round	Benson & Hedges Irish Masters
	v S. Davis	4-5	Quarter-final	Benson & Hedges Irish Masters
	v Kelly	6-2	Quarter-final	Irish Championship
	v Dennis Taylor	5-6	Semi-final	Irish Championship
	v Newbury	10-6	Qualifying	Embassy World Championship
	v Reardon	9-10	1st round	Embassy World Championship
	v Murphy	3-5	3rd round	Goya Matchroom Trophy
	v Simngam	5-1	3rd round	Rothmans Grand Prix
	v Meo	3-5	4th round	Rothmans Grand Prix
	v West	3-9	3rd round	Coral UK Open
1986	v Wych	5-2	3rd round	Mercantile Credit Classic
	v F. Davis	5-3	4th round	Mercantile Credit Classic
	v Johnson	1-5	5th round	Mercantile Credit Classic
	v Longworth	4-5	3rd round	Dulux British Open
	v Reardon	5-2	1st round	Benson & Hedges Irish Masters
	v Thorburn	1-5	Quarter-final	Benson & Hedges Irish Masters
	v Murphy	10-7	Qualifying	Embassy World Championship
	v David Taylor	10-7	1st round	Embassy World Championship
	v Thorburn	6-13	2nd round	Embassy World Championship
	v Sheehan	5-0	1st round	Strongbow Irish Championship
	v Burke	6-3	Quarter-final	Strongbow Irish Championship
	v Higgins	2-6	Semi-final	Strongbow Irish Championship
	v Chappel	5-4	3rd round	BCE International
	v Houlihan	5-1	4th round	BCE International
	v Chaperon	5-0	5th round	BCE International
	v S. Davis	5-4	Quarter-final	BCE International
	v N. Foulds	8-9	Semi-final	BCE International
	v Hendry	1-5	3rd round	Rothmans Grand Prix
	v Roscoe	9-8	3rd round	Tennents UK Open
	v Reardon	9-5	4th round	Tennents UK Open
	v W. Jones	5-9	5th round	Tennents UK Open
1987	v Wright	4-5	3rd round	Mercantile Credit Classic
	v V. Harris	5-0	3rd round	Dulux British Open
	v Johnson	3-5	4th round	Dulux British Open
	v Dennis Taylor	4-5	1st round	Benson & Hedges Irish Masters
	v Medati	10-2	Qualifying	Embassy World Championship
	v Johnson	9-10	1st round	Embassy World Championship
	v Watchorn	5-2	1st round	Matchroom Irish Championship
	v Kearney	6-1	Quarter-final	Matchroom Irish Championship
	v O'Boye	3-6	Semi-final	Matchroom Irish Championship

STEVE JAMES (England)

Born 2.5.61
Turned professional 1986
World ranking 67 (–)
Best professional performance Last 32 1987 Dulux British Open.

1986	v N. Gilbert	5-2	1st round	BCE International
	v Edmonds	2-5	2nd round	BCE International
	v Morra	3-5	1st round	Rothmans Grand Prix
	v Rigitano	9-5	1st round	Tennents UK Open
	v King	8-9	2nd round	Tennents UK Open
1987	v Jonik	4-5	1st round	Mercantile Credit Classic
	v Hargreaves	6-5	1st round	Tolly Ales English Championship
	v F. Davis	6-2	2nd round	Tolly Ales English Championship
	v Longworth	6-2	3rd round	Tolly Ales English Championship
	v Johnson	3-6	4th round	Tolly Ales English Championship
	v Darrington	5-3	1st round	Dulux British Open
	v Miles	5-2	2nd round	Dulux British Open
	v Campbell	5-1	3rd round	Dulux British Open
	v Williams	2-5	4th round	Dulux British Open
	v Watterson	10-2	Qualifying	Embassy World Championship
	v Edmonds	1-10	Qualifying	Embassy World Championship

GREG JENKINS (Australia)

Born –
Turned professional 1985
World ranking 94 (95)

1985	v Wilkinson	2-6	1st round	Australian Championship
	v Burke	9-5	1st round	Coral UK Open
	v Bradley	3-9	2nd round	Coral UK Open
1986	v Watterson	2-5	2nd round	Mercantile Credit Classic
	v Demarco	5-1	1st round	Dulux British Open
	v Meadowcroft	5-2	2nd round	Dulux British Open
	v Wildman	4-5	3rd round	Dulux British Open
	v Gibson	4-10	Qualifying	Embassy World Championship
	v Foldvari	3-6	2nd round	Australian Championship
	v Everton	5-3	1st round	BCE International
	v Gauvreau	1-5	2nd round	BCE International
	v Kearney	3-5	1st round	Rothmans Grand Prix
	v Mienie	9-6	1st round	Tennents UK Open
	v O'Kane	5-9	2nd round	Tennents UK Open
1987	v Parkin	5-2	1st round	Mercantile Credit Classic
	v Scott	5-4	2nd round	Mercantile Credit Classic
	v S. Davis	0-5	3rd round	Mercantile Credit Classic
	v Rowswell	1-5	1st round	Dulux British Open
	v Grace	10-9	Qualifying	Embassy World Championship
	v Murphy	4-10	Qualifying	Embassy World Championship

JOE JOHNSON (England)

Born 29.7.52
Turned professional 1979
World ranking 5 (8)
Best professional performances Winner 1986 Embassy World Championship; runner-up 1987 Embassy World Championship.

1979	v Werbeniuk	3-9	2nd round	Coral UK Championship
1980	v Dunning	9-6	Qualifying	Coral UK Championship
	v Fagan	4-9	1st round	Coral UK Championship
1981	v Knowles	9-2	Qualifying	John Courage English
	Johnson *wo*		1st round	John Courage English
	v Edmonds	5-9	2nd round	John Courage English
	v Meo	8-9	Qualifying	Embassy World Championship
	v Donnelly	5-4	Qualifying	Jameson International
	v Macleod	5-1	Qualifying	Jameson International
	v Wych	5-2	1st round	Jameson International
	v Miles	3-5	2nd round	Jameson International
	v Murphy	9-1	Qualifying	Coral UK Championship
	v Watterson	9-3	Qualifying	Coral UK Championship
	v Wilson	9-5	Qualifying	Coral UK Championship
	v Spencer	9-5	2nd round	Coral UK Championship
	v Reardon	7-9	3rd round	Coral UK Championship
1982	v Harris	9-4	Qualifying	Embassy World Championship
	v Hallett	8-9	Qualifying	Embassy World Championship
	v Wilson	4-5	Qualifying	Jameson International
	v Miles	5-1	1st round	Professional Players Tournament
	v Stevens	5-1	2nd round	Professional Players Tournament
	v Wildman	5-4	3rd round	Professional Players Tournament
	v Virgo	1-5	Quarter-final	Professional Players Tournament
	v V. Harris	9-8	Qualifying	Coral UK Championship
	v Griffiths	1-9	1st round	Coral UK Championship
1983	v Watchorn	10-0	Qualifying	Embassy World Championship
	v Wilson	8-10	Qualifying	Embassy World Championship
	v D. Hughes	5-1	Qualifying	Jameson International
	v Charlton	2-5	1st round	Jameson International
	v Burke	5-3	1st round	Professional Players Tournament
	v White	5-3	2nd round	Professional Players Tournament
	v Charlton	5-0	3rd round	Professional Players Tournament
	v Thorburn	5-1	Quarter-final	Professional Players Tournament
	v Meo	9-6	Semi-final	Professional Players Tournament
	v Knowles	8-9	Final	Professional Players Tournament
	v Gibson	9-6	Qualifying	Coral UK Championship
	v Virgo	9-6	1st round	Coral UK Championship
	v David Taylor	9-3	2nd round	Coral UK Championship
	v Griffiths	2-9	Quarter-final	Coral UK Championship
1984	v Spencer	4-5	Qualifying	Lada Classic
	v Gibson	10-3	Qualifying	Embassy World Championship
	v Dennis Taylor	1-10	1st round	Embassy World Championship

v Morra	5-0	Qualifying	Jameson International
v Charlton	5-1	1st round	Jameson International
v Dennis Taylor	2-5	2nd round	Jameson International
v Medati	5-1	1st round	Rothmans Grand Prix
v Williamson	4-5	2nd round	Rothmans Grand Prix
v John Rea	9-6	Qualifying	Coral UK Open
v Spencer	9-6	1st round	Coral UK Open
v Stevens	2-9	2nd round	Coral UK Open
1985 v Edmonds	5-4	Qualifying	Mercantile Credit Classic
v Knowles	5-1	1st round	Mercantile Credit Classic
v Wilson	5-0	2nd round	Mercantile Credit Classic
v King	5-3	Quarter-final	Mercantile Credit Classic
v Thorburn	2-9	Semi-finals	Mercantile Credit Classic
v Scott	9-1	1st round	Tolly Cobbold English Championship
v Virgo	4-9	2nd round	Tolly Cobbold English Championship
v W. Jones	5-6	1st round	Dulux British Open
v G. Foulds	10-6	Qualifying	Embassy World Championship
v Werbeniuk	8-10	1st round	Embassy World Championship
v White	4-5	Quarter-final	Winfield Australian Masters
v Jim Bear	5-1	3rd round	Goya Matchroom Trophy
v Bradley	5-2	4th round	Goya Matchroom Trophy
v Wilson	5-1	5th round	Goya Matchroom Trophy
v N. Foulds	2-5	Quarter-final	Goya Matchroom Trophy
v Gilbert	5-2	3rd round	Rothmans Grand Prix
v Hallett	5-4	4th round	Rothmans Grand Prix
v Thorburn	1-5	5th round	Rothmans Grand Prix
v Simngam	9-4	3rd round	Coral UK Open
v N. Foulds	8-9	4th round	Coral UK Open
1986 v B. Harris	5-4	3rd round	Mercantile Credit Classic
v Mans	5-2	4th round	Mercantile Credit Classic
v E. Hughes	5-1	5th round	Mercantile Credit Classic
v Thorburn	4-5	Quarter-final	Mercantile Credit Classic
v Thorburn	3-5	1st round	Benson & Hedges Masters
v Fowler	9-7	3rd round	Tolly Cobbold English Championship
v Spencer	9-7	4th round	Tolly Cobbold English Championship
v Hallett	6-9	Quarter-final	Tolly Cobbold English Championship
v J. McLaughlin	5-2	3rd round	Dulux British Open
v Werbeniuk	5-2	4th round	Dulux British Open
v Martin	10-3	1st round	Embassy World Championship
v Hallett	13-6	2nd round	Embassy World Championship
v Griffiths	13-12	Quarter-final	Embassy World Championship
v Knowles	16-8	Semi-final	Embassy World Championship
v S. Davis	**18-12**	**Final**	**Embassy World Championship**
v Dennis Taylor	3-5	1st round	Carlsberg Challenge
v Higgins	2-5	1st round	Langs Scottish Masters
v Murphy	5-4	3rd round	BCE International
v David Taylor	3-5	4th round	BCE International
v Browne	2-5	3rd round	Rothmans Grand Prix
v Higgins	3-5	1st round	BCE Canadian Masters
v Parrott	1-9	3rd round	Tennents UK Open

1987	v Sinclair	5-0	3rd round	Mercantile Credit Classic
	v P. Francisco	3-5	4th round	Mercantile Credit Classic
	v Reardon	5-2	1st round	Benson & Hedges Masters
	v Higgins	1-5	Quarter-final	Benson & Hedges Masters
	v Miles	6-3	3rd round	Tolly Cobbold English Championship
	v James	6-2	4th round	Tolly Cobbold English Championship
	v Williams	6-5	Quarter-final	Tolly Cobbold English Championship
	v Dodd	5-9	Semi-final	Tolly Cobbold English Championship
	v Drago	5-0	3rd round	Dulux British Open
	v E. Hughes	5-3	4th round	Dulux British Open
	v Spencer	3-5	5th round	Dulux British Open
	v Griffiths	0-5	Quarter-final	Benson & Hedges Irish Masters
	v E. Hughes	10-9	1st round	Embassy World Championship
	v Macleod	13-7	2nd round	Embassy World Championship
	v Hendry	13-12	Quarter-final	Embassy World Championship
	v N. Foulds	16-9	Semi-final	Embassy World Championship
	v S. Davis	14-18	Final	Embassy World Championship

TONY JONES (England)

Born 15.4.60
Turned professional 1983
World ranking 46 (55)
Amateur career 1983 English champion.
Best professional performances Last 32 1986 Mercantile Credit Classic, 1986 Tennents UK Open, 1987 Dulux British Open.

1983	v Oliver	5-2	Qualifying	Professional Players Tournament
	v Werbeniuk	4-5	1st round	Professional Players Tournament
	v Sinclair	9-3	Qualifying	Coral UK Championship
	v Knowles	5-9	1st round	Coral UK Championship
1984	v King	9-10	Qualifying	Embassy World Championship
	v French	5-1	Qualifying	Jameson International
	v Duggan	2-5	Qualifying	Jameson International
	v Sinclair	5-4	Qualifying	Rothmans Grand Prix
	v Griffiths	5-3	1st round	Rothmans Grand Prix
	v N. Foulds	0-5	2nd round	Rothmans Grand Prix
	v Chaperon	9-1	Qualifying	Coral UK Open
	v Fagan	9-2	Qualifying	Coral UK Open
	v Wildman	9-2	Qualifying	Coral UK Open
	v Higgins	7-9	1st round	Coral UK Open
1985	v Greaves	5-2	Qualifying	Mercantile Credit Classic
	v Gibson	5-0	Qualifying	Mercantile Credit Classic
	v Dodd	5-1	Qualifying	Mercantile Credit Classic
	v S. Francisco	1-5	Qualifying	Mercantile Credit Classic
	v Houlihan	9-1	Qualifying	Tolly Cobbold English Championship
	v Williams	6-9	1st round	Tolly Cobbold English Championship

v G. Foulds	6-0	Qualifying	Dulux British Open
v White	5-6	1st round	Dulux British Open
v Darrington	10-2	Qualifying	Embassy World Championship
v Duggan	10-8	Qualifying	Embassy World Championship
v Fitzmaurice	10-4	Qualifying	Embassy World Championship
v Sinclair	10-2	Qualifying	Embassy World Championship
v Knowles	8-10	1st round	Embassy World Championship
v Kelly	5-3	2nd round	Goya Matchroom Trophy
v David Taylor	4-5	3rd round	Goya Matchroom Trophy
v Houlihan	5-4	2nd round	Rothmans Grand Prix
v Meo	2-5	3rd round	Rothmans Grand Prix
v Jonik	9-4	2nd round	Coral UK Open
v Griffiths	5-9	3rd round	Coral UK Open
1986 v Gilbert	5-3	2nd round	Mercantile Credit Classic
v Thorne	5-3	3rd round	Mercantile Credit Classic
v Werbeniuk	3-5	4th round	Mercantile Credit Classic
v B. Harris	9-5	2nd round	Tolly Cobbold English Championship
v Virgo	7-9	3rd round	Tolly Cobbold English Championship
v O'Boye	5-2	2nd round	Dulux British Open
v S. Francisco	2-5	3rd round	Dulux British Open
v V. Harris	10-7	Qualifying	Embassy World Championship
v Gilbert	7-10	Qualifying	Embassy World Championship
v Burke	4-5	2nd round	BCE International
v Smith	5-0	2nd round	Rothmans Grand Prix
v White	0-5	3rd round	Rothmans Grand Prix
v Fitzmaurice	9-0	2nd round	Tennents UK Open
v West	9-4	3rd round	Tennents UK Open
v Knowles	2-9	4th round	Tennents UK Open
1987 v Oliver	5-0	2nd round	Mercantile Credit Classic
v Parrott	2-5	3rd round	Mercantile Credit Classic
v Oliver	6-1	2nd round	Tolly Ales English Championship
v Williams	4-6	3rd round	Tolly Ales English Championship
v Donnelly	5-2	2nd round	Dulux British Open
v Macleod	5-4	3rd round	Dulux British Open
v Griffiths	3-5	4th round	Dulux British Open
v Chalmers	10-1	Qualifying	Embassy World Championship
v Van Rensberg	10-0	Qualifying	Embassy World Championship
v Virgo	9-10	Qualifying	Embassy World Championship

WAYNE JONES (Wales)

Born 24.12.59
Turned professional 1984
World ranking 34 (56)
Amateur career 1983 Welsh champion.
Best professional performance Quarter-finals 1986 Tennents UK Open.

1984 v Watchorn	5-0	Qualifying	Jameson International
v Gibson	5-2	Qualifying	Jameson International
v Scott	5-0	Qualifying	Jameson International
v Wildman	5-0	Qualifying	Jameson International
v David Taylor	4-5	1st round	Jameson International
v Watterson	5-3	Qualifying	Rothmans Grand Prix
v Campbell	4-5	1st round	Rothmans Grand Prix
v O'Kane	7-9	Qualifying	Coral UK Open
1985 v O'Kane	5-0	Qualifying	Mercantile Credit Classic
v Duggan	0-5	Qualifying	Mercantile Credit Classic
v Donnelly	6-1	Qualifying	Dulux British Open
v Johnson	6-5	1st round	Dulux British Open
v Chaperon	2-5	2nd round	Dulux British Open
v Jack Rea	10-3	Qualifying	Embassy World Championship
v Dunning	10-6	Qualifying	Embassy World Championship
v Watterson	10-5	Qualifying	Embassy World Championship
v Miles	10-8	Qualifying	Embassy World Championship
v White	4-10	1st round	Embassy World Championship
v Newbury	2-6	1st round	BCE Welsh Championship
v Smith	5-3	2nd round	Goya Matchroom Trophy
v Parrott	3-5	3rd round	Goya Matchroom Trophy
v John Rea	5-0	2nd round	Rothmans Grand Prix
v Thorne	5-0	3rd round	Rothmans Grand Prix
v P. Francisco	3-5	4th round	Rothmans Grand Prix
v Fitzmaurice	9-3	2nd round	Coral UK Open
v Virgo	7-9	3rd round	Coral UK Open
1986 v Van Rensberg	4-5	2nd round	Mercantile Credit Classic
v Everton	6-2	1st round	Zetters Welsh Championship
v Reardon	6-4	Quarter-final	Zetters Welsh Championship
v Mountjoy	7-9	Semi-final	Zetters Welsh Championship
v Rigitano	5-1	2nd round	Dulux British Open
v Mans	2-5	3rd round	Dulux British Open
v Grace	10-3	Qualifying	Embassy World Championship
v Hendry	8-10	Qualifying	Embassy World Championship
v Jack Rea	5-1	2nd round	BCE International
v Reardon	4-5	3rd round	BCE International
v Foldvari	5-3	2nd round	Rothmans Grand Prix
v David Taylor	5-1	3rd round	Rothmans Grand Prix
v S. Francisco	4-5	4th round	Rothmans Grand Prix
v Hargreaves	9-0	2nd round	Tennents UK Open
v Campbell	9-3	3rd round	Tennents UK Open
v Dennis Taylor	9-2	4th round	Tennents UK Open
v E. Hughes	9-5	5th round	Tennents UK Open
v Higgins	5-9	Quarter-final	Tennents UK Open
1987 v Everton	5-0	2nd round	Mercantile Credit Classic
v Dennis Taylor	5-2	3rd round	Mercantile Credit Classic
v Kearney	5-1	4th round	Mercantile Credit Classic
v Wilson	3-5	5th round	Mercantile Credit Classic
v M. Bennett	6-3	1st round	Matchroom Welsh Championship
v Griffiths	2-6	Quarter-final	Matchroom Welsh Championship

v Gilbert	3-5	2nd round	Dulux British Open
v Donnelly	10-3	Qualifying	Embassy World Championship
v M. Bennett	3-10	Qualifying	Embassy World Championship

FRANK JONIK (Canada)

Born 2.12.57
Turned professional 1979
World ranking 96 (98)

1980	v Wildman	9-7	Qualifying	Embassy World Championship
	v Wilson	6-9	Qualifying	Embassy World Championship
1981	v Hallett	1-9	Qualifying	Embassy World Championship
1982	v John Bear	4-9	Qualifying	Embassy World Championship
	v Hallett	2-5	Qualifying	Jameson International
	v Mountjoy	5-3	1st round	Professional Players Tournament
	v Meo	0-5	2nd round	Professional Players Tournament
1983	v Edmonds	4-10	Qualifying	Embassy World Championship
	v Wildman	4-5	1st round	Professional Players Tournament
1984	v Mikkelsen	9-10	Qualifying	Embassy World Championship
	v J. McLaughlin	5-2	Qualifying	Jameson International
	v Gauvreau	1-5	Qualifying	Jameson International
	v Bradley	1-5	Qualifying	Rothmans Grand Prix
	v Newbury	3-9	Qualifying	Coral UK Open
1985	v G. Foulds	2-5	Qualifying	Mercantile Credit Classic
	v J. McLaughlin	6-2	Qualifying	Dulux British Open
	v Spencer	0-6	1st round	Dulux British Open
	v O'Kane	5-10	Qualifying	Embassy World Championship
	v Mikkelsen	6-4	Quarter-final	Canadian Championship
	v Chaperon	3-6	Semi-final	Canadian Championship
	v Newbury	4-5	2nd round	Goya Matchroom Trophy
	v Fowler	4-5	2nd round	Rothmans Grand Prix
	v T. Jones	4-9	2nd round	Coral UK Open
1986	v P. Francisco	2-5	2nd round	Mercantile Credit Classic
	v Dodd	4-5	2nd round	Dulux British Open
	v Chaperon	8-10	Qualifying	Embassy World Championship
	v Rigitano	6-1	1st round	Canadian Championship
	v Chaperon	6-3	2nd round	Canadian Championship
	v Thorburn	3-6	Semi-final	Canadian Championship
	v Miles	1-5	2nd round	Rothmans Grand Prix
	v Wilkinson	8-9	1st round	Tennents UK Open
1987	v James	5-4	1st round	Mercantile Credit Classic
	v Drago	5-2	2nd round	Mercantile Credit Classic
	v West	4-5	3rd round	Mercantile Credit Classic
	v Owers	4-5	1st round	Dulux British Open

TONY KEARNEY (Republic of Ireland)

Born 24.6.54
Turned professional 1984
World ranking 66 (101)
Amateur career 1981 Republic of Ireland champion.
Best professional performance Last 32 1987 Mercantile Credit Classic.

Year	Opponent	Score	Round	Tournament
1984	v Burke	4-5	Qualifying	Jameson International
	v Chaperon	1-5	Qualifying	Rothmans Grand Prix
	v Murphy	2-9	Qualifying	Coral UK Open
1985	v French	5-1	Qualifying	Mercantile Credit Classic
	v Williamson	3-5	Qualifying	Mercantile Credit Classic
	v Watterson	6-4	Qualifying	Dulux British Open
	v S. Francisco	4-6	1st round	Dulux British Open
	v Burke	4-6	Qualifying	Irish Championship
	v Anderson	8-10	Qualifying	Embassy World Championship
	v D. Hughes	1-5	1st round	Goya Matchroom Trophy
	v Jim Bear	5-3	1st round	Rothmans Grand Prix
	v Edmonds	2-5	2nd round	Rothmans Grand Prix
	v D. Hughes	8-9	1st round	Coral UK Open
1986	v Jim Bear	5-0	1st round	Mercantile Credit Classic
	v Medati	2-5	2nd round	Mercantile Credit Classic
	v Smith	5-2	1st round	Dulux British Open
	v Foldvari	5-2	2nd round	Dulux British Open
	v Wilkinson	10-5	Qualifying	Embassy World Championship
	v Scott	8-10	Qualifying	Embassy World Championship
	v Fagan	5-0	1st round	Strongbow Irish Championship
	v Murphy	2-6	Quarter-final	Strongbow Irish Championship
	v Medati	3-5	2nd round	BCE International
	v Jenkins	5-3	1st round	Rothmans Grand Prix
	v Chappel	1-5	2nd round	Rothmans Grand Prix
	v Dunning	6-9	1st round	Tennents UK Open
1987	v Agrawal	5-0	1st round	Mercantile Credit Classic
	v Wildman	5-3	2nd round	Mercantile Credit Classic
	v Macleod	5-0	3rd round	Mercantile Credit Classic
	v W. Jones	1-5	4th round	Mercantile Credit Classic
	v Chappel	3-5	2nd round	Dulux British Open
	v Medati	8-10	Qualifying	Embassy World Championship
	v Murphy	5-1	1st round	Matchroom Irish Championship
	v E. Hughes	1-6	Quarter-final	Matchroom Irish Championship

BILLY KELLY (Republic of Ireland)

Born 1.5.45
Turned professional 1981
World ranking 103 (88)

Year	Opponent	Score	Round	Tournament
1981	v Macleod	1-5	Qualifying	Jameson International
	v G. Foulds	7-9	Qualifying	Coral UK Championship

1982	v Sinclair	8-9	Qualifying	Embassy World Championship
	v G. Foulds	5-4	Qualifying	Jameson International
	v Williamson	5-1	Qualifying	Jameson International
	v Higgins	3-5	1st round	Jameson International
	v Wych	0-5	1st round	Professional Players Tournament
	v Fitzmaurice	8-0	Qualifying	Coral UK Championship
	(*retd*)			
	v Virgo	2-9	1st round	Coral UK Championship
1983	v Dennis Taylor	0-6	Quarter-final	Irish Championship
	v Demarco	10-4	Qualifying	Embassy World Championship
	v S. Francisco	5-10	Qualifying	Embassy World Championship
	v F. Davis	1-5	Qualifying	Jameson International
	v Hallett	0-5	1st round	Professional Players Tournament
1984	v Burke	7-10	Qualifying	Embassy World Championship
	v Hargreaves	5-2	Qualifying	Jameson International
	v King	5-4	Qualifying	Jameson International
	v S. Francisco	3-5	Qualifying	Jameson International
	v O'Kane	4-5	Qualifying	Rothmans Grand Prix
	v Bradley	6-9	Qualifying	Coral UK Open
	v Bales	3-5	Qualifying	Mercantile Credit Classic
	v P. Francisco	3-6	Qualifying	Dulux British Open
	v Watchorn	6-2	Qualifying	Irish Championship
	v E. Hughes	2-6	Quarter-final	Irish Championship
	v Rigitano	6-10	Qualifying	Embassy World Championship
1985	v P. Francisco	3-6	Qualifying	Dulux British Open
	v Watchorn	6-2	Qualifying	Irish Championship
	v E. Hughes	2-6	Quarter-final	Irish Championship
	v Rigitano	6-10	Qualifying	Embassy World Championship
	v T. Jones	3-5	2nd round	Goya Matchroom Trophy
	v Donnelly	5-4	2nd round	Rothmans Grand Prix
	v S. Francisco	2-5	3rd round	Rothmans Grand Prix
	v Medati	1-9	2nd round	Coral UK Open
1986	v F. Davis	3-5	2nd round	Mercantile Credit Classic
	v F. Davis	4-5	2nd round	Dulux British Open
	v Edmonds	0-10	Qualifying	Embassy World Championship
	v Jack Rea	5-0	1st round	Strongbow Irish Championship
	v Dennis Taylor	1-6	Quarter-final	Strongbow Irish Championship
	v Whitthread	5-1	1st round	BCE International
	v Van Rensberg	1-5	2nd round	BCE International
	v Parkin	5-2	1st round	Rothmans Grand Prix
	v V. Harris	3-5	2nd round	Rothmans Grand Prix
	v Watchorn	8-9	1st round	Tennents UK Open
1987	v Jack Rea	3-5	1st round	Mercantile Credit Classic
	v B. Bennett	5-2	1st round	Dulux British Open
	v B. Harris	2-5	2nd round	Dulux British Open
	v B. Bennett	10-0	Qualifying	Embassy World Championship
	v Gibson	9-10	Qualifying	Embassy World Championship
	v O'Boye	0-5	1st round	Matchroom Irish Championship

Joe Johnson

Tony Knowles

WARREN KING (Australia)

Born 1.4.55
Turned professional 1982
World ranking 39 (41)
Amateur career Australian champion 1980, 1981.
Best professional performances Last 32 1987 Embassy World Championship, 1985 Goya Matchroom Trophy, 1986 BCE International, 1986 Rothmans Grand Prix, 1987 Dulux British Open; 1986 Australian champion.

1983	v Anderson	10-6	Qualifying	Embassy World Championship
	v Hallett	6-10	Qualifying	Embassy World Championship
	v Black	5-3	Qualifying	Jameson International
	v Miles	3-5	Qualifying	Jameson International
	v B. Harris	5-3	Qualifying	Professional Players Tournament
	v Meo	2-5	1st round	Professional Players Tournament
1984	v Jones	10-9	Qualifying	Embassy World Championship
	v Watterson	10-8	Qualifying	Embassy World Championship
	v Martin	10-8	Qualifying	Embassy World Championship
	v S. Davis	3-10	1st round	Embassy World Championship
	v Kelly	4-5	Qualifying	Jameson International
	v Greaves	5-0	Qualifying	Rothmans Grand Prix
	v Macleod	4-5	1st round	Rothmans Grand Prix
	v Browne	9-5	Qualifying	Coral UK Open
	v Virgo	9-4	Qualifying	Coral UK Open
	v Dennis Taylor	5-9	1st round	Coral UK Open
1985	v Duggan	5-4	Qualifying	Mercantile Credit Classic
	v Reynolds	5-2	Qualifying	Mercantile Credit Classic
	v Spencer	5-2	1st round	Mercantile Credit Classic
	v White	5-2	2nd round	Mercantile Credit Classic
	v Johnson	3-5	Quarter-final	Mercantile Credit Classic
	v Medati	6-4	Qualifying	Dulux British Open
	v Reardon	5-6	1st round	Dulux British Open
	v Medati	9-10	Qualifying	Embassy World Championship
	v Anderson	8-2	Quarter-final	Australian Championship
	v Campbell	6-9	Semi-final	Australian Championship
	v Caggianello	5-0	2nd round	Goya Matchroom Trophy
	v Williams	5-3	3rd round	Goya Matchroom Trophy
	v White	2-5	4th round	Goya Matchroom Trophy
	v Drago	4-5	2nd round	Rothmans Grand Prix
	v D. Hughes	9-0	2nd round	Coral UK Open
	v Williams	5-9	3rd round	Coral UK Open
1986	v Duggan	5-2	2nd round	Mercantile Credit Classic
	v Mountjoy	4-5	3rd round	Mercantile Credit Classic
	v John Rea	1-5	2nd round	Dulux British Open
	v Sheehan	10-4	Qualifying	Embassy World Championship
	v Roscoe	10-5	Qualifying	Embassy World Championship
	v Reynolds	7-10	Qualifying	Embassy World Championship
	v Charlton	8-6	Semi-final	Australian Championship

	v Campbell	10-3	Final	Australian Championship
	v Rigitano	5-0	2nd round	BCE International
	v Longworth	5-0	3rd round	BCE International
	v S. Davis	4-5	4th round	BCE International
	v Donnelly	5-2	2nd round	Rothmans Grand Prix
	v Werbeniuk	5-2	3rd round	Rothmans Grand Prix
	v Thorne	2-5	4th round	Rothmans Grand Prix
	v James	9-8	2nd round	Tennents UK Open
	v Hallett	5-9	3rd round	Tennents UK Open
1987	v Burke	5-0	2nd round	Mercantile Credit Classic
	v Reynolds	4-5	3rd round	Mercantile Credit Classic
	v Williamson	5-3	2nd round	Dulux British Open
	v Parrott	5-1	3rd round	Dulux British Open
	v N. Foulds	4-5	4th round	Dulux British Open
	v Roe	10-4	Qualifying	Embassy World Championship
	v Owers	10-4	Qualifying	Embassy World Championship
	v Charlton	10-4	Qualifying	Embassy World Championship
	v S. Davis	7-10	1st round	Embassy World Championship

TONY KNOWLES (England)

Born 13.6.55
Turned professional 1980
World ranking 7 (4)
Best professional performances Winner 1982 Jameson International, 1983
Professional Players Tournament.

	v Andrewartha	8-9	Qualifying	Coral UK Championship
1980				
1981	v Johnson	2-9	Qualifying	John Courage English Professional
	v Ross	7-0	Qualifying	Embassy World Championship
	v Wych	9-3	Qualifying	Embassy World Championship
	v Miles	8-10	1st round	Embassy World Championship
	v Hallett	5-2	1st round	Jameson International
	v Virgo	2-5	2nd round	Jameson International
	v G. Foulds	9-1	Qualifying	Coral UK Championship
	v F. Davis	9-6	2nd round	Coral UK Championship
	v Mountjoy	9-6	3rd round	Coral UK Championship
	v Griffiths	5-9	Quarter-final	Coral UK Championship
1982	v Dennis Taylor	2-5	Semi-final	Tolly Cobbold Classic
	v E. Hughes	9-7	Qualifying	Embassy World Championship
	v S. Davis	10-1	1st round	Embassy World Championship
	v Miles	13-7	2nd round	Embassy World Championship
	v Charlton	11-13	Quarter-final	Embassy World Championship
	v S. Davis	4-5	1st round	Langs Scottish Masters
	v Sinclair	5-2	1st round	Jameson International
	v Reardon	5-2	2nd round	Jameson International
	v Wilson	5-4	Quarter-final	Jameson International
	v Stevens	9-8	Semi-final	Jameson International
	v David Taylor	**9-6**	**Final**	**Jameson International**
	v Houlihan	5-4	1st round	Professional Players Tournament

1980 v Andrewartha (first row above belongs to 1980)

	v Wilson	4-5	2nd round	Professional Players Tournament
	v Donnelly	9-6	1st round	Coral UK Championship
	v Spencer	6-9	2nd round	Coral UK Championship
1983	v Stevens	0-5	1st round	Lada Classic
	v Mountjoy	1-5	1st round	Benson & Hedges Irish Masters
	v Miles	10-3	1st round	Embassy World Championship
	v Reardon	13-12	2nd round	Embassy World Championship
	v Meo	13-9	Quarter-final	Embassy World Championship
	v Thorburn	15-16	Semi-final	Embassy World Championship
	v Werbeniuk	0-5	Semi-final	Winfield Masters
	v Meo	5-4	1st round	Langs Scottish Masters
	v Thorburn	6-2	Semi-final	Langs Scottish Masters
	v S. Davis	6-9	Final	Langs Scottish Masters
	v Edmonds	5-1	1st round	Jameson International
	v Spencer	4-5	2nd round	Jameson International
	v Medati	5-1	1st round	Professional Players Tournament
	v Williams	5-4	2nd round	Professional Players Tournament
	v S. Francisco	5-0	3rd round	Professional Players Tournament
	v Campbell	5-3	Quarter-final	Professional Players Tournament
	v Thorne	9-7	Semi-final	Professional Players Tournament
	v Johnson	**9-8**	**Final**	**Professional Players Tournament**
	v T. Jones	9-5	1st round	Coral UK Championship
	v Mountjoy	9-5	2nd round	Coral UK Championship
	v Higgins	5-9	Quarter-final	Coral UK Championship
1984	v E. Hughes	5-1	Qualifying	Lada Classic
	v Hallett	5-3	1st round	Lada Classic
	v Parrott	1-5	Quarter-final	Lada Classic
	v Dennis Taylor	5-2	1st round	Benson & Hedges Masters
	v Higgins	5-1	Quarter-final	Benson & Hedges Masters
	v Griffiths	4-6	Semi-final	Benson & Hedges Masters
	v Griffiths	0-5	Quarter-final	Benson & Hedges Irish Masters
	v White	5-1	1st round	Tolly Cobbold Classic
	v Thorburn	5-3	Semi-final	Tolly Cobbold Classic
	v S. Davis	2-8	Final	Tolly Cobbold Classic
	v Parrott	7-10	1st round	Embassy World Championship
	v White	5-3	Quarter-final	Winfield Australian Masters
	v Charlton	6-0	Semi-final	Winfield Australian Masters
	v Virgo	**7-3**	**Final**	**Winfield Australian Masters**
	v Griffiths	5-3	1st round	Langs Scottish Masters
	v White	5-6	Semi-final	Langs Scottish Masters
	v Higgins	5-3	1st round	Carlsberg Challenge
	v White	7-9	1st round	Carlsberg Challenge
	v Reynolds	5-1	1st round	Jameson International
	v Newbury	5-4	2nd round	Jameson International
	v White	5-4	Quarter-final	Jameson International
	v S. Francisco	9-6	Semi-final	Jameson International
	v S. Davis	2-9	Final	Jameson International
	v V. Harris	5-1	1st round	Rothmans Grand Prix
	v Dunning	5-1	2nd round	Rothmans Grand Prix
	v Williamson	5-2	3rd round	Rothmans Grand Prix

	v N. Foulds	2-5	Quarter-final	Rothmans Grand Prix
	v Gauvreau	9-5	1st round	Coral UK Open
	v Dennis Taylor	9-2	2nd round	Coral UK Open
	v Stevens	7-9	Quarter-final	Coral UK Open
1985	v Johnson	1-5	1st round	Mercantile Credit Classic
	v Mountjoy	3-5	1st round	Benson & Hedges Masters
	v Bradley	9-8	1st round	Tolly Cobbold English Championship
	v Martin	9-3	2nd round	Tolly Cobbold English Championship
	v David Taylor	9-2	Quarter-final	Tolly Cobbold English Championship
	v Longworth	9-6	Semi-final	Tolly Cobbold English Championship
	v S. Davis	2-9	Final	Tolly Cobbold English Championship
	v French	6-2	1st round	Dulux British Open
	v Longworth	5-2	2nd round	Dulux British Open
	v Meo	2-5	3rd round	Dulux British Open
	v Charlton	5-3	Quarter-final	Benson & Hedges Irish Masters
	v White	4-6	Semi-final	Benson & Hedges Irish Masters
	v T. Jones	10-8	1st round	Embassy World Championship
	v Mountjoy	13-6	2nd round	Embassy World Championship
	v White	13-10	Quarter-final	Embassy World Championship
	v Dennis Taylor	5-16	Semi-final	Embassy World Championship
	v S. Francisco	4-5	1st round	Langs Scottish Masters
	v E. McLaughlin	5-1	3rd round	Goya Matchroom Trophy
	v N. Foulds	4-5	4th round	Goya Matchroom Trophy
	v Gibson	5-1	3rd round	Rothmans Grand Prix
	v Edmonds	5-3	4th round	Rothmans Grand Prix
	v Campbell	5-2	5th round	Rothmans Grand Prix
	v Stevens	5-4	Quarter-final	Rothmans Grand Prix
	v Dennis Taylor	6-9	Semi-final	Rothmans Grand Prix
	v Reardon	5-2	1st round	BCE Canadian Masters
	v O'Boye	9-5	3rd round	Coral UK Open
	v Spencer	9-7	4th round	Coral UK Open
	v David Taylor	9-7	5th round	Coral UK Open
	v White	4-9	Quarter-final	Coral UK Open
1986	v Rigitano	5-4	3rd round	Mercantile Credit Classic
	v Macleod	5-4	4th round	Mercantile Credit Classic
	v Williams	2-5	5th round	Mercantile Credit Classic
	v White	5-3	1st round	BCE Belgian Classic
	v Griffiths	2-5	Semi-final	BCE Belgian Classic
	v S. Francisco	5-1	1st round	Benson & Hedges Masters
	v Charlton	5-4	Quarter-final	Benson & Hedges Masters
	v Thorburn	4-6	Semi-final	Benson & Hedges Masters
	v Bales	9-4	3rd round	Tolly Cobbold English Championship
	v Hallett	5-9	4th round	Tolly Cobbold English Championship
	v Williamson	5-1	3rd round	Dulux British Open
	v Wych	4-5	4th round	Dulux British Open
	v Fagan	4-5	Quarter-final	Benson & Hedges Irish Masters
	v N. Foulds	10-9	1st round	Embassy World Championship
	v S. Francisco	13-10	2nd round	Embassy World Championship
	v Stevens	13-9	Quarter-final	Embassy World Championship
	v Johnson	8-16	Semi-final	Embassy World Championship

v Stevens	3-5	1st round	Langs Scottish Masters
v Spencer	5-0	3rd round	BCE International
v Charlton	5-1	4th round	BCE International
v Wilson	4-5	5th round	BCE International
v Roe	5-3	3rd round	Rothmans Grand Prix
v P. Francisco	5-3	4th round	Rothmans Grand Prix
v Mountjoy	5-1	5th round	Rothmans Grand Prix
v S. Francisco	2-5	Quarter-final	Rothmans Grand Prix
v Thorburn	5-1	1st round	BCE Canadian Masters
v Thorne	7-8	Semi-final	BCE Canadian Masters
v John Rea	9-4	3rd round	Tennents UK Open
v T. Jones	9-2	4th round	Tennents UK Open
v Griffiths	9-6	5th round	Tennents UK Open
v Parrott	4-9	Quarter-final	Tennents UK Open
1987 v Fowler	4-5	3rd round	Mercantile Credit Classic
v S. Francisco	2-5	1st round	Benson & Hedges Masters
v Dodd	2-6	3rd round	Tolly Ales English Championship
v Fowler	5-4	3rd round	Dulux British Open
v Reynolds	5-0	4th round	Dulux British Open
v Murphy	5-3	5th round	Dulux British Open
v Dennis Taylor	5-4	Quarter-final	Dulux British Open
v N. Foulds	2-9	Semi-final	Dulux British Open
v Meo	2-5	1st round	Benson & Hedges Irish Masters
v Hallett	6-10	1st round	Embassy World Championship

STEVE LONGWORTH (England)

Born 27.7.48
Turned professional 1984
World ranking 31 (31)
Amateur career 1984 English champion.
Best professional performances Last 16 1987 Embassy World Championship, 1985 Rothmans Grand Prix, 1986 Tennents UK Open.

1984 v Newbury	4-5	Qualifying	Jameson International
v E. McLaughlin	2-5	Qualifying	Rothmans Grand Prix
v Darrington	9-5	Qualifying	Coral UK Open
v Burke	9-4	Qualifying	Coral UK Open
v Morra	1-9	Qualifying	Coral UK Open
1985 v P. Francisco	5-4	Qualifying	Mercantile Credit Classic
v Oliver	5-1	Qualifying	Mercantile Credit Classic
v Fisher	5-1	Qualifying	Mercantile Credit Classic
v N. Foulds	5-3	Qualifying	Mercantile Credit Classic
v David Taylor	5-4	1st round	Mercantile Credit Classic
v Thorburn	3-5	2nd round	Mercantile Credit Classic
v Edmonds	9-4	Qualifying	Tolly Cobbold English Championship
v Wildman	9-3	1st round	Tolly Cobbold English Championship
v Medati	9-7	2nd round	Tolly Cobbold English Championship

	v White	9-5	Quarter-final	Tolly Cobbold English Championship
	v Knowles	6-9	Semi-final	Tolly Cobbold English Championship
	v F. Davis	6-1	Qualifying	Dulux British Open
	v Wilson	6-3	1st round	Dulux British Open
	v Knowles	2-5	2nd round	Dulux British Open
	v Giannaros	10-1	Qualifying	Embassy World Championship
	v Cripsey	10-8	Qualifying	Embassy World Championship
	v Van Rensberg	7-10	Qualifying	Embassy World Championship
	v Wilkinson	5-0	2nd round	Goya Matchroom Trophy
	v Thorburn	3-5	3rd round	Goya Matchroom Trophy
	v Hargreaves	5-2	2nd round	Rothmans Grand Prix
	v Parrott	5-2	3rd round	Rothmans Grand Prix
	v David Taylor	5-1	4th round	Rothmans Grand Prix
	v Stevens	3-5	5th round	Rothmans Grand Prix
	v Gibson	9-2	2nd round	Coral UK Open
	v Meo	5-9	3rd round	Coral UK Open
1986	v O'Boye	1-5	2nd round	Mercantile Credit Classic
	v Duggan	9-4	2nd round	Tolly Cobbold English Championship
	v Reynolds	5-9	3rd round	Tolly Cobbold English Championship
	v Houlihan	5-3	2nd round	Dulux British Open
	v E. Hughes	5-4	3rd round	Dulux British Open
	v P. Francisco	2-5	4th round	Dulux British Open
	v Watchorn	10-7	Qualifying	Embassy World Championship
	v John Rea	10-4	Qualifying	Embassy World Championship
	v Virgo	8-10	Qualifying	Embassy World Championship
	v King	0-5	3rd round	BCE International
	v Wildman	2-5	3rd round	Rothmans Grand Prix
	v Rowswell	9-3	3rd round	Tennents UK Open
	v Mountjoy	9-1	4th round	Tennents UK Open
	v Parrott	6-9	5th round	Tennents UK Open
1987	v Murphy	5-3	3rd round	Mercantile Credit Classic
	v Meo	0-5	4th round	Mercantile Credit Classic
	v James	2-6	3rd round	Tolly Ales English Championship
	v Duggan	2-5	3rd round	Dulux British Open
	v Murphy	10-2	Qualifying	Embassy World Championship
	v Stevens	10-4	1st round	Embassy World Championship
	v Hendry	7-13	2nd round	Embassy World Championship

EDDIE McLAUGHLIN (Scotland)

Born 27.6.52
Turned professional 1981
World ranking 107 (90)

	v Black	5-3	Qualifying	Jameson International
1981	v Black	5-3	Qualifying	Jameson International
	v Wildman	5-3	Qualifying	Jameson International
	v Greaves	5-1	Qualifying	Jameson International
	v Ross	5-3	Quarter-final	Scottish Championship
	v Black	3-6	Semi-final	Scottish Championship
	v Meo	2-5	1st round	Jameson International

	v Medati	5-9	Qualifying	Coral UK Championship
1982	v Macleod	8-9	Qualifying	Embassy World Championship
	v Gibson	3-6	Quarter-final	Scottish Championship
	v Houlihan	5-2	Qualifying	Jameson International
	v Williams	1-5	Qualifying	Jameson International
	v Mans	2-5	1st round	Professional Players Tournament
	v Wilson	6-9	Qualifying	Coral UK Championship
1983	v Greaves	10-7	Qualifying	Embassy World Championship
	v Fisher	9-10	Qualifying	Embassy World Championship
	v Black	4-6	1st round	Scottish Championship
	v Campbell	5-2	Qualifying	Jameson International
	v Edmonds	1-5	Qualifying	Jameson International
	v Charlton	0-5	1st round	Professional Players Tournament
	v B. Harris	8-9	Qualifying	Coral UK Championship
1984	v Stevens	4-5	Qualifying	Lada Classic
	v Hargreaves	10-5	Qualifying	Embassy World Championship
	v Andrewartha	8-10	Qualifying	Embassy World Championship
	v O'Kane	1-5	Qualifying	Jameson International
	v Longworth	5-2	Qualifying	Rothmans Grand Prix
	v Mountjoy	4-5	1st round	Rothmans Grand Prix
	v Bales	4-9	Qualifying	Coral UK Open
1985	v Sheehan	5-2	Qualifying	Mercantile Credit Classic
	v F. Davis	5-1	Qualifying	Mercantile Credit Classic
	v Macleod	4-5	Qualifying	Mercantile Credit Classic
	v Macleod	4-6	1st round	Scottish Championship
	v French	0-6	Qualifying	Dulux British Open
	v Chalmers	9-10	Qualifying	Embassy World Championship
	v Hendry	5-3	2nd round	Goya Matchroom Trophy
	v Knowles	1-5	3rd round	Goya Matchroom Trophy
	v Van Rensberg	4-5	2nd round	Rothmans Grand Prix
1986	v J. McLaughlin	2-5	2nd round	Mercantile Credit Classic
	v West	3-5	2nd round	Dulux British Open
	v Black	4-6	Quarter-final	Canada Dry Scottish Championship
	v John Rea	6-10	Qualifying	Embassy World Championship

Owing to injury, did not play on the 1986–87 circuit

JACK McLAUGHLIN (Northern Ireland)

Born 29.1.59
Turned professional 1984
World ranking 51 (71)
Amateur career Northern Ireland champion 1983, 1984.
Best professional performances Last 32 1986 Rothmans Grand Prix, 1987 Dulux British Open.

1984	v Greaves	5-3	Qualifying	Jameson International
	v Jonik	2-5	Qualifying	Jameson International
	v Meadowcroft	5-1	Qualifying	Rothmans Grand Prix
	v Wildman	3-5	1st round	Rothmans Grand Prix
	v French	9-3	Qualifying	Coral UK Open

	v Roscoe	9-8	Qualifying	Coral UK Open
	v Miles	9-8	Qualifying	Coral UK Open
	v Thorburn	4-9	1st round	Coral UK Open
1985	v Demarco	5-1	Qualifying	Mercantile Credit Classic
	v Black	5-0	Qualifying	Mercantile Credit Classic
	v Scott	4-5	Qualifying	Mercantile Credit Classic
	v Jonik	2-6	Qualifying	Dulux British Open
	v Sheehan	6-3	Qualifying	Irish Championship
	v Williamson	3-5	2nd round	Goya Matchroom Trophy
	v Medati	5-2	2nd round	Rothmans Grand Prix
	v Griffiths	4-5	3rd round	Rothmans Grand Prix
	v Chaperon	9-5	Qualifying	Coral UK Open
	v Reynolds	7-9	1st round	Coral UK Open
1986	v E. McLaughlin	5-2	2nd round	Mercantile Credit Classic
	v Thorburn	1-5	3rd round	Mercantile Credit Classic
	v Fisher	5-3	2nd round	Dulux British Open
	v Johnson	2-5	3rd round	Dulux British Open
	v Murphy	7-10	Qualifying	Embassy World Championship
	v Watchorn	5-0	1st round	Strongbow Irish Championship
	v Higgins	2-6	Quarter-final	Strongbow Irish Championship
	v B. Bennett	5-0	1st round	BCE International
	v Fowler	5-2	2nd round	BCE International
	v Wilson	2-5	3rd round	BCE International
	v Owers	5-2	1st round	Rothmans Grand Prix
	v Gauvreau	5-3	2nd round	Rothmans Grand Prix
	v West	5-1	3rd round	Rothmans Grand Prix
	v White	2-5	4th round	Rothmans Grand Prix
	v Gauvreau	9-8	2nd round	Tennents UK Open
	v Mountjoy	6-9	3rd round	Tennents UK Open
1987	v M. Gibson	5-3	2nd round	Mercantile Credit Classic
	v Werbeniuk	1-5	3rd round	Mercantile Credit Classic
	v Gibson	5-1	2nd round	Dulux British Open
	v Higgins	5-4	3rd round	Dulux British Open
	v David Taylor	2-5	4th round	Dulux British Open
	v Van Rensberg	6-10	Qualifying	Embassy World Championship
	v Sheehan	4-5	1st round	Matchroom Irish Championship

MURDO MACLEOD (Scotland)

Born 14.1.47
Turned professional 1981
World ranking 30 (22)
Best professional performances Last 16 1987 Embassy World Championship, 1985 Goya Matchroom Trophy, 1985 Coral UK Open; Scottish champion 1983, 1985.

1981	v Kelly	5-1	Qualifying	Jameson International
	v Johnson	1-5	Qualifying	Jameson International
	v Black	4-5	Quarter-final	Scottish Championship
	v Roscoe	7-9	Qualifying	Coral UK Championship

1982	v E. McLaughlin	9-8	Qualifying	Embassy World Championship
	v Dunning	4-9	Qualifying	Embassy World Championship
	v Donnelly	6-5	1st round	Scottish Championship
	v Black	0-6	Quarter-final	Scottish Championship
	v Dodd	1-5	Qualifying	Jameson International
	v Thorne	5-2	2nd round	Professional Players Tournament
	v Reardon	2-5	3rd round	Professional Players Tournament
	v Martin	6-9	Qualifying	Coral UK Championship
1983	v M. Owen	10-5	Qualifying	Embassy World Championship
	v Martin	7-10	Qualifying	Embassy World Championship
	v Gibson	6-5	1st round	Scottish Championship
	v Black	6-2	Semi-final	Scottish Championship
	v Sinclair	**11-9**	**Final**	**Scottish Championship**
	v S. Davis	1-5	1st round	Langs Supreme Scottish Masters
	v Medati	5-3	Qualifying	Jameson International
	v Reardon	2-5	1st round	Jameson International
	v Murphy	0-5	1st round	Professional Players Tournament
	v Bennett	9-0	Qualifying	Coral UK Championship
	v Higgins	6-9	1st round	Coral UK Championship
1984	v David Taylor	5-4	Qualifying	Lada Classic
	v Stevens	1-5	1st round	Lada Classic
	v Gauvreau	6-10	Qualifying	Embassy World Championship
	v White	0-5	1st round	Langs Supreme Scottish Masters
	v Black	5-3	Qualifying	Jameson International
	v Meo	1-5	1st round	Jameson International
	v King	5-4	1st round	Rothmans Grand Prix
	v Thorne	3-5	2nd round	Rothmans Grand Prix
	v Scott	9-5	Qualifying	Coral UK Open
	v David Taylor	6-9	1st round	Coral UK Open
1985	v E. McLaughlin	5-4	Qualifying	Mercantile Credit Classic
	v Charlton	5-1	1st round	Mercantile Credit Classic
	v Virgo	0-5	2nd round	Mercantile Credit Classic
	v E. McLaughlin	6-4	1st round	Scottish Championship
	v M. Gibson	6-4	Semi-final	Scottish Championship
	v Sinclair	**10-2**	**Final**	**Scottish Championship**
	v Murphy	6-5	1st round	Dulux British Open
	v Thorne	5-0	2nd round	Dulux British Open
	v E. Hughes	2-5	3rd round	Dulux British Open
	v P. Francisco	10-7	Qualifying	Embassy World Championship
	v Mountjoy	5-10	1st round	Embassy World Championship
	v Thorburn	1-5	1st round	Langs Scottish Masters
	v Fitzmaurice	5-1	3rd round	Goya Matchroom Trophy
	v Chaperon	5-4	4th round	Goya Matchroom Trophy
	v S. Davis	1-5	5th round	Goya Matchroom Trophy
	v Drago	3-5	3rd round	Rothmans Grand Prix
	v Murphy	9-7	3rd round	Coral UK Open
	v Reardon	9-5	4th round	Coral UK Open
	v West	4-9	5th round	Coral UK Open
1986	v Sinclair	5-3	3rd round	Mercantile Credit Classic
	v Knowles	4-5	4th round	Mercantile Credit Classic

v F. Davis	5-4	3rd round	Dulux British Open
v S. Francisco	5-1	4th round	Dulux British Open
v Griffiths	2-5	5th round	Dulux British Open
v Hendry	5-6	Quarter-final	Canada Dry Scottish Championship
v Fowler	6-10	Qualifying	Embassy World Championship
v Gauvreau	4-5	3rd round	BCE International
v M. Bennett	1-5	3rd round	Rothmans Grand Prix
v Grace	6-9	3rd round	Tennents UK Open
1987 v Kearney	0-5	3rd round	Mercantile Credit Classic
v Donnelly	2-6	1st round	Scottish Championship
v T. Jones	4-5	3rd round	Dulux British Open
v Edmonds	10-7	Qualifying	Embassy World Championship
v Williams	10-5	1st round	Embassy World Championship
v Johnson	7-13	2nd round	Embassy World Championship

PERRIE MANS (South Africa)

Born 14.10.40
Turned professional 1961
World ranking 50 (36)
Amateur career 1963 South African champion.
Best professional performances Winner 1979 Benson & Hedges Masters, runner-up 1978 Embassy World Championship.

1973 v Gross	9-2	1st round	World Championship
v Charlton	8-16	2nd round	World Championship
1974 v Anderson	8-1	1st round	World Championship
v Spencer	15-13	2nd round	World Championship
v Williams	4-15	Quarter-final	World Championship
1975 v Dennis Taylor	12-15	1st round	World Championship
1976 v Miles	15-10	1st round	Embassy World Championship
v Meadowcroft	15-8	Quarter-final	Embassy World Championship
v Reardon	10-20	Semi-final	Embassy World Championship
1977 v Dennis Taylor	11-13	1st round	Embassy World Championship
1978 v Barrie	9-6	Qualifying	Embassy World Championship
v Spencer	13-8	1st round	Embassy World Championship
v Miles	13-7	Quarter-final	Embassy World Championship
v F. Davis	18-16	Semi-final	Embassy World Championship
v Reardon	18-25	Final	Embassy World Championship
1979 v Thorburn	5-4	Quarter-final	Benson & Hedges Masters
v Reardon	5-3	Semi-final	Benson & Hedges Masters
v Higgins	**8-4**	**Final**	**Benson & Hedges Masters**
v Griffiths	8-13	1st round	Embassy World Championship
1980 v Higgins	1-5	Quarter-final	Benson & Hedges Masters
v Higgins	6-13	2nd round	Embassy World Championship
1981 v S. Davis	5-3	1st round	Benson & Hedges Masters
v Thorburn	4-5	Quarter-final	Benson & Hedges Masters
v Werbeniuk	5-13	2nd round	Embassy World Championship
v Meo	5-3	2nd round	Jameson International
v S. Davis	3-5	3rd round	Jameson International

1982	v Meo	10-8	1st round	Embassy World Championship
	v White	6-13	2nd round	Embassy World Championship
	v Dodd	5-3	1st round	Jameson International
	v Stevens	2-5	2nd round	Jameson International
	v E. McLaughlin	5-2	1st round	Professional Players Tournament
	v Wildman	4-5	2nd round	Professional Players Tournament
1983	v Black	10-3	1st round	Embassy World Championship
	v Stevens	3-13	2nd round	Embassy World Championship
	v Watterson	4-5	Qualifying	Jameson International
1984	v Parrott	0-10	Qualifying	Embassy World Championship
	v Sinclair	2-5	Qualifying	Jameson International
	v Dunning	4-5	1st round	Rothmans Grand Prix
	v Gauvreau	6-9	Qualifying	Coral UK Open
1985	v Black	4-5	3rd round	Goya Matchroom Trophy
	v O'Boye	3-5	3rd round	Rothmans Grand Prix
	v Fowler	2-9	3rd round	Coral UK Open
1986	v Smith	5-4	3rd round	Mercantile Credit Classic
	v Johnson	2-5	4th round	Mercantile Credit Classic
	v W. Jones	5-2	3rd round	Dulux British Open
	v Stevens	1-5	4th round	Dulux British Open
	v Dodd	10-7	Qualifying	Embassy World Championship
	v Mountjoy	3-10	1st round	Embassy World Championship
	v Ellis	6-7	2nd round	South African Championship
1987	v Morra	0-5	2nd round	Mercantile Credit Classic
	v Wilkinson	2-5	2nd round	Dulux British Open

DAVE MARTIN (England)

Born 9.5.48
Turned professional 1981
World ranking 27 (28)
Best professional performance Semi-finals 1981 Jameson International.

1981	v Anderson	9-3	Qualifying	Embassy World Championship
	v Pulman	9-2	Qualifying	Embassy World Championship
	v Werbeniuk	4-10	1st round	Embassy World Championship
	v Dunning	5-2	1st round	Jameson International
	v Werbeniuk	5-2	2nd round	Jameson International
	v Charlton	5-2	3rd round	Jameson International
	v Miles	5-1	Quarter-final	Jameson International
	v Dennis Taylor	1-9	Semi-final	Jameson International
	v Sinclair	9-7	Qualifying	Coral UK Championship
	v Higgins	7-9	2nd round	Coral UK Championship
1982	v Houlihan	9-3	Qualifying	Embassy World Championship
	v Miles	5-10	Qualifying	Embassy World Championship
	v E. Hughes	4-5	Qualifying	Jameson International
	v Gibson	5-2	1st round	Professional Players Tournament
	v Spencer	3-5	2nd round	Professional Players Tournament
	v Macleod	9-6	Qualifying	Coral UK Championship

	v Higgins	7-9	1st round	Coral UK Championship
1983	v Parkin	10-1	Qualifying	Embassy World Championship
	v Macleod	10-7	Qualifying	Embassy World Championship
	v Werbeniuk	4-10	Qualifying	Embassy World Championship
	v Greaves	5-1	Qualifying	Jameson International
	v Fagan	5-0	Qualifying	Jameson International
	v Higgins	5-2	1st round	Jameson International
	v Mountjoy	0-5	2nd round	Jameson International
	v Fitzmaurice	5-0	1st round	Professional Players Tournament
	v Watterson	5-4	2nd round	Professional Players Tournament
	v Campbell	0-5	3rd round	Professional Players Tournament
	v French	9-3	Qualifying	Coral UK Championship
	v Griffiths	4-9	Qualifying	Coral UK Championship
1984	v King	8-10	Qualifying	Embassy World Championship
	v Fowler	0-5	Qualifying	Jameson International
	v Chaperon	5-4	1st round	Rothmans Grand Prix
	v Meo	4-5	2nd round	Rothmans Grand Prix
	v Murphy	8-9	Qualifying	Coral UK Open
1985	v Foldvari	2-5	Qualifying	Mercantile Credit Classic
	v Miles	9-7	1st round	Tolly Cobbold English Championship
	v Knowles	3-9	2nd round	Tolly Cobbold English Championship
	v Bennett	6-0	1st round	Dulux British Open
	v Reardon	5-4	2nd round	Dulux British Open
	v O'Kane	4-5	3rd round	Dulux British Open
	v O'Kane	8-10	Qualifying	Embassy World Championship
	v Sinclair	5-1	3rd round	Goya Matchroom Trophy
	v Thorburn	3-5	4th round	Goya Matchroom Trophy
	v Morra	5-2	3rd round	Rothmans Grand Prix
	v S. Francisco	3-5	4th round	Rothmans Grand Prix
	v Darrington	9-3	3rd round	Coral UK Open
	v S. Francisco	6-9	4th round	Coral UK Open
1986	v Murphy	5-3	3rd round	Mercantile Credit Classic
	v P. Francisco	2-5	4th round	Mercantile Credit Classic
	v F. Davis	9-8	3rd round	Tolly Cobbold English Championship
	v S. Davis	4-9	4th round	Tolly Cobbold English Championship
	v B. Harris	5-1	3rd round	Dulux British Open
	v S. Davis	1-5	4th round	Dulux British Open
	v Gilbert	10-5	Qualifying	Embassy World Championship
	v Johnson	3-10	1st round	Embassy World Championship
	v Chaperon	4-5	3rd round	BCE International
	v Higgins	2-5	4th round	Rothmans Grand Prix
	v Williamson	9-5	3rd round	Tennents UK Open
	v Higgins	6-9	4th round	Tennents UK Open
1987	v G. Foulds	5-4	3rd round	Mercantile Credit Classic
	v Griffiths	4-5	4th round	Mercantile Credit Classic
	v Spencer	6-5	3rd round	Tolly Ales English Championship
	v Thorne	3-6	4th round	Tolly Ales English Championship
	v Scott	5-3	3rd round	Dulux British Open
	v Spencer	2-5	4th round	Dulux British Open
	v Hendry	7-10	Qualifying	Embassy World Championship

JIM MEADOWCROFT (England)
Born 15.12.46
Turned professional 1971
World ranking 92 (85)
Best professional performances Quarter-finals 1976 Embassy World Championship, 1977 Super Crystalate UK Championship.

1973 v Reardon	10-16	2nd round	World Championship
1974 v Kennerley	8-5	1st round	World Championship
v Reardon	3-15	2nd round	World Championship
1975 v Werbeniuk	9-15	1st round	World Championship
1976 v Wheelwright	8-1	Qualifying	Embassy World Championship
v Gross	8-4	Qualifying	Embassy World Championship
v Thorne	8-5	Qualifying	Embassy World Championship
v Williams	15-7	1st round	Embassy World Championship
v Mans	8-15	Quarter-final	Embassy World Championship
1977 v Fagan	9-11	Qualifying	Embassy World Championship
v Houlihan	5-1	1st round	Super Crystalate UK Championship
v Reardon	5-4	2nd round	Super Crystalate UK Championship
v Fagan	4-5	Quarter-final	Super Crystalate UK Championship
1978 v Houlihan	6-9	Qualifying	Embassy World Championship
v Jack Rea	9-5	Qualifying	Coral UK Championship
v Higgins	6-9	1st round	Coral UK Championship
1979 v Van Rensberg	9-7	Prelim	Embassy World Championship
v Griffiths	6-9	Qualifying	Embassy World Championship
v Edmonds	3-9	2nd round	Coral UK Championship
1980 v Sinclair	9-1	Qualifying	Embassy World Championship
v Virgo	2-10	1st round	Embassy World Championship
v Greaves	9-1	Qualifying	Coral UK Championship
v Thorne	1-9	1st round	Coral UK Championship
1981 v Barrie	9-3	Qualifying	John Courage English
v S. Davis	2-9	1st round	John Courage English
v White	8-9	Qualifying	Embassy World Championship
v Roscoe	5-4	Qualifying	Jameson International
v Wilson	5-4	1st round	Jameson International
v Stevens	1-5	2nd round	Jameson International
v Houlihan	4-9	Qualifying	Coral UK Championship
1982 v Watterson	9-7	Qualifying	Embassy World Championship
v Higgins	5-10	1st round	Embassy World Championship
v Ross	5-0	Qualifying	Jameson International
v White	1-5	1st round	Jameson International
v Bennett	5-4	1st round	Professional Players Tournament
v Sinclair	3-5	2nd round	Professional Players Tournament
v D. Hughes	9-8	Qualifying	Coral UK Championship
v Dennis Taylor	7-9	1st round	Coral UK Championship
1983 v Bennett	10-3	Qualifying	Embassy World Championship
v Cripsey	10-6	Qualifying	Embassy World Championship
v David Taylor	2-10	1st round	Embassy World Championship
v Roscoe	5-4	1st round	Professional Players Tournament

	v Thorburn	1-5	2nd round	Professional Players Tournament
	v N. Foulds	2-9	Qualifying	Coral UK Championship
1984	v Meo	1-5	Qualifying	Lada Classic
	v N. Foulds	2-10	Qualifying	Embassy World Championship
	v Chalmers	5-1	Qualifying	Jameson International
	v Williams	4-5	Qualifying	Jameson International
	v J. McLaughlin	1-5	Qualifying	Rothmans Grand Prix
	v Bradley	7-9	Qualifying	Coral UK Open
1985	v Fowler	2-5	Qualifying	Mercantile Credit Classic
	v Chalmers	3-9	Qualifying	Tolly Cobbold English Championship
	v B. Harris	1-6	Qualifying	Dulux British Open
	v P. Francisco	5-10	Qualifying	Embassy World Championship
	v Chappel	2-5	2nd round	Goya Matchroom Trophy
	v West	2-5	2nd round	Rothmans Grand Prix
	v Hargreaves	9-8	2nd round	Coral UK Open
	v Hallett	1-9	3rd round	Coral UK Open
1986	v West	0-5	2nd round	Mercantile Credit Classic
	v Cripsey	1-9	2nd round	Tolly Cobbold English Championship
	v Jenkins	2-5	2nd round	Dulux British Open
	v Darrington	6-10	Qualifying	Embassy World Championship
	v P. Gibson	2-5	1st round	BCE International
	v Greaves	5-2	1st round	Rothmans Grand Prix
		wo	2nd round	Rothmans Grand Prix
		scr	3rd round	Rothmans Grand Prix
	v Demarco	9-2	1st round	Tennents UK Open
	v Bradley	2-9	2nd round	Tennents UK Open
1987	v Newbury	1-5	2nd round	Mercantile Credit Classic
	v Grace	4-5	1st round	Dulux British Open
	v Mienie	10-3	Qualifying	Embassy World Championship
	v Cripsey	9-10	Qualifying	Embassy World Championship

PAUL MEDATI (England)

Born 14.11.44
Turned professional 1981
World ranking 68 (58)
Best professional performance Last 32 1986 Dulux British Open.

1981	v Watterson	3-5	Qualifying	Jameson International
	v E. McLaughlin	9-5	Qualifying	Coral UK Championship
	v Donnelly	9-7	Qualifying	Coral UK Championship
	v Thorne	6-9	Qualifying	Coral UK Championship
1982	v Phillips	9-3	Qualifying	Embassy World Championship
	v Wilson	5-9	Qualifying	Embassy World Championship
	v Williams	3-5	Qualifying	Jameson International
	v Thorburn	1-5	1st round	Professional Players Tournament
	v Bennett	9-1	Qualifying	Coral UK Championship
	v White	7-9	1st round	Coral UK Championship

1983	v John Bear	10-7	Qualifying	Embassy World Championship
	v Black	4-10	Qualifying	Embassy World Championship
	v V. Harris	5-0	Qualifying	Jameson International
	v Macleod	3-5	Qualifying	Jameson International
	v D. Hughes	5-1	Qualifying	Professional Players Tournament
	v Knowles	1-5	1st round	Professional Players Tournament
	v D. Hughes	9-2	Qualifying	Coral UK Championship
	v Edmonds	9-7	Qualifying	Coral UK Championship
	v Reynolds	9-3	1st round	Coral UK Championship
	v Higgins	1-9	2nd round	Coral UK Championship
1984	v Mikkelsen	8-10	Qualifying	Embassy World Championship
	v Gibson	3-5	Qualifying	Jameson International
	v Dodd	5-4	Qualifying	Rothmans Grand Prix
	v Johnson	1-5	1st round	Rothmans Grand Prix
	v Hargreaves	6-9	Qualifying	Coral UK Open
1985	v Cripsey	5-4	Qualifying	Mercantile Credit Classic
	v Roscoe	5-4	Qualifying	Mercantile Credit Classic
	v Parrott	5-3	Qualifying	Mercantile Credit Classic
	v Stevens	4-5	1st round	Mercantile Credit Classic
	v Hargreaves	9-8	Qualifying	Tolly Cobbold English Championship
	v Spencer	9-4	1st round	Tolly Cobbold English Championship
	v Longworth	7-9	2nd round	Tolly Cobbold English Championship
	v King	4-6	Qualifying	Dulux British Open
	v Bennett	10-4	Qualifying	Embassy World Championship
	v Williamson	10-8	Qualifying	Embassy World Championship
	v King	10-9	Qualifying	Embassy World Championship
	v S. Francisco	7-10	Qualifying	Embassy World Championship
	v Cripsey	2-5	2nd round	Goya Matchroom Trophy
	v J. McLaughlin	2-5	2nd round	Rothmans Grand Prix
	v Kelly	9-1	2nd round	Coral UK Open
	v Campbell	7-9	3rd round	Coral UK Open
1986	v Kearney	5-2	2nd round	Mercantile Credit Classic
	v O'Kane	0-5	3rd round	Mercantile Credit Classic
	v Greaves	9-4	2nd round	Tolly Cobbold English Championship
	v Thorne	2-9	3rd round	Tolly Cobbold English Championship
	v Everton	5-1	2nd round	Dulux British Open
	v David Taylor	5-1	3rd round	Dulux British Open
	v Campbell	4-5	4th round	Dulux British Open
	v Simngam	10-9	Qualifying	Embassy World Championship
	v Gibson	10-6	Qualifying	Embassy World Championship
	v Wilson	6-10	Qualifying	Embassy World Championship
	v Kearney	5-3	2nd round	BCE International
	v Griffiths	3-5	3rd round	BCE International
	v Rigitano	5-1	2nd round	Rothmans Grand Prix
	v P. Francisco	1-5	3rd round	Rothmans Grand Prix
	v Grace	5-9	2nd round	Tennents UK Open
1987	v Dodd	4-5	2nd round	Mercantile Credit Classic
	v N. Gibson	6-2	2nd round	Tolly Ales English Championship
	v Virgo	1-6	3rd round	Tolly Ales English Championship
	v Ellis	5-0	2nd round	Dulux British Open

v Charlton	4-5	3rd round	Dulux British Open
v Kearney	10-8	Qualifying	Embassy World Championship
v Gauvreau	10-3	Qualifying	Embassy World Championship
v E. Hughes	2-10	Qualifying	Embassy World Championship

TONY MEO (England)

Born 4.10.59
Turned professional 1979
World ranking 20 (11)
Best professional performances Runner-up 1984 Lada Classic; English champion 1986, 1987.

1979	v David Taylor	9-7	2nd round	Coral UK Championship
	v Virgo	6-9	3rd round	Coral UK Championship
1980	v Van Rensberg	9-1	Qualifying	Embassy World Championship
	v Houlihan	9-1	Qualifying	Embassy World Championship
	v Higgins	9-10	1st round	Embassy World Championship
	v Hood	9-5	Qualifying	Coral UK Championship
	v Houlihan	9-1	1st round	Coral UK Championship
	v Virgo	9-1	2nd round	Coral UK Championship
	v S. Davis	5-9	Quarter-final	Coral UK Championship
1981	v Virgo	9-6	1st round	John Courage English
	v Miles	9-7	2nd round	John Courage English
	v Thorne	9-8	Semi-final	John Courage English
	v S. Davis	3-9	Final	John Courage English
	v Johnson	9-8	Qualifying	Embassy World Championship
	v Hallett	9-4	Qualifying	Embassy World Championship
	v Virgo	10-6	1st round	Embassy World Championship
	v Griffiths	6-13	2nd round	Embassy World Championship
	v E. McLaughlin	5-2	1st round	Jameson International
	v Mans	3-5	2nd round	Jameson International
	v Williams	9-8	2nd round	Coral UK Championship
	v Thorburn	9-6	3rd round	Coral UK Championship
	v Higgins	9-4	Quarter-final	Coral UK Championship
	v Griffiths	3-9	Semi-final	Coral UK Championship
1982	v David Taylor	5-2	1st round	Benson & Hedges Masters
	v Thorburn	5-0	Quarter-final	Benson & Hedges Masters
	v S. Davis	4-6	Semi-final	Benson & Hedges Masters
	v Spencer	5-3	1st round	Benson & Hedges Irish Masters
	v Griffiths	3-5	Quarter-final	Benson & Hedges Irish Masters
	v D. Hughes	9-4	Qualifying	Embassy World Championship
	v Mans	8-10	1st round	Embassy World Championship
	v Sinclair	3-5	Qualifying	Jameson International
	v M. Owen	5-4	1st round	Professional Players Tournament
	v Jonik	5-0	2nd round	Professional Players Tournament
	v Charlton	3-5	3rd round	Professional Players Tournament
	v Scott	9-5	Qualifying	Coral UK Championship
	v Miles	9-4	1st round	Coral UK Championship

v David Taylor	9-6	2nd round	Coral UK Championship
v Virgo	9-6	Quarter-final	Coral UK Championship
v Griffiths	7-9	Semi-final	Coral UK Championship
1983 v Charlton	3-5	1st round	Benson & Hedges Masters
v Burke	5-0	1st round	Benson & Hedges Irish Masters
v Reardon	4-5	Quarter-final	Benson & Hedges Irish Masters
v V. Harris	10-0	Qualifying	Embassy World Championship
v G. Foulds	10-4	Qualifying	Embassy World Championship
v White	10-8	1st round	Embassy World Championship
v Mountjoy	13-11	2nd round	Embassy World Championship
v Knowles	9-13	Quarter-final	Embassy World Championship
v Knowles	4-5	1st round	Langs Supreme Scottish Masters
v Watterson	3-5	1st round	Jameson International
v King	5-2	1st round	Professional Players Tournament
v Reynolds	5-0	2nd round	Professional Players Tournament
v Hallett	5-3	3rd round	Professional Players Tournament
v Stevens	5-3	Quarter-final	Professional Players Tournament
v Johnson	6-9	Semi-final	Professional Players Tournament
v Parrott	9-7	1st round	Coral UK Championship
v Spencer	9-5	2nd round	Coral UK Championship
v Davis	4-9	Quarter-final	Coral UK Championship
1984 v Meadowcroft	5-1	Qualifying	Lada Classic
v Williams	5-3	1st round	Lada Classic
v Stevens	5-2	Quarter-final	Lada Classic
v Wildman	5-3	Semi-final	Lada Classic
v S. Davis	8-9	Final	Lada Classic
v S. Davis	0-5	1st round	Benson & Hedges Masters
v White	5-4	1st round	Benson & Hedges Irish Masters
v S. Davis	4-5	Quarter-final	Benson & Hedges Irish Masters
v Thorburn	4-5	1st round	Tolly Cobbold Classic
v S. Francisco	5-10	1st round	Embassy World Championship
v Stevens	5-1	Quarter-final	Winfield Australian Masters
v Virgo	2-6	Semi-final	Winfield Australian Masters
v Macleod	5-1	1st round	Jameson International
v White	1-5	2nd round	Jameson International
v Burke	5-1	1st round	Rothmans Grand Prix
v Martin	5-4	2nd round	Rothmans Grand Prix
v Thorburn	4-5	3rd round	Rothmans Grand Prix
v E. Hughes	9-4	1st round	Coral UK Open
v S. Davis	7-9	2nd round	Coral UK Open
1985 v E. Hughes	4-5	1st round	Mercantile Credit Classic
v Fisher	9-3	1st round	Tolly Cobbold English Championship
v Hallett	9-4	2nd round	Tolly Cobbold English Championship
v Reynolds	9-4	Quarter-final	Tolly Cobbold English Championship
v S. Davis	8-9	Semi-final	Tolly Cobbold English Championship
v Foldvari	6-0	1st round	Dulux British Open
v Hallett	5-4	2nd round	Dulux British Open
v Knowles	5-2	3rd round	Dulux British Open
v S. Francisco	4-5	Quarter-final	Dulux British Open
v White	1-5	1st round	Benson & Hedges Irish Masters

	v Virgo	10-6	1st round	Embassy World Championship
	v White	11-13	2nd round	Embassy World Championship
	v Virgo	5-3	Quarter-final	Winfield Australian Masters
	v White	6-3	Semi-final	Winfield Australian Masters
	v Campbell	**7-2**	**Final**	**Winfield Australian Masters**
	v Dunning	5-0	3rd round	Goya Matchroom Trophy
	v Parrott	4-5	4th round	Goya Matchroom Trophy
	v T. Jones	5-2	3rd round	Rothmans Grand Prix
	v E. Hughes	5-3	4th round	Rothmans Grand Prix
	v Dennis Taylor	3-5	5th round	Rothmans Grand Prix
	v Longworth	9-5	3rd round	Coral UK Open
	v Fowler	9-2	4th round	Coral UK Open
	v S. Davis	5-9	5th round	Coral UK Open
1986	v O'Boye	5-3	3rd round	Mercantile Credit Classic
	v West	5-1	4th round	Mercantile Credit Classic
	v Thorburn	1-5	5th round	Mercantile Credit Classic
	v White	4-5	1st round	Benson & Hedges Masters
	v Scott	9-1	3rd round	Tolly Cobbold English Championship
	v Wildman	9-3	4th round	Tolly Cobbold English Championship
	v Reynolds	9-4	Quarter-final	Tolly Cobbold English Championship
	v S. Davis	9-7	Semi-final	Tolly Cobbold English Championship
	v N. Foulds	**9-7**	**Final**	**Tolly Cobbold English Championship**
	v Donnelly	5-3	3rd round	Dulux British Open
	v Newbury	5-0	4th round	Dulux British Open
	v Thorburn	5-3	5th round	Dulux British Open
	v Virgo	3-5	Quarter-final	Dulux British Open
	v Higgins	5-4	1st round	Benson & Hedges Irish Masters
	v White	2-5	Quarter-final	Benson & Hedges Irish Masters
	v Parrott	6-10	1st round	Embassy World Championship
	v Griffiths	3-6	1st round	Matchroom Trophy
	v Houlihan	4-5	3rd round	BCE International
	v Chappel	5-1	3rd round	Rothmans Grand Prix
	v Parrott	5-3	4th round	Rothmans Grand Prix
	v Dennis Taylor	5-2	5th round	Rothmans Grand Prix
	v N. Foulds	3-5	Quarter-final	Rothmans Grand Prix
	v O'Boye	9-3	3rd round	Tennents UK Open
	v Hallett	4-9	4th round	Tennents UK Open
1987	v John Rea	5-4	3rd round	Mercantile Credit Classic
	v Longworth	5-0	4th round	Mercantile Credit Classic
	v S. Davis	2-5	5th round	Mercantile Credit Classic
	v White	5-4	1st round	Benson & Hedges Masters
	v Mountjoy	5-4	Quarter-final	Benson & Hedges Masters
	v Higgins	2-6	Semi-final	Benson & Hedges Masters
	v Duggan	6-3	3rd round	Tolly Ales English Championship
	v Fowler	6-0	4th round	Tolly Ales English Championship
	v Parrott	6-3	Quarter-final	Tolly Ales English Championship
	v Thorne	9-3	Semi-final	Tolly Ales English Championship
	v Dodd	**9-5**	**Final**	**Tolly Ales English Championship**
	v Spencer	1-5	3rd round	Dulux British Open
	v Knowles	5-2	1st round	Benson & Hedges Irish Masters

v S. Davis	2-5	Quarter-final	Benson & Hedges Irish Masters
v Parrott	8-10	1st round	Embassy World Championship

DEREK MIENIE (South Africa)

Born –
Turned professional 1978
World ranking 115 (108)

1979	v Mountjoy	1-9	Prelim	Embassy World Championship
1985	v Edmonds	1-6	Qualifying	Dulux British Open
	v Bradley	4-10	Qualifying	Embassy World Championship
	v Fagan	4-5	2nd round	Goya Matchroom Trophy
	v Simngam	3-5	1st round	Rothmans Grand Prix
	v Hargreaves	7-9	1st round	Coral UK Open
1986	v Smith	1-5	1st round	Mercantile Credit Classic
	v Thornley	3-10	Qualifying	Embassy World Championship
	v Hines	6-5	1st round	South African Championship
	v Van Rensberg	1-7	2nd round	South African Championship
	v Oliver	4-5	1st round	BCE International
	v Fitzmaurice	5-2	1st round	Rothmans Grand Prix
	v M. Gibson	4-5	2nd round	Rothmans Grand Prix
	v Jenkins	6-9	1st round	Tennents UK Open
1987	v Cripsey	0-5	2nd round	Mercantile Credit Classic
	v Roscoe	2-5	1st round	Dulux British Open
	v Meadowcroft	3-10	Qualifying	Embassy World Championship

BERNIE MIKKELSEN (Canada)

Born 11.4.50
Turned professional 1979
World ranking 74 (61)
Best professional performance Last 32 1986 Mercantile Credit Classic.

1981	v White	4-9	Qualifying	Embassy World Championship
1982	v Roscoe	6-9	Qualifying	Embassy World Championship
1984	v Medati	10-8	Qualifying	Embassy World Championship
	v Jonik	10-9	Qualifying	Embassy World Championship
	v Thorne	3-10	Qualifying	Embassy World Championship
	v Chappel	5-4	Qualifying	Jameson International
	v Everton	5-0	Qualifying	Jameson International
	v Roscoe	1-5	Qualifying	Jameson International
	v Sheehan	3-5	Qualifying	Rothmans Grand Prix
1985	v Chalmers	5-1	Prelim	Mercantile Credit Classic
	v Watchorn	1-5	Qualifying	Mercantile Credit Classic
	v D. Hughes	6-0	Qualifying	Dulux British Open
	v Bradley	9-10	Qualifying	Embassy World Championship

	v Watson	5-3	1st round	Canadian Championship
	v Jonik	4-6	Quarter-final	Canadian Championship
	v Fisher	5-3	2nd round	Goya Matchroom Trophy
	v Reynolds	0-5	3rd round	Goya Matchroom Trophy
	v Murphy	5-4	2nd round	Rothmans Grand Prix
	v Hallett	3-5	3rd round	Rothmans Grand Prix
	v Williamson	9-3	2nd round	Coral UK Open
	v David Taylor	6-9	3rd round	Coral UK Open
1986	v Scott	5-1	2nd round	Mercantile Credit Classic
	v Reardon	5-3	3rd round	Mercantile Credit Classic
	v Campbell	2-5	4th round	Mercantile Credit Classic
	v Roscoe	4-5	2nd round	Dulux British Open
	v Hargreaves	10-7	Qualifying	Embassy World Championship
	v Watterson	2-10	Qualifying	Embassy World Championship
	v Sanderson	6-1	1st round	Canadian Championship
	v Wych	3-6	2nd round	Canadian Championship
	v O'Boye	4-5	2nd round	BCE International
	v G. Foulds	1-5	2nd round	Rothmans Grand Prix
	v Sinclair	9-8	2nd round	Tennents UK Open
	v Reynolds	6-9	3rd round	Tennents UK Open
1987	v Foldvari	5-1	2nd round	Mercantile Credit Classic
	v Hallett	3-5	3rd round	Mercantile Credit Classic
	v Foldvari	3-5	2nd round	Dulux British Open
	v M. Bennett	4-10	Qualifying	Embassy World Championship

GRAHAM MILES (England)

Born 11.5.41
Turned professional 1969
World ranking 69 (56)
Best professional performance Runner-up 1974 World Professional Championship.

1972	v Bennett	15-6	Qualifying	World Championship
	v Dunning	5-11	Qualifying	World Championship
1973	v Thompson	9-5	1st round	World Championship
	v Pulman	16-10	2nd round	World Championship
	v Charlton	6-16	Quarter-final	World Championship
1974	v Morgan	15-7	2nd round	World Championship
	v Dunning	15-13	Quarter-final	World Championship
	v Williams	15-7	Semi-final	World Championship
	v Reardon	12-22	Final	World Championship
1975	v Reardon	3-5	Quarter-final	Benson & Hedges Masters
	v Thorburn	2-15	2nd round	World Championship
1976	v Spencer	5-4	Semi-final	Benson & Hedges Masters
	v Reardon	3-7	Final	Benson & Hedges Masters
	v Mans	10-15	1st round	Embassy World Championship
1977	v Reardon	2-5	Semi-final	Benson & Hedges Masters
	v Thorne	13-4	1st round	Embassy World Championship

v Pulman	10-13	Quarter-final	Embassy World Championship
v Ross	5-1	2nd round	Super Crystalate UK Championship
v Virgo	2-5	Quarter-final	Super Crystalate UK Championship
1978 v David Taylor	13-10	1st round	Embassy World Championship
v Mans	7-13	Quarter-final	Embassy World Championship
v Williams	9-8	1st round	Coral UK Championship
v Thorne	9-1	Quarter-final	Coral UK Championship
v Mountjoy	1-9	Semi-final	Coral UK Championship
1979 v Higgins	6-3	Semi-final	Holsten Lager International
v Spencer	7-11	Final	Holsten Lager International
v Williams	9-5	Qualifying	Embassy World Championship
v Reardon	8-13	1st round	Embassy World Championship
v Fagan	5-9	3rd round	Coral UK Championship
1980 v Stevens	3-10	1st round	Embassy World Championship
v Sinclair	5-9	1st round	Coral UK Championship
1981 v Hood	9-1	1st round	John Courage English
v Meo	7-9	2nd round	John Courage English
v Knowles	10-8	1st round	Embassy World Championship
v Thorburn	2-13	2nd round	Embassy World Championship
v Johnson	5-3	2nd round	Jameson International
v Thorburn	5-0	3rd round	Jameson International
v Martin	1-5	Quarter-final	Jameson International
v Houlihan	9-5	2nd round	Coral UK Championship
v Griffiths	4-9	3rd round	Coral UK Championship
1982 v S. Davis	2-5	Semi-final	Tolly Cobbold Classic
v Martin	10-5	1st round	Embassy World Championship
v Knowles	7-13	2nd round	Embassy World Championship
v Edmonds	1-5	Qualifying	Jameson International
v Johnson	1-5	1st round	Professional Players Tournament
v Meo	4-9	1st round	Coral UK Championship
1983 v Morgan	10-6	Qualifying	Embassy World Championship
v Knowles	3-10	1st round	Embassy World Championship
v King	5-3	Qualifying	Jameson International
v Griffiths	2-5	1st round	Jameson International
v Gauvreau	5-3	1st round	Professional Players Tournament
v Campbell	2-5	2nd round	Professional Players Tournament
v Hallett	4-9	1st round	Coral UK Championship
1984 v Williamson	10-6	Qualifying	Embassy World Championship
v Spencer	3-10	1st round	Embassy World Championship
v Newbury	1-5	Qualifying	Jameson International
v Murphy	5-3	1st round	Rothmans Grand Prix
v S. Davis	0-5	2nd round	Rothmans Grand Prix
v J. McLaughlin	8-9	Qualifying	Coral UK Open
1985 v Browne	3-5	Qualifying	Mercantile Credit Classic
v Martin	7-9	1st round	Tolly Cobbold English Championship
v Edmonds	6-1	1st round	Dulux British Open
v Spencer	2-5	2nd round	Dulux British Open
v Stevens	2-5	3rd round	Dulux British Open
v W. Jones	8-10	Qualifying	Embassy World Championship
v O'Boye	5-2	2nd round	Goya Matchroom Trophy

	v Virgo	2-5	3rd round	Goya Matchroom Trophy
	v Rigitano	5-4	2nd round	Rothmans Grand Prix
	v Reynolds	5-3	3rd round	Rothmans Grand Prix
	v Stevens	2-5	4th round	Rothmans Grand Prix
	v Oliver	9-4	2nd round	Coral UK Open
	v Reardon	4-9	3rd round	Coral UK Open
1986	v Hendry	1-5	2nd round	Mercantile Credit Classic
	v Fitzmaurice	9-5	2nd round	Tolly Cobbold English Championship
	v Williams	6-9	3rd round	Tolly Cobbold English Championship
	v Agrawal	5-4	2nd round	Dulux British Open
	v Stevens	3-5	3rd round	Dulux British Open
	v Everton	10-3	Qualifying	Embassy World Championship
	v Foldvari	7-10	Qualifying	Embassy World Championship
	v Roe	5-1	2nd round	BCE International
	v N. Foulds	2-5	3rd round	BCE International
	v Jonik	5-1	2nd round	Rothmans Grand Prix
	v N. Foulds	1-5	3rd round	Rothmans Grand Prix
	v Sheehan	9-8	2nd round	Tennents UK Open
	v Virgo	7-9	3rd round	Tennents UK Open
1987	v Sinclair	1-5	2nd round	Mercantile Credit Classic
	v Johnson	3-6	3rd round	Tolly Ales English Championship
	v Greaves	10-7	Qualifying	Embassy World Championship
	v Murphy	7-10	Qualifying	Embassy World Championship

MARIO MORRA (Canada)

Born 8.9.53
Turned professional 1979
World ranking 78 (75)

1981	v Thorne	5-9	Qualifying	Embassy World Championship
	v Wildman	3-5	Qualifying	Jameson International
1982	v Murphy	9-5	Qualifying	Embassy World Championship
	v Fitzmaurice	7-9	Qualifying	Embassy World Championship
	v Demarco	5-2	Qualifying	Jameson International
	v Reynolds	1-5	Qualifying	Jameson International
	v Wilson	2-5	1st round	Professional Players Tournament
1983	v Black	9-10	Qualifying	Embassy World Championship
	v Watchorn	5-3	Qualifying	Jameson International
	v Hallett	5-3	Qualifying	Jameson International
	v White	5-3	1st round	Jameson International
	v Charlton	3-5	2nd round	Jameson International
	v Hargreaves	5-0	Qualifying	Professional Players Tournament
	v S. Francisco	3-5	1st round	Professional Players Tournament
	v Burke	5-2	Qualifying	Lada Classic
	v Everton	5-0	Qualifying	Lada Classic
	v S. Francisco	1-5	Qualifying	Lada Classic
1984	v G. Foulds	10-2	Qualifying	Embassy World Championship
	v Murphy	10-5	Qualifying	Embassy World Championship

	v Reynolds	10-7	Qualifying	Embassy World Championship
	v Thorburn	3-10	1st round	Embassy World Championship
	v Bradley	5-3	Qualifying	Jameson International
	v Johnson	0-5	Qualifying	Jameson International
	v Cripsey	5-3	Qualifying	Rothmans Grand Prix
	v S. Davis	2-5	1st round	Rothmans Grand Prix
	v Longworth	9-1	Qualifying	Coral UK Open
	v E. Hughes	8-9	Qualifying	Coral UK Open
1985	v Newbury	2-5	Qualifying	Mercantile Credit Classic
	v Bradley	2-6	Qualifying	Dulux British Open
	v Browne	10-6	Qualifying	Embassy World Championship
	v Campbell	9-10	Qualifying	Embassy World Championship
	v John Bear	4-5	1st round	Canadian Championship
	v Oliver	5-1	2nd round	Goya Matchroom Trophy
	v Campbell	2-5	3rd round	Goya Matchroom Trophy
	v D. Hughes	5-2	2nd round	Rothmans Grand Prix
	v Martin	2-5	3rd round	Rothmans Grand Prix
	v Agrawal	9-8	2nd round	Coral UK Open
	v Mountjoy	2-9	3rd round	Coral UK Open
1986	v B. Harris	3-5	2nd round	Mercantile Credit Classic
	v Gilbert	4-5	2nd round	Dulux British Open
	v Gibson	9-10	Qualifying	Embassy World Championship
	v Thornley	4-6	1st round	Canadian Championship
	v Ellis	5-3	1st round	BCE International
	v Drago	3-5	2nd round	BCE International
	v James	5-3	1st round	Rothmans Grand Prix
	v Black	5-4	2nd round	Rothmans Grand Prix
	v Griffiths	3-5	3rd round	Rothmans Grand Prix
	v B. Bennett	9-3	1st round	Tennents UK Open
	v Drago	6-9	2nd round	Tennents UK Open
1987	v Ellis	5-1	1st round	Mercantile Credit Classic
	v Mans	5-0	2nd round	Mercantile Credit Classic
	v Williams	2-5	3rd round	Mercantile Credit Classic
	v M. Bennett	5-4	1st round	Dulux British Open
	v Van Rensberg	5-1	2nd round	Dulux British Open
	v Virgo	3-5	3rd round	Dulux British Open
	v P. Gibson	10-6	Qualifying	Embassy World Championship
	v Chappel	8-10	Qualifying	Embassy World Championship

DOUG MOUNTJOY (Wales)

Born 8.6.42
Turned professional 1976
World ranking 14 (14)
Amateur career 1976 World champion; Welsh champion 1968, 1976.
Best professional performances Winner 1978 Coral UK Championship, 1977 Benson & Hedges Masters, 1979 Benson & Hedges Irish Masters; Welsh champion 1982, 1984, 1987.

1977	v Higgins	5-3	Semi-final	Benson & Hedges Masters
	v Reardon	**7-6**	**Final**	**Benson & Hedges Masters**
	v Jack Rea	11-9	Qualifying	Embassy World Championship
	v Higgins	13-12	1st round	Embassy World Championship
	v Dennis Taylor	11-13	Quarter-final	Embassy World Championship
	v Andrewartha	5-2	1st round	Super Crystalate UK Championship
	v Spencer	5-3	2nd round	Super Crystalate UK Championship
	v Thorne	5-4	Quarter-final	Super Crystalate UK Championship
	v Higgins	9-2	Semi-final	Super Crystalate UK Championship
	v Fagan	9-12	Final	Super Crystalate UK Championship
1978	v Spencer	3-5	Final	Benson & Hedges Irish Masters
	v Andrewartha	9-3	Qualifying	Embassy World Championship
	v Reardon	9-13	1st round	Embassy World Championship
	v Barrie	9-5	Qualifying	Coral UK Championship
	v Dennis Taylor	9-4	1st round	Coral UK Championship
	v Andrewartha	9-4	Quarter-final	Coral UK Championship
	v Miles	9-1	Semi-final	Coral UK Championship
	v David Taylor	**15-9**	**Final**	**Coral UK Championship**
1979	v F. Davis	5-2	1st round	Benson & Hedges Masters
	v Spencer	5-0	Quarter-final	Benson & Hedges Masters
	v Higgins	1-5	Semi-final	Benson & Hedges Masters
	v Reardon	**6-5**	**Final**	**Benson & Hedges Irish Masters**
	v Mienie	9-1	Prelim	Embassy World Championship
	v Houlihan	9-6	Qualifying	Embassy World Championship
	v Charlton	6-13	1st round	Embassy World Championship
	v S. Davis	5-9	3rd round	Coral UK Championship
	v Griffiths	9-6	1st round	Woodpecker Welsh Championship
	v Reardon	**9-6**	**Final**	**Woodpecker Welsh Championship**
1980	v Griffiths	8-9	Final	Benson & Hedges Irish Masters
	v Wilson	10-6	1st round	Embassy World Championship
	v Thorburn	10-13	2nd round	Embassy World Championship
	v Williams	8-9	1st round	Coral UK Championship
1981	v Charlton	5-0	1st round	Benson & Hedges Masters
	v Higgins	1-5	Quarter-final	Benson & Hedges Masters
	v Wilson	6-9	Semi-final	Woodpecker Welsh Championship
	v Thorne	10-6	1st round	Embassy World Championship
	v Charlton	13-7	2nd round	Embassy World Championship
	v Dennis Taylor	13-8	Quarter-final	Embassy World Championship
	v Reardon	16-10	Semi-final	Embassy World Championship
	v S. Davis	12-18	Final	Embassy World Championship
	v S. Davis	0-5	Quarter-final	Langs Supreme Scottish Masters
	v Higgins	1-5	3rd round	Jameson International
	v Dennis Taylor	5-4	1st round	Northern Ireland Classic
	v White	8-9	Semi-final	Northern Ireland Classic
	v Knowles	6-9	3rd round	Coral UK Championship
1982	v Spencer	5-4	1st round	Benson & Hedges Masters
	v S. Davis	2-5	Quarter-final	Benson & Hedges Masters
	v Andrewartha	6-3	1st round	Welsh Championship
	v Reardon	9-7	Semi-final	Welsh Championship
	v Griffiths	**9-8**	**Final**	**Welsh Championship**

John Parrott

Doug Mountjoy

v E. Hughes	5-4	1st round	Benson & Hedges Irish Masters
v S. Davis	2-5	Quarter-final	Benson & Hedges Irish Masters
v Williams	10-3	1st round	Embassy World Championship
v Higgins	12-13	2nd round	Embassy World Championship
v Wilson	4-5	1st round	Jameson International
v Jonik	3-5	1st round	Professional Players Tournament
v Houlihan	9-3	1st round	Coral UK Championship
v Virgo	5-9	2nd round	Coral UK Championship
1983 v Griffiths	5-1	1st round	Lada Classic
v Werbeniuk	2-5	Quarter-final	Lada Classic
v Virgo	5-1	1st round	Benson & Hedges Masters
v S. Davis	5-4	Quarter-final	Benson & Hedges Masters
v Reardon	3-6	Semi-final	Benson & Hedges Masters
v M. Owen	6-0	Quarter-final	Woodpecker Welsh Championship
v Wilson	9-3	Semi-final	Woodpecker Welsh Championship
v Reardon	1-9	Final	Woodpecker Welsh Championship
v Knowles	5-1	1st round	Benson & Hedges Irish Masters
v Griffiths	4-5	Quarter-final	Benson & Hedges Irish Masters
v Wilson	10-2	1st round	Embassy World Championship
v Meo	11-13	2nd round	Embassy World Championship
v Wildman	5-4	1st round	Jameson International
v Martin	5-0	2nd round	Jameson International
v Thorburn	2-5	Quarter-final	Jameson International
v Campbell	3-5	1st round	Professional Players Tournament
v Watterson	9-2	1st round	Coral UK Championship
v Knowles	5-9	2nd round	Coral UK Championship
1984 v Parrott	4-5	Qualifying	Lada Classic
v Higgins	2-5	1st round	Benson & Hedges Masters
v Everton	6-1	1st round	Strongbow Welsh Championship
v Griffiths	9-5	Semi-final	Strongbow Welsh Championship
v Wilson	**9-3**	**Final**	**Strongbow Welsh Championship**
v Hallett	10-4	1st round	Embassy World Championship
v N. Foulds	13-6	2nd round	Embassy World Championship
v Dennis Taylor	8-13	Quarter-final	Embassy World Championship
v E. Hughes	1-5	1st round	Jameson International
v E. McLaughlin	5-4	1st round	Rothmans Grand Prix
v Wildman	5-0	2nd round	Rothmans Grand Prix
v Charlton	5-4	3rd round	Rothmans Grand Prix
v Thorburn	3-5	Quarter-final	Rothmans Grand Prix
v Hallett	9-2	1st round	Coral UK Open
v White	2-9	2nd round	Coral UK Open
1985 v Wilson	4-5	1st round	Mercantile Credit Classic
v Knowles	5-3	1st round	Benson & Hedges Masters
v Meo	5-4	Quarter-final	Benson & Hedges Masters
v Griffiths	6-2	Semi-final	Benson & Hedges Masters
v Thorburn	6-9	Final	Benson & Hedges Masters
v V. Harris	5-6	1st round	Dulux British Open
v Macleod	10-5	1st round	Embassy World Championship
v Knowles	6-13	2nd round	Embassy World Championship
v Newbury	6-5	Quarter-final	BCE Welsh Championship

	v Wilson	9-2	Semi-final	BCE Welsh Championship
	v Griffiths	4-9	Final	BCE Welsh Championship
	v Wych	5-1	3rd round	Goya Matchroom Trophy
	v Campbell	1-5	4th round	Goya Matchroom Trophy
	v Chappel	5-1	3rd round	Rothmans Grand Prix
	v Campbell	2-5	4th round	Rothmans Grand Prix
	v Morra	9-2	3rd round	Coral UK Open
	v West	4-9	4th round	Coral UK Open
1986	v King	5-4	3rd round	Mercantile Credit Classic
	v O'Kane	5-3	4th round	Mercantile Credit Classic
	v Werbeniuk	5-3	5th round	Mercantile Credit Classic
	v N. Foulds	5-3	Quarter-final	Mercantile Credit Classic
	v Thorburn	6-9	Semi-final	Mercantile Credit Classic
	v Dennis Taylor	2-5	1st round	Benson & Hedges Masters
	v Roscoe	6-4	Quarter-final	Zetters Welsh Championship
	v W. Jones	9-7	Semi-final	Zetters Welsh Championship
	v Griffiths	3-9	Final	Zetters Welsh Championship
	v Fagan	1-5	3rd round	Dulux British Open
	v Mans	10-3	1st round	Embassy World Championship
	v S. Davis	5-13	2nd round	Embassy World Championship
	v M. Gibson	5-3	3rd round	BCE International
	v Reynolds	2-5	4th round	BCE International
	v B. Harris	5-2	3rd round	Rothmans Grand Prix
	v Wych	5-1	4th round	Rothmans Grand Prix
	v Knowles	1-5	5th round	Rothmans Grand Prix
	v J. McLaughlin	9-6	3rd round	Tennents UK Open
	v Longworth	1-9	4th round	Tennents UK Open
1987	v Dodd	4-5	3rd round	Mercantile Credit Classic
	v S. Davis	2-5	1st round	Benson & Hedges Masters
	v Meo	4-5	Quarter-final	Benson & Hedges Masters
	v Roscoe	6-2	Quarter-final	Matchroom Welsh Championship
	v Chappel	9-2	Semi-final	Matchroom Welsh Championship
	v Newbury	**9-7**	**Final**	**Matchroom Welsh Championship**
	v Owers	5-3	3rd round	Dulux British Open
	v P. Francisco	5-3	4th round	Dulux British Open
	v Thorburn	4-5	5th round	Dulux British Open
	v David Taylor	10-5	1st round	Embassy World Championship
	v O'Kane	5-13	2nd round	Embassy World Championship

TOMMY MURPHY (Northern Ireland)

Born 8.1.62
Turned professional 1981
World ranking 44 (57)
Amateur career 1981 Northern Ireland champion.
Best professional performance Last 16 1987 Dulux British Open.

1981	v Johnson	1-9	Qualifying	Coral UK Championship
1982	v Fagan	6-2	Quarter-final	Irish Championship

	v Dennis Taylor	0-6	Semi-final	Irish Championship
	v Morra	5-9	Qualifying	Embassy World Championship
	v Fisher	1-5	Qualifying	Jameson International
	v Reardon	0-5	1st round	Professional Players Tournament
	v Everton	9-4	Qualifying	Coral UK Championship
	v Sinclair	5-9	Qualifying	Coral UK Championship
1983	v Fagan	4-6	Quarter-final	Irish Championship
	v Houlihan	10-9	Qualifying	Embassy World Championship
	v Virgo	8-10	Qualifying	Embassy World Championship
	v Sheehan	5-2	Qualifying	Jameson International
	v Thorne	2-5	Qualifying	Jameson International
	v Macleod	5-0	1st round	Professional Players Tournament
	v Stevens	1-5	2nd round	Professional Players Tournament
	v Demarco	9-4	Qualifying	Coral UK Championship
	v Donnelly	9-4	Qualifying	Coral UK Championship
	v Dennis Taylor	6-9	1st round	Coral UK Championship
1984	v Fitzmaurice	10-8	Qualifying	Embassy World Championship
	v Morra	5-10	Qualifying	Embassy World Championship
	v Bales	4-5	Qualifying	Jameson International
	v G. Foulds	5-1	Qualifying	Rothmans Grand Prix
	v Miles	3-5	1st round	Rothmans Grand Prix
	v Kearney	9-2	Qualifying	Coral UK Open
	v Watterson	9-4	Qualifying	Coral UK Open
	v Martin	9-8	Qualifying	Coral UK Open
	v S. Davis	1-9	1st round	Coral UK Open
1985	v Fowler	0-5	Qualifying	Mercantile Credit Classic
	v Sheehan	6-3	Qualifying	Dulux British Open
	v Macleod	5-6	1st round	Dulux British Open
	v Browne	6-3	Qualifying	Irish Championship
	v Fagan	2-6	Quarter-final	Irish Championship
	v P. Francisco	4-10	Qualifying	Embassy World Championship
	v Jack Rea	5-1	2nd round	Goya Matchroom Trophy
	v E. Hughes	5-3	3rd round	Goya Matchroom Trophy
	v Higgins	2-5	4th round	Goya Matchroom Trophy
	v Mikkelsen	4-5	2nd round	Rothmans Grand Prix
	v Everton	9-4	2nd round	Coral UK Open
	v Macleod	7-9	3rd round	Coral UK Open
1986	v Chappel	5-4	2nd round	Mercantile Credit Classic
	v Martin	3-5	3rd round	Mercantile Credit Classic
	v Duggan	1-5	2nd round	Dulux British Open
	v J. McLaughlin	10-7	Qualifying	Embassy World Championship
	v Thornley	10-3	Qualifying	Embassy World Championship
	v E. Hughes	7-10	Qualifying	Embassy World Championship
	v O'Boye	5-0	1st round	Strongbow Irish Championship
	v Kearney	6-2	Quarter-final	Strongbow Irish Championship
	v Dennis Taylor	3-6	Semi-final	Strongbow Irish Championship
	v Donnelly	5-2	2nd round	BCE International
	v Johnson	4-5	3rd round	BCE International
	v Anderson	4-5	2nd round	Rothmans Grand Prix
	v D. Hughes	9-0	2nd round	Tennents UK Open

v Thorne	4-9	3rd round	Tennents UK Open
1987 v Bales	5-2	2nd round	Mercantile Credit Classic
v Longworth	3-5	3rd round	Mercantile Credit Classic
v D. Gilbert	5-4	2nd round	Dulux British Open
v Wych	5-1	3rd round	Dulux British Open
v Reardon	5-4	4th round	Dulux British Open
v Knowles	3-5	5th round	Dulux British Open
v Jenkins	10-4	Qualifying	Embassy World Championship
v Miles	10-7	Qualifying	Embassy World Championship
v Longworth	2-10	Qualifying	Embassy World Championship
v Kearney	1-5	1st round	Matchroom Irish Championship

STEVE NEWBURY (Wales)

Born 21.4.56
Turned professional 1984
World ranking 45 (40)
Amateur career 1980 Welsh champion.
Best professional performances Last 16 1986 Rothmans Grand Prix; runner-up 1987 Matchroom Welsh Championship.

1984 v Longworth	5-4	Qualifying	Jameson International
v Burke	5-0	Qualifying	Jameson International
v Fagan	5-0	Qualifying	Jameson International
v Miles	5-1	Qualifying	Jameson International
v Werbeniuk	5-2	1st round	Jameson International
v Knowles	4-5	2nd round	Jameson International
v Fisher	5-0	Qualifying	Rothmans Grand Prix
v Thorne	2-5	1st round	Rothmans Grand Prix
v Rigitano	9-6	Qualifying	Coral UK Open
v Jonik	9-3	Qualifying	Coral UK Open
v Dodd	6-9	Qualifying	Coral UK Open
1985 v V. Harris	5-3	Qualifying	Mercantile Credit Classic
v Burke	5-1	Qualifying	Mercantile Credit Classic
v Morra	5-2	Qualifying	Mercantile Credit Classic
v E. Hughes	3-5	Qualifying	Mercantile Credit Classic
v Browne	6-0	Qualifying	Dulux British Open
v Sinclair	6-3	1st round	Dulux British Open
v Griffiths	5-3	2nd round	Dulux British Open
v Dennis Taylor	3-5	3rd round	Dulux British Open
v D. Hughes	10-9	Qualifying	Embassy World Championship
v Burke	10-3	Qualifying	Embassy World Championship
v Scott	10-2	Qualifying	Embassy World Championship
v E. Hughes	6-10	Qualifying	Embassy World Championship
v W. Jones	6-2	1st round	BCE Welsh Championship
v Mountjoy	5-6	Quarter-final	BCE Welsh Championship
v Jonik	5-4	2nd round	Goya Matchroom Trophy
v Griffiths	2-5	3rd round	Goya Matchroom Trophy
v Burke	5-3	2nd round	Rothmans Grand Prix

	v David Taylor	2-5	3rd round	Rothmans Grand Prix
	v Houlihan	9-3	2nd round	Coral UK Open
	v Stevens	7-9	3rd round	Coral UK Open
1986	v Cripsey	4-5	2nd round	Mercantile Credit Classic
	v Wilson	4-6	Quarter-final	Zetters Welsh Championship
	v Oliver	5-2	2nd round	Dulux British Open
	v O'Kane	5-3	3rd round	Dulux British Open
	v Meo	0-5	4th round	Dulux British Open
	v Agrawal	10-5	Qualifying	Embassy World Championship
	v Black	10-2	Qualifying	Embassy World Championship
	v Spencer	7-10	Qualifying	Embassy World Championship
	v Dunning	5-4	2nd round	BCE International
	v S. Francisco	4-5	3rd round	BCE International
	v D. Gilbert	5-1	2nd round	Rothmans Grand Prix
	v Reynolds	5-0	3rd round	Rothmans Grand Prix
	v O'Boye	5-2	4th round	Rothmans Grand Prix
	v S. Francisco	2-5	5th round	Rothmans Grand Prix
	v Owers	8-9	2nd round	Tennents UK Open
1987	v Meadowcroft	5-1	2nd round	Mercantile Credit Classic
	v White	4-5	3rd round	Mercantile Credit Classic
	v Wilson	6-2	Quarter-final	Matchroom Welsh Championship
	v Griffiths	9-6	Semi-final	Matchroom Welsh Championship
	v Mountjoy	7-9	Final	Matchroom Welsh Championship
	v Roscoe	3-5	2nd round	Dulux British Open
	v Dodd	10-7	Qualifying	Embassy World Championship
	v Rigitano	10-4	Qualifying	Embassy World Championship
	v Hallett	4-10	Qualifying	Embassy World Championship

JOE O'BOYE (Republic of Ireland)

Born 6.3.60
Turned professional 1985
World ranking 56 (65)
Amateur career 1980 English champion.
Best professional performances Last 32 1985 & 1986 Rothmans Grand Prix.

	v Parkin	5-3	1st round	Goya Matchroom Trophy
1985	v Miles	2-5	2nd round	Goya Matchroom Trophy
	v Hendry	5-4	1st round	Rothmans Grand Prix
	v Chaperon	5-3	2nd round	Rothmans Grand Prix
	v Mans	5-3	3rd round	Rothmans Grand Prix
	v White	4-5	4th round	Rothmans Grand Prix
	v Bennett	9-3	1st round	Coral UK Open
	v Gauvreau	9-5	2nd round	Coral UK Open
	v Knowles	5-9	3rd round	Coral UK Open
1986	v Wilkinson	5-1	1st round	Mercantile Credit Classic
	v Longworth	5-1	2nd round	Mercantile Credit Classic
	v Meo	3-5	3rd round	Mercantile Credit Classic

v Jim Bear	5-1	1st round	Dulux British Open
v T. Jones	2-5	2nd round	Dulux British Open
v Oliver	8-10	Qualifying	Embassy World Championship
v Murphy	0-5	1st round	Strongbow Irish Championship
v Mikkelsen	5-4	2nd round	BCE International
v Williams	0-5	3rd round	BCE International
v Edmonds	5-2	2nd round	Rothmans Grand Prix
v Thorburn	5-4	3rd round	Rothmans Grand Prix
v Newbury	2-5	4th round	Rothmans Grand Prix
v Duggan	9-4	2nd round	Tennents UK Open
v Meo	3-9	3rd round	Tennents UK Open
1987 v V. Harris	5-1	2nd round	Mercantile Credit Classic
v Griffiths	1-5	3rd round	Mercantile Credit Classic
v Bradley	5-1	2nd round	Dulux British Open
v Reardon	5-4	3rd round	Dulux British Open
v N. Gilbert	10-5	Qualifying	Embassy World Championship
v Bradley	7-10	Qualifying	Embassy World Championship
v Kelly	5-0	1st round	Matchroom Irish Championship
v Higgins	wo	Quarter-final	Matchroom Irish Championship
v E. Hughes	6-3	Semi-final	Matchroom Irish Championship
v Dennis Taylor	2-9	Final	Matchroom Irish Championship

DENE O'KANE (New Zealand)

Born 24.2.63
Turned professional 1984
World ranking 35 (39)
Amateur career 1980 New Zealand champion.
Best professional performance Quarter-finals 1987 Embassy World Championship.

1984 v Parkin	5-2	Qualifying	Jameson International
v E. McLaughlin	5-1	Qualifying	Jameson International
v Fitzmaurice	5-4	Qualifying	Jameson International
v Hallett	5-4	Qualifying	Jameson International
v Thorne	3-5	1st round	Jameson International
v Kelly	5-4	Qualifying	Rothmans Grand Prix
v David Taylor	1-5	1st round	Rothmans Grand Prix
v W. Jones	9-7	Qualifying	Coral UK Open
v Duggan	9-6	Qualifying	Coral UK Open
v Scott	7-9	Qualifying	Coral UK Open
1985 v W. Jones	0-5	Qualifying	Mercantile Credit Classic
v Cripsey	6-4	Qualifying	Dulux British Open
v Campbell	6-4	1st round	Dulux British Open
v V. Harris	5-3	2nd round	Dulux British Open
v Martin	5-4	3rd round	Dulux British Open
v S. Davis	1-5	Quarter-final	Dulux British Open

	v J. McLaughlin	*wo*	Qualifying	Embassy World Championship
	v V. Harris	10-5	Qualifying	Embassy World Championship
	v Jonik	10-5	Qualifying	Embassy World Championship
	v Dodd	10-7	Qualifying	Embassy World Championship
	v Martin	10-8	Qualifying	Embassy World Championship
	v David Taylor	4-10	1st round	Embassy World Championship
	v B. Harris	3-5	3rd round	Goya Matchroom Trophy
	v Edmonds	2-5	3rd round	Rothmans Grand Prix
	v Chappel	5-9	3rd round	Coral UK Open
1986	v Medati	5-0	3rd round	Mercantile Credit Classic
	v Mountjoy	3-5	4th round	Mercantile Credit Classic
	v Newbury	3-5	3rd round	Dulux British Open
	v Hendry	9-10	Qualifying	Embassy World Championship
	v Oliver	5-2	2nd round	BCE International
	v Hallett	5-1	3rd round	BCE International
	v Owers	0-5	4th round	BCE International
	v M. Bennett	2-5	2nd round	Rothmans Grand Prix
	v Jenkins	9-5	2nd round	Tennents UK Open
	v Werbeniuk	9-5	3rd round	Tennents UK Open
	v Griffiths	0-9	4th round	Tennents UK Open
1987	v G. Foulds	4-5	2nd round	Mercantile Credit Classic
	v Rowswell	4-5	2nd round	Dulux British Open
	v D. Gilbert	10-2	Qualifying	Embassy World Championship
	v Black	10-2	Qualifying	Embassy World Championship
	v P. Francisco	10-5	Qualifying	Embassy World Championship
	v Thorburn	5-10	1st round	Embassy World Championship
	v Mountjoy	13-5	2nd round	Embassy World Championship
	v White	6-13	Quarter-final	Embassy World Championship

BILL OLIVER (England)

Born 3.12.48
Turned professional 1983
World ranking 85 (84)

1983	v T. Jones	2-5	Qualifying	Professional Players Tournament
	v Andrewartha	1-9	Qualifying	Coral UK Championship
1984	v Dunning	10-3	Qualifying	Embassy World Championship
	v Caggianello	10-7	Qualifying	Embassy World Championship
	v Williams	8-10	Qualifying	Embassy World Championship
	v D. Hughes	5-4	Qualifying	Jameson International
	v Chalmers	4-5	Qualifying	Jameson International
	v Bennett	5-3	Qualifying	Rothmans Grand Prix
	v White	1-5	1st round	Rothmans Grand Prix
	v Fowler	3-9	Qualifying	Coral UK Open
1985	v Longworth	1-5	Qualifying	Mercantile Credit Classic
	v Fowler	7-9	Qualifying	Tolly Cobbold English Championship
	v Thorne	3-6	1st round	Dulux British Open
	v Foldvari	3-10	Qualifying	Embassy World Championship

	v Morra	1-5	2nd round	Goya Matchroom Trophy
	v Fagan	5-4	2nd round	Rothmans Grand Prix
	v Thorburn	0-5	3rd round	Rothmans Grand Prix
	v Miles	4-9	2nd round	Coral UK Open
1986	v Bradley	3-5	2nd round	Mercantile Credit Classic
	v Dodd	9-5	2nd round	Tolly Cobbold English Championship
	v Parrott	0-9	3rd round	Tolly Cobbold English Championship
	v Newbury	2-5	2nd round	Dulux British Open
	v O'Boye	10-8	Qualifying	Embassy World Championship
	v Fowler	8-10	Qualifying	Embassy World Championship
	v Mienie	5-4	1st round	BCE International
	v O'Kane	2-5	2nd round	BCE International
	v Anderson	4-5	1st round	Rothmans Grand Prix
	v Chalmers	9-6	1st round	Tennents UK Open
	v Hendry	1-9	2nd round	Tennents UK Open
1987	v Greaves	5-4	1st round	Mercantile Credit Classic
	v T. Jones	0-5	2nd round	Mercantile Credit Classic
	v T. Jones	1-6	2nd round	Tolly Ales English Championship
	v Jack Rea	5-1	1st round	Dulux British Open
	v Drago	1-5	2nd round	Dulux British Open

KEN OWERS (England)

Born 30.3.53
Turned professional 1986
World ranking 53 (–)
Best professional performance Last 16 1986 BCE International.

	v Scott	5-1	2nd round	BCE International
1986				
	v White	5-2	3rd round	BCE International
	v O'Kane	5-0	4th round	BCE International
	v N. Foulds	1-5	5th round	BCE International
	v J. McLaughlin	2-5	1st round	Rothmans Grand Prix
	v D. Gilbert	9-8	1st round	Tennents UK Open
	v Newbury	9-8	2nd round	Tennents UK Open
	v S. Francisco	3-9	3rd round	Tennents UK Open
1987	v Houlihan	5-1	1st round	Mercantile Credit Classic
	v John Rea	2-5	2nd round	Mercantile Credit Classic
	v Bales	6-5	2nd round	Tolly Ales English Championship
	v N. Foulds	6-3	3rd round	Tolly Ales English Championship
	v Hallett	2-6	4th round	Tolly Ales English Championship
	v Jonik	5-4	1st round	Dulux British Open
	v F. Davis	5-3	2nd round	Dulux British Open
	v Mountjoy	1-5	3rd round	Dulux British Open
	v Fisher	10-5	Qualifying	Embassy World Championship
	v F. Davis	10-5	Qualifying	Embassy World Championship
	v King	4-10	Qualifying	Embassy World Championship

JOHN PARROTT (England)

Born 11.5.64
Turned professional 1983
World ranking 13 (17)
Best professional performances Quarter-finals 1985 Embassy World Championship; semi-finals 1984 Lada Classic.

1983 v Watchorn	5-0	Qualifying	Professional Players Tournament
v Fagan	5-2	1st round	Professional Players Tournament
v Griffiths	1-5	2nd round	Professional Players Tournament
v Scott	9-7	Qualifying	Coral UK Championship
v Fisher	9-0	Qualifying	Coral UK Championship
v Meo	7-9	1st round	Coral UK Championship
1984 v Mountjoy	5-4	Qualifying	Lada Classic
v Higgins	5-2	1st round	Lada Classic
v Knowles	5-1	Quarter-final	Lada Classic
v S. Davis	4-5	Semi-final	Lada Classic
v D. Hughes	10-3	Qualifying	Embassy World Championship
v Everton	10-2	Qualifying	Embassy World Championship
v Mans	10-0	Qualifying	Embassy World Championship
v Knowles	10-7	1st round	Embassy World Championship
v Dennis Taylor	11-13	2nd round	Embassy World Championship
v Gauvreau	4-5	Qualifying	Jameson International
v Gauvreau	5-3	1st round	Rothmans Grand Prix
v Charlton	1-5	2nd round	Rothmans Grand Prix
v Fitzmaurice	9-6	Qualifying	Coral UK Open
v Thorne	7-9	1st round	Coral UK Open
1985 v Medati	3-5	Qualifying	Mercantile Credit Classic
v G. Foulds	9-4	1st round	Tolly Cobbold English Championship
v David Taylor	6-9	2nd round	Tolly Cobbold English Championship
v John Rea	6-4	1st round	Dulux British Open
v Dennis Taylor	2-5	2nd round	Dulux British Open
v Fowler	10-2	Qualifying	Embassy World Championship
v Spencer	10-3	1st round	Embassy World Championship
v Stevens	13-6	2nd round	Embassy World Championship
v Reardon	12-13	Quarter-final	Embassy World Championship
v Thorne	5-0	Quarter-final	Winfield Australian Masters
v Campbell	4-6	Semi-final	Winfield Australian Masters
v White	3-5	Semi-final	Carlsberg Trophy
v W. Jones	5-3	3rd round	Goya Matchroom Trophy
v Meo	5-4	4th round	Goya Matchroom Trophy
v Griffiths	5-1	5th round	Goya Matchroom Trophy
v Dennis Taylor	1-5	Quarter-final	Goya Matchroom Trophy
v Longworth	2-5	3rd round	Rothmans Grand Prix
v Dennis Taylor	1-5	1st round	BCE Canadian Masters
v Sinclair	9-2	3rd round	Coral UK Open
v Thorburn	6-9	4th round	Coral UK Open
1986 v Van Rensberg	3-5	3rd round	Mercantile Credit Classic
v Oliver	9-0	3rd round	Tolly Cobbold English Championship

v Virgo	6-9	4th round	Tolly Cobbold English Championship
v Roscoe	5-2	3rd round	Dulux British Open
v Fagan	5-0	4th round	Dulux British Open
v Wych	4-5	5th round	Dulux British Open
v Foldvari	10-6	Qualifying	Embassy World Championship
v Meo	10-4	1st round	Embassy World Championship
v White	8-13	2nd round	Embassy World Championship
v Thorburn	1-5	1st round	Langs Scottish Masters
v Hendry	3-5	3rd round	BCE International
v Cripsey	5-4	3rd round	Rothmans Grand Prix
v Meo	3-5	4th round	Rothmans Grand Prix
v Bradley	9-4	3rd round	Tennents UK Open
v Johnson	9-1	4th round	Tennents UK Open
v Longworth	9-6	5th round	Tennents UK Open
v Knowles	9-4	Quarter-final	Tennents UK Open
v N. Foulds	3-9	Semi-final	Tennents UK Open
1987 v T. Jones	5-2	3rd round	Mercantile Credit Classic
v Higgins	5-2	4th round	Mercantile Credit Classic
v Charlton	5-4	5th round	Mercantile Credit Classic
v S. Davis	4-5	Quarter-final	Mercantile Credit Classic
v Wildman	6-1	3rd round	Tolly Ales English Championship
v Virgo	6-2	4th round	Tolly Ales English Championship
v Meo	3-6	Quarter-final	Tolly Ales English Championship
v King	1-5	3rd round	Dulux British Open
v Fowler	10-3	Qualifying	Embassy World Championship
v Meo	10-8	1st round	Embassy World Championship
v White	11-13	2nd round	Embassy World Championship

JACK REA (Northern Ireland)

Born 6.4.21
Turned professional 1948
World ranking 112 (103)
Amateur career 1947 Northern Irish champion.
Best professional performance Runner-up 1957 World Championship.

1969 v G. Owen	17-25	Quarter-final	World Championship
1970 v Spencer	15-31	Quarter-final	World Championship
1972 v Higgins	11-19	1st round	World Championship
1973 v Houlihan	2-9	1st round	World Championship
1976 v Anderson	8-5	Qualifying	Embassy World Championship
1977 v John Rea	9-11	Qualifying	Embassy World Championship
v Fagan	1-5	1st round	Super Crystalate UK Championship
1978 v Meadowcroft	5-9	Qualifying	Coral UK Championship
1979 v Dunning	5-9	Prelim	Embassy World Championship
v Bennett	9-8	1st round	Coral UK Championship
v Houlihan	3-9	2nd round	Coral UK Championship
1980 v Thorne	1-9	Qualifying	Embassy World Championship

1981	v D. Hughes	4-5	Qualifying	Jameson International
1982	v E. Hughes	1-6	Quarter-final	Irish Championship
	v Bennett	8-5	Qualifying	Embassy World Championship
	v Werbeniuk	2-5	2nd round	Professional Players Tournament
	v Roscoe	6-9	Qualifying	Coral UK Championship
1983	v Higgins	3-6	Quarter-final	Irish Championship
	v David Taylor	7-8	Qualifying	Embassy World Championship
	v Edmonds	1-5	Qualifying	Jameson International
	v French	5-9	Qualifying	Coral UK Championship
1984	v Bradley	2-5	Qualifying	Jameson International
1985	v Foldvari	4-5	Qualifying	Mercantile Credit Classic
	v Dennis Taylor	0-6	Quarter-final	Irish Championship
	v Murphy	1-5	2nd round	Goya Matchroom Trophy
1986	v Fisher	3-5	2nd round	Mercantile Credit Classic
	v Bradley	1-5	2nd round	Dulux British Open
	v Kelly	0-5	1st round	Strongbow Irish Championship
	v Darrington	5-4	1st round	BCE International
	v W. Jones	1-5	2nd round	BCE International
	v D. Hughes	5-2	1st round	Rothmans Grand Prix
	v B. Harris	0-5	2nd round	Rothmans Grand Prix
	v B. Harris	5-9	2nd round	Tennents UK Open
1987	v Kelly	5-3	1st round	Mercantile Credit Classic
	v Hendry	1-5	2nd round	Mercantile Credit Classic
	v Oliver	1-5	1st round	Dulux British Open
	v Bear	5-10	Qualifying	Embassy World Championship
	v Browne	3-5	1st round	Matchroom Irish Championship

JOHN REA (Scotland)

Born 5.12.51
Turned professional 1984
World ranking 70 (62)
Best professional performance Last 32 1986 Dulux British Open.

1984	v Browne	2-5	Qualifying	Jameson International
	v Fitzmaurice	5-2	Qualifying	Rothmans Grand Prix
	v E. Hughes	5-4	1st round	Rothmans Grand Prix
	v David Taylor	1-5	2nd round	Rothmans Grand Prix
	v Bennett	9-5	Qualifying	Coral UK Open
	v Dunning	9-3	Qualifying	Coral UK Open
	v Edmonds	9-6	Qualifying	Coral UK Open
	v Johnson	6-9	Qualifying	Coral UK Open
1985	v Sheehan	2-5	Qualifying	Mercantile Credit Classic
	v Donnelly	6-2	1st round	Scottish Championship
	v Sinclair	2-6	Semi-final	Scottish Championship
	v Fisher	6-0	Qualifying	Dulux British Open
	v Parrott	4-6	1st round	Dulux British Open
	v W. Jones	3-10	Qualifying	Embassy World Championship
	v Bradley	1-5	2nd round	Goya Matchroom Trophy

	v W. Jones	0-5	2nd round	Rothmans Grand Prix
	v F. Davis	8-9	2nd round	Coral UK Open
1986	v Williamson	5-4	2nd round	Mercantile Credit Classic
	v Hallett	2-5	3rd round	Mercantile Credit Classic
	v King	5-1	2nd round	Dulux British Open
	v Reardon	5-3	3rd round	Dulux British Open
	v Virgo	0-5	4th round	Dulux British Open
	v Donnelly	6-1	Quarter-final	Canada Dry Scottish Championship
	v Gibson	0-6	Semi-final	Canada Dry Scottish Championship
	v E. McLaughlin	10-6	Qualifying	Embassy World Championship
	v Longworth	4-10	Qualifying	Embassy World Championship
	v Anderson	5-1	2nd round	BCE International
	v S. Davis	1-5	3rd round	BCE International
	v Sinclair	5-4	2nd round	Rothmans Grand Prix
	v Wych	2-5	3rd round	Rothmans Grand Prix
	v N. Gilbert	9-8	2nd round	Tennents UK Open
	v Knowles	4-9	3rd round	Tennents UK Open
1987	v Owers	5-2	2nd round	Mercantile Credit Classic
	v Meo	4-5	3rd round	Mercantile Credit Classic
	v Black	6-1	1st round	Scottish Championship
	v Hendry	0-6	Semi-final	Scottish Championship
	v Hargreaves	5-3	2nd round	Dulux British Open
	v Griffiths	2-5	3rd round	Dulux British Open
	v Rempe	9-10	Qualifying	Embassy World Championship

RAY REARDON (Wales)

Born 8.10.32
Turned professional 1967
World ranking 38 (15)
Amateur career 1950–55 Welsh champion, 1964 English champion.
Best professional performances Winner World Championship 1970, 1973–76, 1978, Professional Players Tournament 1982, Benson & Hedges Masters 1976; Welsh champion 1981, 1983.

1969	v F. Davis	24-25	Quarter-final	World Championship
1970	v F. Davis	31-26	Quarter-final	World Championship (Apr)
	v Spencer	37-33	Semi-final	World Championship (Apr)
	v Pulman	**39-34**	**Final**	**World Championship (Apr)**
	v Spencer	15-34	Semi-final	World Championship (Nov)
1972	v Williams	23-25	Quarter-final	World Championship
1973	v Meadowcroft	16-10	2nd round	World Championship
	v G. Owen	16-6	Quarter-final	World Championship
	v Spencer	23-22	Semi-final	World Championship
	v Charlton	**38-32**	**Final**	**World Championship**
1974	v Meadowcroft	15-3	2nd round	World Championship
	v M. Owen	15-11	Quarter-final	World Championship
	v F. Davis	15-3	Semi-final	World Championship
	v Miles	**22-12**	**Final**	**World Championship**

1975	v Miles	5-3	Quarter-final	Benson & Hedges Masters
	v Williams	5-4	Semi-final	Benson & Hedges Masters
	v Spencer	8-9	Final	Benson & Hedges Masters
	v Simpson	15-11	2nd round	World Championship
	v Spencer	19-17	Quarter-final	World Championship
	v Higgins	19-14	Semi-final	World Championship
	v Charlton	**31-30**	**Final**	**World Championship**
1976	v Charlton	5-4	Semi-final	Benson & Hedges Masters
	v Miles	**7-3**	**Final**	**Benson & Hedges Masters**
	v Dunning	15-7	1st round	Embassy World Championship
	v Dennis Taylor	15-2	Quarter-final	Embassy World Championship
	v Mans	20-10	Semi-final	Embassy World Championship
	v Higgins	**27-16**	**Final**	**Embassy World Championship**
1977	v Miles	5-2	Semi-final	Benson & Hedges Masters
	v Mountjoy	6-7	Final	Benson & Hedges Masters
	v Fagan	13-7	1st round	Embassy World Championship
	v Spencer	6-13	Quarter-final	Embassy World Championship
	v Meadowcroft	4-5	2nd round	Super Crystalate UK Championship
1978	v Higgins	1-5	Semi-final	Benson & Hedges Masters
	v Mountjoy	13-9	1st round	Embassy World Championship
	v Werbeniuk	13-6	Quarter-final	Embassy World Championship
	v Charlton	18-14	Semi-final	Embassy World Championship
	v Mans	**25-18**	**Final**	**Embassy World Championship**
	v Thorne	6-9	1st round	Coral UK Championship
1979	v David Taylor	5-2	Quarter-final	Benson & Hedges Masters
	v Mans	3-5	Semi-final	Benson & Hedges Masters
	v Mountjoy	5-6	Final	Benson & Hedges Irish Masters
	v Miles	13-8	1st round	Embassy World Championship
	v Dennis Taylor	8-13	Quarter-final	Embassy World Championship
1980	v Dennis Taylor	5-3	Quarter-final	Benson & Hedges Masters
	v Higgins	2-5	Semi-final	Benson & Hedges Masters
	v Higgins	1-5	Final	British Gold Cup
	v Wilson	9-3	1st round	Woodpecker Welsh Championship
	v Mountjoy	6-9	Final	Woodpecker Welsh Championship
	v Werbeniuk	13-6	2nd round	Embassy World Championship
	v David Taylor	11-13	Quarter-final	Embassy World Championship
	v Andrewartha	9-3	2nd round	Coral UK Championship
	v Williams	9-4	Quarter-final	Coral UK Championship
	v Higgins	7-9	Semi-final	Coral UK Championship
1981	v Spencer	1-5	Quarter-final	Benson & Hedges Masters
	v Griffiths	9-6	Semi-final	Woodpecker Welsh Championship
	v Wilson	**9-6**	**Final**	**Woodpecker Welsh Championship**
	v Higgins	6-5	Semi-final	Benson & Hedges Irish Masters
	v Griffiths	7-9	Final	Benson & Hedges Irish Masters
	v Spencer	13-11	2nd round	Embassy World Championship
	v Werbeniuk	13-10	Quarter-final	Embassy World Championship
	v Mountjoy	10-16	Semi-final	Embassy World Championship
	v White	4-5	Quarter-final	Langs Supreme Scottish Masters
	v Virgo	3-5	3rd round	Jameson International
	v Johnson	9-7	3rd round	Coral UK Championship

	v White	8-9	Quarter-final	Coral UK Championship
1982	v David Taylor	5-1	1st round	Lada Classic
	v S. Davis	4-5	Semi-final	Lada Classic
	v Dennis Taylor	5-3	1st round	Benson & Hedges Masters
	v Griffiths	3-5	Quarter-final	Benson & Hedges Masters
	v Everton	6-1	1st round	Welsh Championship
	v Mountjoy	7-9	Semi-final	Welsh Championship
	v Dennis Taylor	5-4	Quarter-final	Benson & Hedges Irish Masters
	v Griffiths	3-6	Semi-final	Benson & Hedges Irish Masters
	v Donnelly	10-5	1st round	Embassy World Championship
	v Virgo	13-8	2nd round	Embassy World Championship
	v S. Francisco	13-8	Quarter-final	Embassy World Championship
	v Charlton	16-11	Semi-final	Embassy World Championship
	v Higgins	15-18	Final	Embassy World Championship
	v Griffiths	3-5	1st round	Langs Supreme Scottish Masters
	v E. Hughes	5-3	1st round	Jameson International
	v Knowles	2-5	2nd round	Jameson International
	v Murphy	5-0	1st round	Professional Players Tournament
	v Higgins	5-2	2nd round	Professional Players Tournament
	v Macleod	5-2	3rd round	Professional Players Tournament
	v Werbeniuk	5-3	Quarter-final	Professional Players Tournament
	v Charlton	10-7	Semi-final	Professional Players Tournament
	v White	**10-5**	**Final**	**Professional Players Tournament**
	v Wildman	9-5	1st round	Coral UK Championship
	v Hallett	9-8	2nd round	Coral UK Championship
	v White	9-8	Quarter-final	Coral UK Championship
	v Higgins	6-9	Semi-final	Coral UK Championship
1983	v Spencer	3-5	1st round	Lada Classic
	v Reynolds	5-1	1st round	Benson & Hedges Masters
	v White	5-2	Quarter-final	Benson & Hedges Masters
	v Mountjoy	6-3	Semi-final	Benson & Hedges Masters
	v Thorburn	7-9	Final	Benson & Hedges Masters
	v White	**9-6**	**Final**	**Yamaha International Masters**
	v Andrewartha	6-2	Quarter-final	Woodpecker Welsh Championship
	v Griffiths	9-4	Semi-final	Woodpecker Welsh Championship
	v Mountjoy	**9-1**	**Final**	**Woodpecker Welsh Championship**
	v Meo	5-4	Quarter-final	Benson & Hedges Irish Masters
	v Higgins	6-3	Semi-final	Benson & Hedges Irish Masters
	v S. Davis	2-9	Final	Benson & Hedges Irish Masters
	v E. Hughes	10-7	1st round	Embassy World Championship
	v Knowles	12-13	2nd round	Embassy World Championship
	v Macleod	5-2	1st round	Jameson International
	v Thorne	0-5	2nd round	Jameson International
	v Ganim	5-4	1st round	Professional Players Tournament
	v Duggan	5-2	2nd round	Professional Players Tournament
	v Thorne	3-5	3rd round	Professional Players Tournament
	v B. Harris	9-7	1st round	Coral UK Championship
	v Wilson	9-4	2nd round	Coral UK Championship
	v White	4-9	Quarter-final	Coral UK Championship
1984	v Williams	4-5	Qualifying	Lada Classic

	v Virgo	5-3	1st round	Benson & Hedges Masters
	v White	3-5	Quarter-final	Benson & Hedges Masters
	v M. Owen	6-1	1st round	Strongbow Welsh Championship
	v Wilson	4-9	Semi-final	Strongbow Welsh Championship
	v Higgins	2-5	Quarter-final	Benson & Hedges Irish Masters
	v Wych	10-7	1st round	Embassy World Championship
	v S. Francisco	13-8	2nd round	Embassy World Championship
	v Stevens	2-13	Quarter-final	Embassy World Championship
	v Dodd	5-4	1st round	Jameson International
	v E. Hughes	1-5	2nd round	Jameson International
	v Roscoe	5-1	1st round	Rothmans Grand Prix
	v Wilson	5-4	2nd round	Rothmans Grand Prix
	v Dennis Taylor	3-5	3rd round	Rothmans Grand Prix
	v Fowler	9-2	1st round	Coral UK Open
	v David Taylor	9-4	2nd round	Coral UK Open
	v Thorburn	8-9	Quarter-final	Coral UK Open
1985	v Hallett	5-3	1st round	Mercantile Credit Classic
	v E. Hughes	5-1	2nd round	Mercantile Credit Classic
	v S. Davis	1-5	Quarter-final	Mercantile Credit Classic
	v David Taylor	5-1	1st round	Benson & Hedges Masters
	v Thorburn	0-5	Quarter-final	Benson & Hedges Masters
	v King	6-5	1st round	Dulux British Open
	v Martin	4-5	2nd round	Dulux British Open
	v E. Hughes	0-5	1st round	Benson & Hedges Irish Masters
	v E. Hughes	10-9	1st round	Embassy World Championship
	v Fagan	13-9	2nd round	Embassy World Championship
	v Parrott	13-12	Quarter-final	Embassy World Championship
	v S. Davis	5-16	Semi-final	Embassy World Championship
	v Everton	6-2	Quarter-final	BCE Welsh Championship
	v Griffiths	3-9	Semi-final	BCE Welsh Championship
	v Duggan	3-5	3rd round	Goya Matchroom Trophy
	v Scott	4-5	3rd round	Rothmans Grand Prix
	v Knowles	5-2	1st round	BCE Canadian Masters
	v Dennis Taylor	3-8	Semi-final	BCE Canadian Masters
	v Miles	9-4	3rd round	Coral UK Open
	v Macleod	5-9	4th round	Coral UK Open
	v Griffiths	2-5	1st round	Kit Kat
1986	v Mikkelsen	3-5	3rd round	Mercantile Credit Classic
	v Stevens	1-5	1st round	BCE Belgian Classic
	v Thorne	4-5	1st round	Benson & Hedges Masters
	v W. Jones	4-6	Quarter-final	Zetters Welsh Championship
	v John Rea	3-5	3rd round	Dulux British Open
	v E. Hughes	2-5	1st round	Benson & Hedges Irish Masters
	v Campbell	8-10	1st round	Embassy World Championship
	v W. Jones	5-4	3rd round	BCE International
	v Gauvreau	2-5	4th round	BCE International
	v Chaperon	3-5	3rd round	Rothmans Grand Prix
	v M. Gibson	9-6	3rd round	Tennents UK Open
	v E. Hughes	5-9	4th round	Tennents UK Open
1987	v Hendry	3-5	3rd round	Mercantile Credit Classic

v Johnson	2-5	1st round	Benson & Hedges Masters
v Chappel	4-6	Quarter-final	Matchroom Welsh Championship
v O'Boye	5-4	3rd round	Dulux British Open
v Murphy	4-5	4th round	Dulux British Open
v West	10-5	1st round	Embassy World Championship
v S. Davis	4-13	2nd round	Embassy World Championship

JIM REMPE (USA)

Born 4.11.47
Turned professional 1980
World ranking 102 (110)

1985	v Burke	5-3	1st round	Goya Matchroom Trophy
	v Wych	1-5	2nd round	Goya Matchroom Trophy
	v Agrawal	2-5	1st round	Rothmans Grand Prix
1987	v Smith	10-9	Qualifying	Embassy World Championship
	v John Rea	10-9	Qualifying	Embassy World Championship
	v Hendry	4-10	Qualifying	Embassy World Championship

DEAN REYNOLDS (England)

Born 11.1.63
Turned professional 1981
World ranking 15 (29)
Best professional performance Semi-finals 1987 Mercantile Credit Classic.

1982	v Sheehan	9-5	Qualifying	Embassy World Championship
	v Edmonds	9-6	Qualifying	Embassy World Championship
	v F. Davis	10-7	1st round	Embassy World Championship
	v S. Francisco	8-13	2nd round	Embassy World Championship
	v Morra	5-1	Qualifying	Jameson International
	v Thorne	5-3	1st round	Jameson International
	v S. Davis	0-5	2nd round	Jameson International
	v Fitzmaurice	5-0	2nd round	Professional Players Tournament
	v Wilson	5-1	3rd round	Professional Players Tournament
	v Charlton	2-5	Quarter-final	Professional Players Tournament
	v Fisher	9-6	1st round	Coral UK Championship
	v Higgins	8-9	2nd round	Coral UK Championship
1983	v Reardon	1-5	1st round	Benson & Hedges Masters
	v Edmonds	10-6	Qualifying	Embassy World Championship
	v Higgins	4-10	1st round	Embassy World Championship

	v Williams	5-3	Qualifying	Jameson International
	v Dennis Taylor	3-5	1st round	Jameson International
	v Greaves	5-1	1st round	Professional Players Tournament
	v Meo	0-5	2nd round	Professional Players Tournament
	v Medati	3-9	1st round	Coral UK Championship
1984	v Griffiths	2-5	Qualifying	Lada Classic
	v Morra	7-10	Qualifying	Embassy World Championship
	v Bales	5-4	Qualifying	Jameson International
	v Knowles	1-5	1st round	Jameson International
	v Fowler	5-2	1st round	Rothmans Grand Prix
	v P. Francisco	5-4	2nd round	Rothmans Grand Prix
	v S. Francisco	5-1	3rd round	Rothmans Grand Prix
	v S. Davis	0-5	Quarter-final	Rothmans Grand Prix
	v Chappel	6-9	Qualifying	Coral UK Open
1985	v King	2-5	Qualifying	Mercantile Credit Classic
	v Fitzmaurice	9-2	1st round	Tolly Cobbold English Championship
	v Thorne	9-6	2nd round	Tolly Cobbold English Championship
	v Meo	4-9	Quarter-final	Tolly Cobbold English Championship
	v Giannaros	6-3	1st round	Dulux British Open
	v Thorburn	3-5	2nd round	Dulux British Open
	v Gauvreau	10-1	Qualifying	Embassy World Championship
	v Higgins	4-10	1st round	Embassy World Championship
	v Mikkelsen	5-0	3rd round	Goya Matchroom Trophy
	v Gibson	5-0	4th round	Goya Matchroom Trophy
	v White	1-5	5th round	Goya Matchroom Trophy
	v Miles	3-5	3rd round	Rothmans Grand Prix
	v J. McLaughlin	9-7	3rd round	Coral UK Open
	v Griffiths	7-9	4th round	Coral UK Open
1986	v Houlihan	5-1	3rd round	Mercantile Credit Classic
	v Dennis Taylor	4-5	4th round	Mercantile Credit Classic
	v Longworth	9-5	3rd round	Tolly Cobbold English Championship
	v Thorne	9-8	4th round	Tolly Cobbold English Championship
	v Meo	4-9	Quarter-final	Tolly Cobbold English Championship
	v Wych	3-5	3rd round	Dulux British Open
	v Stevens	6-10	1st round	Embassy World Championship
	v Dodd	5-2	3rd round	BCE International
	v Mountjoy	5-2	4th round	BCE International
	v David Taylor	5-1	5th round	BCE International
	v N. Foulds	2-5	Quarter-final	BCE International
	v Newbury	0-5	3rd round	Rothmans Grand Prix
	v Mikkelsen	9-6	3rd round	Tennents UK Open
	v S. Francisco	9-8	4th round	Tennents UK Open
	v S. Davis	5-9	5th round	Tennents UK Open
1987	v King	5-4	3rd round	Mercantile Credit Classic
	v Thorburn	5-4	4th round	Mercantile Credit Classic
	v West	5-3	5th round	Mercantile Credit Classic
	v Wilson	5-1	Quarter-final	Mercantile Credit Classic
	v White	8-9	Semi-final	Mercantile Credit Classic
	v Edmonds	6-3	3rd round	Tolly Ales English Championship
	v White	6-5	4th round	Tolly Ales English Championship

v Thorne	4-6	Quarter-final	Tolly Ales English Championship
v N. Gilbert	5-3	3rd round	Dulux British Open
v Knowles	0-5	4th round	Dulux British Open
v Oliver	10-7	Qualifying	Embassy World Championship
v White	8-10	1st round	Embassy World Championship

GINO RIGITANO (Canada)

Born 14.8.57
Turned professional 1983
World ranking 86 (86)

1984	v Gibson	7-10	Qualifying	Embassy World Championship
	v Foldvari	2-5	Qualifying	Jameson International
	v Edmonds	5-3	Qualifying	Rothmans Grand Prix
	v Thorburn	4-5	1st round	Rothmans Grand Prix
	v Newbury	6-9	Qualifying	Coral UK Open
1985	v Fowler	0-5	Qualifying	Mercantile Credit Classic
	v Thorburn	3-6	1st round	Dulux British Open
	v Sheehan	10-9	Qualifying	Embassy World Championship
	v B. Harris	10-4	Qualifying	Embassy World Championship
	v Kelly	10-6	Qualifying	Embassy World Championship
	v Fisher	10-2	Qualifying	Embassy World Championship
	v N. Foulds	8-10	Qualifying	Embassy World Championship
	v Black	4-5	2nd round	Goya Matchroom Trophy
	v Miles	4-5	2nd round	Rothmans Grand Prix
1986	v Dodd	5-3	2nd round	Mercantile Credit Classic
	v Knowles	4-5	3rd round	Mercantile Credit Classic
	v W. Jones	1-5	2nd round	Dulux British Open
	v Foldvari	6-10	Qualifying	Embassy World Championship
	v Jonik	1-6	1st round	Canadian Championship
	v Greaves	5-3	1st round	BCE International
	v King	0-5	2nd round	BCE International
	v Everton	5-1	1st round	Rothmans Grand Prix
	v Medati	1-5	2nd round	Rothmans Grand Prix
	v James	5-9	1st round	Tennents UK Open
1987	v Grace	5-4	1st round	Mercantile Credit Classic
	v Gauvreau	0-5	2nd round	Mercantile Credit Classic
	v Demarco	5-1	1st round	Dulux British Open
	v Browne	5-4	2nd round	Dulux British Open
	v Hallett	0-5	3rd round	Dulux British Open
	v Morgan	4-0 *retd*	Qualifying	Embassy World Championship
	v V. Harris	10-6	Qualifying	Embassy World Championship
	v Newbury	4-10	Qualifying	Embassy World Championship

DAVID ROE (England)

Born 11.9.65
Turned professional 1986
World ranking 84 (–)

1986	v D. Hughes	5-2	1st round	BCE International
	v Miles	1-5	2nd round	BCE International
	v Hargreaves	5-1	1st round	Rothmans Grand Prix
	v Van Rensberg	5-3	2nd round	Rothmans Grand Prix
	v Knowles	3-5	3rd round	Rothmans Grand Prix
	v G. Foulds	7-1	1st round	Tennents UK Open
	v Van Rensberg	9-6	2nd round	Tennents UK Open
	v Dennis Taylor	6-9	3rd round	Tennents UK Open
1987	v Darrington	5-0	1st round	Mercantile Credit Classic
	v Chaperon	4-5	2nd round	Mercantile Credit Classic
	v Greaves	6-1	1st round	Tolly Ales English Championship
	v Williamson	4-6	2nd round	Tolly Ales English Championship
	v Watterson	5-3	1st round	Dulux British Open
	v Black	5-0	2nd round	Dulux British Open
	v N. Foulds	1-5	3rd round	Dulux British Open
	v King	4-10	Qualifying	Embassy World Championship

COLIN ROSCOE (Wales)

Born 30.6.45
Turned professional 1981
World ranking 79 (74)
Amateur career 1981 Welsh champion.

1981	v Macleod	9-7	Qualifying	Coral UK Championship
	v Williams	4-9	Qualifying	Coral UK Championship
	v Andrewartha	5-2	Qualifying	Jameson International
	v Sheehan	5-1	Qualifying	Jameson International
	v Meadowcroft	4-5	Qualifying	Jameson International
1982	v Griffiths	2-6	1st round	Welsh Championship
	v Mikkelsen	9-6	Qualifying	Embassy World Championship
	v Thorne	1-9	Qualifying	Embassy World Championship
	v Dunning	5-2	Qualifying	Jameson International
	v French	5-2	Qualifying	Jameson International
	v S. Davis	0-5	1st round	Jameson International
	v Griffiths	1-5	1st round	Professional Players Tournament
	v Jack Rea	9-6	Qualifying	Coral UK Championship
	v Wildman	4-9	Qualifying	Coral UK Championship
1983	v Wilson	4-6	Quarter-final	Woodpecker Welsh Championship
	v Sinclair	2-10	Qualifying	Embassy World Championship
	v Hallett	2-5	Qualifying	Jameson International
	v Meadowcroft	4-5	1st round	Professional Players Tournament
	v N. Foulds	2-9	Qualifying	Coral UK Championship

1984	v Ganim	5-3	Qualifying	Lada Classic
	v Miles	5-2	Qualifying	Lada Classic
	v Werbeniuk	5-4	1st round	Lada Classic
	v Griffiths	2-5	2nd round	Lada Classic
	v Wilson	2-6	1st round	Strongbow Welsh Championship
	v Demarco	10-7	Qualifying	Embassy World Championship
	v Browne	4-10	Qualifying	Embassy World Championship
	v Mikkelsen	5-1	Qualifying	Jameson International
	v French	5-0	Qualifying	Rothmans Grand Prix
	v Reardon	1-5	1st round	Rothmans Grand Prix
	v J. McLaughlin	8-9	Qualifying	Coral UK Open
1985	v Medati	4-5	Qualifying	Mercantile Credit Classic
	v Giannaros	1-6	Qualifying	Dulux British Open
	v G. Foulds	7-10	Qualifying	Embassy World Championship
	v Wilson	3-6	Quarter-final	BCE Welsh Championship
	v G. Foulds	5-3	2nd round	Goya Matchroom Trophy
	v Wilson	1-5	3rd round	Goya Matchroom Trophy
	v Watson	2-5	2nd round	Rothmans Grand Prix
	v West	5-9	2nd round	Coral UK Open
1986	v V. Harris	1-5	2nd round	Mercantile Credit Classic
	v Mountjoy	4-6	Quarter-final	Zetters Welsh Championship
	v Mikkelsen	5-4	2nd round	Dulux British Open
	v Parrott	2-5	3rd round	Dulux British Open
	v G. Foulds	10-3	Qualifying	Embassy World Championship
	v King	5-10	Qualifying	Embassy World Championship
	v Parkin	5-1	1st round	BCE International
	v Chappel	3-5	2nd round	BCE International
	v Burke	3-5	1st round	Rothmans Grand Prix
	v Parkin	9-1	1st round	Tennents UK Open
	v Wildman	9-6	2nd round	Tennents UK Open
	v E. Hughes	8-9	3rd round	Tennents UK Open
1987	v Whitthread	5-1	1st round	Mercantile Credit Classic
	Roscoe *wo* Fran *scr*		2nd round	Mercantile Credit Classic
	v Higgins	2-5	3rd round	Mercantile Credit Classic
	v Everton	6-2	1st round	Matchroom Welsh Championship
	v Mountjoy	2-6	Quarter-final	Matchroom Welsh Championship
	v Mienie	5-2	1st round	Dulux British Open
	v Newbury	5-3	2nd round	Dulux British Open
	v Dennis Taylor	1-5	3rd round	Dulux British Open
	v Whitthread	10-2	Qualifying	Embassy World Championship
	v Duggan	7-10	Qualifying	Embassy World Championship

BRIAN ROWSWELL (England)

Born 18.3.67
Turned professional 1986
World ranking 91 (–)

1986	v Sheehan	5-4	1st round	BCE International
	v Wildman	2-5	2nd round	BCE International

v D. Gilbert	1-5	1st round	Rothmans Grand Prix
v F. Davis	9-4	2nd round	Tennents UK Open
v Longworth	3-9	3rd round	Tennents UK Open
1987 v Watterson	5-1	1st round	Mercantile Credit Classic
v Bradley	4-5	2nd round	Mercantile Credit Classic
v Smith	5-6	1st round	Tolly Ales English Championship
v Jenkins	5-1	1st round	Dulux British Open
v O'Kane	5-4	2nd round	Dulux British Open
v S. Francisco	0-5	3rd round	Dulux British Open
v Bradley	6-10	Qualifying	Embassy World Championship

GEORGE SCOTT (England)

Born 16.9.29
Turned professional 1981
World ranking 61 (44)
Best professional performance Last 32 1985 Goya Matchroom Trophy,
1985 Rothmans Grand Prix.

1982 v B. Harris	5-4	Qualifying	Jameson International
v Thorburn	1-5	1st round	Jameson International
v Meo	5-9	Qualifying	Coral UK Championship
1983 v Houlihan	5-0	Qualifying	Jameson International
v Gibson	5-3	Qualifying	Jameson International
v Werbeniuk	5-3	1st round	Jameson International
v Griffiths	0-5	2nd round	Jameson International
v Dennis Taylor	5-4	1st round	Professional Players Tournament
v S. Francisco	1-5	2nd round	Professional Players Tournament
v Parrott	7-9	Qualifying	Coral UK Championship
1984 v Heywood	10-7	Qualifying	Embassy World Championship
v Wych	6-10	Qualifying	Embassy World Championship
v W. Jones	0-5	Qualifying	Jameson International
v Chappel	1-5	Qualifying	Rothmans Grand Prix
v O'Kane	9-7	Qualifying	Coral UK Open
v Macleod	5-9	Qualifying	Coral UK Open
1985 v J. McLaughlin	5-4	Qualifying	Mercantile Credit Classic
v Campbell	5-4	Qualifying	Mercantile Credit Classic
v Thorburn	1-5	1st round	Mercantile Credit Classic
v V. Harris	9-7	Qualifying	Tolly Cobbold English Championship
v Johnson	1-9	1st round	Tolly Cobbold English Championship
v Darrington	6-3	Qualifying	Dulux British Open
v Dennis Taylor	2-6	1st round	Dulux British Open
v Newbury	2-10	Qualifying	Embassy World Championship
v Van Rensberg	5-4	2nd round	Goya Matchroom Trophy
v Wildman	5-1	3rd round	Goya Matchroom Trophy
v Thorne	1-5	4th round	Goya Matchroom Trophy
v Chalmers	5-2	2nd round	Rothmans Grand Prix
v Reardon	5-4	3rd round	Rothmans Grand Prix
v Wilson	3-5	4th round	Rothmans Grand Prix
v Sheehan	6-9	2nd round	Coral UK Open

1986	v Mikkelsen	1-5	2nd round	Mercantile Credit Classic
	v Bennett	9-1	2nd round	Tolly Cobbold English Championship
	v Meo	1-9	3rd round	Tolly Cobbold English Championship
	v Chalmers	5-1	2nd round	Dulux British Open
	v Griffiths	3-5	3rd round	Dulux British Open
	v Kearney	10-8	Qualifying	Embassy World Championship
	v Fowler	7-10	Qualifying	Embassy World Championship
	v Owers	1-5	2nd round	BCE International
	v Dodd	2-5	2nd round	Rothmans Grand Prix
	v Watchorn	9-7	2nd round	Tennents UK Open
	v Stevens	2-9	3rd round	Tennents UK Open
1987	v Jenkins	4-5	2nd round	Mercantile Credit Classic
	v Fitzmaurice	2-6	2nd round	Tolly Ales English Championship
	v Burke	5-2	2nd round	Dulux British Open
	v Martin	3-5	3rd round	Dulux British Open
	v Dunning	10-7	Qualifying	Embassy World Championship
	v Oliver	5-10	Qualifying	Embassy World Championship

DESSIE SHEEHAN (Republic of Ireland)

Born 3.9.49
Turned professional 1981
World ranking 95 (81)
Amateur career 1980 Republic of Ireland champion.

1981	v V. Harris	5-1	Qualifying	Jameson International
	v Roscoe	1-5	Qualifying	Jameson International
1982	v E. Hughes	1-6	1st round	Irish Championship
	v V. Harris	3-5	Qualifying	Jameson International
	v Dennis Taylor	3-5	1st round	Benson & Hedges Irish Masters
	v Reynolds	5-9	Qualifying	Embassy World Championship
	v Fitzmaurice	1-5	1st round	Professional Players Tournament
1983	v Donnelly	6-10	Qualifying	Embassy World Championship
	v Murphy	2-5	Qualifying	Jameson International
	v Houlihan	5-2	Qualifying	Professional Players Tournament
	v Williams	1-5	1st round	Professional Players Tournament
1984	v B. Harris	3-10	Qualifying	Embassy World Championship
	v Bales	2-5	Qualifying	Jameson International
	v Mikkelsen	5-3	Qualifying	Rothmans Grand Prix
	v Hallett	1-5	1st round	Rothmans Grand Prix
	v P. Francisco	5-9	Qualifying	Coral UK Open
1985	v John Rea	5-2	Qualifying	Mercantile Credit Classic
	v E. McLaughlin	2-5	Qualifying	Mercantile Credit Classic
	v Murphy	3-6	Qualifying	Dulux British Open
	v J. McLaughlin	3-6	Qualifying	Irish Championship
	v Rigitano	9-10	Qualifying	Embassy World Championship
	v Smith	2-5	1st round	Goya Matchroom Trophy
	v Watson	1-5	1st round	Rothmans Grand Prix
	v Watchorn	9-7	1st round	Coral UK Open
	v Scott	9-6	2nd round	Coral UK Open

	v S. Davis	1-9	3rd round	Coral UK Open
1986	v Hendry	2-5	1st round	Mercantile Credit Classic
	v Simngam	5-2	1st round	Dulux British Open
	Sheehan wo			
	Watterson scr		2nd round	Dulux British Open
	v Thorburn	0-5	3rd round	Dulux British Open
	v Houlihan	10-7	Qualifying	Embassy World Championship
	v King	4-10	Qualifying	Embassy World Championship
	v E. Hughes	0-5	1st round	Strongbow Irish Championship
	v Rowswell	4-5	1st round	BCE International
	v Demarco	5-1	1st round	Rothmans Grand Prix
	v Browne	4-5	2nd round	Rothmans Grand Prix
	v M. Bennett	9-8	1st round	Tennents UK Open
	v Miles	8-9	2nd round	Tennents UK Open
1987	v M. Bennett	3-5	1st round	Mercantile Credit Classic
	v Wright	5-2	1st round	Dulux British Open
	v V. Harris	4-5	2nd round	Dulux British Open
	v N. Gilbert	6-10	Qualifying	Embassy World Championship
	v J. McLaughlin	5-4	1st round	Matchroom Irish Championship
	v Dennis Taylor	3-6	Quarter-final	Matchroom Irish Championship

EDDIE SINCLAIR (Scotland)

Born 5.5.37
Turned professional 1979
World ranking 77 (70)
Amateur career 7 times Scottish champion between 1960 and 1976.
Best professional performance Scottish champion 1980, 1982.

1980	v Meadowcroft	1-9	Qualifying	Embassy World Championship
	v Kennerley	9-1	Qualifying	Coral UK Championship
	v Miles	9-5	1st round	Coral UK Championship
	v Dennis Taylor	6-9	2nd round	Coral UK Championship
1981	v Donnelly	0-5	Quarter-final	Scottish Championship
	v Morgan	9-8	Qualifying	Embassy World Championship
	v Wilson	4-9	Qualifying	Embassy World Championship
	v E. Hughes	2-5	Qualifying	Jameson International
	v Wildman	9-8	Qualifying	Coral UK Championship
	v Hood	9-0	Qualifying	Coral UK Championship
	v Martin	7-9	Qualifying	Coral UK Championship
1982	v Kelly	9-8	Qualifying	Embassy World Championship
	v Donnelly	8-9	Qualifying	Embassy World Championship
	v Phillips	6-3	Quarter-final	Scottish Championship
	v Gibson	6-2	Semi-final	Scottish Championship
	v Black	**11-7**	**Final**	**Scottish Championship**
	v Higgins	1-5	1st round	Langs Supreme Scottish Masters
	v Anderson	5-2	Qualifying	Jameson International
	v Meo	5-3	Qualifying	Jameson International
	v Knowles	2-5	1st round	Jameson International

v F. Davis	5-2	1st round	Professional Players Tournament
v Meadowcroft	5-3	2nd round	Professional Players Tournament
v Griffiths	3-5	3rd round	Professional Players Tournament
v Murphy	9-5	Qualifying	Coral UK Championship
v Spencer	8-9	1st round	Coral UK Championship
1983 v Roscoe	10-2	Qualifying	Embassy World Championship
v E. Hughes	8-10	Qualifying	Embassy World Championship
v Donnelly	6-5	Semi-final	Scottish Championship
v Macleod	9-11	Final	Scottish Championship
v Andrewartha	5-4	Qualifying	Jameson International
v Thorburn	0-5	1st round	Jameson International
v E. Hughes	4-5	1st round	Professional Players Tournament
v T. Jones	3-9	Qualifying	Coral UK Championship
1984 v S. Davis	2-5	Qualifying	Lada Classic
v Browne	10-1	Qualifying	Embassy World Championship
v Stevens	1-10	1st round	Embassy World Championship
v Duggan	5-0	Qualifying	Jameson International
v Mans	5-2	Qualifying	Jameson International
v Higgins	1-5	1st round	Jameson International
v T. Jones	4-5	Qualifying	Rothmans Grand Prix
v P. Francisco	9-8	Qualifying	Coral UK Open
v S. Francisco	4-9	Qualifying	Coral UK Open
v Demarco	6-3	1st round	Scottish Championship
v John Rea	6-2	Semi-final	Scottish Championship
v Macleod	2-10	Final	Scottish Championship
1985 v Newbury	3-6	1st round	Dulux British Open
v T. Jones	2-10	Qualifying	Embassy World Championship
v Darrington	5-0	2nd round	Goya Matchroom Trophy
v Martin	1-5	3rd round	Goya Matchroom Trophy
v Fitzmaurice	3-5	2nd round	Rothmans Grand Prix
v G. Foulds	9-4	2nd round	Coral UK Open
v Parrott	2-9	3rd round	Coral UK Open
1986 v Greaves	5-1	2nd round	Mercantile Credit Classic
v Macleod	2-5	3rd round	Mercantile Credit Classic
v B. Harris	3-5	2nd round	Dulux British Open
v Gibson	4-6	Quarter-final	Canada Dry Scottish Championship
v Morgan	10-8	Qualifying	Embassy World Championship
v Van Rensberg	2-10	Qualifying	Embassy World Championship
v Fagan	5-0	2nd round	BCE International
v Higgins	3-5	3rd round	BCE International
v John Rea	4-5	2nd round	Rothmans Grand Prix
v Mikkelsen	8-9	2nd round	Tennents UK Open
1987 v Miles	5-1	2nd round	Mercantile Credit Classic
v Johnson	0-5	3rd round	Mercantile Credit Classic
v M. Gibson	6-2	1st round	Scottish Championship
v Donnelly	4-6	Semi-final	Scottish Championship
v Hendry	5-2	2nd round	Dulux British Open
v P. Francisco	3-5	3rd round	Dulux British Open
v Drago	10-9	Qualifying	Embassy World Championship
v Edmonds	6-10	Qualifying	Embassy World Championship

Dean Reynolds

Dennis Taylor

MARTIN SMITH (England)

Born –
Turned professional 1985
World ranking 108 (94)

1985 v Sheehan	5-2	1st round	Goya Matchroom Trophy
v W. Jones	3-5	2nd round	Goya Matchroom Trophy
v Bales	1-5	1st round	Rothmans Grand Prix
v Wilkinson	9-4	1st round	Coral UK Open
1986 v Mienie	5-1	1st round	Mercantile Credit Classic
v Edmonds	5-2	2nd round	Mercantile Credit Classic
v Mans	4-5	3rd round	Mercantile Credit Classic
v Edmonds	8-9	2nd round	Tolly Cobbold English Championship
v Kearney	2-5	1st round	Dulux British Open
v Greaves	10-4	Qualifying	Embassy World Championship
v Donnelly	6-10	Qualifying	Embassy World Championship
v M. Bennett	4-5	1st round	BCE International
v Hines	5-2	1st round	Rothmans Grand Prix
v T. Jones	0-5	2nd round	Rothmans Grand Prix
v Wright	7-9	1st round	Tennents UK Open
1987 v N. Gilbert	2-5	1st round	Mercantile Credit Classic
v Rowswell	6-5	1st round	Tolly Ales English Championship
v Dodd	3-6	2nd round	Tolly Ales English Championship
v Ellis	2-5	1st round	Dulux British Open
v Rempe	9-10	Qualifying	Embassy World Championship

JOHN SPENCER (England)

Born 18.9.35
Turned professional 1967
World ranking 28 (34)
Amateur career 1964 English amateur champion.
Best professional performances Winner World Championship 1969, 1970, 1977, Benson & Hedges Masters 1975, Benson & Hedges Irish Masters 1978.

1969 v Pulman	30-19	Quarter-final	World Championship
v Williams	55-18	Semi-final	World Championship
v G. Owen	**46-27**	**Final**	**World Championship**
1970 v Jack Rea	31-15	Quarter-final	World Championship (Apr)
v Reardon	33-37	Semi-final	World Championship (Apr)
v Reardon	34-15	Semi-final	World Championship (Nov)
v Simpson	**42-31**	**Final**	**World Championship (Nov)**
1972 v F. Davis	31-21	Quarter-final	World Championship
v Charlton	37-32	Semi-final	World Championship
v Higgins	32-37	Final	World Championship
1973 v David Taylor	16-5	2nd round	World Championship
v Williams	16-7	Quarter-final	World Championship

v Reardon	22-23	Semi-final	World Championship
1974 v Mans	13-15	2nd round	World Championship
1975 v Pulman	5-3	Quarter-final	Benson & Hedges Masters
v Charlton	5-2	Semi-final	Benson & Hedges Masters
v Reardon	**9-8**	**Final**	**Benson & Hedges Masters**
v Pulman	15-10	2nd round	World Championship
v Reardon	17-19	Quarter-final	World Championship
1976 v Miles	4-5	Semi-final	Benson & Hedges Masters
v David Taylor	15-5	1st round	Embassy World Championship
v Higgins	14-15	Quarter-final	Embassy World Championship
1977 v Virgo	13-9	1st round	Embassy World Championship
v Reardon	13-6	Quarter-final	Embassy World Championship
v Pulman	18-16	Semi-final	Embassy World Championship
v Thorburn	**25-21**	**Final**	**Embassy World Championship**
v Mountjoy	3-5	2nd round	Super Crystalate UK Championship
1978 v Thorburn	3-5	Semi-final	Benson & Hedges Masters
v Mountjoy	**5-3**	**Final**	**Benson & Hedges Irish Masters**
v Mans	8-13	1st round	Embassy World Championship
v Andrewartha	8-9	1st round	Coral UK Championship
1979 v Williams	6-2	Semi-final	Holsten Lager International
v Miles	**11-7**	**Final**	**Holsten Lager International**
v Mountjoy	0-5	Quarter-final	Benson & Hedges Masters
v Werbeniuk	11-13	1st round	Embassy World Championship
v Werbeniuk	8-9	3rd round	Coral UK Championship
1980 v Charlton	5-2	Quarter-final	Benson & Hedges Masters
v Griffiths	0-5	Semi-final	Benson & Hedges Masters
v Stevens	8-13	2nd round	Embassy World Championship
v Wildman	7-9	1st round	Coral UK Championship
1981 v Dennis Taylor	5-2	1st round	Benson & Hedges Masters
v Reardon	5-1	Quarter-final	Benson & Hedges Masters
v Griffiths	5-6	Semi-final	Benson & Hedges Masters
v Houlihan	9-1	1st round	John Courage English
v S. Davis	7-9	2nd round	John Courage English
v Edmonds	10-9	1st round	Embassy World Championship
v Reardon	11-13	2nd round	Embassy World Championship
v Edmonds	5-3	2nd round	Jameson International
v Griffiths	2-5	3rd round	Jameson International
v Johnson	5-9	2nd round	Coral UK Championship
1982 v S. Davis	2-5	1st round	Lada Classic
v Mountjoy	4-5	1st round	Benson & Hedges Masters
v Meo	3-5	1st round	Benson & Hedges Irish Masters
v Dunning	10-4	1st round	Embassy World Championship
v Thorne	5-13	2nd round	Embassy World Championship
v Edmonds	5-2	1st round	Jameson International
v Virgo	4-5	2nd round	Jameson International
v G. Foulds	5-1	1st round	Professional Players Tournament
v Martin	5-3	2nd round	Professional Players Tournament
v Virgo	1-5	3rd round	Professional Players Tournament
v Sinclair	9-8	1st round	Coral UK Championship

	v Knowles	9-6	2nd round	Coral UK Championship
	v Higgins	5-9	Quarter-final	Coral UK Championship
1983	v Reardon	5-3	1st round	Lada Classic
	v David Taylor	5-2	Quarter-final	Lada Classic
	v S. Davis	4-5	Semi-final	Lada Classic
	v Hallett	10-7	1st round	Embassy World Championship
	v Charlton	11-13	2nd round	Embassy World Championship
	v Higgins	2-3	1st round	Winfield Masters
	v Morgan	5-1	1st round	Jameson International
	v Knowles	5-4	2nd round	Jameson International
	v Griffiths	4-5	Quarter-final	Jameson International
	v Black	5-2	1st round	Professional Players Tournament
	v Thorne	1-5	2nd round	Professional Players Tournament
	v Dunning	9-7	1st round	Coral UK Championship
	v Meo	5-9	2nd round	Coral UK Championship
1984	v Johnson	5-4	Qualifying	Lada Classic
	v S. Davis	1-5	1st round	Lada Classic
	v Thorburn	5-4	1st round	Benson & Hedges Masters
	v Griffiths	4-5	Quarter-final	Benson & Hedges Masters
	v Miles	10-3	1st round	Embassy World Championship
	v S. Davis	5-13	2nd round	Embassy World Championship
	v S. Francisco	2-5	1st round	Jameson International
	v P. Francisco	2-5	1st round	Rothmans Grand Prix
	v Johnson	6-9	1st round	Coral UK Open
1985	v King	2-5	1st round	Mercantile Credit Classic
	v Charlton	5-3	1st round	Benson & Hedges Masters
	v White	2-5	Quarter-final	Benson & Hedges Masters
	v Medati	4-9	1st round	Tolly Cobbold English Championship
	v Jonik	6-0	1st round	Dulux British Open
	v Miles	3-5	2nd round	Dulux British Open
	v Parrott	3-10	1st round	Embassy World Championship
	v Foldvari	5-4	3rd round	Goya Matchroom Trophy
	v Griffiths	1-5	4th round	Goya Matchroom Trophy
	v B. Harris	2-5	3rd round	Rothmans Grand Prix
	v V. Harris	9-5	3rd round	Coral UK Open
	v Knowles	7-9	4th round	Coral UK Open
	v S. Davis	2-5	1st round	Kit Kat
1986	v Cripsey	1-5	3rd round	Mercantile Credit Classic
	v Houlihan	9-5	3rd round	Tolly Cobbold English Championship
	v Johnson	7-9	4th round	Tolly Cobbold English Championship
	v Browne	0-5	3rd round	Dulux British Open
	v Higgins	7-10	1st round	Embassy World Championship
	v Williamson	5-2	2nd round	BCE International
	v Knowles	0-5	3rd round	BCE International
	v Burke	5-3	2nd round	Rothmans Grand Prix
	v S. Francisco	4-5	3rd round	Rothmans Grand Prix
	v Foldvari	9-6	2nd round	Tennents UK Open
	v Wilson	9-5	3rd round	Tennents UK Open
	v Stevens	9-4	4th round	Tennents UK Open

	v Thorburn	2-9	5th round	Tennents UK Open
1987	v D. Gilbert	5-4	2nd round	Mercantile Credit Classic
	v Thorne	5-3	3rd round	Mercantile Credit Classic
	v Campbell	3-5	4th round	Mercantile Credit Classic
	v Wright	6-1	2nd round	Tolly Ales English Championship
	v Martin	5-6	3rd round	Tolly Ales English Championship
	v Whitthread	5-2	2nd round	Dulux British Open
	v Meo	5-1	3rd round	Dulux British Open
	v Martin	5-2	4th round	Dulux British Open
	v Johnson	5-3	5th round	Dulux British Open
	v White	3-5	Quarter-final	Dulux British Open
	v Bales	10-3	Qualifying	Embassy World Championship
	v Chaperon	10-4	Qualifying	Embassy World Championship
	v West	5-10	Qualifying	Embassy World Championship

KIRK STEVENS (Canada)

Born 17.8.58
Turned professional 1978
World ranking 21 (9)
Best professional performances Semi-finals Embassy World Championship 1980, 1984; runner-up 1985 Dulux British Open.

1979	v Amdor	9-1	Prelim	Embassy World Championship
	v Pulman	9-0	Qualifying	Embassy World Championship
	v F. Davis	8-13	1st round	Embassy World Championship
1980	v Hallett	9-3	Qualifying	Embassy World Championship
	v Miles	10-3	1st round	Embassy World Championship
	v Spencer	13-8	2nd round	Embassy World Championship
	v Charlton	13-7	Quarter-final	Embassy World Championship
	v Higgins	13-16	Semi-final	Embassy World Championship
1981	v F. Davis	4-5	1st round	Benson & Hedges Masters
	v David Taylor	3-5	Semi-final	Yamaha International Masters
	v Dunning	10-4	1st round	Embassy World Championship
	v Dennis Taylor	11-13	2nd round	Embassy World Championship
	v Thorburn	1-5	Quarter-final	Langs Supreme Scottish Masters
	v Meadowcroft	5-1	2nd round	Jameson International
	v David Taylor	0-5	3rd round	Jameson International
	v Griffiths	0-5	1st round	Northern Ireland Classic
	v Hallett	9-4	2nd round	Coral UK Championship
	v Werbeniuk	7-9	3rd round	Coral UK Championship
1982	v Fitzmaurice	10-4	1st round	Embassy World Championship
	v Fagan	13-7	2nd round	Embassy World Championship
	v White	9-13	Quarter-final	Embassy World Championship
	v Watterson	5-3	1st round	Jameson International
	v Mans	5-2	2nd round	Jameson International
	v Griffiths	5-3	Quarter-final	Jameson International
	v Knowles	3-9	Semi-final	Jameson International
	v E. Hughes	5-2	1st round	Professional Players Tournament

v Johnson	1-5	2nd round	Professional Players Tournament
1983 v Knowles	5-0	1st round	Lada Classic
v Thorburn	5-3	Quarter-final	Lada Classic
v Werbeniuk	2-5	Semi-final	Lada Classic
v Griffiths	3-5	1st round	Benson & Hedges Masters
v Fisher	10-2	1st round	Embassy World Championship
v Mans	13-3	2nd round	Embassy World Championship
v Thorburn	12-13	Quarter-final	Embassy World Championship
v Thorburn	2-5	Semi-final	Winfield Masters
v Edmonds	5-1	1st round	Professional Players Tournament
v Murphy	5-1	2nd round	Professional Players Tournament
v Wildman	5-0	3rd round	Professional Players Tournament
v Meo	3-5	Quarter-final	Professional Players Tournament
1984 v E. McLaughlin	5-4	Qualifying	Lada Classic
v Macleod	5-1	1st round	Lada Classic
v Meo	2-5	Quarter-final	Lada Classic
v David Taylor	5-1	1st round	Benson & Hedges Masters
v S. Davis	5-3	Quarter-final	Benson & Hedges Masters
v White	4-6	Semi-final	Benson & Hedges Masters
v Charlton	5-3	1st round	Tolly Cobbold Classic
v S. Davis	4-5	Semi-final	Tolly Cobbold Classic
v Sinclair	10-1	1st round	Embassy World Championship
v David Taylor	13-10	2nd round	Embassy World Championship
v Reardon	13-2	Quarter-final	Embassy World Championship
v White	14-16	Semi-final	Embassy World Championship
v Meo	1-5	Quarter-final	Winfield Australian Masters
v Higgins	2-5	1st round	Langs Supreme Scottish Masters
v White	0-5	1st round	Carlsberg Challenge
v Gauvreau	1-5	1st round	Jameson International
v Chappel	5-3	1st round	Rothmans Grand Prix
v Williams	5-3	2nd round	Rothmans Grand Prix
v Hallett	5-3	3rd round	Rothmans Grand Prix
v Dennis Taylor	2-5	Quarter-final	Rothmans Grand Prix
v Chappel	9-7	1st round	Coral UK Open
v Johnson	9-2	2nd round	Coral UK Open
v Knowles	9-7	Quarter-final	Coral UK Open
v S. Davis	2-9	Semi-final	Coral UK Open
1985 v Medati	5-4	1st round	Mercantile Credit Classic
v Thorne	1-5	2nd round	Mercantile Credit Classic
v Meo	2-5	1st round	Benson & Hedges Masters
v Gauvreau	6-3	1st round	Dulux British Open
v Wildman	5-2	2nd round	Dulux British Open
v Miles	5-2	3rd round	Dulux British Open
v Dennis Taylor	5-2	Quarter-final	Dulux British Open
v S. Davis	9-7	Semi-final	Dulux British Open
v S. Francisco	9-12	Final	Dulux British Open
v Higgins	3-5	Quarter-final	Benson & Hedges Irish Masters
v Edmonds	10-8	1st round	Embassy World Championship
v Parrott	6-13	2nd round	Embassy World Championship
v Chaperon	4-6	Quarter-final	Canadian Championship

v Chappel	3-5	3rd round	Goya Matchroom Trophy
v Watson	5-0	3rd round	Rothmans Grand Prix
v Miles	5-2	4th round	Rothmans Grand Prix
v Longworth	5-3	5th round	Rothmans Grand Prix
v Knowles	4-5	Quarter-final	Rothmans Grand Prix
v Newbury	9-7	3rd round	Coral UK Open
v Hallett	9-5	4th round	Coral UK Open
v Williams	9-7	5th round	Coral UK Open
v Dennis Taylor	1-9	Quarter-final	Coral UK Open
1986 v F. Davis	2-5	3rd round	Mercantile Credit Classic
v Reardon	5-1	1st round	BCE Belgian Classic
v Higgins	5-4	Semi-final	BCE Belgian Classic
v Griffiths	7-9	Final	BCE Belgian Classic
v Charlton	4-5	1st round	Benson & Hedges Masters
v Miles	5-3	3rd round	Dulux British Open
v Wilson	5-0	4th round	Dulux British Open
v Thorne	4-5	5th round	Dulux British Open
v Reynolds	10-6	1st round	Embassy World Championship
v Charlton	13-12	2nd round	Embassy World Championship
v Knowles	9-13	Quarter-final	Embassy World Championship
v Thornley	6-2	2nd round	Canadian Championship
v Wych	2-6	Semi-final	Canadian Championship
v Knowles	5-3	1st round	Langs Scottish Masters
v Higgins	2-6	Semi-final	Langs Scottish Masters
v Bales	3-5	3rd round	BCE International
v Dodd	4-5	3rd round	Rothmans Grand Prix
v Scott	9-2	3rd round	Tennents UK Open
v Spencer	4-9	4th round	Tennents UK Open
1987 v Chaperon	5-3	3rd round	Mercantile Credit Classic
v West	3-5	4th round	Mercantile Credit Classic
v Thorne	3-5	1st round	Benson & Hedges Masters
v Chaperon	5-4	3rd round	Dulux British Open
v West	5-4	4th round	Dulux British Open
v David Taylor	2-5	5th round	Dulux British Open
v Thorne	1-5	1st round	Benson & Hedges Irish Masters
v Longworth	4-10	1st round	Embassy World Championship

DAVID TAYLOR (England)

Born 29.7.43
Turned professional 1968
World ranking 25 (21)
Amateur career 1968 World and English champion.
Best professional performances Semi-finals 1980 Embassy World Championship; runner-up 1978 Coral UK, 1982 Jameson International.

1970 v Bennett	11-8	1st round	World Championship
v Pulman	22-39	Quarter-final	World Championship
1972 v Charlton	25-31	Quarter-final	World Championship

1973	v Dunning	9-4	1st round	World Championship
	v Spencer	5-16	2nd round	World Championship
1974	v Dunning	6-8	1st round	World Championship
1975	v King	15-8	1st round	World Championship
	v Higgins	2-15	2nd round	World Championship
1976	v Greaves	8-1	Qualifying	Embassy World Championship
	v Jack Rea	8-7	Qualifying	Embassy World Championship
	v Spencer	5-15	1st round	Embassy World Championship
1977	v Greaves	11-0	Qualifying	Embassy World Championship
	v Charlton	5-13	1st round	Embassy World Championship
	v Greaves	5-4	1st round	Super Crystalate UK Championship
	v Higgins	4-5	2nd round	Super Crystalate UK Championship
1978	v Morgan	9-7	Qualifying	Embassy World Championship
	v Miles	10-13	1st round	Embassy World Championship
	v Parkin	9-2	Qualifying	Coral UK Championship
	v Fagan	9-7	1st round	Coral UK Championship
	v Virgo	9-2	Quarter-final	Coral UK Championship
	v Higgins	9-5	Semi-final	Coral UK Championship
	v Mountjoy	9-15	Final	Coral UK Championship
1979	v Fagan	5-4	1st round	Benson & Hedges Masters
	v Reardon	2-5	Quarter-final	Benson & Hedges Masters
	v Dunning	9-8	Qualifying	Embassy World Championship
	v Higgins	5-13	1st round	Embassy World Championship
	v Meo	7-9	2nd round	Coral UK Championship
1980	v Edmonds	10-3	1st round	Embassy World Championship
	v F. Davis	13-5	2nd round	Embassy World Championship
	v Reardon	13-11	Quarter-final	Embassy World Championship
	v Thorburn	7-16	Semi-final	Embassy World Championship
	v Williams	7-9	2nd round	Coral UK Championship
1981	v Stevens	5-3	Semi-final	Yamaha International Masters
	v S. Davis	6-9	Final	Yamaha International Masters
	v Dunning	8-9	1st round	John Courage English
	v Wilson	10-6	1st round	Embassy World Championship
	v F. Davis	13-3	2nd round	Embassy World Championship
	v Thorburn	6-13	Quarter-final	Embassy World Championship
	v Stevens	5-0	3rd round	Jameson International
	v S. Davis	1-5	Quarter-final	Jameson International
	v Higgins	5-9	3rd round	Coral UK Championship
1982	v Reardon	1-5	1st round	Lada Classic
	v Meo	2-5	1st round	Benson & Hedges Masters
	v Fagan	9-10	1st round	Embassy World Championship
	v Fisher	5-1	1st round	Jameson International
	v Werbeniuk	5-2	2nd round	Jameson International
	v S. Davis	5-3	Quarter-final	Jameson International
	v Virgo	9-5	Semi-final	Jameson International
	v Knowles	6-9	Final	Jameson International
	v Anderson	5-1	1st round	Professional Players Tournament
	v Dennis Taylor	1-5	2nd round	Professional Players Tournament
	v Dodd	9-7	1st round	Coral UK Championship
	v Meo	6-9	2nd round	Coral UK Championship

1983	v White	5-3	1st round	Lada Classic
	v Spencer	2-5	Quarter-final	Lada Classic
	v White	2-5	1st round	Benson & Hedges Masters
	v Charlton	4-5	1st round	Benson & Hedges Irish Masters
	v Meadowcroft	10-2	1st round	Embassy World Championship
	v Werbeniuk	10-13	2nd round	Embassy World Championship
	v Donnelly	3-5	1st round	Jameson International
	v Morgan	5-3	1st round	Professional Players Tournament
	v Wildman	3-5	2nd round	Professional Players Tournament
	v N. Foulds	9-4	1st round	Coral UK Championship
	v Johnson	3-9	2nd round	Coral UK Championship
1984	v Macleod	4-5	Qualifying	Lada Classic
	v Stevens	1-5	1st round	Benson & Hedges Masters
	v Gauvreau	10-5	1st round	Embassy World Championship
	v Stevens	10-13	2nd round	Embassy World Championship
	v Charlton	4-5	Quarter-final	Winfield Australian Masters
	v W. Jones	5-4	1st round	Jameson International
	v S. Davis	1-5	2nd round	Jameson International
	v O'Kane	5-1	1st round	Rothmans Grand Prix
	v John Rea	5-1	2nd round	Rothmans Grand Prix
	v S. Davis	1-5	3rd round	Rothmans Grand Prix
	v Macleod	9-6	1st round	Coral UK Open
	v Reardon	4-9	2nd round	Coral UK Open
1985	v Longworth	4-5	1st round	Mercantile Credit Classic
	v Reardon	1-5	1st round	Benson & Hedges Masters
	v Cripsey	9-5	1st round	Tolly Cobbold English Championship
	v Parrott	9-6	2nd round	Tolly Cobbold English Championship
	v Knowles	2-9	Quarter-final	Tolly Cobbold English Championship
	v Bradley	3-6	1st round	Dulux British Open
	v O'Kane	10-4	1st round	Embassy World Championship
	v S. Davis	4-13	2nd round	Embassy World Championship
	v White	0-4	1st round	Winfield Australian Masters
	v T. Jones	5-4	3rd round	Goya Matchroom Trophy
	v Werbeniuk	5-4	4th round	Goya Matchroom Trophy
	v N. Foulds	4-5	5th round	Goya Matchroom Trophy
	v Newbury	5-2	3rd round	Rothmans Grand Prix
	v Longworth	1-5	4th round	Rothmans Grand Prix
	v Mikkelsen	9-6	3rd round	Coral UK Open
	v Campbell	9-4	4th round	Coral UK Open
	v Knowles	7-9	5th round	Coral UK Open
1986	v Gauvreau	3-5	3rd round	Mercantile Credit Classic
	v S. Davis	4-5	1st round	Benson & Hedges Masters
	v Edmonds	6-9	3rd round	Tolly Cobbold English Championship
	v Medati	1-5	3rd round	Dulux British Open
	v E. Hughes	7-10	1st round	Embassy World Championship
	v Edmonds	5-4	3rd round	BCE International
	v Johnson	5-3	4th round	BCE International
	v Reynolds	1-5	5th round	BCE International
	v W. Jones	1-5	3rd round	Rothmans Grand Prix
	v Chaperon	9-8	3rd round	Tennents UK Open

	v Thorburn	4-9	4th round	Tennents UK Open
1987	v Bradley	1-5	3rd round	Mercantile Credit Classic
	v Fitzmaurice	6-1	3rd round	Tolly Ales English Championship
	v Williams	2-6	4th round	Tolly Ales English Championship
	v Wilkinson	5-4	3rd round	Dulux British Open
	v J. McLaughlin	5-2	4th round	Dulux British Open
	v Stevens	5-2	5th round	Dulux British Open
	v Thorburn	3-5	Quarter-final	Dulux British Open
	v Cripsey	10-7	Qualifying	Embassy World Championship
	v Mountjoy	5-10	1st round	Embassy World Championship

DENNIS TAYLOR (Northern Ireland)

Born 19.1.49
Turned professional 1971
World ranking 8 (3)
Best professional performances Winner 1985 Embassy World Championship, 1984 Rothmans Grand Prix, 1987 Benson & Hedges Masters; Irish champion 1982, 1985, 1986, 1987.

1973	v Thorburn	8-9	1st round	World Championship
1974	v M. Owen	1-8	Qualifying	World Championship
1975	v Mans	15-12	1st round	World Championship
	v F. Davis	15-14	2nd round	World Championship
	v G. Owen	19-9	Quarter-final	World Championship
	v Charlton	12-19	Semi-final	World Championship
1976	v G. Owen	15-9	1st round	Embassy World Championship
	v Reardon	2-15	Quarter-final	Embassy World Championship
1977	v Karnehm	11-0	Qualifying	Embassy World Championship
	v Mans	13-11	1st round	Embassy World Championship
	v Mountjoy	13-11	Quarter-final	Embassy World Championship
	v Thorburn	16-18	Semi-final	Embassy World Championship
1978	v F. Davis	9-13	1st round	Embassy World Championship
	v Mountjoy	4-9	1st round	Coral UK Championship
1979	v S. Davis	13-11	1st round	Embassy World Championship
	v Reardon	13-8	Quarter-final	Embassy World Championship
	v Virgo	19-12	Semi-final	Embassy World Championship
	v Griffiths	16-24	Final	Embassy World Championship
	v Thorne	9-8	3rd round	Coral UK Championship
	v Fagan	9-6	Quarter-final	Coral UK Championship
	v Virgo	4-9	Semi-final	Coral UK Championship
1980	v Reardon	3-5	Quarter-final	Benson & Hedges Masters
	v Wych	10-13	2nd round	Embassy World Championship
	v Sinclair	9-6	2nd round	Coral UK Championship
	v Griffiths	2-9	Quarter-final	Coral UK Championship
1981	v Spencer	2-5	1st round	Benson & Hedges Masters
	v S. Davis	2-5	Semi-final	Yamaha International Masters
	v Stevens	13-11	2nd round	Embassy World Championship
	v Mountjoy	8-13	Quarter-final	Embassy World Championship

	v Williams	5-1	3rd round	Jameson International
	v Virgo	5-2	Quarter-final	Jameson International
	v Martin	9-1	Semi-final	Jameson International
	v S. Davis	0-9	Final	Jameson International
	v Mountjoy	4-5	1st round	Northern Ireland Classic
	v White	5-9	3rd round	Coral UK Championship
1982	v Higgins	1-5	1st round	Lada Classic
	v Reardon	3-5	1st round	Benson & Hedges Masters
	v Knowles	5-2	Semi-final	Tolly Cobbold Classic
	v S. Davis	3-8	Final	Tolly Cobbold Classic
	v Murphy	6-0	Semi-final	Irish Championship
	v Higgins	**16-13**	**Final**	**Irish Championship**
	v Sheehan	5-3	1st round	Benson & Hedges Irish Masters
	v Reardon	4-5	Quarter-final	Benson & Hedges Irish Masters
	v S. Francisco	7-10	1st round	Embassy World Championship
	v White	5-4	1st round	Langs Supreme Scottish Masters
	v S. Davis	1-6	Semi-final	Langs Supreme Scottish Masters
	v Wildman	5-2	1st round	Jameson International
	v Thorburn	5-2	2nd round	Jameson International
	v Virgo	3-5	Quarter-final	Jameson International
	v Edmonds	5-4	1st round	Professional Players Tournament
	v David Taylor	5-1	2nd round	Professional Players Tournament
	v White	3-5	3rd round	Professional Players Tournament
	v Meadowcroft	9-7	1st round	Coral UK Championship
	v Griffiths	7-9	2nd round	Coral UK Championship
1983	v S. Davis	2-5	1st round	Lada Classic
	v S. Davis	1-5	Semi-final	Tolly Cobbold Classic
	v Kelly	6-0	Quarter-final	Irish Championship
	v Fagan	6-1	Semi-final	Irish Championship
	v Higgins	11-16	Final	Irish Championship
	v White	4-5	1st round	Benson & Hedges Irish Masters
	v S. Francisco	10-9	1st round	Embassy World Championship
	v S. Davis	11-13	2nd round	Embassy World Championship
	v Reynolds	5-3	1st round	Jameson International
	v Thorburn	3-5	2nd round	Jameson International
	v Scott	4-5	1st round	Professional Players Tournament
	v Murphy	9-6	1st round	Coral UK Championship
	v White	4-9	2nd round	Coral UK Championship
1984	v Hallett	4-5	Qualifying	Lada Classic
	v Knowles	2-5	1st round	Benson & Hedges Masters
	v E. Hughes	5-1	1st round	Benson & Hedges Irish Masters
	v Thorburn	5-2	Quarter-final	Benson & Hedges Irish Masters
	v Griffiths	4-5	Semi-final	Benson & Hedges Irish Masters
	v Johnson	10-1	1st round	Embassy World Championship
	v Parrott	13-11	2nd round	Embassy World Championship
	v Mountjoy	13-8	Quarter-final	Embassy World Championship
	v S. Davis	9-16	Semi-final	Embassy World Championship
	v Fowler	5-0	1st round	Jameson International
	v Watchorn	5-1	1st round	Rothmans Grand Prix
	v Virgo	5-3	2nd round	Rothmans Grand Prix

	v Reardon	5-3	3rd round	Rothmans Grand Prix
	v Stevens	5-2	Quarter-final	Rothmans Grand Prix
	v N. Foulds	9-3	Semi-final	Rothmans Grand Prix
	v Thorburn	**10-2**	**Final**	**Rothmans Grand Prix**
	v King	9-5	1st round	Coral UK Open
	v Knowles	2-9	2nd round	Coral UK Open
1985	v Williams	3-5	1st round	Mercantile Credit Classic
	v Thorburn	3-5	1st round	Benson & Hedges Masters
	v Scott	6-2	1st round	Dulux British Open
	v Parrott	5-2	2nd round	Dulux British Open
	v Newbury	5-3	3rd round	Dulux British Open
	v Stevens	2-5	Quarter-final	Dulux British Open
	v Charlton	4-5	1st round	Benson & Hedges Irish Masters
	v Jack Rea	6-0	Quarter-final	Irish Championship
	v E. Hughes	6-5	Semi-final	Irish Championship
	v Higgins	**10-5**	**Final**	**Irish Championship**
	v S. Francisco	10-2	1st round	Embassy World Championship
	v Charlton	13-6	2nd round	Embassy World Championship
	v Thorburn	13-5	Quarter-final	Embassy World Championship
	v Knowles	16-5	Semi-final	Embassy World Championship
	v S. Davis	**18-17**	**Final**	**Embassy World Championship**
	v Thorne	3-5	1st round	Langs Scottish Masters
	v Cripsey	5-1	3rd round	Goya Matchroom Trophy
	v B. Harris	5-3	4th round	Goya Matchroom Trophy
	v Higgins	5-1	5th round	Goya Matchroom Trophy
	v Parrott	5-1	Quarter-final	Goya Matchroom Trophy
	v Thorburn	5-9	Semi-final	Goya Matchroom Trophy
	v West	5-1	3rd round	Rothmans Grand Prix
	v Williams	5-2	4th round	Rothmans Grand Prix
	v Meo	5-3	5th round	Rothmans Grand Prix
	v Wilson	5-2	Quarter-final	Rothmans Grand Prix
	v Knowles	9-6	Semi-final	Rothmans Grand Prix
	v S. Davis	9-10	Final	Rothmans Grand Prix
	v Parrott	5-1	1st round	BCE Canadian Masters
	v Reardon	8-3	Semi-final	BCE Canadian Masters
	v S. Davis	**9-5**	**Final**	**BCE Canadian Masters**
	v Jim Bear	9-3	3rd round	Coral UK Open
	v Cripsey	9-2	4th round	Coral UK Open
	v N. Foulds	9-5	5th round	Coral UK Open
	v Stevens	9-1	Quarter-final	Coral UK Open
	v Thorne	7-9	Semi-final	Coral UK Open
	v F. Davis	5-0	1st round	Kit Kat
	v Griffiths	6-4	Semi-final	Kit Kat
	v S. Davis	**9-5**	**Final**	**Kit Kat**
1986	v Fitzmaurice	5-1	3rd round	Mercantile Credit Classic
	v Reynolds	5-4	4th round	Mercantile Credit Classic
	v Higgins	4-5	5th round	Mercantile Credit Classic
	v Higgins	1-5	1st round	BCE Belgian Classic
	v Mountjoy	5-2	1st round	Benson & Hedges Masters
	v White	3-5	Quarter-final	Benson & Hedges Masters

		4-5	3rd round	Dulux British Open
	v Bales	4-5	3rd round	Dulux British Open
	v Thorne	2-5	Quarter-final	Benson & Hedges Irish Masters
	v Hallett	6-10	1st round	Embassy World Championship
	v Kelly	6-1	Quarter-final	Strongbow Irish Championship
	v Murphy	6-3	Semi-final	Strongbow Irish Championship
	v Higgins	**10-7**	**Final**	**Strongbow Irish Championship**
	v Griffiths	5-4	Semi-final	Camus Hong Kong Masters
	v Thorne	3-8	Final	Camus Hong Kong Masters
	v Johnson	5-3	1st round	Carlsberg Challenge
	v White	**8-3**	**Final**	**Carlsberg Challenge**
	v Thorne	5-6	Semi-final	Matchroom Trophy
	v Foldvari	5-1	3rd round	BCE International
	v Hendry	5-3	4th round	BCE International
	v S. Francisco	0-5	5th round	BCE International
	v Wright	5-3	3rd round	Rothmans Grand Prix
	v Virgo	5-3	4th round	Rothmans Grand Prix
	v Meo	2-5	5th round	Rothmans Grand Prix
	v Thorne	4-5	1st round	BCE Canadian Masters
	v Roe	9-6	3rd round	Tennents UK Open
	v W. Jones	2-9	4th round	Tennents UK Open
1987	v W. Jones	2-5	3rd round	Mercantile Credit Classic
	v N. Foulds	5-2	1st round	Benson & Hedges Masters
	v S. Francisco	5-3	Quarter-final	Benson & Hedges Masters
	v Thorburn	6-5	Semi-final	Benson & Hedges Masters
	v Higgins	**9-8**	**Final**	**Benson & Hedges Masters**
	v Roscoe	5-1	3rd round	Dulux British Open
	v Charlton	5-1	4th round	Dulux British Open
	v Griffiths	5-4	5th round	Dulux British Open
	v Knowles	4-5	Quarter-final	Dulux British Open
	v E. Hughes	5-4	1st round	Benson & Hedges Irish Masters
	v Thorburn	5-1	Quarter-final	Benson & Hedges Irish Masters
	v Thorne	6-2	Semi-final	Benson & Hedges Irish Masters
	v M. Bennett	10-4	1st round	Embassy World Championship
	v N. Foulds	10-13	2nd round	Embassy World Championship
	v Sheehan	6-3	Quarter-final	Matchroom Irish Championship
	v Browne	6-1	Semi-final	Matchroom Irish Championship
	v O'Boye	**9-2**	**Final**	**Matchroom Irish Championship**

CLIFF THORBURN (Canada)

Born 16.1.48
Turned professional 1973
World ranking 4 (2)
Best professional performances Winner Embassy World Championship 1980, Goya Matchroom Trophy 1985, Benson & Hedges Masters 1983, 1985, 1986; Canadian champion 1985, 1986.

1973	v Dennis Taylor	9-8	1st round	World Championship
	v Williams	15-16	2nd round	World Championship

1974	v Morgan	4-8	1st round	World Championship
1975	v Pulman	3-5	1st round	Benson & Hedges Masters
	v Morgan	15-6	1st round	World Championship
	v Miles	15-2	2nd round	World Championship
	v Charlton	12-19	Quarter-final	World Championship
1976	v Higgins	14-15	1st round	Embassy World Championship
1977	v Ross	11-0	Qualifying	Embassy World Championship
	v Williams	13-6	1st round	Embassy World Championship
	v Charlton	13-12	Quarter-final	Embassy World Championship
	v Dennis Taylor	18-16	Semi-final	Embassy World Championship
	v Spencer	21-25	Final	Embassy World Championship
1978	v Mountjoy	4-2	Quarter-final	Benson & Hedges Masters
	v Spencer	5-3	Semi-final	Benson & Hedges Masters
	v Higgins	5-7	Final	Benson & Hedges Masters
	v Houlihan	13-8	1st round	Embassy World Championship
	v Charlton	12-13	Quarter-final	Embassy World Championship
1979	v Mans	4-5	Quarter-final	Benson & Hedges Masters
	v Virgo	10-13	1st round	Embassy World Championship
1980	v Virgo	5-3	1st round	Benson & Hedges Masters
	v Griffiths	3-5	Quarter-final	Benson & Hedges Masters
	v Mountjoy	13-10	2nd round	Embassy World Championship
	v Wych	13-6	Quarter-final	Embassy World Championship
	v David Taylor	16-7	Semi-final	Embassy World Championship
	v Higgins	**18-16**	**Final**	**Embassy World Championship**
1981	v Mans	5-4	Quarter-final	Benson & Hedges Masters
	v Higgins	5-6	Semi-final	Benson & Hedges Masters
	v Griffiths	5-6	Semi-final	Benson & Hedges Irish Masters
	v Miles	13-2	2nd round	Embassy World Championship
	v David Taylor	13-6	Quarter-final	Embassy World Championship
	v S. Davis	10-16	Semi-final	Embassy World Championship
	v Stevens	5-1	Quarter-final	Langs Scottish Masters
	v Higgins	6-2	Semi-final	Langs Scottish Masters
	v White	4-9	Final	Langs Scottish Masters
	v Miles	0-5	3rd round	Jameson International
	v White	2-5	1st round	Northern Ireland Classic
	v Meo	6-9	3rd round	Coral UK Championship
1982	v Griffiths	1-5	1st round	Lada Classic
	v Meo	0-5	Quarter-final	Benson & Hedges Masters
	v Higgins	4-5	Quarter-final	Benson & Hedges Irish Masters
	v White	4-10	1st round	Embassy World Championship
	v Scott	5-1	1st round	Jameson International
	v Dennis Taylor	2-5	2nd round	Jameson International
	v Medati	5-1	1st round	Professional Players Tournament
	v Everton	5-2	2nd round	Professional Players Tournament
	v Werbeniuk	2-5	3rd round	Professional Players Tournament
1983	v Wilson	5-3	1st round	Lada Classic
	v Stevens	3-5	Quarter-final	Lada Classic
	v Johnson	5-2	1st round	Benson & Hedges Masters
	v Griffiths	5-3	Quarter-final	Benson & Hedges Masters
	v Charlton	6-5	Semi-final	Benson & Hedges Masters

v **Reardon**	**9-7**	**Final**	**Benson & Hedges Masters**
v Campbell	10-5	1st round	Embassy World Championship
v Griffiths	13-12	2nd round	Embassy World Championship
v Stevens	13-12	Quarter-final	Embassy World Championship
v Knowles	16-15	Semi-final	Embassy World Championship
v S. Davis	6-18	Final	Embassy World Championship
v Stevens	5-2	Semi-final	Winfield Masters
v **Werbeniuk**	**7-3**	**Final**	**Winfield Masters**
v Griffiths	5-1	1st round	Langs Scottish Masters
v Knowles	2-6	Semi-final	Langs Scottish Masters
v Sinclair	5-0	1st round	Jameson International
v Dennis Taylor	5-3	2nd round	Jameson International
v Mountjoy	5-2	Quarter-final	Jameson International
v Griffiths	9-8	Semi-final	Jameson International
v S. Davis	4-9	Final	Jameson International
v V. Harris	5-1	1st round	Professional Players Tournament
v Meadowcroft	5-1	2nd round	Professional Players Tournament
v Wilson	5-3	3rd round	Professional Players Tournament
v Johnson	1-5	Quarter-final	Professional Players Tournament
1984 v S. Francisco	1-5	Qualifying	Lada Classic
v Spencer	4-5	1st round	Benson & Hedges Masters
v Dennis Taylor	2-5	Quarter-final	Benson & Hedges Irish Masters
v Meo	5-4	1st round	Tolly Cobbold Classic
v Knowles	3-5	Semi-final	Tolly Cobbold Classic
v Morra	10-3	1st round	Embassy World Championship
v Thorne	13-11	2nd round	Embassy World Championship
v White	8-13	Quarter-final	Embassy World Championship
v S. Davis	2-5	1st round	Langs Scottish Masters
v Virgo	0-5	1st round	Jameson International
v Rigitano	5-4	1st round	Rothmans Grand Prix
v Campbell	5-1	2nd round	Rothmans Grand Prix
v Meo	5-4	3rd round	Rothmans Grand Prix
v Mountjoy	5-3	Quarter-final	Rothmans Grand Prix
v S. Davis	9-7	Semi-final	Rothmans Grand Prix
v Dennis Taylor	2-10	Final	Rothmans Grand Prix
v J. McLaughlin	9-4	1st round	Coral UK Open
v Wilson	9-3	2nd round	Coral UK Open
v Reardon	9-8	Quarter-final	Coral UK Open
v Higgins	7-9	Semi-final	Coral UK Open
1985 v Scott	5-1	1st round	Mercantile Credit Classic
v Longworth	5-3	2nd round	Mercantile Credit Classic
v Griffiths	5-4	Quarter-final	Mercantile Credit Classic
v Johnson	9-2	Semi-final	Mercantile Credit Classic
v Thorne	8-13	Final	Mercantile Credit Classic
v Dennis Taylor	5-3	1st round	Benson & Hedges Masters
v Reardon	5-0	Quarter-final	Benson & Hedges Masters
v White	6-4	Semi-final	Benson & Hedges Masters
v **Mountjoy**	**9-6**	**Final**	**Benson & Hedges Masters**
v Rigitano	6-3	1st round	Dulux British Open
v Reynolds	5-3	2nd round	Dulux British Open

v Higgins	2-5	3rd round	Dulux British Open
v White	3-5	Quarter-final	Benson & Hedges Irish Masters
v Hallett	10-8	1st round	Embassy World Championship
v Werbeniuk	13-3	2nd round	Embassy World Championship
v Dennis Taylor	5-13	Quarter-final	Embassy World Championship
v Caggianello	6-2	Quarter-final	Canadian Championship
v Wych	6-5	Semi-final	Canadian Championship
v Chaperon	**6-4**	**Final**	**Canadian Championship**
v Higgins	4-5	Semi-final	Carlsberg Trophy
v Macleod	5-1	1st round	Langs Scottish Masters
v S. Francisco	6-0	Semi-final	Langs Scottish Masters
v Thorne	**9-7**	**Final**	**Langs Scottish Masters**
v Longworth	5-3	3rd round	Goya Matchroom Trophy
v Martin	5-3	4th round	Goya Matchroom Trophy
v Campbell	5-0	5th round	Goya Matchroom Trophy
v Duggan	5-2	Quarter-final	Goya Matchroom Trophy
v Dennis Taylor	9-5	Semi-final	Goya Matchroom Trophy
v White	**12-10**	**Final**	**Goya Matchroom Trophy**
v Oliver	5-0	3rd round	Rothmans Grand Prix
v Wildman	5-2	4th round	Rothmans Grand Prix
v Johnson	5-1	5th round	Rothmans Grand Prix
v Griffiths	5-1	Quarter-final	Rothmans Grand Prix
v S. Davis	5-9	Semi-final	Rothmans Grand Prix
v White	5-3	1st round	BCE Canadian Masters
v S. Davis	1-8	Semi-final	BCE Canadian Masters
v Dodd	9-4	3rd round	Coral UK Open
v Parrott	9-6	4th round	Coral UK Open
v Thorne	7-9	5th round	Coral UK Open
v Higgins	4-5	1st round	Kit Kat
1986 v J. McLaughlin	5-1	3rd round	Mercantile Credit Classic
v Hallett	5-3	4th round	Mercantile Credit Classic
v Meo	5-1	5th round	Mercantile Credit Classic
v Johnson	5-4	Quarter-final	Mercantile Credit Classic
v Mountjoy	9-6	Semi-final	Mercantile Credit Classic
v White	12-13	Final	Mercantile Credit Classic
v Johnson	5-3	1st round	Benson & Hedges Masters
v Griffiths	5-2	Quarter-final	Benson & Hedges Masters
v Knowles	6-4	Semi-final	Benson & Hedges Masters
v White	**9-5**	**Final**	**Benson & Hedges Masters**
v Sheehan	5-0	3rd round	Dulux British Open
v Wildman	5-1	4th round	Dulux British Open
v Meo	3-5	5th round	Dulux British Open
v E. Hughes	5-1	Quarter-final	Benson & Hedges Irish Masters
v Thorne	4-6	Semi-final	Benson & Hedges Irish Masters
v Werbeniuk	10-5	1st round	Embassy World Championship
v E. Hughes	13-6	2nd round	Embassy World Championship
v Thorne	13-6	Quarter-final	Embassy World Championship
v S. Davis	12-16	Semi-final	Embassy World Championship
v Watson	6-1	Quarter-final	Canadian Championship
v Jonik	6-3	Semi-final	Canadian Championship

	v Wych	6-2	Final	Canadian Championship
	v Parrott	5-1	1st round	Langs Scottish Masters
	v White	6-2	Semi-final	Langs Scottish Masters
	v Higgins	9-8	Final	Langs Scottish Masters
	v Burke	5-0	3rd round	BCE International
	v Wych	5-3	4th round	BCE International
	v Griffiths	5-4	5th round	BCE International
	v Wilson	5-1	Quarter-final	BCE International
	v P. Francisco	9-7	Semi-final	BCE International
	v N. Foulds	9-12	Final	BCE International
	v O'Boye	4-5	3rd round	Rothmans Grand Prix
	v Knowles	1-5	1st round	BCE Canadian Masters
	v Fowler	9-7	3rd round	Tennents UK Open
	v David Taylor	9-4	4th round	Tennents UK Open
	v Spencer	9-2	5th round	Tennents UK Open
	v N. Foulds	2-9	Quarter-final	Tennents UK Open
1987	v Cripsey	5-0	3rd round	Mercantile Credit Classic
	v Reynolds	4-5	4th round	Mercantile Credit Classic
	v Williams	5-1	1st round	Benson & Hedges Masters
	v Thorne	5-3	Quarter-final	Benson & Hedges Masters
	v Dennis Taylor	5-6	Semi-final	Benson & Hedges Masters
	v Wildman	5-3	3rd round	Dulux British Open
	v Cripsey	5-2	4th round	Dulux British Open
	v Mountjoy	5-4	5th round	Dulux British Open
	v David Taylor	5-3	Quarter-final	Dulux British Open
	v White	5-9	Semi-final	Dulux British Open
	v Dennis Taylor	1-5	Quarter-final	Benson & Hedges Irish Masters
	v O'Kane	5-10	1st round	Embassy World Championship

WILLIE THORNE (England)

Born 4.3.54
Turned professional 1975
World ranking 11 (7)
Best professional performance Winner 1985 Mercantile Credit Classic.

1976	v Condo	8-3	Qualifying	Embassy World Championship
	v Meadowcroft	5-8	Qualifying	Embassy World Championship
1977	v Bennett	11-4	Qualifying	Embassy World Championship
	v Miles	4-13	1st round	Embassy World Championship
	v Bennett	5-1	1st round	Super Crystalate UK Championship
	v Williams	5-4	2nd round	Super Crystalate UK Championship
	v Mountjoy	4-5	Quarter-final	Super Crystalate UK Championship
1978	v Williams	9-3	Qualifying	Embassy World Championship
	v Charlton	12-13	1st round	Embassy World Championship
	v Bennett	9-4	Qualifying	Coral UK Championship
	v Reardon	9-6	1st round	Coral UK Championship
	v Miles	1-9	Quarter-final	Coral UK Championship

1979	v Jim Charlton	9-3	Prelim	Embassy World Championship
	v Virgo	8-9	Qualifying	Embassy World Championship
	v Andrewartha	9-4	2nd round	Coral UK Championship
	v Dennis Taylor	8-9	3rd round	Coral UK Championship
1980	v Jack Rea	9-1	Qualifying	Embassy World Championship
	v Werbeniuk	9-10	1st round	Embassy World Championship
	v Meadowcroft	9-1	1st round	Coral UK Championship
	v Higgins	7-9	2nd round	Coral UK Championship
1981	v Wildman	9-2	1st round	John Courage English
	v Dunning	9-0	2nd round	John Courage English
	v Meo	8-9	Semi-final	John Courage English
	v Morra	9-5	Qualifying	Embassy World Championship
	v Greaves	9-3	Qualifying	Embassy World Championship
	v Mountjoy	6-10	1st round	Embassy World Championship
	v Medati	9-6	Qualifying	Coral UK Championship
	v Edmonds	9-4	2nd round	Coral UK Championship
	v S. Davis	2-9	3rd round	Coral UK Championship
1982	v Roscoe	9-1	Qualifying	Embassy World Championship
	v Griffiths	10-6	1st round	Embassy World Championship
	v Spencer	13-5	2nd round	Embassy World Championship
	v Higgins	10-13	Quarter-final	Embassy World Championship
	v Reynolds	3-5	1st round	Jameson International
	v Demarco	5-3	1st round	Professional Players Tournament
	v Macleod	4-5	2nd round	Professional Players Tournament
	v Wilson	7-9	1st round	Coral UK Championship
	v Virgo	10-3	1st round	Embassy World Championship
	v Higgins	8-13	2nd round	Embassy World Championship
1983	v Murphy	5-2	Qualifying	Jameson International
	v Virgo	5-2	1st round	Jameson International
	v Reardon	5-0	2nd round	Jameson International
	v Charlton	0-5	Quarter-final	Jameson International
	v Everton	5-1	1st round	Professional Players Tournament
	v Spencer	5-1	2nd round	Professional Players Tournament
	v Reardon	5-3	3rd round	Professional Players Tournament
	v E. Hughes	5-1	Quarter-final	Professional Players Tournament
	v Knowles	7-9	Semi-final	Professional Players Tournament
	v Wildman	9-5	1st round	Coral UK Championship
	v S. Davis	3-9	2nd round	Coral UK Championship
1984	v S. Davis	2-5	1st round	Tolly Cobbold Classic
	v Mikkelsen	10-3	Qualifying	Embassy World Championship
	v Virgo	10-9	1st round	Embassy World Championship
	v Thorburn	11-13	2nd round	Embassy World Championship
	v Virgo	3-5	Quarter-final	Winfield Australian Masters
	v O'Kane	5-3	1st round	Jameson International
	v Gauvreau	5-3	2nd round	Jameson International
	v E. Hughes	2-5	Quarter-final	Jameson International
	v Newbury	5-2	1st round	Rothmans Grand Prix
	v Macleod	5-3	2nd round	Rothmans Grand Prix
	v N. Foulds	1-5	3rd round	Rothmans Grand Prix
	v Parrott	9-7	1st round	Coral UK Open

v Charlton	9-7	2nd round	Coral UK Open
v Higgins	5-9	Quarter-final	Coral UK Open
1985 v Foldvari	5-2	1st round	Mercantile Credit Classic
v Stevens	5-1	2nd round	Mercantile Credit Classic
v Virgo	5-1	Quarter-final	Mercantile Credit Classic
v S. Davis	9-8	Semi-final	Mercantile Credit Classic
v Thorburn	**13-8**	**Final**	**Mercantile Credit Classic**
v White	2-5	1st round	Benson & Hedges Masters
v Dodd	9-1	1st round	Tolly Cobbold English Championship
v Reynolds	6-9	2nd round	Tolly Cobbold English Championship
v Oliver	6-3	1st round	Dulux British Open
v Macleod	0-5	2nd round	Dulux British Open
v Fagan	6-10	1st round	Embassy World Championship
v Parrott	0-5	Quarter-final	Winfield Australian Masters
v Dennis Taylor	5-3	1st round	Langs Scottish Masters
v White	6-2	Semi-final	Langs Scottish Masters
v Thorburn	7-9	Final	Langs Scottish Masters
v Fowler	5-1	3rd round	Goya Matchroom Trophy
v Scott	5-1	4th round	Goya Matchroom Trophy
v Duggan	4-5	5th round	Goya Matchroom Trophy
v W. Jones	0-5	3rd round	Rothmans Grand Prix
v Browne	9-6	3rd round	Coral UK Open
v Virgo	9-8	4th round	Coral UK Open
v Thorburn	9-7	5th round	Coral UK Open
v Griffiths	9-7	Quarter-final	Coral UK Open
v Dennis Taylor	9-7	Semi-final	Coral UK Open
v S. Davis	14-16	Final	Coral UK Open
1986 v T. Jones	3-5	3rd round	Mercantile Credit Classic
v Reardon	5-4	1st round	Benson & Hedges Masters
v S. Davis	4-5	Quarter-final	Benson & Hedges Masters
v Medati	9-2	3rd round	Tolly Cobbold English Championship
v Reynolds	8-9	4th round	Tolly Cobbold English Championship
v Dodd	5-2	3rd round	Dulux British Open
v Mans	5-1	4th round	Dulux British Open
v Stevens	5-4	5th round	Dulux British Open
v Griffiths	5-4	Quarter-final	Dulux British Open
v Virgo	9-4	Semi-final	Dulux British Open
v S. Davis	7-12	Final	Dulux British Open
v Griffiths	5-2	1st round	Benson & Hedges Irish Masters
v Dennis Taylor	5-2	Quarter-final	Benson & Hedges Irish Masters
v Thorburn	6-4	Semi-final	Benson & Hedges Irish Masters
v White	5-9	Final	Benson & Hedges Irish Masters
v Hendry	10-8	1st round	Embassy World Championship
v Campbell	13-9	2nd round	Embassy World Championship
v Thorburn	6-13	Quarter-final	Embassy World Championship
v S. Davis	5-2	Semi-final	Camus Hong Kong Masters
v Dennis Taylor	**8-3**	**Final**	**Camus Hong Kong Masters**
v N. Foulds	6-3	1st round	Matchroom Trophy
v Dennis Taylor	6-5	Semi-final	Matchroom Trophy

v S. Davis	10-9	**Final**	**Matchroom Trophy**
v Drago	2-5	3rd round	BCE International
v Duggan	5-0	3rd round	Rothmans Grand Prix
v King	5-2	4th round	Rothmans Grand Prix
v N. Foulds	3-5	5th round	Rothmans Grand Prix
v Dennis Taylor	5-4	1st round	BCE Canadian Masters
v Knowles	8-7	Semi-final	BCE Canadian Masters
v S. Davis	3-9	Final	BCE Canadian Masters
v Murphy	9-4	3rd round	Tennents UK Open
v Grace	9-1	4th round	Tennents UK Open
v Drago	5-9	5th round	Tennents UK Open
1987 v Spencer	3-5	3rd round	Mercantile Credit Classic
v Stevens	5-3	1st round	Benson & Hedges Masters
v Thorburn	3-5	Quarter-final	Benson & Hedges Masters
v B. Harris	6-2	3rd round	Tolly Ales English Championship
v Martin	6-3	4th round	Tolly Ales English Championship
v Reynolds	6-4	Quarter-final	Tolly Ales English Championship
v Meo	3-9	Semi-final	Tolly Ales English Championship
v R. Harris	5-1	3rd round	Dulux British Open
v Duggan	5-2	4th round	Dulux British Open
v N. Foulds	2-5	5th round	Dulux British Open
v Stevens	5-1	1st round	Benson & Hedges Irish Masters
v White	5-4	Quarter-final	Benson & Hedges Irish Masters
v Dennis Taylor	6-2	Semi-final	Benson & Hedges Irish Masters
v S. Davis	1-9	Final	Benson & Hedges Irish Masters
v Hendry	7-10	1st round	Embassy World Championship

PAUL THORNLEY (Canada)

Born –
Turned professional 1979
World ranking 110 (97)

1984 v Fisher	8-10	Qualifying	Embassy World Championship
v Cripsey	3-5	Qualifying	Jameson International
v Williamson	2-5	Qualifying	Rothmans Grand Prix
1985 v Chaperon	1-5	1st round	Canadian Championship
v Mienie	10-3	Qualifying	Embassy World Championship
v Fagan	10-7	Qualifying	Embassy World Championship
v Murphy	3-10	Qualifying	Embassy World Championship
1986 v Morra	6-4	1st round	Canadian Championship
v Stevens	2-6	2nd round	Canadian Championship
1987 v Greaves	6-10	Qualifying	Embassy World Championship

Cliff Thorburn

Willie Thorne

JIMMY VAN RENSBERG (South Africa)

Born 24.10.31
Turned professional 1978
World ranking 72 (59)
Amateur career South African champion (11 times).
Best professional performance Last 32 1986 Mercantile Credit Classic.

1979	v Meadowcroft	7-9	Prelim	Embassy World Championship
1980	v Meo	1-9	Qualifying	Embassy World Championship
1984	v V. Harris	10-7	Qualifying	Embassy World Championship
	v Edmonds	10-9	Qualifying	Embassy World Championship
	v S. Francisco	3-10	Qualifying	Embassy World Championship
1985	v Longworth	10-7	Qualifying	Embassy World Championship
	v Gauvreau	9-10	Qualifying	Embassy World Championship
	v Scott	4-5	2nd round	Goya Matchroom Trophy
	v E. McLaughlin	5-4	2nd round	Rothmans Grand Prix
	v Campbell	4-5	3rd round	Rothmans Grand Prix
	v Edmonds	5-9	2nd round	Coral UK Open
1986	v W. Jones	5-4	2nd round	Mercantile Credit Classic
	v Parrott	5-3	3rd round	Mercantile Credit Classic
	v S. Davis	1-5	4th round	Mercantile Credit Classic
	v Wych	0-5	2nd round	Dulux British Open
	v Williamson	10-9	Qualifying	Embassy World Championship
	v Sinclair	10-2	Qualifying	Embassy World Championship
	v Campbell	6-10	Qualifying	Embassy World Championship
	v Mienie	7-1	2nd round	South African Championship
	v Ellis	2-8	Semi-final	South African Championship
	v Kearney	5-3	2nd round	BCE International
	v West	3-5	3rd round	BCE International
	v Roe	3-5	2nd round	Rothmans Grand Prix
	v Roe	6-9	2nd round	Tennents UK Open
1987	v N. Gilbert	5-3	2nd round	Mercantile Credit Classic
	v S. Francisco	4-5	3rd round	Mercantile Credit Classic
	v Morra	1-5	2nd round	Dulux British Open
	v J. McLaughlin	10-6	Qualifying	Embassy World Championship
	v T. Jones	0-10	Qualifying	Embassy World Championship

JOHN VIRGO (England)

Born 3.4.46
Turned professional 1976
World ranking 19 (19)
Best professional performance Winner 1979 Coral UK Championship.

1977	v Andrewartha	11-1	Prelim	Embassy World Championship
	v Dunning	11-6	Qualifying	Embassy World Championship
	v Spencer	9-13	1st round	Embassy World Championship
	v Dennis Taylor	5-2	2nd round	Super Crystalate UK Championship

	v Miles	5-2	Quarter-final	Super Crystalate UK Championship
	v Fagan	8-9	Semi-final	Super Crystalate UK Championship
1978	v F. Davis	8-9	Qualifying	Embassy World Championship
	v Edmonds	9-4	Qualifying	Coral UK Championship
	v Pulman	9-3	1st round	Coral UK Championship
	v David Taylor	2-9	Quarter-final	Coral UK Championship
1979	v Parkin	9-0	Prelim	Embassy World Championship
	v Thorne	9-8	Qualifying	Embassy World Championship
	v Thorburn	13-10	1st round	Embassy World Championship
	v Werbeniuk	13-9	Quarter-final	Embassy World Championship
	v Dennis Taylor	12-19	Semi-final	Embassy World Championship
	v Meo	9-6	3rd round	Coral UK Championship
	v S. Davis	9-7	Quarter-final	Coral UK Championship
	v Dennis Taylor	9-4	Semi-final	Coral UK Championship
	v Griffiths	**14-13**	**Final**	**Coral UK Championship**
1980	v Thorburn	3-5	1st round	Benson & Hedges Masters
	v Meadowcroft	10-2	1st round	Embassy World Championship
	v Charlton	12-13	2nd round	Embassy World Championship
	v Meo	1-9	2nd round	Coral UK Championship
1981	v Meo	6-9	1st round	John Courage English
	v Meo	6-10	1st round	Embassy World Championship
	v Knowles	5-2	2nd round	Jameson International
	v Reardon	5-3	3rd round	Jameson International
	v Dennis Taylor	2-5	Quarter-final	Jameson International
	v White	6-9	2nd round	Coral UK Championship
1982	v Hallett	10-4	1st round	Embassy World Championship
	v Reardon	8-13	2nd round	Embassy World Championship
	v V. Harris	5-2	Qualifying	Jameson International
	v Charlton	5-4	1st round	Jameson International
	v Spencer	5-4	2nd round	Jameson International
	v Dennis Taylor	5-3	Quarter-final	Jameson International
	v David Taylor	5-9	Semi-final	Jameson International
	v Black	5-2	1st round	Professional Players Tournament
	v Hallett	5-2	2nd round	Professional Players Tournament
	v Spencer	5-1	3rd round	Professional Players Tournament
	v Johnson	5-1	Quarter-final	Professional Players Tournament
	v White	4-10	Semi-final	Professional Players Tournament
	v Kelly	9-2	1st round	Coral UK Championship
	v Mountjoy	9-5	2nd round	Coral UK Championship
	v Meo	6-9	Quarter-final	Coral UK Championship
1983	v Charlton	2-5	1st round	Lada Classic
	v Mountjoy	1-5	1st round	Benson & Hedges Masters
	v Murphy	10-8	Qualifying	Embassy World Championship
	v Thorne	3-10	1st round	Embassy World Championship
	v Thorne	2-5	1st round	Jameson International
	v French	5-4	1st round	Professional Players Tournament
	v Wilson	2-5	2nd round	Professional Players Tournament
	v Johnson	6-9	1st round	Coral UK Championship
1984	v Wildman	2-5	Qualifying	Lada Classic
	v Reardon	3-5	1st round	Benson & Hedges Masters

v Thorburn	9-10	1st round	Embassy World Championship
v Thorne	5-3	Quarter-final	Winfield Australian Masters
v Meo	6-2	Semi-final	Winfield Australian Masters
v Knowles	3-7	Final	Winfield Australian Masters
v F. Davis	5-3	Qualifying	Jameson International
v Thorburn	5-0	1st round	Jameson International
v S. Francisco	2-5	2nd round	Jameson International
v Bradley	5-0	1st round	Rothmans Grand Prix
v Dennis Taylor	3-5	2nd round	Rothmans Grand Prix
v King	4-9	Qualifying	Coral UK Open
1985 v Bales	5-1	Qualifying	Mercantile Credit Classic
v Werbeniuk	5-2	1st round	Mercantile Credit Classic
v Macleod	5-0	2nd round	Mercantile Credit Classic
v Thorne	1-5	Quarter-final	Mercantile Credit Classic
v Darrington	9-0	1st round	Tolly Cobbold English Championship
v Johnson	9-4	2nd round	Tolly Cobbold English Championship
v S. Davis	2-9	Quarter-final	Tolly Cobbold English Championship
v P. Francisco	6-2	1st round	Dulux British Open
v S. Davis	2-5	2nd round	Dulux British Open
v Wych	10-4	Qualifying	Embassy World Championship
v Meo	6-10	1st round	Embassy World Championship
v Meo	3-5	Quarter-final	Winfield Australian Masters
v Miles	5-2	3rd round	Goya Matchroom Trophy
v S. Davis	1-5	4th round	Goya Matchroom Trophy
v P. Francisco	4-5	3rd round	Rothmans Grand Prix
v W. Jones	9-7	3rd round	Coral UK Open
v Thorne	8-9	4th round	Coral UK Open
1986 v Gibson	5-3	3rd round	Mercantile Credit Classic
v White	2-5	4th round	Mercantile Credit Classic
v T. Jones	9-7	3rd round	Tolly Cobbold English Championship
v Parrott	9-6	4th round	Tolly Cobbold English Championship
v S. Davis	2-9	Quarter-final	Tolly Cobbold English Championship
v Fowler	5-1	3rd round	Dulux British Open
v John Rea	5-0	4th round	Dulux British Open
v Charlton	5-4	5th round	Dulux British Open
v Meo	5-3	Quarter-final	Dulux British Open
v Thorne	4-9	Semi-final	Dulux British Open
v White	7-10	1st round	Embassy World Championship
v Newbury	5-4	3rd round	BCE International
v S. Francisco	0-5	4th round	BCE International
v Fagan	5-2	3rd round	Rothmans Grand Prix
v Dennis Taylor	3-5	4th round	Rothmans Grand Prix
v Miles	9-7	3rd round	Tennents UK Open
v Drago	6-9	4th round	Tennents UK Open
1987 v M. Bennett	5-3	3rd round	Mercantile Credit Classic
v S. Davis	2-5	4th round	Mercantile Credit Classic
v Medati	6-1	3rd round	Tolly Ales English Championship
v Parrott	2-6	4th round	Tolly Ales English Championship
v Morra	5-3	3rd round	Dulux British Open
v S. Davis	5-4	4th round	Dulux British Open

v Wilson	5-2	5th round	Dulux British Open
v N. Foulds	3-5	Quarter-final	Dulux British Open
v T. Jones	10-9	Qualifying	Embassy World Championship
v N. Foulds	4-10	1st round	Embassy World Championship

PAUL WATCHORN (Republic of Ireland)
Born 19.7.58
Turned professional 1982
World ranking 14 (106)

1983 v Johnson	0-10	Qualifying	Embassy World Championship
v Morra	3-5	Qualifying	Jameson International
v Parrott	0-5	Qualifying	Professional Players Tournament
1984 v Donnelly	7-10	Qualifying	Embassy World Championship
v W. Jones	0-5	Qualifying	Jameson International
v Dennis Taylor	1-5	1st round	Rothmans Grand Prix
v B. Harris	9-7	Qualifying	Coral UK Open
v Everton	9-6	Qualifying	Coral UK Open
v Fisher	5-9	Qualifying	Coral UK Open
1985 v D. Hughes	5-0	Prelim	Mercantile Credit Classic
v Mikkelsen	5-1	Qualifying	Mercantile Credit Classic
v Donnelly	1-5	Qualifying	Mercantile Credit Classic
v Fitzmaurice	6-1	Qualifying	Dulux British Open
v E. Hughes	4-6	1st round	Dulux British Open
v Kelly	2-6	Qualifying	Irish Championship
v Hines	4-10	Qualifying	Embassy World Championship
v Agrawal	2-5	1st round	Goya Matchroom Trophy
v Drago	2-5	1st round	Rothmans Grand Prix
v Sheehan	9-7	1st round	Coral UK Open
1986 v Greaves	4-5	1st round	Mercantile Credit Classic
v Wilkinson	4-5	1st round	Dulux British Open
v Longworth	7-10	Qualifying	Embassy World Championship
v J. McLaughlin	0-5	1st round	Strongbow Irish Championship
v Bear	1-5	1st round	BCE International
v Darrington	5-2	1st round	Rothmans Grand Prix
v Drago	3-5	2nd round	Rothmans Grand Prix
v Kelly	9-8	1st round	Tennents UK Open
v Scott	7-9	2nd round	Tennents UK Open
1987 v Donnelly	5-0	1st round	Mercantile Credit Classic
v Duggan	1-5	2nd round	Mercantile Credit Classic
v Dunning	5-2	1st round	Dulux British Open
v Cripsey	4-5	2nd round	Dulux British Open
v G. Foulds	6-10	Qualifying	Embassy World Championship
v E. Hughes	2-5	1st round	Matchroom Irish Championship

GERRY WATSON (Canada)

Born 28.9.49
Turned professional 1983
World ranking 109 (unranked)

1984	v Anderson	4-10	Qualifying	Embassy World Championship
	v Mikkelsen	3-5	1st round	Canadian Championship
	v Sheehan	5-1	1st round	Rothmans Grand Prix
	v Roscoe	5-2	2nd round	Rothmans Grand Prix
	v Stevens	0-5	3rd round	Rothmans Grand Prix
	v Houlihan	4-9	1st round	Coral UK Open
1986	v Gilbert	4-5	1st round	Mercantile Credit Classic
	Did not play on the 1986–87 circuit			

MIKE WATTERSON (England)

Born 26.8.42
Turned professional 1981
World ranking 82 (47)

1981	v Medati	5-3	Qualifying	Jameson International
	v Everton	5-4	Qualifying	Jameson International
	v Fagan	2-5	Qualifying	Jameson International
	v Bennett	9-4	Qualifying	Coral UK Championship
	v Johnson	3-9	Qualifying	Coral UK Championship
1982	v Demarco	9-6	Qualifying	Embassy World Championship
	v Meadowcroft	7-9	Qualifying	Embassy World Championship
	v Everton	5-1	Qualifying	Jameson International
	v Fagan	5-1	Qualifying	Jameson International
	v Stevens	3-5	1st round	Jameson International
	v Donnelly	5-4	1st round	Professional Players Tournament
	v Griffiths	2-5	2nd round	Professional Players Tournament
	v B. Harris	3-9	Qualifying	Coral UK Championship
1983	v Campbell	6-10	Qualifying	Embassy World Championship
	v Demarco	5-3	Qualifying	Jameson International
	v Mans	5-4	Qualifying	Jameson International
	v Meo	5-3	1st round	Jameson International
	v S. Davis	0-5	2nd round	Jameson International
	v Higgins	5-2	1st round	Professional Players Tournament
	v Martin	4-5	2nd round	Professional Players Tournament
	v Everton	9-6	Qualifying	Coral UK Championship
	v F. Davis	9-6	Qualifying	Coral UK Championship
	v Mountjoy	2-9	1st round	Coral UK Championship
1984	v Bennett	10-5	Qualifying	Embassy World Championship
	v King	8-10	Qualifying	Embassy World Championship
	v Black	3-5	Qualifying	Jameson International
	v W. Jones	3-5	Qualifying	Rothmans Grand Prix
	v Murphy	4-9	Qualifying	Coral UK Open

1985 v Edmonds	2-5	Qualifying	Mercantile Credit Classic
v Kearney	4-6	Qualifying	Dulux British Open
v W. Jones	5-10	Qualifying	Embassy World Championship
v Fitzmaurice	2-5	2nd round	Goya Matchroom Trophy
v Caggianello	5-1	2nd round	Rothmans Grand Prix
v Williams	2-5	3rd round	Rothmans Grand Prix
v Jim Bear	0-9	2nd round	Coral UK Open
1986 v Jenkins	5-2	2nd round	Mercantile Credit Classic
v Williams	0-5	3rd round	Mercantile Credit Classic
v G. Foulds	1-9	2nd round	Tolly Cobbold English Championship
v Mikkelsen	10-2	Qualifying	Embassy World Championship
v Dodd	1-10	Qualifying	Embassy World Championship
v Wright	1-5	1st round	BCE International
v M. Bennett	1-5	1st round	Rothmans Grand Prix
v Burke	9-0	1st round	Tennents UK Open
v Black	9-3	2nd round	Tennents UK Open
v P. Francisco	4-9	3rd round	Tennents UK Open
1987 v Rowswell	1-5	1st round	Mercantile Credit Classic
v Roe	3-5	1st round	Dulux British Open
v James	2-10	Qualifying	Embassy World Championship

BILL WERBENIUK (Canada)

Born 14.1.47
Turned professional 1973
World ranking 33 (24)
Best professional performances Semi-finals 1983 Lada Classic, 1979 Coral UK Championship.

1974 v Thompson	8-3	1st round	World Championship
v F. Davis	5-15	2nd round	World Championship
1975 v Higgins	0-5	1st round	Benson & Hedges Masters
v Meadowcroft	15-9	1st round	Embassy World Championship
v Charlton	11-15	2nd round	Embassy World Championship
1976 v F. Davis	12-15	1st round	Embassy World Championship
1978 v Parkin	9-2	Qualifying	Embassy World Championship
v Pulman	13-4	1st round	Embassy World Championship
v Reardon	6-13	Quarter-final	Embassy World Championship
1979 v Andrewartha	9-2	Qualifying	Embassy World Championship
v Spencer	13-11	1st round	Embassy World Championship
v Virgo	9-13	Quarter-final	Embassy World Championship
v Johnson	9-3	2nd round	Coral UK Championship
v Spencer	9-8	3rd round	Coral UK Championship
v Edmonds	9-8	Quarter-final	Coral UK Championship
v Griffiths	3-9	Semi-final	Coral UK Championship
1980 v Thorne	10-9	1st round	Embassy World Championship
v Reardon	6-13	2nd round	Embassy World Championship
v S. Davis	3-9	2nd round	Coral UK Championship
1981 v Martin	10-4	1st round	Embassy World Championship

	v Mans	13-5	2nd round	Embassy World Championship
	v Reardon	10-13	Quarter-final	Embassy World Championship
	v Martin	2-5	2nd round	Jameson International
	v Stevens	9-7	3rd round	Coral UK Championship
	v S. Davis	5-9	Quarter-final	Coral UK Championship
1982	v John Bear	10-7	1st round	Embassy World Championship
	v Charlton	5-13	2nd round	Embassy World Championship
	v Wych	5-3	1st round	Jameson International
	v David Taylor	2-5	2nd round	Jameson International
	v Morgan	5-3	1st round	Professional Players Tournament
	v Jack Rea	5-2	2nd round	Professional Players Tournament
	v Thorburn	5-2	3rd round	Professional Players Tournament
	v Reardon	3-5	Quarter-final	Professional Players Tournament
1983	v Higgins	5-4	1st round	Lada Classic
	v Mountjoy	5-2	Quarter-final	Lada Classic
	v Stevens	5-2	Semi-final	Lada Classic
	v S. Davis	5-9	Final	Lada Classic
	v Higgins	5-4	1st round	Benson & Hedges Masters
	v Charlton	3-5	Quarter-final	Benson & Hedges Masters
	v Griffiths	3-5	Semi-final	Tolly Cobbold Classic
	v Martin	10-4	1st round	Embassy World Championship
	v David Taylor	13-10	2nd round	Embassy World Championship
	v Higgins	11-13	Quarter-final	Embassy World Championship
	v Knowles	5-0	Semi-final	Winfield Masters
	v Thorburn	3-7	Final	Winfield Masters
	v Scott	3-5	1st round	Jameson International
	v T. Jones	5-4	1st round	Professional Players Tournament
	v E. Hughes	0-5	2nd round	Professional Players Tournament
1984	v Roscoe	4-5	Qualifying	Lada Classic
	v Griffiths	1-5	1st round	Benson & Hedges Masters
	v Griffiths	2-5	1st round	Benson & Hedges Irish Masters
	v F. Davis	10-4	1st round	Embassy World Championship
	v Griffiths	5-10	2nd round	Embassy World Championship
	v Williamson	2-5	1st round	Rothmans Grand Prix
	v Williams	1-9	1st round	Coral UK Open
1985	v Virgo	2-5	1st round	Mercantile Credit Classic
	v Griffiths	2-5	1st round	Benson & Hedges Masters
	v Chaperon	1-6	1st round	Dulux British Open
	v Johnson	10-8	1st round	Embassy World Championship
	v Thorburn	3-13	2nd round	Embassy World Championship
	v Williamson	5-2	3rd round	Goya Matchroom Trophy
	v David Taylor	4-5	4th round	Goya Matchroom Trophy
	v Fowler	1-5	3rd round	Rothmans Grand Prix
	v F. Davis	7-9	3rd round	Coral UK Open
1986	v G. Foulds	5-3	3rd round	Mercantile Credit Classic
	v T. Jones	5-3	4th round	Mercantile Credit Classic
	v Mountjoy	3-5	5th round	Mercantile Credit Classic
	v Foldvari	5-4	3rd round	Dulux British Open
	v Johnson	5-3	4th round	Dulux British Open
	v Williams	5-3	5th round	Dulux British Open

v Higgins	1-5	Quarter-final	Dulux British Open
v Thorburn	5-10	1st round	Embassy World Championship
v G. Foulds	2-5	3rd round	BCE International
v King	2-5	3rd round	Rothmans Grand Prix
v O'Kane	5-9	3rd round	Tennents UK Open
1987 v J. McLaughlin	5-1	3rd round	Mercantile Credit Classic
v Duggan	0-5	4th round	Mercantile Credit Classic
v Cripsey	2-5	3rd round	Dulux British Open
v M. Bennett	8-10	Qualifying	Embassy World Championship

BARRY WEST (England)

Born 24.10.58
Turned professional 1985
World ranking 29 (30)
Best professional performance Quarter-finals 1985 Coral UK Championship.

1985 v Hendry	4-5	1st round	Goya Matchroom Trophy
v Meadowcroft	5-2	2nd round	Rothmans Grand Prix
v Dennis Taylor	1-5	3rd round	Rothmans Grand Prix
v Roscoe	9-5	2nd round	Coral UK Open
v E. Hughes	9-3	3rd round	Coral UK Open
v Mountjoy	9-4	4th round	Coral UK Open
v Macleod	9-4	5th round	Coral UK Open
v S. Davis	1-9	Quarter-final	Coral UK Open
1986 v Darrington	5-0	1st round	Mercantile Credit Classic
v Meadowcroft	5-0	2nd round	Mercantile Credit Classic
v Wildman	5-2	3rd round	Mercantile Credit Classic
v Meo	1-5	4th round	Mercantile Credit Classic
v Gilbert	8-9	1st round	Tolly Cobbold English Championship
v Bennett	5-1	1st round	Dulux British Open
v E. McLaughlin	5-3	2nd round	Dulux British Open
v Campbell	4-5	3rd round	Dulux British Open
v Dunning	10-3	Qualifying	Embassy World Championship
v Donnelly	10-5	Qualifying	Embassy World Championship
v Werbeniuk	8-10	Qualifying	Embassy World Championship
v Van Rensberg	5-3	3rd round	BCE International
v Griffiths	1-5	4th round	BCE International
v J. McLaughlin	1-5	3rd round	Rothmans Grand Prix
v T. Jones	4-9	3rd round	Tennents UK Open
1987 v Jonik	5-4	3rd round	Mercantile Credit Classic
v Stevens	5-3	4th round	Mercantile Credit Classic
v Reynolds	3-5	5th round	Mercantile Credit Classic
v V. Harris	6-3	3rd round	Tolly Ales English Championship
v Dodd	3-6	4th round	Tolly Ales English Championship
v Grace	5-2	3rd round	Dulux British Open
v Stevens	4-5	4th round	Dulux British Open
v Spencer	10-5	Qualifying	Embassy World Championship
v Reardon	5-10	1st round	Embassy World Championship

JIMMY WHITE (England)

Born 2.5.62
Turned professional 1980
World ranking 2 (5)
Amateur career 1980 World champion, 1979 English champion.
Best professional performances Winner 1986 Mercantile Credit Classic, 1986 Rothmans Grand Prix, 1987 Dulux British Open, 1984 Benson & Hedges Masters, 1985 & 1986 Benson & Hedges Irish Masters.

1981	v Mikkelsen	9-4	Qualifying	Embassy World Championship
	v Meadowcroft	9-8	Qualifying	Embassy World Championship
	v S. Davis	8-10	1st round	Embassy World Championship
	v Reardon	5-4	Quarter-final	Langs Supreme Scottish Masters
	v S. Davis	6-5	Semi-final	Langs Supreme Scottish Masters
	v Thorburn	**9-4**	**Final**	**Langs Supreme Scottish Masters**
	v Williams	1-5	1st round	Jameson International
	v Thorburn	5-2	1st round	Northern Ireland Classic
	v Mountjoy	9-8	Semi-final	Northern Ireland Classic
	v S. Davis	**11-9**	**Final**	**Northern Ireland Classic**
	v Everton	9-4	Qualifying	Coral UK Championship
	v Virgo	9-6	2nd round	Coral UK Championship
	v Dennis Taylor	9-5	3rd round	Coral UK Championship
	v Reardon	9-8	Quarter-final	Coral UK Championship
	v S. Davis	0-9	Semi-final	Coral UK Championship
1982	v Charlton	4-5	1st round	Benson & Hedges Masters
	v Wildman	9-4	Qualifying	Embassy World Championship
	v Thorburn	10-4	1st round	Embassy World Championship
	v Mans	13-6	2nd round	Embassy World Championship
	v Stevens	13-9	Quarter-final	Embassy World Championship
	v Higgins	15-16	Semi-final	Embassy World Championship
	v Dennis Taylor	4-5	1st round	Langs Supreme Scottish Masters
	v Meadowcroft	5-1	1st round	Jameson International
	v Wilson	2-5	2nd round	Jameson International
	v Wych	5-0	2nd round	Professional Players Tournament
	v Dennis Taylor	5-3	3rd round	Professional Players Tournament
	v Griffiths	5-2	Quarter-final	Professional Players Tournament
	v Virgo	10-4	Semi-final	Professional Players Tournament
	v Reardon	5-10	Final	Professional Players Tournament
	v Medati	9-7	1st round	Coral UK Championship
	v Wilson	9-5	2nd round	Coral UK Championship
	v Reardon	8-9	Quarter-final	Coral UK Championship
1983	v David Taylor	3-5	1st round	Lada Classic
	v David Taylor	5-2	1st round	Benson & Hedges Masters
	v Reardon	2-5	Quarter-final	Benson & Hedges Masters
	v Reardon	6-9	Final	Yamaha International Masters
	v Dennis Taylor	5-4	1st round	Benson & Hedges Irish Masters
	v Higgins	2-5	Quarter-final	Benson & Hedges Irish Masters
	v Meo	8-10	1st round	Embassy World Championship
	v Higgins	3-5	1st round	Langs Supreme Scottish Masters

v Morra	3-5	1st round	Jameson International
v Williamson	5-2	1st round	Professional Players Tournament
v Johnson	3-5	2nd round	Professional Players Tournament
v Black	9-1	1st round	Coral UK Championship
v Dennis Taylor	9-4	2nd round	Coral UK Championship
v Reardon	9-4	Quarter-final	Coral UK Championship
v S. Davis	4-9	Semi-final	Coral UK Championship
1984 v Campbell	5-1	Qualifying	Lada Classic
v Charlton	3-5	1st round	Lada Classic
v Charlton	5-2	1st round	Benson & Hedges Masters
v Reardon	5-3	Quarter-final	Benson & Hedges Masters
v Stevens	6-4	Semi-final	Benson & Hedges Masters
v Griffiths	**9-5**	**Final**	**Benson & Hedges Masters**
v Meo	4-5	1st round	Benson & Hedges Irish Masters
v Knowles	1-5	1st round	Tolly Cobbold Classic
v Williams	10-6	1st round	Embassy World Championship
v Charlton	13-7	2nd round	Embassy World Championship
v Thorburn	13-8	Quarter-final	Embassy World Championship
v Stevens	16-14	Semi-final	Embassy World Championship
v S. Davis	16-18	Final	Embassy World Championship
v Knowles	3-5	Quarter-final	Winfield Australian Masters
v Macleod	5-0	1st round	Langs Supreme Scottish Masters
v Knowles	6-5	Semi-final	Langs Supreme Scottish Masters
v S. Davis	4-9	Final	Langs Supreme Scottish Masters
v Stevens	5-0	1st round	Carlsberg Challenge
v Knowles	**9-7**	**Final**	**Carlsberg Challenge**
v Williams	5-3	1st round	Jameson International
v Meo	5-1	2nd round	Jameson International
v Knowles	4-5	Quarter-final	Jameson International
v Oliver	5-1	1st round	Rothmans Grand Prix
v S. Francisco	1-5	2nd round	Rothmans Grand Prix
v Campbell	9-7	1st round	Coral UK Open
v Mountjoy	9-2	2nd round	Coral UK Open
v S. Davis	4-9	Quarter-final	Coral UK Open
1985 v Browne	5-2	1st round	Mercantile Credit Classic
v King	2-5	2nd round	Mercantile Credit Classic
v Thorne	5-2	1st round	Benson & Hedges Masters
v Spencer	5-2	Quarter-final	Benson & Hedges Masters
v Thorburn	4-6	Semi-final	Benson & Hedges Masters
v Chalmers	9-5	1st round	Tolly Cobbold English Championship
v N. Foulds	9-7	2nd round	Tolly Cobbold English Championship
v Longworth	5-9	Quarter-final	Tolly Cobbold English Championship
v T. Jones	6-5	1st round	Dulux British Open
v S. Francisco	4-5	2nd round	Dulux British Open
v Meo	5-1	1st round	Benson & Hedges Irish Masters
v Thorburn	5-3	Quarter-final	Benson & Hedges Irish Masters
v Knowles	6-4	Semi-final	Benson & Hedges Irish Masters
v Higgins	**9-5**	**Final**	**Benson & Hedges Irish Masters**
v W. Jones	10-4	1st round	Embassy World Championship

v Meo	13-11	2nd round	Embassy World Championship
v Knowles	10-13	Quarter-final	Embassy World Championship
v Johnson	5-4	Quarter-final	Winfield Australian Masters
v Meo	3-6	Semi-final	Winfield Australian Masters
v Higgins	5-0	1st round	Langs Scottish Masters
v Thorne	2-6	Semi-final	Langs Scottish Masters
v Parrott	5-3	Semi-final	Carlsberg Challenge
v Higgins	**8-3**	**Final**	**Carlsberg Challenge**
v Fagan	5-2	3rd round	Goya Matchroom Trophy
v King	5-2	4th round	Goya Matchroom Trophy
v Reynolds	5-1	5th round	Goya Matchroom Trophy
v S. Davis	5-3	Quarter-final	Goya Matchroom Trophy
v N. Foulds	9-5	Semi-final	Goya Matchroom Trophy
v Thorburn	10-12	Final	Goya Matchroom Trophy
v Fitzmaurice	5-0	3rd round	Rothmans Grand Prix
v O'Boye	5-4	4th round	Rothmans Grand Prix
v S. Francisco	4-5	5th round	Rothmans Grand Prix
v Thorburn	3-5	1st round	BCE Canadian Masters
v Bradley	9-4	3rd round	Coral UK Open
v Chappel	9-5	4th round	Coral UK Open
v Higgins	9-6	5th round	Coral UK Open
v Knowles	9-4	Quarter-final	Coral UK Open
v S. Davis	5-9	Semi-final	Coral UK Open
1986 v Fowler	5-1	3rd round	Mercantile Credit Classic
v Virgo	5-2	4th round	Mercantile Credit Classic
v Gauvreau	5-2	5th round	Mercantile Credit Classic
v S. Davis	5-2	Quarter-final	Mercantile Credit Classic
v Williams	9-7	Semi-final	Mercantile Credit Classic
v Thorburn	**13-12**	**Final**	**Mercantile Credit Classic**
v Knowles	3-5	1st round	BCE Belgian Classic
v Meo	5-4	1st round	Benson & Hedges Masters
v Dennis Taylor	5-3	Quarter-final	Benson & Hedges Masters
v S. Davis	6-3	Semi-final	Benson & Hedges Masters
v Thorburn	5-9	Final	Benson & Hedges Masters
v Williamson	9-1	3rd round	Tolly Cobbold English Championship
v Williams	9-5	4th round	Tolly Cobbold English Championship
v N. Foulds	4-9	Quarter-final	Tolly Cobbold English Championship
v P. Francisco	4-5	3rd round	Dulux British Open
v Meo	5-2	Quarter-final	Benson & Hedges Irish Masters
v Fagan	6-0	Semi-final	Benson & Hedges Irish Masters
v Thorne	**9-5**	**Final**	**Benson & Hedges Irish Masters**
v Virgo	10-7	1st round	Embassy World Championship
v Parrott	13-8	2nd round	Embassy World Championship
v S. Davis	5-13	Quarter-final	Embassy World Championship
v Higgins	5-1	1st round	Carlsberg Challenge
v Dennis Taylor	3-8	Final	Carlsberg Challenge
v Hendry	5-1	1st round	Langs Scottish Masters
v Thorburn	2-6	Semi-final	Langs Scottish Masters
v Owers	2-5	3rd round	BCE International

v T. Jones	5-0	3rd round	Rothmans Grand Prix
v J. McLaughlin	5-2	4th round	Rothmans Grand Prix
v Hallett	5-3	5th round	Rothmans Grand Prix
v Hendry	5-4	Quarter-final	Rothmans Grand Prix
v S. Francisco	9-6	Semi-final	Rothmans Grand Prix
v Williams	**10-6**	**Final**	**Rothmans Grand Prix**
v S. Davis	2-5	1st round	BCE Canadian Masters
v Edmonds	9-4	3rd round	Tennents UK Open
v P. Francisco	9-5	4th round	Tennents UK Open
v N. Foulds	7-9	5th round	Tennents UK Open
1987 v Newbury	5-4	3rd round	Mercantile Credit Classic
v Bradley	5-0	4th round	Mercantile Credit Classic
v Duggan	5-2	5th round	Mercantile Credit Classic
v Griffiths	5-3	Quarter-final	Mercantile Credit Classic
v Reynolds	9-8	Semi-final	Mercantile Credit Classic
v S. Davis	12-13	Final	Mercantile Credit Classic
v Meo	4-5	1st round	Benson & Hedges Masters
v Cripsey	6-4	3rd round	Tolly Ales English Championship
v Reynolds	5-6	4th round	Tolly Ales English Championship
v Chappel	5-1	3rd round	Dulux British Open
v Hallett	5-2	4th round	Dulux British Open
v Williams	5-0	5th round	Dulux British Open
v Spencer	5-3	Quarter-final	Dulux British Open
v Thorburn	9-5	Semi-final	Dulux British Open
v N. Foulds	**13-9**	**Final**	**Dulux British Open**
v Thorne	4-5	Quarter-final	Benson & Hedges Irish Masters
v Reynolds	10-8	1st round	Embassy World Championship
v Parrott	13-11	2nd round	Embassy World Championship
v O'Kane	13-6	Quarter-final	Embassy World Championship
v S. Davis	11-16	Semi-final	Embassy World Championship

TERRY WHITTHREAD (England)

Born 7.7.64
Turned professional 1986
World ranking 116 (–)
Amateur career 1985 English champion.

1986 v Kelly	1-5	1st round	BCE International
v Duggan	1-5	1st round	Rothmans Grand Prix
v Darrington	8-9	1st round	Tennents UK Open
1987 v Roscoe	1-5	1st round	Mercantile Credit Classic
v Fisher	3-6	1st round	Tolly Ales English Championship
v D. Hughes	5-1	1st round	Dulux British Open
v Spencer	2-5	2nd round	Dulux British Open
v Roscoe	2-10	Qualifying	Embassy World Championship

Rex Williams

Jimmy White

MARK WILDMAN (England)

Born 25.1.36
Turned professional 1979
World ranking 47 (43)
Best professional performance Semi-final 1984 Lada Classic.

1980	v Jonik	7-9	Qualifying	Embassy World Championship
	v Wilson	9-8	Qualifying	Coral UK Championship
	v Spencer	9-7	1st round	Coral UK Championship
	v F. Davis	6-9	2nd round	Coral UK Championship
1981	v Bennett	9-3	Qualifying	John Courage English
	v Thorne	2-9	1st round	John Courage English
	v Edmonds	3-9	Qualifying	Embassy World Championship
	v Morra	5-3	Qualifying	Jameson International
	v E. McLaughlin	3-5	Qualifying	Jameson International
	v Sinclair	8-9	Qualifying	Coral UK Championship
1982	v G. Foulds	9-8	Qualifying	Embassy World Championship
	v White	4-9	Qualifying	Embassy World Championship
	v Gibson	5-1	Qualifying	Jameson International
	v Hallett	5-2	Qualifying	Jameson International
	v Dennis Taylor	2-5	1st round	Jameson International
	v Dunning	5-4	1st round	Professional Players Tournament
	v Mans	5-4	2nd round	Professional Players Tournament
	v Johnson	4-5	3rd round	Professional Players Tournament
	v Roscoe	9-4	Qualifying	Coral UK Championship
	v Reardon	5-9	1st round	Coral UK Championship
1983	v S. Davis	2-5	1st round	Benson & Hedges Masters
	v B. Harris	10-7	Qualifying	Embassy World Championship
	v Griffiths	8-10	1st round	Embassy World Championship
	v B. Harris	5-2	Qualifying	Jameson International
	v Mountjoy	4-5	1st round	Jameson International
	v Jonik	5-4	1st round	Professional Players Tournament
	v David Taylor	5-3	2nd round	Professional Players Tournament
	v Stevens	0-5	3rd round	Professional Players Tournament
	v Greaves	9-5	Qualifying	Coral UK Championship
	v Thorne	5-9	1st round	Coral UK Championship
1984	v Virgo	5-2	Qualifying	Lada Classic
	v S. Francisco	5-1	1st round	Lada Classic
	v Charlton	5-4	Quarter-final	Lada Classic
	v Meo	3-5	Semi-final	Lada Classic
	v Andrewartha	9-10	Qualifying	Embassy World Championship
	v W. Jones	0-5	Qualifying	Jameson International
	v J. McLaughlin	5-3	1st round	Rothmans Grand Prix
	v Mountjoy	0-5	2nd round	Rothmans Grand Prix
	v T. Jones	2-9	Qualifying	Coral UK Open
1985	v Fagan	3-5	Qualifying	Mercantile Credit Classic
	v Longworth	3-9	1st round	Tolly Cobbold English Championship
	v Gibson	6-1	1st round	Dulux British Open
	v Stevens	2-5	2nd round	Dulux British Open

	v Edmonds	7-10	Qualifying	Embassy World Championship
	v Scott	1-5	3rd round	Goya Matchroom Trophy
	v Duggan	5-4	3rd round	Rothmans Grand Prix
	v Thorburn	2-5	4th round	Rothmans Grand Prix
	v Drago	5-9	3rd round	Coral UK Open
1986	v West	2-5	3rd round	Mercantile Credit Classic
	v Cripsey	9-5	3rd round	Tolly Cobbold English Championship
	v Meo	3-9	4th round	Tolly Cobbold English Championship
	v Jenkins	5-4	3rd round	Dulux British Open
	v Thorburn	1-5	4th round	Dulux British Open
	v Edmonds	9-10	Qualifying	Embassy World Championship
	v Rowswell	5-2	2nd round	BCE International
	v P. Francisco	2-5	3rd round	BCE International
	v Ellis	5-1	2nd round	Rothmans Grand Prix
	v Longworth	5-2	3rd round	Rothmans Grand Prix
	v Williams	1-5	4th round	Rothmans Grand Prix
	v Roscoe	6-9	2nd round	Tennents UK Open
1987	v Kearney	3-5	2nd round	Mercantile Credit Classic
	v Parrott	1-6	3rd round	Tolly Ales English Championship
	v Chalmers	5-0	2nd round	Dulux British Open
	v Thorburn	3-5	3rd round	Dulux British Open
	v Foldvari	10-5	Qualifying	Embassy World Championship
	v Wright	0-10	Qualifying	Embassy World Championship

GLEN WILKINSON (Australia)

Born 4.7.59
Turned professional 1985
World ranking 97 (102)
Amateur career 1985 Australian champion.

1985	v Jenkins	6-2	1st round	Australian Championship
	v Heywood	7-3	2nd round	Australian Championship
	v Charlton	2-8	Quarter-final	Australian Championship
	v Demarco	5-2	1st round	Goya Matchroom Trophy
	v Longworth	0-5	2nd round	Goya Matchroom Trophy
	v Gilbert	4-5	1st round	Rothmans Grand Prix
	v Smith	9-4	1st round	Coral UK Open
	v Fowler	6-9	2nd round	Coral UK Open
1986	v O'Boye	1-5	1st round	Mercantile Credit Classic
	v Watchorn	5-4	1st round	Dulux British Open
	v Donnelly	4-5	2nd round	Dulux British Open
	v Kearney	5-10	Qualifying	Embassy World Championship
	v Heywood	6-0	2nd round	Australian Championship
	v Campbell	1-6	Quarter-final	Australian Championship
	v Bradley	4-5	2nd round	BCE International
	v G. Foulds	3-5	1st round	Rothmans Grand Prix
	v Jonik	9-8	1st round	Tennents UK Open
	v Chappel	2-9	2nd round	Tennents UK Open

1987 v Fitzmaurice	5-2	1st round	Mercantile Credit Classic
v Fowler	1-5	2nd round	Mercantile Credit Classic
v Fitzmaurice	5-0	1st round	Dulux British Open
v Mans	5-2	2nd round	Dulux British Open
v David Taylor	4-5	3rd round	Dulux British Open

REX WILLIAMS (England)

Born 20.7.33
Turned professional 1951
World ranking 12 (16)
Amateur career 1951 English champion.
Best professional performance Runner-up 1986 Rothmans Grand Prix.

1969 v Bennett	38-11	Quarter-final	World Championship
v Spencer	18-55	Semi-final	World Championship
1970 v G. Owen	11-31	Quarter-final	World Championship (Apr)
1972 v Reardon	25-23	Quarter-final	World Championship
v Higgins	30-31	Semi-final	World Championship
1973 v Thorburn	16-15	2nd round	World Championship
v Spencer	7-16	Quarter-final	World Championship
1974 v Pulman	15-12	2nd round	World Championship
v Mans	15-4	Quarter-final	World Championship
v Miles	7-15	Semi-final	World Championship
1975 v Higgins	5-3	Quarter-final	Benson & Hedges Masters
v Reardon	4-5	Semi-final	Benson & Hedges Masters
v Anderson	15-4	2nd round	World Championship
v Higgins	12-19	Quarter-final	World Championship
1976 v Meadowcroft	7-15	1st round	Embassy World Championship
1977 v Thorburn	6-13	1st round	Embassy World Championship
1978 v Thorne	3-9	Qualifying	Embassy World Championship
v Griffiths	9-8	Qualifying	Coral UK Championship
v Miles	8-9	1st round	Coral UK Championship
1979 v Spencer	2-6	Semi-final	Holsten Lager International
v Greaves	9-2	Prelim	Embassy World Championship
v Miles	5-9	Qualifying	Embassy World Championship
1980 v Wych	7-9	Qualifying	Embassy World Championship
v Barrie	9-1	Qualifying	Coral UK Championship
v Mountjoy	9-8	1st round	Coral UK Championship
v David Taylor	9-7	2nd round	Coral UK Championship
v Reardon	4-9	Quarter-final	Coral UK Championship
1981 v Hood	9-4	Qualifying	Embassy World Championship
v Edmonds	7-9	Qualifying	Embassy World Championship
v French	5-0	Qualifying	Jameson International
v White	5-1	1st round	Jameson International
v F. Davis	5-0	2nd round	Jameson International
v Dennis Taylor	1-5	3rd round	Jameson International
v French	9-3	Qualifying	Coral UK Championship

	v Roscoe	9-4	Qualifying	Coral UK Championship
	v Dunning	9-4	Qualifying	Coral UK Championship
	v Meo	8-9	2nd round	Coral UK Championship
1982	v Black	9-2	Qualifying	Embassy World Championship
	v Mountjoy	3-10	1st round	Embassy World Championship
	v Medati	5-3	Qualifying	Jameson International
	v E. McLaughlin	5-1	Qualifying	Jameson International
	v Griffiths	2-5	1st round	Jameson International
	v Ross	5-0	1st round	Professional Players Tournament
	v Charlton	2-5	2nd round	Professional Players Tournament
	v G. Foulds	9-7	Qualifying	Coral UK Championship
	v S. Davis	6-9	1st round	Coral UK Championship
	v Darrington	10-0	Qualifying	Embassy World Championship
	v F. Davis	10-1	Qualifying	Embassy World Championship
	v S. Davis	4-10	1st round	Embassy World Championship
1983	v French	5-1	Qualifying	Jameson International
	v Reynolds	3-5	Qualifying	Jameson International
	v Sheehan	5-1	1st round	Professional Players Tournament
	v Knowles	4-5	2nd round	Professional Players Tournament
	v V. Harris	9-6	Qualifying	Coral UK Championship
	v Wilson	4-9	1st round	Coral UK Championship
1984	v Reardon	5-4	Qualifying	Lada Classic
	v Meo	3-5	1st round	Lada Classic
	v Oliver	10-8	Qualifying	Embassy World Championship
	v White	6-10	1st round	Embassy World Championship
	v Meadowcroft	5-4	Qualifying	Jameson International
	v White	3-5	Qualifying	Jameson International
	v Chalmers	5-0	1st round	Rothmans Grand Prix
	v Stevens	3-5	2nd round	Rothmans Grand Prix
	v Fisher	9-8	Qualifying	Coral UK Open
	v Werbeniuk	9-1	1st round	Coral UK Open
	v Higgins	7-9	2nd round	Coral UK Open
1985	v Donnelly	5-3	Qualifying	Mercantile Credit Classic
	v Dennis Taylor	5-3	1st round	Mercantile Credit Classic
	v Griffiths	3-5	2nd round	Mercantile Credit Classic
	v T. Jones	9-6	1st round	Tolly Cobbold English Championship
	v S. Davis	2-9	2nd round	Tolly Cobbold English Championship
	v Fowler	4-6	1st round	Dulux British Open
	v F. Davis	10-6	Qualifying	Embassy World Championship
	v Griffiths	3-10	1st round	Embassy World Championship
	v King	3-5	3rd round	Goya Matchroom Trophy
	v Watterson	5-2	3rd round	Rothmans Grand Prix
	v Dennis Taylor	2-5	4th round	Rothmans Grand Prix
	v King	9-5	3rd round	Coral UK Open
	v P. Francisco	9-7	4th round	Coral UK Open
	v Stevens	7-9	5th round	Coral UK Open
1986	v Watterson	5-0	3rd round	Mercantile Credit Classic
	v V. Harris	5-1	4th round	Mercantile Credit Classic
	v Knowles	5-2	5th round	Mercantile Credit Classic
	v Higgins	5-2	Quarter-final	Mercantile Credit Classic

	v White	7-9	Semi-final	Mercantile Credit Classic
	v Miles	9-6	3rd round	Tolly Cobbold English Championship
	v White	5-9	4th round	Tolly Cobbold English Championship
	v Drago	5-1	3rd round	Dulux British Open
	v Bales	5-4	4th round	Dulux British Open
	v Werbeniuk	3-5	5th round	Dulux British Open
	v S. Francisco	4-10	1st round	Embassy World Championship
	v O'Boye	5-0	3rd round	BCE International
	v Duggan	5-4	4th round	BCE International
	v S. Davis	4-5	5th round	BCE International
	v Bear	5-2	3rd round	Rothmans Grand Prix
	v Wildman	5-1	4th round	Rothmans Grand Prix
	v Higgins	5-1	5th round	Rothmans Grand Prix
	v S. Davis	5-1	Quarter-final	Rothmans Grand Prix
	v N. Foulds	9-8	Semi-final	Rothmans Grand Prix
	v White	6-10	Final	Rothmans Grand Prix
	v Drago	7-9	3rd round	Tennents UK Open
1987	v Morra	5-2	3rd round	Mercantile Credit Classic
	v Charlton	4-5	4th round	Mercantile Credit Classic
	v Thorburn	1-5	1st round	Benson & Hedges Masters
	v T. Jones	6-4	3rd round	Tolly Ales English Championship
	v David Taylor	6-2	4th round	Tolly Ales English Championship
	v Johnson	5-4	Quarter-final	Tolly Ales English Championship
	v Foldvari	5-4	3rd round	Dulux British Open
	v James	5-2	4th round	Dulux British Open
	v White	0-5	5th round	Dulux British Open
	v Macleod	5-10	1st round	Embassy World Championship

IAN WILLIAMSON (England)

Born 1.12.58
Turned professional 1982
World ranking 81 (67)

	v Donnelly	5-3	Qualifying	Jameson International
1982	v Donnelly	5-3	Qualifying	Jameson International
	v Kelly	1-5	Qualifying	Jameson International
	v Dodd	1-9	Qualifying	Coral UK Championship
1983	v French	10-8	Qualifying	Embassy World Championship
	v Dodd	9-10	Qualifying	Embassy World Championship
	v Darrington	3-5	Qualifying	Jameson International
	v White	2-5	1st round	Professional Players Tournament
	v Hargreaves	9-4	Qualifying	Coral UK Championship
	v Black	6-9	Qualifying	Coral UK Championship
1984	v Houlihan	10-5	Qualifying	Embassy World Championship
	v Hines	10-6	Qualifying	Embassy World Championship
	v Miles	6-10	Qualifying	Embassy World Championship
	v V. Harris	5-0	Qualifying	Jameson International
	v G. Foulds	4-5	Qualifying	Jameson International
	v Thornley	5-2	Qualifying	Rothmans Grand Prix

v Werbeniuk	5-2	1st round	Rothmans Grand Prix
v Johnson	5-4	2nd round	Rothmans Grand Prix
v Knowles	2-5	3rd round	Rothmans Grand Prix
v P. Francisco	2-9	Qualifying	Coral UK Open
1985 v Kearney	5-3	Qualifying	Mercantile Credit Classic
v Fagan	1-5	Qualifying	Mercantile Credit Classic
v Bradley	8-9	Qualifying	Tolly Cobbold English Championship
v Chappel	5-6	Qualifying	Dulux British Open
v Medati	8-10	Qualifying	Embassy World Championship
v J. McLaughlin	5-3	2nd round	Goya Matchroom Trophy
v Werbeniuk	2-5	3rd round	Goya Matchroom Trophy
v Gilbert	4-5	2nd round	Rothmans Grand Prix
v Mikkelsen	3-9	2nd round	Coral UK Championship
1986 v John Rea	4-5	2nd round	Mercantile Credit Classic
v Parkin	9-4	2nd round	Tolly Cobbold English Championship
v White	1-9	3rd round	Tolly Cobbold English Championship
v Cripsey	5-4	2nd round	Dulux British Open
v Knowles	1-5	3rd round	Dulux British Open
v Van Rensberg	9-10	Qualifying	Embassy World Championship
v Spencer	4-5	2nd round	BCE International
v Hendry	1-5	2nd round	Rothmans Grand Prix
v Browne	9-4	2nd round	Tennents UK Open
v Martin	5-9	3rd round	Tennents UK Open
1987 v Edmonds	5-2	2nd round	Mercantile Credit Classic
v Wilson	4-5	3rd round	Mercantile Credit Classic
v Roe	6-4	2nd round	Tolly Ales English Championship
v Hallett	2-6	3rd round	Tolly Ales English Championship
v King	3-5	2nd round	Dulux British Open
v Black	8-10	Qualifying	Embassy World Championship

CLIFF WILSON (Wales)

Born 10.5.34
Turned professional 1979
World ranking 17 (23)
Amateur career Welsh champion 1956, 1977, 1979.
Best professional performances Quarter-finals 1982 Jameson International, 1986 BCE International, 1985 Rothmans Grand Prix, 1987 Mercantile Credit Classic.

1979 v Pulman	9-7	2nd round	Coral UK Championship
v Griffiths	4-9	3rd round	Coral UK Championship
v Reardon	3-9	1st round	Woodpecker Welsh Championship
1980 v Jonik	9-6	Qualifying	Embassy World Championship
v Mountjoy	6-10	1st round	Embassy World Championship
v Wildman	8-9	Qualifying	Coral UK Championship
1981 v Andrewartha	6-5	Prelim	Woodpecker Welsh Championship
v Mountjoy	9-6	Semi-final	Woodpecker Welsh Championship

	v Reardon	6-9	Final	Woodpecker Welsh Championship
	v Andrewartha	9-4	Qualifying	Embassy World Championship
	v Sinclair	9-4	Qualifying	Embassy World Championship
	v David Taylor	6-10	1st round	Embassy World Championship
	v Meadowcroft	4-5	1st round	Jameson International
	v Johnson	5-9	Qualifying	Coral UK Championship
1982	v M. Owen	6-0	1st round	Welsh Championship
	v Griffiths	6-9	Semi-final	Welsh Championship
	v Medati	9-5	Qualifying	Embassy World Championship
	v Charlton	5-10	1st round	Embassy World Championship
	v Johnson	5-4	Qualifying	Jameson International
	v Mountjoy	5-4	1st round	Jameson International
	v White	5-2	2nd round	Jameson International
	v Knowles	4-5	Quarter-final	Jameson International
	v Morra	5-2	1st round	Professional Players Tournament
	v Knowles	5-4	2nd round	Professional Players Tournament
	v Reynolds	1-5	3rd round	Professional Players Tournament
	v E. McLaughlin	9-6	Qualifying	Coral UK Championship
	v Thorne	9-7	1st round	Coral UK Championship
	v White	5-9	2nd round	Coral UK Championship
1983	v Thorburn	3-5	1st round	Lada Classic
	v Roscoe	6-4	Quarter-final	Woodpecker Welsh Championship
	v Mountjoy	3-9	Semi-final	Woodpecker Welsh Championship
	v Everton	10-1	Qualifying	Embassy World Championship
	v Johnson	10-8	Qualifying	Embassy World Championship
	v Mountjoy	2-10	1st round	Embassy World Championship
	v Donnelly	1-5	Qualifying	Jameson International
	v Bennett	5-1	1st round	Professional Players Tournament
	v Virgo	5-2	2nd round	Professional Players Tournament
	v Thorburn	3-5	3rd round	Professional Players Tournament
	v Williams	9-4	1st round	Coral UK Championship
	v Reardon	4-9	2nd round	Coral UK Championship
1984	v Charlton	0-5	Qualifying	Lada Classic
	v Roscoe	6-2	1st round	Strongbow Welsh Championship
	v Reardon	9-4	Semi-final	Strongbow Welsh Championship
	v Mountjoy	3-9	Final	Strongbow Welsh Championship
	v Mifsud	8-10	Qualifying	Embassy World Championship
	v Dodd	1-5	Qualifying	Jameson International
	v Donnelly	5-2	1st round	Rothmans Grand Prix
	v Reardon	4-5	2nd round	Rothmans Grand Prix
	v Dodd	9-8	Qualifying	Coral UK Open
	v Griffiths	9-6	1st round	Coral UK Open
	v Thorburn	3-9	2nd round	Coral UK Open
1985	v Fowler	5-4	Qualifying	Mercantile Credit Classic
	v Mountjoy	5-4	1st round	Mercantile Credit Classic
	v Johnson	0-5	2nd round	Mercantile Credit Classic
	v Longworth	3-6	1st round	Dulux British Open
	v Fagan	9-10	Qualifying	Embassy World Championship
	v Roscoe	6-3	Quarter-final	BCE Welsh Championship
	v Mountjoy	2-9	Semi-final	BCE Welsh Championship

	v Roscoe	5-1	3rd round	Goya Matchroom Trophy
	v Chappel	5-0	4th round	Goya Matchroom Trophy
	v Johnson	1-5	5th round	Goya Matchroom Trophy
	v Bales	5-1	3rd round	Rothmans Grand Prix
	v Scott	5-3	4th round	Rothmans Grand Prix
	v Drago	5-2	5th round	Rothmans Grand Prix
	v Dennis Taylor	2-5	Quarter-final	Rothmans Grand Prix
	v Cripsey	7-9	3rd round	Coral UK Open
1986	v Browne	3-5	3rd round	Mercantile Credit Classic
	v Newbury	6-4	Quarter-final	Zetters Welsh Championship
	v Griffiths	1-9	Semi-final	Zetters Welsh Championship
	v Chaperon	5-3	3rd round	Dulux British Open
	v Stevens	0-5	4th round	Dulux British Open
	v Charlton	6-10	1st round	Embassy World Championship
	v J. McLaughlin	5-2	3rd round	BCE International
	v Bales	5-1	4th round	BCE International
	v Knowles	5-4	5th round	BCE International
	v Thorburn	1-5	Quarter-final	BCE International
	v Anderson	5-4	3rd round	Rothmans Grand Prix
	v N. Foulds	0-5	4th round	Rothmans Grand Prix
	v Spencer	5-9	3rd round	Tennents UK Open
1987	v Williamson	5-4	3rd round	Mercantile Credit Classic
	v Dodd	5-4	4th round	Mercantile Credit Classic
	v W. Jones	5-3	5th round	Mercantile Credit Classic
	v Reynolds	1-5	Quarter-final	Mercantile Credit Classic
	v Newbury	2-6	Quarter-final	Matchroom Welsh Championship
	v G. Foulds	5-3	3rd round	Dulux British Open
	v S. Francisco	5-4	4th round	Dulux British Open
	v Virgo	2-5	5th round	Dulux British Open
	v Wright	4-10	Qualifying	Embassy World Championship

JON WRIGHT (England)

Born 10.8.62
Turned professional 1986
World ranking 54 (–)
Best professional performances Last 32 1987 Embassy World Championship, 1987 Mercantile Credit Classic.

1986	v Watterson	5-1	1st round	BCE International
	v Black	1-5	2nd round	BCE International
	v Fisher	5-1	1st round	Rothmans Grand Prix
	v Bradley	5-0	2nd round	Rothmans Grand Prix
	v Dennis Taylor	3-5	3rd round	Rothmans Grand Prix
	v Smith	9-7	1st round	Tennents UK Open
	v Fagan	9-0	2nd round	Tennents UK Open
	v Johnson	1-9	3rd round	Tennents UK Open

1987	v D. Hughes	5-2	1st round	Mercantile Credit Classic
	v Chappel	5-4	2nd round	Mercantile Credit Classic
	v E. Hughes	5-4	3rd round	Mercantile Credit Classic
	v Hendry	1-5	4th round	Mercantile Credit Classic
	v Chalmers	6-5	1st round	Tolly Ales English Championship
	v Spencer	1-6	2nd round	Tolly Ales English Championship
	v Sheehan	2-5	1st round	Dulux British Open
	v Houlihan	10-4	Qualifying	Embassy World Championship
	v Browne	10-6	Qualifying	Embassy World Championship
	v Wildman	10-0	Qualifying	Embassy World Championship
	v Wilson	10-4	Qualifying	Embassy World Championship
	v Higgins	6-10	1st round	Embassy World Championship

JIM WYCH (Canada)

Born 11.1.55
Turned professional 1979
World ranking 36 (32)
Best professional performances Quarter-finals 1980 Embassy World Championship, 1986 Dulux British Open.

1980	v John Bear	9-5	Qualifying	Embassy World Championship
	v Williams	9-7	Qualifying	Embassy World Championship
	v Pulman	10-5	1st round	Embassy World Championship
	v Dennis Taylor	13-10	2nd round	Embassy World Championship
	v Thorburn	6-13	Quarter-final	Embassy World Championship
1981	v Knowles	3-9	Qualifying	Embassy World Championship
	v Johnson	2-5	1st round	Jameson International
1982	v Higgins	3-5	1st round	Benson & Hedges Irish Masters
	v John Bear	4-9	Qualifying	Embassy World Championship
	v Bennett	5-0	Qualifying	Jameson International
	v Werbeniuk	3-5	1st round	Jameson International
	v Kelly	5-0	1st round	Professional Players Tournament
	v White	0-5	2nd round	Professional Players Tournament
1984	v Ganim	10-1	Qualifying	Embassy World Championship
	v Scott	10-6	Qualifying	Embassy World Championship
	v Fagan	10-3	Qualifying	Embassy World Championship
	v Reardon	7-10	1st round	Embassy World Championship
1985	v Bradley	10-7	Qualifying	Embassy World Championship
	v Virgo	4-10	Qualifying	Embassy World Championship
	v Sanderson	5-2	1st round	Canadian Championship
	v John Bear	6-3	Quarter-final	Canadian Championship
	v Thorburn	5-6	Semi-final	Canadian Championship
	v Rempe	5-1	2nd round	Goya Matchroom Trophy
	v Mountjoy	1-5	3rd round	Goya Matchroom Trophy
	v V. Harris	3-5	2nd round	Rothmans Grand Prix
	v Duggan	9-5	2nd round	Coral UK Open
	v S. Francisco	8-9	3rd round	Coral UK Open

1986	v Demarco	5-0	2nd round	Mercantile Credit Classic
	v E. Hughes	2-5	3rd round	Mercantile Credit Classic
	v Van Rensberg	5-0	2nd round	Dulux British Open
	v Reynolds	5-3	3rd round	Dulux British Open
	v Knowles	5-4	4th round	Dulux British Open
	v Parrott	5-4	5th round	Dulux British Open
	v S. Davis	2-5	Quarter-final	Dulux British Open
	v Chappel	10-6	Qualifying	Embassy World Championship
	v Duggan	10-5	Qualifying	Embassy World Championship
	v Hallett	7-10	Qualifying	Embassy World Championship
	v Mikkelsen	6-3	2nd round	Canadian Championship
	v Stevens	6-2	Semi-final	Canadian Championship
	v Thorburn	2-6	Final	Canadian Championship
	v Bradley	5-2	3rd round	BCE International
	v Thorburn	3-5	4th round	BCE International
	v John Rea	5-2	3rd round	Rothmans Grand Prix
	v Mountjoy	1-5	4th round	Rothmans Grand Prix
	v B. Harris	9-6	3rd round	Tennents UK Open
	v N. Foulds	3-9	4th round	Tennents UK Open
1987	v B. Harris	3-5	3rd round	Mercantile Credit Classic
	v Murphy	1-5	3rd round	Dulux British Open
	v Bradley	10-7	Qualifying	Embassy World Championship
	v Griffiths	4-10	1st round	Embassy World Championship

At the end of the 1986–87 season, the following players became non-tournament playing members of the WPBSA: Bernard Bennett (England), Bert Demarco (Scotland), James Giannaros (Australia), Mike Hines (South Africa), Paddy Morgan (Australia), Maurice Parkin (England).

Other non-tournament members are: Lou Condo (Australia), Mannie Francisco (South Africa), George Ganim (Australia), Steve Mizerak (USA), Alan Robidoux (Canada), Wayne Sanderson (Canada).

Omprakesh Agrawal (India) and Sakchai Simngam (Thailand) both resigned during the 1986–87 season.

The nine players who qualified for professional status from 1987–88 are: Jim Chambers, Martin Clark, Anthony Harris, Derek Heaton, Eric Lawlor, Robert Marshall, Steve Meakin, Jason Smith and Gary Wilkinson (all England).

SNOOKER GREATS

JOE DAVIES O.B.E. (1901–1978)
Although only one of the 'Big Four' at billiards, Joe Davis was un-doubtedly the number one at snooker. With his friend Bill Camkin, a Birmingham billiard trader, he promoted and won the first World Professional Snooker Championship in 1927. He went on to win the title every year until 1940. The championship was suspended until 1946, at which point Davis beat Horace Lindrum 78-67 to take the title for the 15th time.

Davis then retired from Championship play. He continued to play in other tournaments and in the public's mind he was still the champion, whoever had won the World Championship in his absence.

His expertise at the three-ball game carried him to four World Pro-fessional Billiards titles but his name will always be synonymous with snooker. It was he who developed the modern break-making methods, using the black as the key colour, and it was he who brought the sport to the public's attention.

WALTER DONALDSON (1907–1973)
Consistent and steady, Walter Donaldson reached eight consecutive World Championship finals between 1948 and 1954. In 1947 and 1950 he beat Fred Davis to take the title.

As professional snooker's appeal dwindled in the mid-1950s, a dis-illusioned Donaldson turned his billiard room into a cowshed and broke up the slates of his table for crazy paving.

JOHN PULMAN (born 1926)
After winning the English Amateur Championship in 1946, John Pulman turned professional but was at his peak when the professional game was going through a period in the doldrums. He was never able to capitalise fully on his natural talent.

He won the world title in 1957 and then successfully withstood a series of challengers. When the influx of new professionals led to the Championship being restored to a tournament format, he once reached the final, losing to Ray Reardon.

An accident led to his retirement from playing in 1982 but he is still involved on the circuit as a member of ITV's commentary team.

THE CIRCUIT

WINFIELD AUSTRALIAN MASTERS

Having existed for four years as the Australian version of Pot Black, the Winfield Australian Masters was expanded in 1983 to an authentic tournament format although the final stages were still played in a television studio. In 1986, however, the event reverted to its original format and consequently those results are not listed.

1983
First round: C. Thorburn beat W. King 3-1; J. White beat I. Anderson 3-2; K. Stevens beat D. Mountjoy 3-1; E. Charlton beat P. Morgan 3-2; A. Higgins beat J. Spencer 3-2; B. Werbeniuk beat Dennis Taylor 3-2; T. Meo beat David Taylor 3-0; A. Knowles beat J. Campbell 3-1

Quarter-finals: Thorburn beat White 4-2; Stevens beat Charlton 4-1; Werbeniuk beat Higgins 4-0; Knowles beat Meo 4-3

Semi-finals: Thorburn beat Stevens 5-2; Werbeniuk beat Knowles 5-0

Final: Thorburn beat Werbeniuk 7-3

1984
First round: W. Thorne beat C. Thorburn 4-1; J. Virgo beat D. Mountjoy 4-1; T. Meo beat B. Werbeniuk 4-0; K. Stevens beat P. Morgan 4-2; E. Charlton beat W. King 4-1; David Taylor beat I. Anderson 4-2; J. White beat J. Campbell 4-0; A. Knowles beat Dennis Taylor 4-2

Quarter-finals: Virgo beat Thorne 5-3; Charlton beat David Taylor 5-4; Meo beat Stevens 5-1; Knowles beat White 5-3

Semi-finals: Virgo beat Meo 6-2; Knowles beat Charlton 6-0

Final: Knowles beat Virgo 7-3

1985
First round: E. Charlton beat I. Anderson 4-2; J. Campbell beat A. Higgins 4-1; W. Thorne beat P. Morgan 4-2; J. Parrott beat S. Francisco 4-3; J. Johnson beat B. Werbeniuk 4-1; J. White beat David Taylor 4-0; T. Meo beat W. King 4-1; J. Virgo beat A. Knowles 4-1

Quarter-finals: Campbell beat Charlton 5-4; Parrott beat Thorne 5-0; White beat Johnson 5-4; Meo beat Virgo 5-3

Semi-finals: Campbell beat Parrott 6-4; Meo beat White 6-3

Final: Meo beat Campbell 7-2

CAMUS HONG KONG MASTERS

First staged 1984*
Sponsors Camus
Venue Queen Elizabeth Stadium
Prize-money last season £86,800
TV Hong Kong
The first two events, in 1984 and 1985, were small, pathfinding events which do not meet the conditions required for full inclusion in this book.

1986
Semi-finals: Dennis Taylor beat T. Griffiths 5-4; W. Thorne beat S. Davis 5-2

Final: Thorne beat Dennis Taylor 8-3

CARLSBERG CHALLENGE

First staged 1984
Sponsors Carlsberg
Venue RTE Studios
Initial prize-money £20,000
Prize-money last season £33,000
TV RTE

1984
First round: A. Knowles beat A. Higgins 5-3; J. White beat K. Stevens 5-0

Final: White beat Knowles 9-7

1985
First round: J. White beat J. Parrott 5-3; A. Higgins beat C. Thorburn 5-4

Final: White beat Higgins 8-3

1986
First round: J. White beat A. Higgins 5-1; Dennis Taylor beat J. Johnson 5-3

Final: Dennis Taylor beat White 8-3

MATCHROOM TROPHY

First staged 1986
Sponsors Matchroom
Venue Cliffs Pavilion, Southend
Initial prize-money £100,000
Prize-money last season £100,000
TV None

1986
First round: T. Griffiths beat T. Meo 6-3; W. Thorne beat N. Foulds 6-3

Semi-finals: S. Davis beat Griffiths 6-2; Thorne beat Dennis Taylor 6-5

Final: Thorne beat S. Davis 10-9

LANGS SCOTTISH MASTERS

First staged 1981
Sponsors Langs
Venue Kelvin Hall, Glasgow (1981), Holiday Inn, Glasgow (1982),
Skean Dhu Hotel (re-named Hospitality Inn), Glasgow (1983–)
Initial prize-money £20,500
Prize-money this season £40,000
TV BBC Scotland

1981
Preliminary round: V. Harris beat I. Black 4-0

First round: J. White beat R. Reardon 5-4; S. Davis beat D. Mountjoy 5-0;
C. Thorburn beat K. Stevens 5-1; A. Higgins beat V. Harris 5-3

Semi-finals: White beat Davis 6-5; Thorburn beat Higgins 6-2

Final: White beat Thorburn 9-4

1982
First round: Dennis Taylor beat J. White 5-4; S. Davis beat A. Knowles 5-4;
T. Griffiths beat R. Reardon 5-3; A. Higgins beat E. Sinclair 5-1

Semi-finals: S. Davis beat Dennis Taylor 6-1; Higgins beat Griffiths 6-5

Final: S. Davis beat Higgins 9-4

1983
First round: C. Thorburn beat T. Griffiths 5-1; S. Davis beat M. Macleod 5-1;
A. Knowles beat T. Meo 5-4; A. Higgins beat J. White 5-3

Semi-finals: Knowles beat Thorburn 6-2; S. Davis beat Higgins 6-2

Final: S. Davis beat Knowles 9-6

1984
First round: A. Knowles beat T. Griffiths 5-3; J. White beat M. Macleod 5-0;
S. Davis beat C. Thorburn 5-2; A. Higgins beat K. Stevens 5-2

Semi-finals: White beat Knowles 6-5; S. Davis beat Higgins 6-4

Final: S. Davis beat White 9-4

1985
First round: J. White beat A. Higgins 5-0; C. Thorburn beat M. Macleod 5-1;
S. Francisco beat A. Knowles 5-4; W. Thorne beat Dennis Taylor 5-2

Semi-finals: Thorne beat White 6-2; Thorburn beat Francisco 6-0

Final: Thorburn beat Thorne 9-7

1986
First round: C. Thorburn beat J. Parrott 5-1; J. White beat S. Hendry 5-1;
K. Stevens beat A. Knowles 5-3; A. Higgins beat J. Johnson 5-2

Semi-finals: Thorburn beat White 6-2; Higgins beat Stevens 6-2

Final: Thorburn beat Higgins 9-8

BCE INTERNATIONAL

First staged 1981
Sponsors Jameson (1981-84), Goya (1985), BCE (1986)
Venue Assembly Rooms, Derby (1981-82), Eldon Square Recreation
Centre (1983-84), Trentham Gardens, Stoke (1985-)
Initial prize-money £66,000
Prize-money last season £175,000
TV ITV

1981 (*Jameson*)
Qualifying groups
1 M. Gibson beat S. Hood 5-3; Gibson beat M. Parkin 5-3; J. Dunning beat
  Gibson 5-3
2 C. Roscoe beat R. Andrewartha 5-2; D. Sheehan beat V. Harris 5-1;
  Roscoe beat Sheehan 5-1; J. Meadowcroft beat Roscoe 5-4
3 C. Everton beat K. Kennerley 5-4; M. Watterson beat P. Medati 5-3;
  Watterson beat Everton 5-4; P. Fagan beat Watterson 5-2

4 P. Houlihan *wo* J. Barrie *scr*; D. French beat G. Foulds 5-2; French beat Houlihan 5-3; R. Williams beat French 5-0
5 B. Demarco *wo* B. Mikkelsen *scr*; D. Hughes beat Jack Rea 5-4; Demarco beat Hughes 5-1; M. Hallett beat Demarco 5-4
6 E. Hughes beat M. Owen 5-1; J. Fitzmaurice beat B. Bennett 5-1; E. Hughes beat Fitzmaurice 5-3; E. Hughes beat E. Sinclair 5-2
7 E. McLaughlin beat I. Black 5-3; M. Wildman beat M. Morra 5-3; E. McLaughlin beat Wildman 5-3; E. McLaughlin beat D. Greaves 5-1
8 M. Macleod beat B. Kelly 5-1; J. Johnson beat J. Donnelly 5-4; Johnson beat Macleod 5-1; Johnson *wo* J. Pulman *scr*

First round: J. Johnson beat J. Wych 5-2; D. Martin beat J. Dunning 5-2; R. Williams beat J. White 5-1; A. Knowles beat M. Hallett 5-2; R. Edmonds beat E. Hughes 5-4; J. Meadowcroft beat C. Wilson 5-4; T. Meo beat E. McLaughlin 5-2

Second round: G. Miles beat Johnson 5-3; Martin beat B. Werbeniuk 5-2; Williams beat F. Davis 5-0; A. Higgins beat P. Fagan 5-3; J. Spencer beat Edmonds 5-3; J. Virgo beat Knowles 5-2; K. Stevens beat Meadowcroft 5-1; P. Mans beat Meo 5-3

Third round: Miles beat C. Thorburn 5-0; Martin beat E. Charlton 5-2; Virgo beat R. Reardon 5-3; David Taylor beat Stevens 5-0; Dennis Taylor beat Williams 5-1; Higgins beat D. Mountjoy 5-1; T. Griffiths beat Spencer 5-2; S. Davis beat Mans 5-3

Quarter-finals: Martin beat Miles 5-1; Higgins beat Griffiths 5-2; Dennis Taylor beat Virgo 5-2; S. Davis beat David Taylor 5-1

Semi-finals: Dennis Taylor beat Martin 9-1; S. Davis beat Higgins 9-8

Final: S. Davis beat Dennis Taylor 9-0

1982 (*Jameson*)
Qualifying groups
1 R. Edmonds beat D. Hughes 5-0; Edmonds beat G. Miles 5-1
2 V. Harris beat D. Sheehan 5-3; J. Virgo beat Harris 5-2
3 M. Fisher beat T. Murphy 5-1; Fisher beat F. Davis 5-3
4 B. Bennett beat M. Owen 5-2; J. Wych beat Bennett 5-0
5 M. Morra beat B. Demarco 5-2; D. Reynolds beat Morra 5-1
6 M. Watterson beat C. Everton 5-1; Watterson beat P. Fagan 5-1
7 E. Sinclair beat I. Anderson 5-2; Sinclair beat T. Meo 5-3
8 G. Scott beat B. Harris 5-4; Scott *wo* John Bear *scr*
9 J. Johnson *wo* J. Phillips *scr*; C. Wilson beat Johnson 5-4
10 E. Hughes beat M. Parkin 5-2; Hughes beat D. Martin 5-4
11 C. Ross *wo* D. Greaves *scr*; J. Meadowcroft beat Ross 5-0
12 I. Williamson beat J. Donnelly 5-3; B. Kelly beat G. Foulds 5-4; Kelly beat Williamson 5-1
13 C. Roscoe beat J. Dunning 5-2; D. French beat G. Cripsey 5-1; Roscoe beat French 5-2

14   M. Hallett beat F. Jonik 5-2; M. Wildman beat M. Gibson 5-1; Wildman
     beat Hallett 5-2
15   J. Fitzmaurice beat I. Black 5-3; L. Dodd beat M. Macleod 5-1; Dodd beat
     Fitzmaurice 5-3
16   R. Williams beat P. Medati 5-3; E. McLaughlin beat P. Houlihan 5-2;
     Williams beat McLaughlin 5-1

First round: A. Knowles beat Sinclair 5-2; Reynolds beat W. Thorne 5-3;
S. Davis beat Roscoe 5-0; B. Werbeniuk beat Wych 5-3; David Taylor beat
Fisher 5-1; K. Stevens beat Watterson 5-3; T. Griffiths beat Williams 5-2;
J. Spencer beat Edmonds 5-2; Dennis Taylor beat Wildman 5-2; Virgo beat
E. Charlton 5-4; P. Mans beat Dodd 5-3; J. White beat Meadowcroft 5-1;
R. Reardon beat E. Hughes 5-3; C. Thorburn beat Scott 5-1; A. Higgins beat
Kelly 5-3; Wilson beat D. Mountjoy 5-4

Second round: S. Davis beat Reynolds 5-0; David Taylor beat Werbeniuk 5-2;
Stevens beat Mans 5-2; Griffiths beat Higgins 5-2; Dennis Taylor beat
Thorburn 5-2; Wilson beat White 5-2; Virgo beat Spencer 5-4; Knowles beat
Reardon 5-2

Quarter-finals: Virgo beat Dennis Taylor 5-3; David Taylor beat S. Davis 5-3;
Knowles beat Wilson 5-4; Stevens beat Griffiths 5-3

Semi-finals: Knowles beat Stevens 9-3; David Taylor beat Virgo 9-5

Final: Knowles beat David Taylor 9-6

1983 (*Jameson*)
Qualifying groups
1   M. Watterson beat B. Demarco 5-3; Watterson beat P. Mans 5-4
2   T. Murphy beat D. Sheehan 5-2; W. Thorne beat Murphy 5-2
3   R. Williams beat D. French 5-1; D. Reynolds beat Williams 5-3
4   J. Donnelly beat B. Bennett 5-1; Donnelly beat C. Wilson 5-1
5   M. Darrington beat I. Williamson 5-3; S. Francisco beat Darrington 5-2
6   W. King beat I. Black 5-3; G. Miles beat King 5-3
7   D. Hughes beat M. Parkin 5-0; J. Johnson beat Hughes 5-1
8   B. Harris beat J. Dunning 5-3; M. Wildman beat Harris 5-2
9   D. Martin beat D. Greaves 5-1; Martin beat P. Fagan 5-0
10 R. Andrewartha beat C. Everton 5-1; E. Sinclair beat Andrewartha 5-4
11 P. Medati beat V. Harris 5-0; M. Macleod beat Medati 5-3
12 F. Davis beat B. Kelly 5-1; P. Morgan beat J. Fitzmaurice 5-4; Morgan
    beat Davis 5-3
13 M. Hallett beat C. Roscoe 5-2; M. Morra beat P. Watchorn 5-3; Morra beat
    Hallett 5-3
14 G. Foulds beat P. Burke 5-2; E. Hughes beat M. Fisher 5-4; Hughes beat
    Foulds 5-1
15 M. Gibson beat L. Dodd 5-1; G. Scott beat P. Houlihan 5-0; Scott beat
    Gibson 5-3
16 E. McLaughlin beat J. Campbell 5-2; R. Edmonds beat Jack Rea 5-1;
    Edmonds beat McLaughlin 5-1

First round: Dennis Taylor beat Reynolds 5-3; R. Reardon beat Macleod 5-2; Thorne beat J. Virgo 5-2; Morra beat J. White 5-3; D. Mountjoy beat Wildman 5-4; Martin beat A. Higgins 5-2; Watterson beat T. Meo 5-3; Scott beat B. Werbeniuk 5-3; T. Griffiths beat Miles 5-2; S. Davis beat Hughes 5-1; Donnelly beat David Taylor 5-3; Francisco *wo* K. Stevens *scr*; E. Charlton beat Johnson 5-2; C. Thorburn beat Sinclair 5-0; J. Spencer beat Morgan 5-1; A. Knowles beat Edmonds 5-1

Second round: Griffiths beat Scott 5-0; Spencer beat Knowles 5-4; Thorburn beat Dennis Taylor 5-3; Mountjoy beat Martin 5-0; Charlton beat Morra 5-3; Thorne beat Reardon 5-0; S. Francisco beat Donnelly 5-1; S. Davis beat Watterson 5-0

Quarter-finals: Griffiths beat Spencer 5-4; Thorburn beat Mountjoy 5-2; Charlton beat Thorne 5-0; S. Davis beat S. Francisco 5-1

Semi-finals: Thorburn beat Griffiths 9-8; S. Davis beat Charlton 9-2

Final: S. Davis beat Thorburn 9-4

1984 (*Jameson*)
Qualifying groups
1   G. Foulds beat P. Francisco 5-4; I. Williamson beat V. Harris 5-0; Foulds beat Williamson 5-4; Foulds beat J. Donnelly 5-3; J. Campbell beat Foulds 5-3
2   W. Jones beat P. Watchorn 5-0; M. Gibson beat P. Medati 5-3; Jones beat Gibson 5-2; Jones beat G. Scott 5-0; Jones beat M. Wildman 5-0
3   T. Jones beat D. French 5-1; S. Duggan beat Jones 5-2; E. Sinclair beat Duggan 5-0; Sinclair beat P. Mans 5-2
4   B. Bennett beat B. Demarco 5-1; Bennett *wo* P. Morgan *scr*; Bennett *wo* J. Wych *scr*; N. Foulds beat Bennett 5-0
5   R. Foldvari beat G. Rigitano 5-2; Foldvari beat R. Edmonds 5-1; L. Dodd beat Foldvari 5-3; Dodd beat C. Wilson 5-1
6   B. Mikkelsen beat T. Chappel 5-4; Mikkelsen beat C. Everton 5-0; C. Roscoe beat Mikkelsen 5-1; E. Hughes beat Roscoe 5-1
7   D. O'Kane beat M. Parkin 5-2; O'Kane beat E. McLaughlin 5-1; O'Kane beat J. Fitzmaurice 5-4; O'Kane beat M. Hallett 5-4
8   J. McLaughlin beat D. Greaves 5-3; F. Jonik beat McLaughlin 5-2; M. Gauvreau beat Jonik 5-1; Gauvreau beat J. Parrott 5-4
9   G. Cripsey beat P. Thornley 5-3; J. Dunning beat Cripsey 5-3; F. Davis beat Dunning 5-4; J. Virgo beat Davis 5-3
10   J. Hargreaves beat P. Houlihan 5-2; B. Kelly beat Hargreaves 5-2; Kelly beat W. King 5-4; S. Francisco beat Kelly 5-3
11   D. Fowler beat R. Chaperon 5-0; Fowler *wo* P. Mifsud *scr*; Fowler beat R. Andrewartha 5-0; Fowler beat D. Martin 5-0
12   M. Bradley beat M. Darrington 5-3; Bradley beat Jack Rea 5-2; M. Morra beat Bradley 5-3; J. Johnson beat Morra 5-0
13   D. Chalmers *wo* Condo *scr*; W. Oliver beat D. Hughes 5-4; Chalmers beat Oliver 5-4; J. Meadowcroft beat Chalmers 5-1; R. Williams beat Meadowcroft 5-4

14 P. Browne beat John Rea 5-2; I. Black beat Browne 5-4; Black beat
M. Watterson 5-3; M. Macleod beat Black 5-3
15 S. Newbury beat S. Longworth 5-4; P. Burke beat A. Kearney 5-4;
Newbury beat Burke 5-0; Newbury beat P. Fagan 5-0; Newbury beat
G. Miles 5-1
16 R. Bales beat D. Sheehan 5-2; Bales beat T. Murphy 5-4; Bales beat
M. Fisher 5-3; D. Reynolds beat Bales 5-4

First round: S. Davis beat Campbell 5-1; A. Higgins beat Sinclair 5-1;
T. Griffiths beat N. Foulds 5-3; R. Reardon beat Dodd 5-4; E. Hughes beat
D. Mountjoy 5-1; W. Thorne beat O'Kane 5-3; Gauvreau beat K. Stevens 5-1;
Virgo beat C. Thorburn 5-0; S. Francisco beat J. Spencer 5-2; Dennis Taylor
beat Fowler 5-0; Johnson beat E. Charlton 5-1; J. White beat Williams 5-3;
T. Meo beat Macleod 5-1; Newbury beat B. Werbeniuk 5-2; A. Knowles beat
Reynolds 5-1; David Taylor beat W. Jones 5-4

Second round: S. Davis beat David Taylor 5-1; Higgins beat Griffiths 5-4;
E. Hughes beat Reardon 5-1; Thorne beat Gauvreau 5-3; S. Francisco beat
Virgo 5-2; Dennis Taylor beat Johnson 5-2; White beat Meo 5-1; Knowles beat
Newbury 5-4

Quarter-finals: S. Davis beat Higgins 5-1; E. Hughes beat Thorne 5-2;
S. Francisco *wo* Dennis Taylor *scr*; Knowles beat White 5-4

Semi-finals: S. Davis beat E. Hughes 9-3; Knowles beat S. Francisco 9-6

Final: S. Davis beat Knowles 9-2

1985 (*Goya Matchroom*)
First round: M. Darrington beat D. Gilbert 5-2; O. Agrawal beat P. Watchorn
5-2; M. Smith beat D. Sheehan 5-2; S. Simngam beat D. Greaves 5-2;
G. Wilkinson beat B. Demarco 5-2; J. Rempe beat P. Burke 5-3; S. Hendry beat
B. West 5-4; Jim Bear beat P. Houlihan 5-2; J. Caggianello beat J. Hargreaves
5-2; D. Mienie *wo* G. Watson *scr*; J. O'Boye beat M. Parkin 5-3; R. Bales beat
T. Drago 5-2; D. Hughes beat A. Kearney 5-1; G. Cripsey beat B. Bennett 5-3

Second round: B. Mikkelsen beat M. Fisher 5-3; M. Gibson beat P. Francisco
5-4; P. Fagan beat Mienie 5-4; W. King beat Caggianello 5-0; R. Chaperon beat
D. Chalmers 5-2; Bales beat R. Edmonds 5-0; G. Miles beat O'Boye 5-2;
J. Fitzmaurice beat M. Watterson 5-2; T. Chappel beat J. Meadowcroft 5-2;
C. Roscoe beat G. Foulds 5-3; E. McLaughlin beat Hendry 5-3; Jim Bear beat
J. Donnelly 5-2; T. Jones beat W. Kelly 5-3; M. Bradley beat John Rea 5-1;
L. Dodd beat Simngam 5-4; Williamson beat J. McLaughlin 5-3; J. Dunning
beat C. Everton 5-2; M. Morra beat B. Oliver 5-1; D. Fowler beat Agrawal 5-2;
J. Wych beat Rempe 5-1; E. Sinclair beat Darrington 5-0; S. Longworth beat
Wilkinson 5-0; Cripsey beat P. Medati 5-2; S. Newbury beat F. Jonik 5-4; S.
Duggan beat F. Davis 5-1; I. Black beat G. Rigitano 5-4; R. Foldvari beat
V. Harris 5-4; G. Scott beat J. Van Rensberg 5-4; T. Murphy beat Jack Rea 5-1;
B. Harris beat P. Browne 5-3; W. Jones beat Smith 5-3; D. Hughes beat
M. Gauvreau 5-4

Third round: S. Davis beat Bales 5-2; J. Virgo beat Miles 5-2; Chaperon beat S. Francisco 5-3; M. Macleod beat Fitzmaurice 5-1; Gibson beat E. Charlton 5-4; D. Reynolds beat Mikkelsen 5-0; J. White beat Fagan 5-2; King beat R. Williams 5-3; Chappel beat K. Stevens 5-3; C. Wilson beat Roscoe 5-1; J. Johnson beat Jim Bear 5-1; Bradley beat M. Hallett 5-4; David Taylor beat T. Jones 5-4; B. Werbeniuk beat Williamson 5-2; A. Knowles beat E. McLaughlin 5-1; N. Foulds beat Dodd 5-3; C. Thorburn beat Longworth 5-3; D. Martin beat Sinclair 5-1; D. Mountjoy beat Wych 5-1; J. Campbell beat Morra 5-2; W. Thorne beat Fowler 5-1; Scott beat M. Wildman 5-1; Duggan beat R. Reardon 5-4; Black beat P. Mans 5-4; T. Griffiths beat Newbury 5-2; J. Spencer beat Foldvari 5-4; T. Meo beat Dunning 5-0; J. Parrott beat W. Jones 5-3; A. Higgins beat D. Hughes 5-1; Murphy beat E. Hughes 5-3; Dennis Taylor beat Cripsey 5-1; B. Harris beat D. O'Kane 5-3

Fourth round: S. Davis beat Virgo 5-1; Macleod beat Chaperon 5-4; Reynolds beat Gibson 5-0; White beat King 5-2; Wilson beat Chappel 5-0; Johnson beat Bradley 5-2; David Taylor beat Werbeniuk 5-4; N. Foulds beat Knowles 5-3; Thorburn beat Martin 5-3; Campbell beat Mountjoy 5-1; Thorne beat Scott 5-1; Duggan beat Black 5-1; Griffiths beat Spencer 5-1; Parrott beat Meo 5-4; Higgins beat Murphy 5-2; Dennis Taylor beat B. Harris 5-3

Fifth round: S. Davis beat Macleod 5-1; White beat Reynolds 5-1; Johnson beat Wilson 5-1; N. Foulds beat David Taylor 5-4; Thorburn beat Campbell 5-0; Duggan beat Thorne 5-4; Parrott beat Griffiths 5-1; Dennis Taylor beat Higgins 5-1

Quarter-finals: White beat S. Davis 5-3; N. Foulds beat Johnson 5-2; Thorburn beat Duggan 5-2; Dennis Taylor beat Parrott 5-1

Semi-finals: White beat N. Foulds 9-5; Thorburn beat Dennis Taylor 9-5

Final: Thorburn beat White 12-10

1986
First round: P. Burke beat J. Fitzmaurice 5-4; G. Wilkinson *wo* F. Jonik *scr*; A. Kearney *wo* S. Simngam *scr*; B. Kelly beat T. Whitthread 5-1; J. McLaughlin beat B. Bennett 5-0; J. Wright beat M. Watterson 5-1; B. Rowswell beat D. Sheehan 5-4; Jack Rea beat M. Darrington 5-4; G. Jenkins beat C. Everton 5-3; J. Dunning beat B. Demarco 5-4; M. Bennett beat M. Smith 5-4; P. Gibson beat J. Meadowcroft 5-2; I. Anderson *wo* E. McLaughlin *scr*; G. Rigitano beat D. Greaves 5-3; J. Bear beat P. Watchorn 5-1; P. Houlihan beat D. Chalmers 5-1; C. Roscoe beat M. Parkin 5-1; M. Morra beat F. Ellis 5-3; N. Gilbert beat O. Agrawal 5-0; K. Owers beat J. Hargreaves 5-3; B. Oliver beat D. Mienie 5-4; D. Roe beat D. Hughes 5-2; G. Foulds *wo* L. Heywood *scr*; M. Hines beat M. Fisher 5-2; J. Donnelly *wo* R. Grace *scr*; S. James beat D. Gilbert 5-2

Second round: Burke beat T. Jones 5-4; M. Bradley beat Wilkinson 5-4; P. Medati beat Kearney 5-3; J. Van Rensberg beat Kelly 5-1; R. Bales beat F. Davis 5-4; J. McLaughlin beat D. Fowler 5-2; J. Spencer beat I. Williamson

5-4; I. Black beat Wright 5-1; E. Sinclair beat P. Fagan 5-0; M. Wildman beat Rowswell 5-2; W. Jones beat Jack Rea 5-1; M. Gauvreau beat Jenkins 5-1; S. Newbury beat Dunning 5-4; M. Bennett beat P. Browne 5-1; R. Foldvari beat B. Harris 5-0; S. Hendry beat P. Gibson 5-2; John Rea beat Anderson 5-1; W. King beat Rigitano 5-0; J. O'Boye beat B. Mikkelsen 5-4; S. Duggan beat Bear 5-4; Houlihan beat G. Cripsey 5-1; T. Chappel beat Roscoe 5-3; J. Drago beat Morra 5-3; R. Chaperon beat N. Gilbert 5-3; Owers beat G. Scott 5-1; D. O'Kane beat Oliver 5-2; G. Miles beat Roe 5-1; G. Foulds beat V. Harris 5-4; M. Gibson beat Hines 5-1; L. Dodd *wo* P. Mans *scr*; T. Murphy beat Donnelly 5-2; R. Edmonds beat James 5-2

Third round: C. Thorburn beat Burke 5-0; J. Wych beat Bradley 5-2; T. Griffiths beat Medati 5-3; B. West beat Van Rensberg 5-3; Bales beat K. Stevens 5-3; C. Wilson beat J. McLaughlin 5-2; T. Knowles beat Spencer 5-0; E. Charlton beat Black 5-0; A. Higgins beat Sinclair 5-3; P. Francisco beat Wildman 5-2; R. Reardon beat W. Jones 5-4; Gauvreau beat M. Macleod 5-4; S. Francisco beat Newbury 5-4; J. Virgo beat M. Bennett 5-1; Dennis Taylor beat Foldvari 5-1; Hendry beat J. Parrott 5-3; S. Davis beat John Rea 5-1; King beat S. Longworth 5-0; R. Williams beat O'Boye 5-0; Duggan beat J. Campbell 5-3; Houlihan beat T. Meo 5-4; E. Hughes beat Chappel 5-4; Drago beat W. Thorne 5-2; Chaperon beat D. Martin 5-4; Owers beat J. White 5-2; O'Kane beat M. Hallett 5-1; N. Foulds beat Miles 5-2; G. Foulds beat B. Werbeniuk 5-2; D. Mountjoy beat M. Gibson 5-3; D. Reynolds beat Dodd 5-2; J. Johnson beat Murphy 5-4; David Taylor beat Edmonds 5-4

Fourth round: Thorburn beat Wych 5-3; Griffiths beat West 5-1; Wilson beat Bales 5-1; Knowles beat Charlton 5-1; P. Francisco beat Higgins 5-4; Gauvreau beat Reardon 5-2; S. Francisco beat Virgo 5-0; Dennis Taylor beat Hendry 5-3; S. Davis beat King 5-4; Williams beat Duggan 5-4; E. Hughes beat Houlihan 5-1; Chaperon beat Drago 5-1; Owers beat O'Kane 5-0; N. Foulds beat G. Foulds 5-0; Reynolds beat Mountjoy 5-2; David Taylor beat Johnson 5-3

Fifth round: Thorburn beat Griffiths 5-4; Wilson beat Knowles 5-4; P. Francisco beat Gauvreau 5-2; S. Francisco beat Dennis Taylor 5-0; S. Davis beat Williams 5-4; E. Hughes beat Chaperon 5-0; N. Foulds beat Owers 5-1; Reynolds beat David Taylor 5-1

Quarter-finals: Thorburn beat Wilson 5-1; P. Francisco beat S. Francisco 5-3; E. Hughes beat S. Davis 5-4; N. Foulds beat Reynolds 5-2

Semi-finals: Thorburn beat P. Francisco 9-7; N. Foulds beat E. Hughes 9-8

Final: N. Foulds beat Thorburn 12-9

This event will be sponsored by Fidelity Unit Trusts in 1987.

ROTHMANS GRAND PRIX

First staged 1982
Sponsors WPBSA (1982–83 when entitled Professional Players Tournament), Rothmans (1984–)
Venue La Reserve, Sutton Coldfield & International Snooker Club, Aston, Birmingham (1982), Redwood Lodge Country Club (1983), Hexagon, Reading (1984–)
Initial prize-money £32,000
Prize-money last season £275,000
TV BBC

1982 (*Professional Players Tournament*)
First round: E. Sinclair beat F. Davis 5-2; J. Meadowcroft beat B. Bennett 5-4; M. Watterson beat J. Donnelly 5-4; T. Griffiths beat C. Roscoe 5-1; A. Higgins beat D. French 5-3; R. Reardon beat T. Murphy 5-0; B. Werbeniuk beat P. Morgan 5-3; C. Everton beat P. Fagan 5-2; C. Thorburn beat P. Medati 5-1; David Taylor beat I. Anderson 5-1; Dennis Taylor beat R. Edmonds 5-4; J. Wych beat B. Kelly 5-0; R. Williams beat C. Ross 5-0; P. Mans beat E. McLaughlin 5-2; W. Thorne beat B. Demarco 5-3; M. Wildman beat J. Dunning 5-4; J. Johnson beat G. Miles 5-1; E. Charlton beat D. Hughes 5-2; F. Jonik beat D. Mountjoy 5-3; K. Stevens beat E. Hughes 5-2; T. Meo beat M. Owen 5-4; C. Wilson beat M. Morra 5-2; A. Knowles beat P. Houlihan 5-4; J. Virgo beat I. Black 5-2; M. Hallett beat V. Harris 5-3; D. Martin beat M. Gibson 5-2; J. Fitzmaurice beat D. Sheehan 5-1; J. Spencer beat G. Foulds 5-1

Second round: Werbeniuk beat Jack Rea 5-2; Sinclair beat Meadowcroft 5-3; Thorburn beat Everton 5-2; Griffiths beat Watterson 5-2; Reardon beat Higgins 5-2; Dennis Taylor beat David Taylor 5-1; Wildman beat Mans 5-4; Charlton beat Williams 5-2; M. Macleod beat Thorne 5-4; White beat Wych 5-0; Johnson beat Stevens 5-1; Meo beat Jonik 5-0; Wilson beat Knowles 5-4; Virgo beat Hallett 5-2; Spencer beat Martin 5-3; Reynolds beat Fitzmaurice 5-0

Third round: Werbeniuk beat Thorburn 5-2; Johnson beat Wildman 5-4; Reynolds beat Wilson 5-1; Virgo beat Spencer 5-1; Charlton beat Meo 5-3; White beat Dennis Taylor 5-3; Griffiths beat Sinclair 5-3; Reardon beat Macleod 5-2

Quarter-finals: White beat Griffiths 5-2; Virgo beat Johnson 5-1; Reardon beat Werbeniuk 5-3; Charlton beat Reynolds 5-1

Semi-finals: White beat Virgo 10-4; Reardon beat Charlton 10-7

Final: Reardon beat White 10-5

1983 (*Professional Players Tournament*)
Qualifying: G. Ganim Jr beat G. Cripsey 5-4; S. Duggan beat M. Darrington 5-4; T. Jones beat W. Oliver 5-2; D. French beat N. Foulds 5-2; B. Bennett beat

B. Demarco 5-4; P. Burke beat G. Foulds 5-4; V. Harris *wo* P. Mifsud *scr*;
P. Medati beat D. Hughes 5-1; T. Murphy beat P. Browne 5-2; J. Parrott beat
P. Watchorn 5-0; D. Sheehan beat P. Houlihan 5-2; M. Morra beat
J. Hargreaves 5-0; D. Greaves beat R. Andrewartha 5-2; W. King beat
B. Harris 5-3; P. Morgan beat M. Gibson 5-4

First round: R. Reardon beat Ganim 5-4; C. Thorburn beat V. Harris 5-1;
J. Meadowcroft beat C. Roscoe 5-4; Duggan beat J. Dunning 5-2; J. Virgo beat
French 5-4; J. Spencer beat I. Black 5-2; W. Thorne beat C. Everton 5-1;
C. Wilson beat Bennett 5-1; T. Griffiths beat L. Dodd 5-3; J. White beat
I. Williamson 5-2; Parrott beat P. Fagan 5-2; J. Johnson beat Burke 5-3;
E. Hughes beat E. Sinclair 5-4; M. Fisher beat F. Davis 5-4; B. Werbeniuk beat
T. Jones 5-4; E. Charlton beat E. McLaughlin 5-0; M. Watterson beat
A. Higgins 5-2; K. Stevens beat R. Edmonds 5-1; D. Martin beat J. Fitzmaurice
5-0; T. Murphy beat M. Macleod 5-0; J. Campbell beat D. Mountjoy 5-3; David
Taylor beat P. Morgan 5-3; G. Miles beat M. Gauvreau 5-3; M. Wildman beat
F. Jonik 5-4; G. Scott beat Dennis Taylor 5-4; T. Meo beat W. King 5-2;
S. Francisco beat M. Morra 5-3; D. Reynolds beat D. Greaves 5-1; R. Williams
beat D. Sheehan 5-1; M. Hallett beat B. Kelly 5-0; A. Knowles beat P. Medati
5-1; S. Davis beat J. Donnelly 5-1

Second round: Reardon beat Duggan 5-2; Thorburn beat Meadowcroft 5-1;
Thorne beat Spencer 5-1; Wilson beat Virgo 5-2; Griffiths beat Parrot 5-1;
Johnson beat White 5-3; E. Hughes beat Werbeniuk 5-0; Charlton beat Fisher
5-4; Stevens beat Murphy 5-1; Martin beat Watterson 5-4; Wildman beat David
Taylor 5-3; Campbell beat Miles 5-2; Meo beat Reynolds 5-0; S. Francisco beat
Scott 5-1; Knowles beat Williams 5-4; Hallett beat S. Davis 5-2

Third round: Thorne beat Reardon 5-3; Thorburn beat Wilson 5-3; E. Hughes
beat Griffiths 5-2; Johnson beat Charlton 5-0; Stevens beat Wildman 5-0;
Campbell beat Martin 5-0; Knowles beat S. Francisco 5-0; Meo beat Hallett 5-3

Quarter-finals: Johnson beat Thorburn 5-1; Thorne beat E. Hughes 5-1; Meo
beat Stevens 5-3; Knowles beat Campbell 5-3

Semi-finals: Knowles beat Thorne 9-7; Johnson beat Meo 9-6

Final: Knowles beat Johnson 9-8

1984
Qualifying: I. Williamson beat P. Thornley 5-2; J. Donnelly beat J. Hargreaves
5-4; B. Demarco *wo* P. Fagan *scr*; V. Harris beat F. Davis 5-1; J. Dunning beat
D. Hughes 5-0; D. O'Kane beat B. Kelly 5-4; M. Gauvreau beat R. Foldvari
5-2; E. McLaughlin beat S. Longworth 5-2; M. Morra beat G. Cripsey 5-3;
S. Duggan beat P. Browne 5-2; D. Sheehan *wo* L. Condo *scr*; Sheehan beat
B. Mikkelsen 5-3; P. Burke beat M. Darrington 5-3; D. Chalmers beat
R. Andrewartha 5-2; W. King beat D. Greaves 5-0; P. Medati beat L. Dodd 5-4;
R. Chaperon beat A. Kearney 5-1; Chaperon beat M. Gibson 5-4; P. Francisco
beat I. Black 5-4; G. Rigitano beat R. Edmonds 5-3; M. Bradley beat F. Jonik

5-1; W. Jones beat M. Watterson 5-3; John Rea beat J. Fitzmaurice 5-2;
R. Bales *wo* J. Wych *scr*; S. Newbury beat M. Fisher 5-0; W. Oliver beat
B. Bennett 5-3; C. Everton beat P. Houlihan 5-3; J. McLaughlin beat
J. Meadowcroft 5-1; T. Chappel beat G. Scott 5-1; T. Murphy beat G. Foulds
5-1; T. Jones beat E. Sinclair 5-4; C. Roscoe beat D. French 5-0; P. Watchorn
wo P. Morgan *scr*; D. Fowler *wo* P. Mifsud *scr*

First round: A. Knowles beat V. Harris 5-1; Dunning beat P. Mans 5-4;
Williamson beat B. Werbeniuk 5-2; J. Johnson beat Medati 5-1; W. Thorne beat
Newbury 5-2; M. Macleod beat King 5-4; N. Foulds beat Demarco 5-2;
T. Jones beat T. Griffiths 5-3; R. Reardon beat Roscoe 5-1; C. Wilson beat
Donnelly 5-2; Dennis Taylor beat Watchorn 5-1; J. Virgo beat Bradley 5-0;
A. Higgins beat Bales 5-1; M. Hallett beat Sheehan 5-1; R. Williams beat
Chalmers 5-0; K. Stevens beat Chappel 5-3; C. Thorburn beat Rigitano 5-4;
J. Campbell beat W. Jones 5-4; T. Meo beat Burke 5-1; D. Martin beat
Chaperon 5-4; D. Mountjoy beat E. McLaughlin 5-4; M. Wildman beat
J. McLaughlin 5-3; J. Parrott beat Gauvreau 5-3; E. Charlton beat Everton 5-1;
J. White beat Oliver 5-1; S. Francisco beat Duggan 5-3; P. Francisco beat
J. Spencer 5-2; D. Reynolds beat Fowler 5-2; David Taylor beat O'Kane 5-1;
John Rea beat E. Hughes 5-4; G. Miles beat Murphy 5-3; S. Davis beat Morra
5-2

Second round: Knowles beat Dunning 5-1; Williamson beat Johnson 5-4;
Thorne beat Macleod 5-3; N. Foulds beat T. Jones 5-0; Reardon beat Wilson
5-4; Dennis Taylor beat Virgo 5-3; Hallett beat Higgins 5-3; Stevens beat
Williams 5-3; Thorburn beat Campbell 5-1; Meo beat Martin 5-4; Mountjoy
beat Wildman 5-0; Charlton beat Parrott 5-1; S. Francisco beat White 5-1;
David Taylor beat John Rea 5-1; S. Davis beat Miles 5-0; Reynolds beat
P. Francisco 5-4

Third round: Knowles beat Williamson 5-2; N. Foulds beat Thorne 5-1; Dennis
Taylor beat Reardon 5-3; Stevens beat Hallett 5-3; Thorburn beat Meo 5-4;
Mountjoy beat Charlton 5-4; Reynolds beat S. Francisco 5-1; S. Davis beat
David Taylor 5-1

Quarter-finals: N. Foulds beat Knowles 5-2; Dennis Taylor beat Stevens 5-2;
Thorburn beat Mountjoy 5-3; S. Davis beat Reynolds 5-0

Semi-finals: Dennis Taylor beat N. Foulds 9-3; Thorburn beat S. Davis 9-7

Final: Dennis Taylor beat Thorburn 10-2

1985
First round: B. West beat B. Demarco 5-2; P. Houlihan *wo* G. Robinson *scr*;
S. Simngam beat D. Mienie 5-3; T. Drago beat P. Watchorn 5-2; R. Bales beat
M. Smith 5-1; G. Watson beat D. Sheehan 5-1; J. Hargreaves beat G. Cripsey
5-1; A. Kearney beat Jim Bear 5-3; D. Gilbert beat G. Wilkinson 5-4; J. O'Boye
beat S. Hendry 5-4; D. Hughes beat B. Bennett 5-4; M. Darrington beat
D. Greaves 5-2; O. Agrawal beat J. Rempe 5-2

Second round: West beat J. Meadowcroft 5-2; M. Watterson beat J. Caggianello 5-1; T. Jones beat Houlihan 5-4; Simngam beat F. Davis 5-3; G. Foulds beat Black 5-3; Drago beat W. King 5-4; G. Scott beat D. Chalmers 5-2; Bales beat M. Fisher 5-3; Watson beat C. Roscoe 5-2; G. Miles beat Rigitano 5-4; S. Newbury beat P. Burke 5-3; S. Longworth beat Hargreaves 5-2; T. Chappel beat L. Dodd 5-2; J. Van Rensberg beat E. McLaughlin 5-4; M. Gibson beat M. Bradley 5-4; R. Edmonds beat Kearney 5-2; B. Oliver beat P. Fagan 5-4; S. Duggan beat M. Gauvreau 5-4; Gilbert beat I. Williams 5-4; B. Mikkelsen beat T. Murphy 5-4; W. Jones beat John Rea 5-0; P. Francisco beat C. Everton 5-0; J. McLaughlin beat P. Medati 5-2; B. Harris beat P. Browne 5-3; J. Fitzmaurice beat E. Sinclair 5-3; O'Boye beat R. Chaperon 5-3; B. Kelly beat J. Donnelly 5-4; M. Morra beat D. Hughes 5-2; V. Harris beat J. Wych 5-3; Darrington beat R. Foldvari 5-3; Agrawal *wo* J. Dunning *scr*; D. Fowler beat F. Jonik 5-4

Third round: Dennis Taylor beat West 5-1; R. Williams beat Watterson 5-2; T. Meo beat T. Jones 5-2; E. Hughes beat Simngam 5-1; E. Charlton beat G. Foulds 5-1; Drago beat M. Macleod 5-3; Scott beat R. Reardon 5-4; C. Wilson beat Bales 5-1; K. Stevens beat Watson 5-0; Miles beat D. Reynolds 5-3; David Taylor beat Newbury 5-2; Longworth beat J. Parrott 5-2; D. Mountjoy beat Chappel 5-1; J. Campbell beat Van Rensberg 5-4; A. Knowles beat Gibson 5-1; Edmonds beat D. O'Kane 5-2; C. Thorburn beat Oliver 5-0; M. Wildman beat Duggan 5-4; J. Johnson beat Gilbert 5-2; M. Hallett beat Mikkelsen 5-3; W. Jones beat W. Thorne 5-0; P. Francisco beat J. Virgo 5-4; T. Griffiths beat J. McLaughlin 5-4; B. Harris beat J. Spencer 5-2; J. White beat Fitzmaurice 5-0; O'Boye beat P. Mans 5-3; S. Francisco beat Kelly 5-2; D. Martin beat Morra 5-2; A. Higgins beat V. Harris 5-1; N. Foulds beat Darrington 5-0; S. Davis beat Agrawal 5-0; Fowler beat B. Werbeniuk 5-1

Fourth round: Dennis Taylor beat Williams 5-2; Meo beat E. Hughes 5-3; Drago beat Charlton 5-3; Wilson beat Scott 5-3; Stevens beat Miles 5-2; Longworth beat David Taylor 5-1; Campbell beat Mountjoy 5-2; Knowles beat Edmonds 5-3; Thorburn beat Wildman 5-2; Johnson beat Hallett 5-4; P. Francisco beat W. Jones 5-3; Griffiths beat B. Harris 5-3; White beat O'Boye 5-4; S. Francisco beat Martin 5-3; Higgins beat N. Foulds 5-3; S. Davis beat Fowler 5-1

Fifth round: Dennis Taylor beat Meo 5-3; Wilson beat Drago 5-2; Stevens beat Longworth 5-3; Knowles beat Campbell 5-4; Thorburn beat Johnson 5-1; Griffiths beat P. Francisco 5-2; S. Francisco beat White 5-4; S. Davis beat Higgins 5-0

Quarter-finals: Dennis Taylor beat Wilson 5-2; Knowles beat Stevens 5-4; Thorburn beat Griffiths 5-1; S. Davis beat S. Francisco 5-2

Semi-finals: Dennis Taylor beat Knowles 9-6; S. Davis beat Thorburn 9-5

Final: S. Davis beat Dennis Taylor 10-9

1986

First round: D. Mienie beat J. Fitzmaurice 5-2; P. Watchorn beat
M. Darrington 5-2; M. Morra beat S. James 5-3; G. Foulds beat G. Wilkinson
5-3; J. Bear beat B. Bennett 5-2; F. Ellis *wo* E. McLaughlin *scr*;
J. Meadowcroft beat D. Greaves 5-2; T. Whitthread *wo* S. Simngam *scr*;
J. Donnelly beat N. Gilbert 5-1; F. Jonik *wo* L. Heywood *scr*; I. Anderson beat
B. Oliver 5-4; A. Kearney beat G. Jenkins 5-3; P. Gibson beat J. Dunning 5-1;
J. Wright beat M. Fisher 5-1; R. Grace beat P. Houlihan 5-1; D. Gilbert beat
B. Rowswell 5-1; P. Burke beat C. Roscoe 5-3; Jack Rea beat D. Hughes 5-2;
D. Roe beat J. Hargreaves 5-1; G. Rigitano beat C. Everton 5-1; M. Smith beat
M. Hines 5-2; J. McLaughlin beat K. Owers 5-2; B. Kelly beat M. Parkin 5-2;
D. Chalmers beat O. Agrawal 5-1; D. Sheehan beat B. Demarco 5-1;
M. Bennett beat M. Watterson 5-1

Second round: M. Gibson beat Mienie 5-4; T. Drago beat Watchorn 5-3; Morra
beat I. Black 5-4; G. Foulds beat B. Mikkelsen 5-1; Bear beat D. Fowler 5-2;
M. Wildman beat Ellis 5-1; F. Davis beat R. Bales 5-4; Meadowcroft *wo*
P. Mans *scr*; S. Duggan beat Whitthread 5-1; W. King beat Donnelly 5-2;
G. Miles beat Jonik 5-1; Anderson beat T. Murphy 5-4; T. Chappel beat
Kearney 5-1; G. Cripsey beat P. Gibson 5-3; Wright beat M. Bradley 5-0;
P. Fagan beat Grace 5-3; J. O'Boye beat R. Edmonds 5-2; S. Newbury beat
D. Gilbert 5-1; J. Spencer beat Burke 5-3; W. Jones beat R. Foldvari 5-3;
B. Harris beat Jack Rea 5-0; John Rea beat E. Sinclair 5-4; Roe beat J. Van
Rensberg 5-3; P. Medati beat Rigitano 5-1; T. Jones beat Smith 5-0;
J. McLaughlin beat M. Gauvreau 5-3; L. Dodd beat G. Scott 5-2; V. Harris
beat Kelly 5-3; R. Chaperon beat Chalmers 5-2; S. Hendry beat I. Williamson
5-1; P. Browne beat Sheehan 5-4; M. Bennett beat D. O'Kane 5-2

Third round: S. Davis beat M. Gibson 5-1; Drago beat E. Charlton 5-4;
T. Griffiths beat Morra 5-3; J. Campbell beat G. Foulds 5-0; R. Williams beat
Bear 5-2; Wildman beat S. Longworth 5-2; A. Higgins beat F. Davis 5-0;
D. Martin *wo* Meadowcroft *scr*; W. Thorne beat Duggan 5-0; King beat
B. Werbeniuk 5-2; N. Foulds beat Miles 5-1; C. Wilson beat Anderson 5-4;
T. Meo beat Chappel 5-1; J. Parrott beat Cripsey 5-4; Dennis Taylor beat
Wright 5-3; J. Virgo beat Fagan 5-2; O'Boye beat C. Thorburn 5-4; Newbury
beat D. Reynolds 5-0; S. Francisco beat Spencer 5-4; W. Jones beat David
Taylor 5-1; D. Mountjoy beat B. Harris 5-2; J. Wych beat John Rea 5-2;
A. Knowles beat Roe 5-3; P. Francisco beat Medati 5-1; J. White beat T. Jones
5-0; J. McLaughlin beat B. West 5-1; Dodd beat K. Stevens 5-4; M. Hallett beat
V. Harris 5-2; Chaperon beat R. Reardon 5-3; Hendry beat E. Hughes 5-1;
Browne beat J. Johnson 5-2; M. Bennett beat M. Macleod 5-1

Fourth round: S. Davis beat Drago 5-1; Griffiths beat Campbell 5-1; Williams
beat Wildman 5-1; Higgins beat Martin 5-2; Thorne beat King 5-2; N. Foulds
beat Wilson 5-0; Meo beat Parrott 5-3; Dennis Taylor beat Virgo 5-3; Newbury
beat O'Boye 5-2; S. Francisco beat W. Jones 5-4; Mountjoy beat Wych 5-1;
Knowles beat P. Francisco 5-3; White beat J. McLaughlin 5-2; Hallett beat
Dodd 5-2; Hendry beat Chaperon 5-2; Browne beat M. Bennett 5-0

Fifth round: S. Davis beat Griffiths 5-2; Williams beat Higgins 5-1; N. Foulds beat Thorne 5-3; Meo beat Dennis Taylor 5-2; S. Francisco beat Newbury 5-2; Knowles beat Mountjoy 5-1; White beat Hallett 5-3; Hendry beat Browne 5-3

Quarter-finals: Williams beat S. Davis 5-1; N. Foulds beat Meo 5-3; S. Francisco beat Knowles 5-2; White beat Hendry 5-4

Semi-finals: Williams beat N. Foulds 9-8; White beat S. Francisco 9-6

Final: White beat Williams 10-6

BCE CANADIAN MASTERS

First staged 1985
Sponsors BCE
Venue CBC Studios, Toronto
Initial prize-money £50,000
Prize-money last season £62,500
Television CBC

1985
First round: Dennis Taylor beat J. Parrott 5-1; R. Reardon beat A. Knowles 5-2; C. Thorburn beat J. White 5-3; S. Davis beat T. Griffiths 5-4

Semi-finals: Taylor beat Reardon 8-3; S. Davis beat Thorburn 8-1

Final: Taylor beat S. Davis 9-5

1986
First round: W. Thorne beat Dennis Taylor 5-4; A. Knowles beat C. Thorburn 5-1; S. Davis beat J. White 5-2; A. Higgins beat J. Johnson 5-3

Semi-finals: Thorne beat Knowles 8-7; S. Davis beat Higgins 8-2

Final: S. Davis beat Thorne 9-3

TENNENTS UK OPEN

First staged 1977
Sponsors Super Crystalate (1977), Coral (1979–85), Tennents (1986–)
Venue Blackpool Tower Circus (1977), Guild Hall, Preston (1978–)
Initial prize-money £7,000
Prize-money last season £300,000
TV BBC

1977 (*Super Crystalate UK Championship*)
First round: J. Virgo *wo* J. Barrie *scr*; C. Ross beat J. Karnehm 5-4; P. Fagan

beat Jack Rea 5-1; J. Meadowcroft beat P. Houlihan 5-1; D. Mountjoy beat
R. Andrewartha 5-2; W. Thorne beat B. Bennett 5-1; J. Dunning beat M. Parkin
5-4; David Taylor beat D. Greaves 5-4

Second round: Virgo beat Dennis Taylor 5-2; G. Miles beat Ross 5-1; Fagan
beat F. Davis 5-0; Meadowcroft beat R. Reardon 5-4; Mountjoy beat J. Spencer
5-3; Thorne beat R. Williams 5-4; Dunning *wo* J. Pulman *scr*; A. Higgins beat
David Taylor 5-4

Quarter-finals: Virgo beat Miles 5-2; Fagan beat Meadowcroft 5-4; Mountjoy
beat Thorne 5-4; Higgins beat Dunning 5-0

Semi-finals: Fagan beat Virgo 9-8; Mountjoy beat Higgins 9-2

Final: Fagan beat Mountjoy 12-9

1978 (*Coral UK Championship*)
Qualifying: W. Thorne beat B. Bennett 9-4; R. Andrewartha beat P. Houlihan
9-3; D. Mountjoy beat J. Barrie 9-5; R. Williams beat T. Griffiths 9-8;
J. Dunning beat D. Greaves 9-3; J. Virgo beat R. Edmonds 9-4; David Taylor
beat M. Parkin 9-2; J. Meadowcroft beat Jack Rea 9-5

First round: David Taylor beat Fagan 9-7; Virgo beat J. Pulman 9-3; F. Davis
beat Dunning 9-2; A. Higgins beat Meadowcroft 9-6; Thorne beat R. Reardon
9-6; G. Miles beat Williams 9-8; Mountjoy beat Dennis Taylor 9-4;
Andrewartha beat J. Spencer 9-8

Quarter-finals: David Taylor beat Virgo 9-2; Higgins beat F. Davis 9-4; Miles
beat Thorne 9-1; Mountjoy beat Andrewartha 9-4

Semi-finals: David Taylor beat Higgins 9-5; Mountjoy beat Miles 9-1

Final: Mountjoy beat David Taylor 15-9

1979 (*Coral UK Championship*)
Qualifying: Jack Rea beat B. Bennett 9-8; M. Hallett beat M. Parkin 9-1;
J. Dunning beat D. Greaves 9-8

First round: W. Thorne beat R. Andrewartha 9-4; P. Houlihan beat Jack Rea
9-3; S. Davis beat Dunning 9-3; P. Fagan beat Hallett 9-4; B. Werbeniuk beat
J. Johnson 9-3; R. Edmonds beat J. Meadowcroft 9-3; T. Meo beat David
Taylor 9-7; C. Wilson beat J. Pulman 9-7

Second round: S. Davis beat D. Mountjoy 9-5; T. Griffiths beat Wilson 9-4;
A. Higgins beat Houlihan 9-3; Fagan beat G. Miles 9-5; Werbeniuk beat
J. Spencer 9-8; Dennis Taylor beat Thorne 9-8; J. Virgo beat Meo 9-6;
Edmonds beat F. Davis 9-6

Quarter-finals: Werbeniuk beat Edmonds 9-8; Dennis Taylor beat Fagan 9-6;
Virgo beat S. Davis 9-7; Griffiths beat Higgins 9-7

Semi-finals: Virgo beat Dennis Taylor 9-4; Griffiths beat Werbeniuk 9-3

Final: Virgo beat Griffiths 14-13

1980 (*Coral UK Championship*)
Preliminary round: M. Hallett beat B. Bennett 9-4; S. Hood beat C. Ross 9-3

Qualifying: Hallett beat R. Edmonds 9-8; E. Sinclair beat K. Kennerley 9-1;
M. Wildman beat C. Wilson 9-8; J. Meadowcroft beat D. Greaves 9-1;
R. Andrewartha beat A. Knowles 9-8; R. Williams beat J. Barrie 9-1;
J. Johnson beat J. Dunning 9-6; T. Meo beat Hood 9-5

First round: Meo beat P. Houlihan 9-1; S. Davis beat Hallett 9-1; P. Fagan beat
Johnson 9-4; Sinclair beat G. Miles 9-5; Thorne beat Meadowcroft 9-1;
Wildman beat J. Spencer 9-7; Williams beat D. Mountjoy 9-8; Andrewartha
beat J. Pulman 9-6

Second round: Meo beat J. Virgo 9-1; S. Davis beat B. Werbeniuk 9-3; Dennis
Taylor beat Sinclair 9-6; T. Griffiths beat Fagan 9-8; A. Higgins beat Thorne
9-7; F. Davis beat Wildman 9-6; R. Reardon beat Andrewartha 9-3; Williams
beat David Taylor 9-7

Quarter-finals: S. Davis beat Meo 9-5; Griffiths beat Dennis Taylor 9-2; Higgins
beat F. Davis 9-6; Reardon beat Williams 9-4

Semi-finals: S. Davis beat Griffiths 9-0; Higgins beat Reardon 9-7

Final: S. Davis beat Higgins 16-6

1981 (*Coral UK Championship*)
Qualifying groups
1 P. Medati beat E. McLaughlin 9-5; Medati beat J. Donnelly 9-7;
   W. Thorne beat Medati 9-6
2 M. Hallett beat V. Harris 9-4; Hallett beat D. Hughes 9-6; Hallett beat
   P. Fagan 9-5
3 M. Gibson beat J. Fitzmaurice 9-6; C. Everton beat Gibson 9-7; J. White
   beat Everton 9-4
4 J. Johnson beat T. Murphy 9-1; M. Watterson beat B. Bennett 9-4;
   Johnson beat Watterson 9-3; Johnson beat C. Wilson 9-5
5 P. Houlihan beat K. Kennerley 9-1; Houlihan beat I. Black 9-4; Houlihan
   beat J. Meadowcroft 9-4
6 G. Foulds beat B. Kelly 9-7; A. Knowles beat Foulds 9-1
7 E. Sinclair beat M. Wildman 9-8; Sinclair beat S. Hood 9-0; D. Martin beat
   Sinclair 9-7
8 R. Williams beat D. French 9-3; C. Roscoe beat M. Macleod 9-7; Williams
   beat Roscoe 9-4; Williams beat J. Dunning 9-4

First round: Thorne beat R. Edmonds 9-4; K. Stevens beat Hallett 9-4; White beat J. Virgo 9-6; Johnson beat J. Spencer 9-5; G. Miles beat Houlihan 9-5; Knowles beat F. Davis 9-6; A. Higgins beat Martin 9-7; T. Meo beat Williams 9-8

Second round: S. Davis beat Thorne 9-2; B. Werbeniuk beat Stevens 9-7; White beat Dennis Taylor 9-5; R. Reardon beat Johnson 9-7; T. Griffiths beat Miles 9-4; Knowles beat D. Mountjoy 9-6; Higgins beat David Taylor 9-5; Meo beat C. Thorburn 9-6

Quarter-finals: S. Davis beat Werbeniuk 9-5; White beat Reardon 9-8; Griffiths beat Knowles 9-5; Meo beat Higgins 9-4

Semi-finals: S. Davis beat White 9-0; Griffiths beat Meo 9-3

Final: S. Davis beat Griffiths 16-3

1982 (*Coral UK Championship*)
Qualifying groups
1   T. Meo beat G. Scott 9-5
2   C. Wilson beat E. McLaughlin 9-6
3   D. Martin beat M. Macleod 9-6
4   J. Meadowcroft beat D. Hughes 9-8
5   J. Donnelly beat C. Ross 9-5
6   P. Houlihan *wo* J. Dunning *scr*
7   M. Hallett beat B. Demarco 9-1
8   B. Kelly beat J. Fitzmaurice 9-0
9   G. Foulds beat M. Gibson 9-2; R. Williams beat Foulds 9-7
10 V. Harris beat M. Owen 9-4; J. Johnson beat Harris 9-8
11 T. Murphy beat C. Everton 9-4; E. Sinclair beat Murphy 9-5
12 B. Harris beat G. Cripsey 9-6; Harris beat M. Watterson 9-3
13 M. Fisher beat I. Black 9-3; Fisher beat R. Edmonds 9-8
14 L. Dodd beat I. Williamson 9-1; Dodd beat D. French 9-7
15 B. Bennett *wo* J. Phillips *scr*; P. Medati beat Bennett 9-1
16 C. Roscoe beat Jack Rea 9-6; M. Wildman beat Roscoe 9-4

First round: S. Davis beat Williams 9-6; P. Fagan beat B. Harris 9-6; T. Griffiths beat Johnson 9-1; Dennis Taylor beat Meadowcroft 9-7; David Taylor beat Dodd 9-7; Meo beat G. Miles 9-4; J. Virgo beat Kelly 9-2; D. Mountjoy beat Houlihan 9-3; R. Reardon beat Wildman 9-5; Hallett beat F. Davis 9-7; Wilson beat W. Thorne 9-7; J. White beat Medati 9-7; J. Spencer beat Sinclair 9-8; A. Knowles beat Donnelly 9-6; D. Reynolds beat Fisher 9-6; A. Higgins beat Martin 9-7

Second round: S. Davis beat Fagan 9-3; Griffiths beat Dennis Taylor 9-7; Meo beat David Taylor 9-6; Virgo beat Mountjoy 9-5; Reardon beat Hallett 9-8; White beat Wilson 9-5; Spencer beat Knowles 9-6; Higgins beat Reynolds 9-8

Quarter-finals: Griffiths beat S. Davis 9-6; Meo beat Virgo 9-6; Reardon beat White 9-8; Higgins beat Spencer 9-5

Semi-finals: Griffiths beat Meo 9-7; Higgins beat Reardon 9-6

Final: Griffiths beat Higgins 16-15

1983 (*Coral UK Championship*)
Qualifying groups
1   J. Johnson beat M. Gibson 9-6
2   T. Jones beat E. Sinclair 9-3
3   M. Wildman beat D. Greaves 9-5
4   M. Macleod beat B. Bennett 9-0
5   M. Watterson beat C. Everton 9-6; Watterson beat F. Davis 9-6
6   M. Darrington beat G. Cripsey 9-3; M. Hallett beat Darrington 9-1
7   N. Foulds beat C. Roscoe 9-2; Foulds beat J. Meadowcroft 9-2
8   V. Harris beat P. Houlihan 9-6; R. Williams beat Harris 9-6
9   D. French beat Jack Rea 9-5; D. Martin beat French 9-3
10   G. Foulds beat S. Duggan 9-8; Foulds beat L. Dodd 9-7
11   J. Parrott beat G. Scott 9-7; Parrott beat M. Fisher 9-0
12   R. Andrewartha beat W. Oliver 9-1; J. Dunning beat Andrewartha 9-2
13   T. Murphy beat B. Demarco 9-4; Murphy beat Donnelly 9-4
14   P. Medati beat D. Hughes 9-3; Medati beat R. Edmonds 9-7
15   B. Harris beat E. McLaughlin 9-8; Harris beat J. Fitzmaurice 9-3
16   I. Williamson beat J. Hargreaves 9-4; I. Black beat Williamson 9-6

First round: T. Griffiths beat Martin 9-4; Hallett beat G. Miles 9-4; Johnson beat J. Virgo 9-6; David Taylor beat N. Foulds 9-4; A. Knowles beat J. Jones 9-5; D. Mountjoy beat Watterson 9-2; A. Higgins beat Macleod 9-6; Medati beat D. Reynolds 9-3; C. Wilson beat Williams 9-4; R. Reardon beat B. Harris 9-7; Dennis Taylor beat Murphy 9-6; J. White beat Black 9-1; J. Spencer beat Dunning 9-7; T. Meo beat Parrott 9-7; W. Thorne beat Wildman 9-5; S. Davis beat G. Foulds 9-1

Second round: Griffiths beat Hallett 9-5; Johnson beat David Taylor 9-3; Knowles beat Mountjoy 9-5; Higgins beat Medati 9-1; Reardon beat Wilson 9-4; White beat Dennis Taylor 9-4; Meo beat Spencer 9-5; S. Davis beat Thorne 9-3

Quarter-finals: White beat Reardon 9-4; Griffiths beat Johnson 9-2; Higgins beat Knowles 9-5; S. Davis beat Meo 9-4

Semi-finals: Higgins beat Griffiths 9-4; S. Davis beat White 9-4

Final: Higgins beat S. Davis 16-15

1984 (*Coral UK Open*)
Qualifying rounds
1   T. Jones beat R. Chaperon 9-1; Jones beat P. Fagan 9-2; Jones beat M. Wildman 9-2
2   P. Watchorn beat B. Harris 9-7; Watchorn beat C. Everton 9-6; M. Fisher beat Watchorn 9-5; R. Williams beat Fisher 9-8

3   R. Foldvari beat D. Greaves 9-5; G. Cripsey beat Foldvari 9-7;
    J. Fitzmaurice beat Cripsey 9-8; J. Parrott beat Fitzmaurice 9-6
4   P. Francisco beat D. Sheehan 9-5; P. Francisco beat I. Williamson 9-2;
    E. Sinclair beat P. Francisco 9-8; S. Francisco beat Sinclair 9-4
5   D. Fowler beat B. Demarco 9-3; Fowler beat W. Oliver 9-3; Fowler beat
    F. Davis 9-4; Fowler beat N. Foulds 9-6
6   D. O'Kane beat W. Jones 9-7; O'Kane beat S. Duggan 9-6; G. Scott beat
    O'Kane 9-7; M. Macleod beat Scott 9-5
7   S. Newbury beat G. Rigitano 9-6; Newbury beat F. Jonik 9-3; L. Dodd
    beat Newbury 9-6; C. Wilson beat Dodd 9-8
8   J. McLaughlin beat D. French 9-3; McLaughlin *wo* P. Morgan *scr*;
    McLaughlin beat C. Roscoe 9-8; McLaughlin beat G. Miles 9-8
9   R. Bales beat D. Chalmers 9-2; Bales beat E. McLaughlin 9-4;
    M. Gauvreau beat Bales 9-8; Gauvreau beat P. Mans 9-6
10 G. Foulds beat D. Hughes 9-7; P. Browne beat Foulds 9-5; W. King beat
    Browne 9-5; King beat J. Virgo 9-4
11 John Rea beat B. Bennett 9-5; Rea beat F. Dunning 9-3; Rea beat
    R. Edmonds 9-6; J. Johnson beat Rea 9-6
12 T. Chappel beat P. Houlihan 9-3; Chappel beat I. Black 9-3; Chappel *wo*
    R. Andrewartha *scr*; Chappel beat D. Reynolds 9-6
13 J. Hargreaves beat P. Medati 9-6; M. Gibson beat Hargreaves 9-8;
    J. Donnelly beat Gibson 9-6; J. Campbell beat Donnelly 9-6
14 M. Bradley beat V. Harris 9-8; Bradley beat B. Kelly 9-6; Bradley beat
    J. Meadowcroft 9-7; M. Hallett beat Bradley 9-8
15 S. Longworth beat M. Darrington 9-5; Longworth beat P. Burke 9-4;
    M. Morra beat Longworth 9-1; E. Hughes beat Morra 9-8
16 T. Murphy beat A. Kearney 9-2; Murphy beat M. Watterson 9-4; Murphy
    beat D. Martin 9-8

First round: A. Higgins beat T. Jones 9-7; S. Davis beat Murphy 9-1; J. White
beat Campbell 9-7; Williams beat B. Werbeniuk 9-1; W. Thorne beat Parrott
9-7; E. Charlton beat S. Francisco 9-4; D. Mountjoy beat Hallett 9-2; T. Meo
beat E. Hughes 9-4; R. Reardon beat Fowler 9-2; K. Stevens beat Chappel 9-7;
Dennis Taylor beat King 9-5; Wilson beat T. Griffiths 9-6; Johnson beat
J. Spencer 9-6; David Taylor beat Macleod 9-6; A. Knowles beat Gauvreau 9-5;
C. Thorburn beat J. McLaughlin 9-4

Second round: Thorne beat Charlton 9-7; White beat Mountjoy 9-2; Higgins
beat Williams 9-7; Stevens beat Johnson 9-2; Reardon beat David Taylor 9-4;
Thorburn beat Wilson 9-3; Knowles beat Dennis Taylor 9-2; S. Davis beat Meo
9-7

Quarter-finals: Higgins beat Thorne 9-5; S. Davis beat White 9-4; Thorburn
beat Reardon 9-8; Stevens beat Knowles 9-7

Semi-finals: Higgins beat Thorburn 9-7; S. Davis beat Stevens 9-2

Final: S. Davis beat Higgins 16-8

1985 (*Coral UK Open*)
First round: D. Sheehan beat P. Watchorn 9-7; T. Drago beat D. Gilbert 9-5;
G. Wilkinson beat M. Smith 9-4; O. Agrawal beat S. Hendry 9-2; B. West *wo*
G. Robinson *scr*; G. Jenkins beat P. Burke 9-5; J. O'Boye beat B. Bennett 9-3;
M. Darrington *wo* M. Parkin *scr*; P. Houlihan beat G. Watson 9-4;
J. Hargreaves beat D. Mienie 9-7; D. Hughes beat A. Kearney 9-8; S. Simngam
beat R. Bales 9-2; Jim Bear beat B. Demarco 9-1; G. Cripsey beat D. Greaves
9-4

Second round: Sheehan beat G. Scott 9-6; Drago beat J. Donnelly 9-8;
S. Longworth beat M. Gibson 9-2; D. Fowler beat Wilkinson 9-6; M. Morra
beat Agrawal 9-8; West beat C. Roscoe 9-5; G. Miles beat B. Oliver 9-4;
T. Murphy beat C. Everton 9-4; M. Bradley beat Jenkins 9-3; T. Chappell *wo*
J. McLaughlin *scr*; R. Edmonds beat J. Van Rensberg 9-5; F. Davis beat
John Rea 9-8; B. Mikkelsen beat I. Williamson 9-3; P. Medati beat W. Kelly
9-1; O'Boye beat M. Gauvreau 9-5; V. Harris beat I. Black 9-3; L. Dodd *wo*
Jack Rea *scr*; E. Sinclair beat G. Foulds 9-4; P. Browne beat D. Chalmers 9-4;
W. Jones beat J. Fitzmaurice 9-3; J. Wych beat S. Duggan 9-5; Darrington beat
R. Foldvari 9-6; T. Jones beat F. Jonik 9-4; J. McLaughlin beat R. Chaperon
9-5; S. Newbury beat Houlihan 9-3; J. Meadowcroft beat Hargreaves 9-8;
P. Francisco *wo* G. Rigitano *scr*; W. King beat D. Hughes 9-0; Simngam beat
M. Fisher 9-4; P. Fagan beat B. Harris 9-2; Jim Bear beat M. Watterson 9-0;
Cripsey *wo* J. Dunning *scr*

Third round: S. Davis beat Sheehan 9-1; Drago beat M. Wildman 9-5; T. Meo
beat Longworth 9-5; Fowler beat P. Mans 9-2; D. Mountjoy beat Morra 9-2;
West beat E. Hughes 9-3; R. Reardon beat Miles 9-4; M. Macleod beat Murphy
9-7; J. White beat Bradley 9-4; Chappel beat D. O'Kane 9-5; A. Higgins beat
Edmonds 9-8; F. Davis beat B. Werbeniuk 9-7; David Taylor beat Mikkelsen
9-6; J. Campbell beat Medati 9-7; A. Knowles beat O'Boye 9-5; J. Spencer beat
V. Harris 9-5; C. Thorburn beat Dodd 9-4; J. Parrott beat Sinclair 9-2;
W. Thorne beat Browne 9-6; J. Virgo beat W. Jones 9-7; S. Francisco beat
Wych 9-8; D. Martin beat Darrington 9-3; T. Griffiths beat T. Jones 9-5;
D. Reynolds beat J. McLaughlin 9-7; K. Stevens beat Newbury 9-7; M. Hallett
beat Meadowcroft 9-1; P. Francisco beat E. Charlton 9-5; R. Williams beat
King 9-5; J. Johnson beat Simngam 9-4; N. Foulds beat Fagan 9-5;
Dennis Taylor beat Jim Bear 9-3; Cripsey beat C. Wilson 9-7

Fourth round: S. Davis beat Drago 9-2; Meo beat Fowler 9-2; West beat
Mountjoy 9-4; Macleod beat Reardon 9-5; White beat Chappel 9-5; Higgins
beat F. Davis 9-2; David Taylor beat Campbell 9-4; Knowles beat Spencer 9-7;
Thorburn beat Parrott 9-6; Thorne beat Virgo 9-8; S. Francisco beat Martin 9-6;
Griffiths beat Reynolds 9-7; Stevens beat Hallett 9-5; Williams beat
P. Francisco 9-7; N. Foulds beat Johnson 9-8; Dennis Taylor beat Cripsey 9-2

Fifth round: S. Davis beat Meo 9-5; West beat Macleod 9-4; White beat Higgins
9-6; Knowles beat David Taylor 9-7; Thorne beat Thorburn 9-7; Griffiths beat
S. Francisco 9-5; Stevens beat Williams 9-7; Dennis Taylor beat N. Foulds 9-5

Quarter-finals: S. Davis beat West 9-1; White beat Knowles 9-4; Thorne beat Griffiths 9-7; Dennis Taylor beat Stevens 9-1

Semi-finals: S. Davis beat White 9-5; Thorne beat Dennis Taylor 9-7

Final: S. Davis beat Thorne 16-14

1986

First round: G. Wilkinson beat F. Jonik 9-8; M. Fisher beat D. Greaves 9-4; K. Owers beat D. Gilbert 9-8; M. Morra beat B. Bennett 9-3; D. Sheehan beat M. Bennett 9-8; D. Hughes beat F. Ellis 9-6; R. Grace beat P. Houlihan 9-6; B. Oliver beat D. Chalmers 9-6; S. James beat G. Rigitano 9-5; J. Dunning beat A. Kearney 9-6; C. Roscoe beat M. Parkin 9-1; D. Roe beat G. Foulds 7-1 (*retd*); J. Hargreaves *wo* L. Heywood *scr*; M. Darrington beat T. Whitthread 9-8; P. Watchorn beat B. Kelly 9-8; Jack Rea *wo* S. Simngam *scr*; J. Bear beat C. Everton 9-1; M. Watterson beat P. Burke 9-0; N. Gilbert beat J. Donnelly 9-8; J. Fitzmaurice beat M. Hines 9-4; P. Gibson beat O. Agrawal 9-6; G. Jenkins beat D. Mienie 9-6; B. Rowswell *wo* E. McLaughlin *scr*; J. Wright beat M. Smith 9-7; J. Meadowcroft beat B. Demarco 9-2

Second round: T. Chappel beat Wilkinson 9-2; V. Harris beat Fisher 9-4; Owers beat S. Newbury 9-8; B. Mikkelsen beat E. Sinclair 9-8; T. Drago beat Morra 9-6; G. Miles beat Sheehan 9-8; T. Murphy beat D. Hughes 9-0; Grace beat P. Medati 9-5; S. Hendry beat Oliver 9-1; I. Williamson beat P. Browne 9-4; J. O'Boye beat S. Duggan 9-4; W. King beat James 9-8; M. Gibson beat Dunning 9-2; Roscoe beat M. Wildman 9-6; Roe beat J. Van Rensberg 9-6; W. Jones beat Hargreaves 9-0; D. Fowler beat Darrington 9-6; R. Chaperon beat Dodd 9-4; G. Scott beat Watchorn 9-7; J. Spencer beat R. Foldvari 9-6; G. Cripsey beat R. Bales 9-6; B. Harris beat Jack Rea 9-5; R. Edmonds beat Bear 9-6; Watterson beat I. Black 9-3; John Rea beat N. Gilbert 9-8; T. Jones beat Fitzmaurice 9-0; P. Gibson *wo* P. Mans *scr*; D. O'Kane beat Jenkins 9-5; J. McLaughlin beat Gauvreau 9-8; Rowswell beat F. Davis 9-4; Wright beat P. Fagan 9-0; M. Bradley beat Meadowcroft 9-2

Third round: S. Davis beat Chappel 9-7; E. Charlton beat V. Harris 9-2; S. Francisco beat Owers 9-3; D. Reynolds beat Mikkelsen 9-6; Drago beat R. Williams 9-7; J. Virgo beat Miles 9-7; W. Thorne beat Murphy 9-4; Grace beat M. Macleod 9-6; A. Higgins beat Hendry 9-8; D. Martin beat Williamson 9-5; T. Meo beat O'Boye 9-3; M. Hallett beat King 9-5; R. Reardon beat M. Gibson 9-6; E. Hughes beat Roscoe 9-8; Dennis Taylor beat Roe 9-6; W. Jones beat J. Campbell 9-3; C. Thorburn beat Fowler 9-7; David Taylor beat Chaperon 9-8; K. Stevens beat Scott 9-2; Spencer beat C. Wilson 9-5; N. Foulds beat Cripsey 9-7; J. Wych beat B. Harris 9-6; J. White beat Edmonds 9-4; P. Francisco beat Watterson 9-4; A. Knowles beat John Rea 9-4; T. Jones beat B. West 9-4; T. Griffiths beat P. Gibson 9-3; O'Kane beat B. Werbeniuk 9-5; D. Mountjoy beat J. McLaughlin 9-6; S. Longworth beat Rowswell 9-3; J. Johnson beat Wright 9-1; J. Parrott beat Bradley 9-4

Fourth round: S. Davis beat Charlton 9-6; Reynolds beat S. Francisco 9-8; Drago beat Virgo 9-6; Thorne beat Grace 9-1; Higgins beat Martin 9-6; Hallett beat Meo 9-4; E. Hughes beat Reardon 9-5; W. Jones beat Dennis Taylor 9-2; Thorburn beat David Taylor 9-4; Spencer beat Stevens 9-4; N. Foulds beat Wych 9-3; White beat P. Francisco 9-5; Knowles beat T. Jones 9-2; Griffiths beat O'Kane 9-0; Longworth beat Mountjoy 9-1; Parrott beat Johnson 9-1

Fifth round: S. Davis beat Reynolds 9-5; Drago beat Thorne 9-5; Higgins beat Hallett 9-7; W. Jones beat E. Hughes 9-5; Thorburn beat Spencer 9-2; N. Foulds beat White 9-7; Knowles beat Griffiths 9-6; Parrott beat Longworth 9-6

Quarter-finals: S. Davis beat Drago 9-8; Higgins beat W. Jones 9-5; N. Foulds beat Thorburn 9-2; Parrott beat Knowles 9-4

Semi-finals: S. Davis beat Higgins 9-3; N. Foulds beat Parrott 9-3

Final: S. Davis beat N. Foulds 16-7

HOFMEISTER WORLD DOUBLES CHAMPIONSHIP

First staged 1982
Sponsors Hofmeister
Venue Crystal Palace (1982), Derngate, Northampton (1983–)
Initial prize-money £60,000
Prize-money last season £200,000
TV ITV

1982
Qualifying groups
1 J. Johnson & C. Wilson *wo* M. Morra & F. Jonik *scr*; Johnson & Wilson beat R. Edmonds & J. Meadowcroft 6-4; R. Reardon & J. Spencer beat Johnson & Wilson 6-2
2 D. Martin & Dennis Taylor beat L. Dodd & D. French 6-2; T. Griffiths & D. Mountjoy beat Martin & Taylor 6-0
3 F. Davis & P. Medati beat J. Dunning & B. Demarco 6-0; A. Higgins & E. Charlton beat Davis & Medati 6-3
4 P. Houlihan & B. Bennett beat E. Sinclair & I. Black 6-2; D. Reynolds & M. Watterson beat Houlihan & Bennett 6-3; S. Davis & T. Meo beat Reynolds & Watterson 6-3
5 M. Hallett & G. Cripsey beat M. Macleod & E. McLaughlin 6-3; Hallett & Cripsey beat P. Fagan & G. Foulds 6-2; K. Stevens & J. Wych beat Hallett & Cripsey 6-4
6 V. Harris & I. Williamson beat T. Murphy & E. Hughes 6-1; R. Williams & J. Fitzmaurice beat Harris & Williamson 6-1; G. Miles & B. Werbeniuk beat Williams & Fitzmaurice 6-5
7 J. White & A. Knowles beat G. Scott & D. Hughes 6-2; White & Knowles beat David Taylor & W. Thorne 6-1

8 M. Fisher & M. Wildman beat C. Everton & C. Roscoe 6-3; Fisher & Wildman beat J. Donnelly & M. Gibson 6-5; C. Thorburn & J. Virgo beat Fisher & Wildman 6-2

First round: Griffiths & Mountjoy beat Stevens & Wych 6-1; S. Davis & Meo beat Thorburn & Virgo 6-2; White & Knowles beat Reardon & Spencer 6-2; Higgins & Charlton beat Miles & Werbeniuk 6-3

Semi-finals: Griffiths & Mountjoy beat Charlton & Higgins 10-7; S. Davis & Meo beat White & Knowles 10-5

Final: S. Davis & Meo beat Griffiths & Mountjoy 13-2

1983
Preliminary round: B. Bennett & P. Houlihan beat M. Gibson & M. Macleod 5-2; S. Duggan & J. Hargreaves beat W. Oliver & P. Browne 5-1; G. Scott & J. Parrott beat G. Foulds & N. Foulds 5-4; B. Harris & M. Morra beat D. Sheehan & E. McLaughlin 5-2

Qualifying: T. Murphy & P. Morgan beat P. Burke & D. Martin 5-4; J. Fitzmaurice & V. Harris beat Bennett & Houlihan 5-4; J. Donnelly & C. Roscoe beat W. King & J. Campbell 5-3; Duggan & Hargreaves beat D. Hughes & B. Kelly 5-0; J. Dunning & B. Demarco beat M. Hallett & G. Cripsey 5-4; R. Edmonds & J. Meadowcroft beat D. French & C. Everton 5-2; E. Hughes & L. Dodd beat Scott & Parrott 5-2; B. Harris & Morra beat M. Darrington & I. Williamson 5-1

First round: Murphy & Morgan beat I. Black & E. Sinclair 5-1; Dennis Taylor & R. Williams beat Fitzmaurice & V. Harris 5-1; T. Jones & S. Francisco beat Donnelly & Roscoe 5-2; G. Miles & G. Ganim beat Duggan & Hargreaves 5-3; F. Davis & M. Watterson beat Dunning & Demarco 5-3; D. Reynolds & P. Fagan beat Edmonds & Meadowcroft 5-0; E. Hughes & Dodd beat C. Wilson & J. Johnson 5-1; B. Harris & Morra beat M. Fisher & M. Wildman 5-2

Second round: S. Davis & T. Meo beat Murphy & Morgan 5-2; David Taylor & W. Thorne beat Dennis Taylor & Williams 5-4; E. Charlton & B. Werbeniuk beat T. Jones & S. Francisco 5-3; A. Higgins & K. Stevens *wo* Miles & Ganim *scr*; R. Reardon & J. Spencer beat F. Davis & Watterson 5-2; J. Virgo & C. Thorburn beat Reynolds & Fagan 5-2; T. Griffiths & D. Mountjoy beat E. Hughes & Dodd 5-3; A. Knowles & J. White beat B. Harris & Morra 5-4

Quarter-finals: S. Davis & Meo beat David Taylor & Thorne 5-3; Charlton & Werbeniuk beat Higgins & Stevens 5-1; Thorburn & Virgo beat Reardon & Spencer 5-0; Knowles & White beat Griffiths & Mountjoy 5-0

Semi-finals: S. Davis & Meo beat Charlton & Werbeniuk 9-1; Knowles & White beat Thorburn & Virgo 9-7

Final: S. Davis & Meo beat Knowles & White 10-2

1984
Qualifying: J. Donnelly & C. Roscoe beat S. Longworth & D. French 5-3;
D. Chalmers & J. McLaughlin beat P. Fagan & B. Harris 5-0; M. Morra &
M. Bradley beat I. Williamson & M. Darrington 5-1; G. Miles & P. Francisco
beat J. Hargreaves & S. Duggan 5-1; T. Chappel & S. Newbury beat
G. Rigitano & G. Scott 5-0; M. Gauvreau & D. Fowler beat B. Bennett &
P. Houlihan 5-1; R. Bales & W. Oliver beat John Rea & E. McLaughlin 5-2;
J. Meadowcroft & R. Edmonds beat F. Jonik and R. Chaperon 5-4; V. Harris &
J. Fitzmaurice beat P. Burke and B. Kelly 5-2; D. Sheehan & P. Watchorn beat
M. Macleod & M. Gibson 5-0; F. Davis & M. Watterson beat C. Everton &
R. Foldvari 5-3; P. Medati & P. Browne beat I. Black & E. Sinclair 5-1;
D. Hughes & A. Kearney *wo* J. Dunning & B. Demarco *scr*

First round: D. Mountjoy & W. Jones beat Chappel & Newbury 5-1;
S. Francisco & T. Jones beat J. Campbell & W. King 5-4; A. Higgins &
J. White beat D. Martin & G. Cripsey 5-2; David Taylor & M. Hallett beat
E. Hughes & L. Dodd 5-3; P. Francisco & Miles beat C. Wilson & J. Johnson
5-4; D. Reynolds & D. O'Kane beat Gauvreau & Fowler 5-4; Dennis Taylor &
R. Williams beat Medati & Browne 5-0; Bales & Oliver beat G. Foulds &
N. Foulds 5-2; S. Davis & T. Meo beat D. Hughes & Kearney 5-2; R. Reardon
& T. Murphy beat F. Davis & Watterson 5-2; M. Fisher & M. Wildman beat
Edmonds & Meadowcroft 5-3; E. Charlton & B. Werbeniuk beat Sheehan &
Watchorn 5-2; T. Griffiths & J. Parrott beat Chalmers & J. McLaughlin 5-0;
J. Virgo & K. Stevens beat Morra & Bradley 5-1; A. Knowles & J. Spencer
beat V. Harris & Fitzmaurice 5-2

Second round: S. Davis & Meo beat Miles & P. Francisco 5-2; Virgo & Stevens
beat Dennis Taylor & Williams 5-3; Higgins & White beat Reynolds & O'Kane
5-4; Thorburn & Thorne beat Mountjoy & W. Jones 5-3; Reardon & Murphy
beat S. Francisco & T. Jones 5-3; Griffiths & Parrot beat Bales & Oliver 5-4;
David Taylor & Hallett beat Charlton & Werbeniuk 5-4; Knowles & Spencer
beat Fisher & Wildman 5-4

Quarter-finals: Knowles & Spencer beat Reardon & Murphy 5-4; Higgins &
White beat Griffiths & Parrott 5-2; Thorburn & Thorne beat Virgo & Stevens
5-3; S. Davis & Meo beat Hallett & David Taylor 5-1

Semi-finals: Thorburn & Thorne beat Knowles & Spencer 9-1; Higgins & White
beat S. Davis & Meo 9-6

Final: Higgins & White beat Thorburn & Thorne 10-2

1985
First round: P. Watchorn & D. Sheehan beat D. Greaves & G. Jenkins 5-4;
G. Cripsey & G. Wilkinson beat P. Houlihan & B. Bennett 5-2; R. Bales &
J. McLaughlin beat S. Simngam & O. Agrawal 5-3; J. Hargreaves & P. Burke
beat T. Drago & J. O'Boye 5-3

Second round: D. Fowler & B. West beat R. Chaperon & M. Gauvreau 5-4;
P. Mans & J. Campbell beat Watchorn & Sheehan 5-1; P. Medati & B. Browne

beat R. Foldvari & M. Fisher 5-3; Cripsey & Wilkinson beat M. Gibson &
D. O'Kane 5-4; T. Murphy & P. Fagan beat A. Kearney & D. Hughes 5-2;
M. Bradley & D. Chalmers beat W. Oliver & M. Darrington 5-4; Bales &
J. McLaughlin beat B. Mikkelsen & J. Meadowcroft 5-4; M. Wildman &
R. Edmonds beat S. Hendry & G. Rigitano 5-3; T. Chappel & F. Jonik beat
E. Sinclair & I. Black 5-1; I. Williamson & S. Duggan beat D. Gilbert &
B. Harris 5-1; M. Watterson & F. Davis *wo* J. Fitzmaurice & V. Harris *scr*;
D. Reynolds & S. Longworth beat J. Van Rensberg & D. Mienie 5-4; Jim Bear
& L. Dodd beat M. Morra & J. Wych 5-1; J. Donnelly & C. Roscoe beat
Hargreaves & Burke 5-4; John Rea & E. McLaughlin beat G. Scott &
G. Foulds 5-0; R. Williams & G. Miles *wo* J. Dunning & B. Demarco *scr*

Third round: Fowler & West beat A. Higgins & J. White 5-4; Mans & Campbell
beat D. Martin & M. Macleod; M. Hallett & David Taylor beat Medati &
Browne 5-4; T. Jones & R. Reardon beat Cripsey & Wilkinson 5-3; A. Knowles
& J. Johnson beat Murphy & Fagan 5-2; W. Jones & D. Mountjoy beat Bradley
& Chalmers 5-2; J. Spencer & S. Newbury beat Bales & J. McLaughlin 5-4;
T. Griffiths & Dennis Taylor beat Wildman & Edmonds 5-4; C. Thorburn &
W. Thorne beat Chappel & Jonik 5-1; W. King & C. Wilson beat Williamson &
Duggan 5-3; P. Francisco & S. Francisco beat Watterson & F. Davis 5-0;
J. Virgo & K. Stevens beat Reynolds & Longworth 5-0; E. Charlton &
B. Werbeniuk beat Jim Bear & Dodd 5-4; N. Foulds & J. Parrott beat Donnelly
& Roscoe 5-1; E. Hughes & M. Smith beat John Rea & E. McLaughlin 5-4;
S. Davis & T. Meo beat Williams & Miles 5-2

Fourth round: Mans & Campbell beat Fowler & West 5-4; T. Jones & Reardon
beat Hallett & David Taylor 5-0; W. Jones & Mountjoy beat Knowles &
Johnson 5-4; Griffiths & Dennis Taylor beat Spencer & Newbury 5-0;
Thorburn & Thorne beat King & Wilson 5-2; P. Francisco & S. Francisco beat
Virgo & Stevens 5-3; N. Foulds & Parrott beat Charlton & Werbeniuk 5-4;
S. Davis & Meo beat E. Hughes & Smith 5-1

Quarter-finals: T. Jones & Reardon beat Mans & Campbell 5-4; Griffiths &
Dennis Taylor beat W. Jones & Mountjoy 5-2; Thorburn & Thorne beat
P. Francisco & S. Francisco 5-3; S. Davis & Meo beat N. Foulds & Parrott 5-3

Semi-finals: T. Jones & Reardon beat Griffiths & Dennis Taylor 9-6; S. Davis &
Meo beat Thorburn & Thorne 9-6

Final: S. Davis & Meo beat T. Jones & Reardon 12-5

1986
First round: J. Hargreaves & P. Burke beat J. Meadowcroft & M. Morra 5-0;
J. Wright & T. Whitthread beat B. Mikkelsen & F. Jonik 5-4; M. Darrington &
B. Oliver beat D. Greaves & O. Agrawal 5-3; S. James & D. Roe beat
J. Fitzmaurice & B. Rowswell 5-1; I. Williamson & R. Grace beat G. Jenkins &
P. Gibson 5-2; B. Kelly & Jack Rea *wo* E. McLaughlin & John Rea *scr*;
B. Bennett & P. Houlihan beat J. Bear & D. Mienie 5-2; J. Donnelly &
C. Roscoe beat N. Gilbert & M. Fisher 5-1; J. Dunning & B. Demarco *wo*

R. Foldvari & L. Heywood *scr*; P. Watchorn & D. Sheehan beat D. Hughes & A. Kearney 5-2

Second round: J. Spencer & G. Rigitano beat Hargreaves & Burke 5-1; S. Duggan & B. West beat Wright & Whitthread 5-3; M. Gauvreau & R. Chaperon beat J. O'Boye & J. McLaughlin 5-4; V. Harris & D. Gilbert beat D. Reynolds & S. Longworth 5-4; Darrington & Oliver beat B. Harris & M. Smith 5-1; James & Roe beat F. Davis & M. Watterson 5-0; Williamson & Grace beat T. Chappel & M. Bennett 5-2; G. Scott & G. Foulds beat I. Black & E. Sinclair 5-4; M. Wildman & R. Edmonds beat Kelly & Jack Rea 5-0; T. Drago & K. Owers beat B. Bennett & Houlihan 5-2; M. Gibson & D. Chalmers *wo* E. Hughes & S. Simngam *scr*; P. Fagan & T. Murphy beat G. Cripsey & G. Wilkinson 5-1; S. Newbury & R. Bales beat L. Dodd & M. Bradley 5-2; Donnelly & Roscoe beat P. Browne & P. Medati 5-1; M. Hallett & S. Hendry beat Dunning & Demarco 5-1; J. Wych & D. O'Kane beat Watchorn & Sheehan 5-1

Third round: S. Davis & T. Meo beat Spencer & Rigitano 5-1; Duggan & West beat C. Wilson & W. King 5-4; David Taylor & E. Charlton beat Gauvreau & Chaperon 5-1; S. Francisco & P. Francisco beat V. Harris & D. Gilbert 5-4; Dennis Taylor & T. Griffiths beat Darrington & Oliver 5-1; James & Roe beat J. Campbell & P. Mans 5-2; R. Williams & G. Miles beat Williamson & Grace 5-3; J. White & A. Higgins beat G. Scott & G. Foulds 5-2; J. Johnson & A. Knowles beat Wildman & Edmonds 5-2; R. Reardon & T. Jones beat Drago & Owers 5-3; D. Mountjoy & W. Jones beat M. Gibson & Chalmers 5-1; J. Virgo & K. Stevens beat Fagan & Murphy 5-1; J. Parrott & N. Foulds beat Newbury & Bales 5-3; D. Martin & M. Macleod beat Donnelly & Roscoe 5-0; Hallett & Hendry beat B. Werbeniuk & D. Fowler 5-3; W. Thorne & C. Thorburn beat Wych & O'Kane 5-2

Fourth round: S. Davis & Meo beat Duggan & West 5-3; S. Francisco & P. Francisco beat David Taylor & Charlton 5-1; Dennis Taylor & Griffiths beat James & Roe 5-2; White & Higgins beat Williams & Miles 5-2; Reardon & T. Jones beat Johnson & Knowles 5-4; Virgo & Stevens beat Mountjoy & W. Jones 5-4; Parrott & N. Foulds beat Martin & Macleod 5-2; Hallett & Hendry beat Thorne & Thorburn 5-4

Quarter-finals: S. Davis & Meo beat S. Francisco & P. Francisco 5-0; Dennis Taylor & Griffiths beat White & Higgins 5-4; Virgo & Stevens beat Reardon & T. Jones 5-2; Hallett & Hendry beat N. Foulds & Parrott 5-1

Semi-finals: S. Davis & Meo beat Dennis Taylor & Griffiths 9-6; Hallett & Hendry beat Virgo & Stevens 9-2

Final: S. Davis & Meo beat Hallett & Hendry 12-3

MERCANTILE CREDIT CLASSIC

First staged 1980*
Sponsors Wilsons (1980–82), Lada (1983–84), Mercantile Credit (1985–)
Venue Civic Centre, Oldham (1982), Spectrum Arena, Warrington (1983–86), Norbreck Castle Hotel, Blackpool (1987–)
Initial prize-money £15,000 (1982)
Prize-money last season £250,000
TV ITV
The first two events, both in 1980, were small invitation events which do not meet the conditions required for full inclusion in this book.

1982 (*Lada Classic*)
First round: T. Griffiths beat C. Thorburn 5-1; A. Higgins beat Dennis Taylor 5-1; R. Reardon beat David Taylor 5-1; S. Davis beat J. Spencer 5-2

Semi-finals: Griffiths beat Higgins 5-1; S. Davis beat Reardon 5-4

Final: Griffiths beat S. Davis 9-8

1983 (*Lada Classic*)
First round: E. Charlton beat J. Virgo 5-2; J. Spencer beat R. Reardon 5-3; C. Thorburn beat C. Wilson 5-3; D. Mountjoy beat T. Griffiths 5-1; David Taylor beat J. White 5-3; B. Werbeniuk beat A. Higgins 5-4; K. Stevens beat A. Knowles 5-0; S. Davis beat Dennis Taylor 5-2

Quarter-finals: Spencer beat David Taylor 5-2; Werbeniuk beat Mountjoy 5-2; Stevens beat Thorburn 5-3; S. Davis beat Charlton 5-4

Semi-finals: S. Davis beat Spencer 5-4; Werbeniuk beat Stevens 5-2

Final: S. Davis beat Werbeniuk 9-5

1984 (*Lada Classic*)
First qualifying round: G. Foulds beat M. Gauvreau 5-2; B. Demarco beat M. Gibson 5-2; N. Foulds beat P. Houlihan 5-3; M. Morra beat P. Burke 5-2; G. Ganim beat D. Hughes 5-2; I. Williamson beat D. French 5-1; J. Hargreaves beat W. King 5-3; W. Oliver beat D. Sheehan 5-3; T. Jones beat P. Mifsud 5-3; P. Morgan beat M. Darrington 5-3; G. Cripsey beat V. Harris 5-4; J. Parrott beat B. Bennett 5-0; P. Browne beat D. Greaves 5-2; P. Watchorn beat R. Andrewartha 5-2; S. Duggan beat B. Harris 5-2; P. Medati beat T. Murphy 5-4

Second qualifying round: E. McLaughlin beat G. Foulds 5-1; G. Scott beat Demarco 5-2; N. Foulds beat Jack Rea 5-1; Morra beat C. Everton 5-0; C. Roscoe beat Ganim 5-3; F. Jonik beat Williamson 5-1; Hargreaves beat B. Kelly 5-4; Oliver beat J. Donnelly 5-4; Morgan beat M. Watterson 5-3; T. Jones beat I. Black 5-0; J. Campbell beat Cripsey 5-3; Parrott beat

J. Fitzmaurice 5-2; R. Edmonds beat Browne 5-1; M. Fisher beat Watchorn 5-4; L. Dodd beat Duggan 5-2; E. Hughes beat Medati 5-1

Third qualifying round: E. McLaughlin beat W. Thorne 5-3; D. Reynolds beat Scott 5-3; C. Wilson beat N. Foulds 5-4; S. Francisco beat Morra 5-1; Roscoe beat G. Miles 5-2; J. Johnson beat Jonik 5-2; M. Wildman beat Hargreaves 5-1; P. Fagan beat Oliver 5-1; E. Sinclair beat Morgan 5-2; M. Macleod beat T. Jones 5-2; Campbell beat F. Davis 5-0; Parrott beat D. Martin 5-1; R. Williams beat Edmonds 5-1; J. Meadowcroft beat Fisher 5-0; M. Hallett beat Dodd 5-1; E. Hughes beat J. Dunning 5-4

First round: K. Stevens beat E. McLaughlin 5-4; T. Griffiths beat Reynolds 5-2; E. Charlton beat Wilson 5-0; S. Francisco beat C. Thorburn 5-1; Roscoe beat B. Werbeniuk 5-4; J. Spencer beat Johnson 5-4; Wildman beat J. Virgo 5-2; A. Higgins beat Fagan 5-3; S. Davis beat Sinclair 5-2; Macleod beat David Taylor 5-4; J. White beat Campbell 5-1; Parrott beat D. Mountjoy 5-4; Williams beat R. Reardon 5-4; T. Meo beat Meadowcroft 5-1; Hallett beat Dennis Taylor 5-4; A. Knowles beat E. Hughes 5-1

Second round: S. Davis beat Spencer 5-1; Charlton beat White 5-2; Wildman beat S. Francisco 5-1; Knowles beat Hallett 5-3; Stevens beat Macleod 5-1; Griffiths beat Roscoe 5-2; Meo beat Williams 5-3; Parrot beat Higgins 5-2

Quarter-finals: Wildman beat Charlton 5-4; S. Davis beat Griffiths 5-4; Meo beat Stevens 5-2; Parrott beat Knowles 5-1

Semi-finals: Meo beat Wildman 5-3; S. Davis beat Parrott 5-4

Final: S. Davis beat Meo 9-8

1985
Preliminary round: P. Watchorn beat D. Hughes 5-0; B. Mikkelsen beat D. Chalmers 5-1

First qualifying round: T. Jones beat D. Greaves 5-2; J. Giannaros beat T. Chappel 5-2; S. Newbury beat V. Harris 5-3; G. Foulds beat R. Chaperon 5-3; D. Sheehan beat John Rea 5-2; R. Bales beat B. Bennett 5-1; R. Foldvari beat P. Houlihan 5-1; P. Medati beat G. Cripsey 5-4; J. McLaughlin beat B. Demarco 5-1; S. Longworth beat P. Francisco 5-4; A. Kearney beat D. French 5-1; P. Browne beat M. Bradley 5-3; W. Jones beat D. O'Kane 5-0; D. Fowler beat Rigitano 5-0; J. Hargreaves beat Darrington 5-2

Second qualifying round: T. Jones beat M. Gibson 5-0; Newbury beat P. Burke 5-1; G. Foulds beat F. Jonik 5-2; E. McLaughlin beat Sheehan 5-2; Bales beat B. Kelly 5-3; Foldvari beat Jack Rea 5-4; J. McLaughlin beat I. Black 5-0; Longworth beat B. Oliver 5-1; Watchorn beat Mikkelsen 5-1; I. Williamson beat Kearney 5-3; Browne beat C. Everton 5-0; S. Duggan beat W. Jones 5-0; Fowler beat T. Murphy 5-0; R. Edmonds beat Hargreaves 5-2

Third qualifying round: T. Jones beat L. Dodd 5-1; M. Gauvreau beat Giannaros 5-3; Newbury beat M. Morra 5-2; G. Foulds beat J. Fitzmaurice 5-1; E. McLaughlin beat F. Davis 5-1; Medati beat C. Roscoe 5-4; G. Scott beat J. McLaughlin 5-4; Longworth beat M. Fisher 5-1; J. Donnelly beat Watchorn 5-1; P. Fagan beat Williamson 5-1; W. King beat Duggan 5-4; Fowler beat J. Meadowcroft 5-2; Edmonds beat M. Watterson 5-2

Fourth qualifying round: S. Francisco beat T. Jones 5-1; Fagan beat M. Wildman 5-3; M. Hallett beat G. Foulds 5-4; M. Macleod beat E. McLaughlin 5-4; Medati beat J. Parrott 5-3; C. Wilson beat Fowler 5-4; Gauvreau beat E. Sinclair 5-1; J. Johnson beat Edmonds 5-4; Scott beat J. Campbell 5-4; E. Hughes beat Newbury 5-3; King beat D. Reynolds 5-2; R. Williams beat Donnelly 5-3; J. Virgo beat Bales 5-1; Longworth beat N. Foulds 5-3; Foldvari beat D. Martin 5-2; Browne beat G. Miles 5-3

First round: Longworth beat David Taylor 5-4; Johnson beat A. Knowles 5-1; C. Thorburn beat Scott 5-1; King beat J. Spencer 5-2; T. Griffiths beat Fagan 5-0; J. White beat Browne 5-2; E. Hughes beat T. Meo 5-4; Macleod beat Charlton 5-1; A. Higgins beat Gauvreau 5-3; Virgo beat B. Werbeniuk 5-2; Wilson beat D. Mountjoy 5-4; Williams beat Dennis Taylor 5-3; R. Reardon beat Hallett 5-3; S. Davis beat S. Francisco 5-0; W. Thorne beat Foldvari 5-2; K. Stevens beat Medati 5-4

Second round: Reardon beat E. Hughes 5-1; S. Davis beat Higgins 5-2; Virgo beat Macleod 5-0; Thorne beat Stevens 5-1; Thorburn beat Longworth 5-3; Griffiths beat Williams 5-3; Johnson beat Wilson 5-0; King beat White 5-2

Quarter-finals: S. Davis beat Reardon 5-1; Thorburn beat Griffiths 5-4; Johnson beat King 5-3; Thorne beat Virgo 5-1

Semi-finals: Thorne beat S. Davis 9-8; Thorburn beat Johnson 9-2

Final: Thorne beat Thorburn 13-8

1986
First round: D. Gilbert beat G. Watson 5-4; A. Kearney beat Jim Bear 5-0; S. Hendry beat D. Sheehan 5-2; B. Demarco beat O. Agrawal 5-4; M. Smith beat D. Mienie 5-1; J. O'Boye beat G. Wilkinson 5-1; B. West beat M. Darrington 5-0; P. Burke beat D. Hughes 5-3; S. Simngam beat J. Hargreaves 5-1; R. Bales beat M. Parkin 5-0; D. Greaves beat P. Watchorn 5-4; G. Jenkins *wo* G. Robinson *scr*; G. Cripsey beat T. Drago 5-4; P. Houlihan beat B. Bennett 5-0

Second round: T. Jones beat Gilbert 5-3; G. Foulds beat I. Black 5-2; W. King beat S. Duggan 5-2; P. Medati beat Kearney 5-2; Hendry beat G. Miles 5-1; M. Bradley beat B. Oliver 5-3; B. Mikkelsen beat G. Scott 5-1; J. Donnelly beat D. Chalmers 5-0; F. Davis beat B. Kelly 5-3; J. Wych beat Demarco 5-0; B. Harris beat M. Morra 5-3; Smith beat R. Edmonds 5-2; O'Boye beat S. Longworth 5-1; West beat J. Meadowcroft 5-0; J. McLaughlin beat E. McLaughlin 5-2; John Rea beat I. Williamson 5-4; R. Chaperon beat Burke

5-2; J. Van Rensberg beat W. Jones 5-4; P. Francisco beat F. Jonik 5-2;
T. Murphy beat T. Chappel 5-4; M. Gauvreau beat Simngam 5-1; M. Gibson *wo*
J. Dunning *scr*; P. Browne beat C. Everton 5-0; D. Fowler beat Bales 5-4;
G. Rigitano beat L. Dodd 5-3; E. Sinclair beat Greaves 5-1; V. Harris beat
C. Roscoe 5-1; M. Watterson beat Jenkins 5-2; M. Fisher beat Jack Rea 5-3;
Cripsey beat S. Newbury 5-4; J. Fitzmaurice beat P. Fagan 5-3; Houlihan beat
R. Foldvari 5-4

Third round: T. Jones beat W. Thorne 5-3; B. Werbeniuk beat G. Foulds 5-3;
D. Mountjoy beat King 5-4; D. O'Kane beat Medati 5-0; Hendry beat
S. Francisco 5-4; N. Foulds beat Bradley 5-3; Mikkelsen beat R. Reardon 5-3;
J. Campbell beat Donnelly 5-2; F. Davis beat K. Stevens 5-2; E. Hughes beat
Wych 5-2; J. Johnson beat B. Harris 5-4; P. Mans beat Smith 5-4; T. Meo beat
O'Boye 5-3; West beat M. Wildman 5-2; C. Thorburn beat J. McLaughlin 5-1;
M. Hallett beat John Rea 5-2; S. Davis beat Chaperon 5-1; Van Rensberg beat
J. Parrott 5-3; P. Francisco beat E. Charlton 5-1; D. Martin beat Murphy 5-3;
Gauvreau beat David Taylor 5-3; Browne beat C. Wilson 5-3; J. White beat
Fowler 5-1; J. Virgo beat Gibson 5-3; A. Knowles beat Rigitano 5-4;
M. Macleod beat Sinclair 5-2; V. Harris beat T. Griffiths 5-3; R. Williams beat
Watterson 5-0; A. Higgins beat Fisher 5-0; Cripsey beat J. Spencer 5-1;
Dennis Taylor beat Fitzmaurice 5-1; D. Reynolds beat Houlihan 5-1

Fourth round: Werbeniuk beat T. Jones 5-3; Mountjoy beat O'Kane 5-3;
N. Foulds beat Hendry 5-4; Campbell beat Mikkelsen 5-2; E. Hughes beat
F. Davis 5-3; Johnson beat Mans 5-2; Meo beat West 5-1; Thorburn beat
Hallett 5-3; S. Davis beat Van Rensberg 5-1; P. Francisco beat Martin 5-2;
Gauvreau beat Browne 5-3; White beat Virgo 5-2; Knowles beat Macleod 5-4;
Williams beat V. Harris 5-1; Higgins beat Cripsey 5-2; Dennis Taylor beat
Reynolds 5-4

Fifth round: Mountjoy beat Werbeniuk 5-3; N. Foulds beat Campbell 5-1;
Johnson beat E. Hughes 5-1; Thorburn beat Meo 5-1; S. Davis beat
P. Francisco 5-0; White beat Gauvreau 5-2; Williams beat Knowles 5-2;
Higgins beat Dennis Taylor 5-4

Quarter-finals: Mountjoy beat N. Foulds 5-3; Thorburn beat Johnson 5-4;
White beat S. Davis 5-2; Williams beat Higgins 5-2

Semi-finals: Thorburn beat Mountjoy 9-6; White beat Williams 9-7

Final: White beat Thorburn 13-12

1987
First round: J. Meadowcroft *wo* L. Heywood *scr*; B. Rowswell beat
M. Watterson 5-1; P. Watchorn beat J. Donnelly 5-0; G. Foulds beat
B. Bennett 5-2; C. Everton *wo* E. McLaughlin *scr*; A. Kearney beat
O. Agrawal 5-0; D. Roe beat M. Darrington 5-0; F. Jonik beat S. James 5-4;
D. Mienie *wo* J. Hargreaves *scr*; P. Burke *wo* J. Bear *scr*; G. Jenkins beat
M. Parkin 5-2; M. Bennett beat D. Sheehan 5-3; K. Owers beat P. Houlihan
5-1; M. Morra beat F. Ellis 5-1; M. Fisher beat B. Demarco 5-0; C. Roscoe beat

T. Whitthread 5-1; B. Oliver beat D. Greaves 5-4; G. Wilkinson beat
J. Fitzmaurice 5-2; Jack Rea beat B. Kelly 5-3; J. Wright beat D. Hughes 5-2;
N. Gilbert beat M. Smith 5-0; P. Gibson *wo* S. Simngam *scr*; G. Rigitano beat
R. Grace 5-4

Second round: S. Newbury beat Meadowcroft 5-1; M. Bradley beat Rowswell
5-4; S. Duggan beat Watchorn 5-1; J. McLaughlin beat M. Gibson 5-3;
J. O'Boye beat V. Harris 5-1; G. Foulds beat D. O'Kane 5-4; J. Spencer beat
D. Gilbert 5-4; P. Browne beat Dunning 5-1; W. Jones beat Everton 5-0;
Kearney beat M. Wildman 5-3; L. Dodd beat Medati 5-4; I. Williamson beat
R. Edmonds 5-2; R. Chaperon beat Roe 5-4; Jonik beat T. Drago 5-2;
G. Cripsey beat Mienie 5-0; W. King beat Burke 5-0; Jenkins beat G. Scott 5-4;
M. Bennett beat I. Black 5-3; John Rea beat Owers 5-2; T. Murphy beat
R. Bales 5-2; Morra *wo* P. Mans *scr*; Fisher beat F. Davis 5-2; Roscoe *wo*
P. Fagan *scr*; T. Jones beat Oliver 5-0; D. Fowler beat Wilkinson 5-1;
B. Mikkelsen beat R. Foldvari 5-1; S. Hendry beat Jack Rea 5-1; Wright beat
T. Chappel 5-4; J. Van Rensberg beat N. Gilbert 5-3; R. Harris beat P. Gibson
5-3; E. Sinclair beat G. Miles 5-1; M. Gauvreau beat Rigitano 5-0

Third round: J. White beat Newbury 5-4; Bradley beat David Taylor 5-1;
Duggan beat N. Foulds 5-3; B. Werbeniuk beat J. McLaughlin 5-1; T. Griffiths
beat O'Boye 5-1; D. Martin beat G. Foulds 5-4; Spencer beat W. Thorne 5-3;
J. Campbell beat Browne 5-2; W. Jones beat Dennis Taylor 5-2; Kearney beat
M. Macleod 5-0; Dodd beat D. Mountjoy 5-4; C. Wilson beat Williamson 5-4;
K. Stevens beat Chaperon 5-3; B. West beat Jonik 5-4; C. Thorburn beat
Cripsey 5-0; D. Reynolds beat King 5-4; S. Davis beat Jenkins 5-0; J. Virgo
beat M. Bennett 5-3; T. Meo beat John Rea 5-4; S. Longworth beat Murphy
5-3; R. Williams beat Morra 5-2; E. Charlton beat Fisher 5-0; A. Higgins beat
Roscoe 5-2; J. Parrott beat T. Jones 5-2; Fowler beat A. Knowles 5-4;
M. Hallett beat Mikkelsen 5-3; Hendry beat R. Reardon 5-3; Wright beat
E. Hughes 5-4; S. Francisco beat Van Rensberg 5-4; B. Harris beat J. Wych
5-3; J. Johnson beat Sinclair 5-0; P. Francisco beat Gauvreau 5-3

Fourth round: White beat Bradley 5-0; Duggan beat Werbeniuk 5-0; Griffiths
beat Martin 5-4; Campbell beat Spencer 5-3; W. Jones beat Kearney 5-1;
Wilson beat Dodd 5-4; West beat Stevens 5-3; Reynolds beat Thorburn 5-4;
Davis beat Virgo 5-2; Meo beat Longworth 5-0; Charlton beat Williams 5-4;
Parrott beat Higgins 5-2; Fowler beat Hallett 5-4; Hendry beat Wright 5-1;
S. Francisco beat N. Harris 5-3; P. Francisco beat Johnson 5-3

Fifth round: White beat Duggan 5-2; Griffiths beat Campbell 5-3; Wilson beat
W. Jones 5-3; Reynolds beat West 5-3; S. Davis beat Meo 5-2; Parrott beat
Charlton 5-4; Hendry beat Fowler 5-4; S. Francisco beat P. Francisco 5-1

Quarter-finals: White beat Griffiths 5-3; Reynolds beat Wilson 5-1; S. Davis
beat Parrott 5-4; Hendry beat S. Francisco 5-0

Semi-finals: White beat Reynolds 9-8; S. Davis beat Hendry 9-3

Final: S. Davis beat White 13-12

BENSON AND HEDGES MASTERS

First staged 1975
Sponsors Benson and Hedges
Venue West Centre Hotel (1975), New London Theatre (1976-78),
Wembley Conference Centre (1979-)
Initial prize-money £5,000
Prize-money last season £200,000
TV BBC

1975
First round: J. Pulman beat C. Thorburn 5-3; A. Higgins beat B. Werbeniuk 5-0

Quarter-finals: E. Charlton beat F. Davis 5-3; J. Spencer beat Pulman 5-3;
R. Reardon beat G. Miles 5-3; R. Williams beat Higgins 5-3

Semi-finals: Spencer beat Charlton 5-2; Reardon beat Williams 5-4

Final: Spencer beat Reardon 9-8

1976
First round: F. Davis beat C. Thorburn 4-2; J. Pulman beat Dennis Taylor 4-2

Quarter-finals: G. Miles beat A. Higgins 4-1; R. Reardon beat Pulman 4-1;
J. Spencer beat F. Davis 4-0; E. Charlton beat R. Williams 4-1

Semi-finals: Miles beat Spencer 5-4; Reardon beat Charlton 5-4

Final: Reardon beat Miles 7-3

1977
First round: D. Mountjoy beat J. Pulman 4-2; J. Spencer beat Dennis Taylor 4-2

Quarter-finals: R. Reardon beat R. Williams 4-1; G. Miles beat Spencer 4-1;
A. Higgins beat P. Mans 4-2; Mountjoy beat F. Davis 4-2

Semi-finals: Mountjoy beat Higgins 5-3; Reardon beat Miles 5-2

Final: Mountjoy beat Reardon 7-6

1978
First round: J. Pulman beat P. Fagan 4-2; G. Miles beat F. Davis 4-3

Quarter-finals: J. Spencer beat Pulman 4-2; A. Higgins beat Dennis Taylor 4-3;
C. Thorburn beat D. Mountjoy 4-2; R. Reardon beat Miles 4-1

Semi-finals: Higgins beat Reardon 5-1; Thorburn beat Spencer 5-3

Final: Higgins beat Thorburn 7-5

1979
First round: D. Mountjoy beat F. Davis 5-2; David Taylor beat P. Fagan 5-4

Quarter-finals: A. Higgins beat E. Charlton 5-2; P. Mans beat C. Thorburn 5-4; Mountjoy beat Spencer 5-0; R. Reardon beat Taylor 5-2

Semi-finals: Higgins beat Mountjoy 5-1; Mans beat Reardon 5-3

Final: Mans beat Higgins 8-4

1980
First round: C. Thorburn beat J. Virgo 5-3; A. Higgins beat F. Davis 5-1

Quarter-finals: R. Reardon beat Dennis Taylor 5-3; T. Griffiths beat Thorburn 5-3; J. Spencer beat E. Charlton 5-2; Higgins beat P. Mans 5-1

Semi-finals: Griffiths beat Spencer 5-0; Higgins beat Reardon 5-2

Final: Griffiths beat Higgins 9-5

1981
First round: P. Mans beat S. Davis 5-3; D. Mountjoy beat E. Charlton 5-0; F. Davis beat K. Stevens 5-4; J. Spencer beat Dennis Taylor 5-2

Quarter-finals: A. Higgins beat Mountjoy 5-1; C. Thorburn beat Mans 5-4; Spencer beat R. Reardon 5-1; T. Griffiths beat F. Davis 5-2

Semi-finals: Higgins beat Thorburn 6-5; Griffiths beat Spencer 6-5

Final: Higgins beat Griffiths 9-6

1982
First round: R. Reardon beat Dennis Taylor 5-3; D. Mountjoy beat J. Spencer 5-4; T. Meo beat David Taylor 5-2; E. Charlton beat J. White 5-4

Quarter-finals: Meo beat C. Thorburn 5-0; S. Davis beat Mountjoy 5-2; A. Higgins beat Charlton 5-1; T. Griffiths beat Reardon 5-3

Semi-finals: S. Davis beat Meo 6-4; Griffiths beat Higgins 6-5

Final: S. Davis beat Griffiths 9-5

1983
First round: B. Werbeniuk beat A. Higgins 5-4; E. Charlton beat T. Meo 5-3; T. Griffiths beat K. Stevens 5-3; C. Thorburn beat J. Johnson 5-2; R. Reardon beat D. Reynolds 5-1; D. Mountjoy beat J. Virgo 5-1; S. Davis beat M. Wildman 5-2; J. White beat David Taylor 5-2

Quarter-finals: Charlton beat Werbeniuk 5-3; Thorburn beat Griffiths 5-3; Reardon beat White 5-2; Mountjoy beat S. Davis 5-4

Semi-finals: Thorburn beat Charlton 6-5; Reardon beat Mountjoy 6-3

Final: Thorburn beat Reardon 9-7

1984
First round: A. Knowles beat Dennis Taylor 5-2; R. Reardon beat J. Virgo 5-3; J. Spencer beat C. Thorburn 5-4; T. Griffiths beat B. Werbeniuk 5-1; J. White beat E. Charlton 5-2; A. Higgins beat D. Mountjoy 5-2; K. Stevens beat David Taylor 5-1; S. Davis beat T. Meo 5-0

Quarter-finals: Griffiths beat Spencer 5-4; Knowles beat Higgins 5-1; White beat Reardon 5-3; Stevens beat S. Davis 5-3

Semi-finals: Griffiths beat Knowles 6-4; White beat Stevens 6-4

Final: White beat Griffiths 9-5

1985
First round: J. White beat W. Thorne 5-2; J. Spencer beat E. Charlton 5-3; R. Reardon beat David Taylor 5-1; C. Thorburn beat Dennis Taylor 5-3; D. Mountjoy beat A. Knowles 5-3; T. Meo beat K. Stevens 5-2; T. Griffiths beat B. Werbeniuk 5-2; A. Higgins beat S. Davis 5-4

Quarter-finals: White beat Spencer 5-2; Thorburn beat Reardon 5-0; Mountjoy beat Meo 5-4; Griffiths beat Higgins 5-1

Semi-finals: Thorburn beat White 6-4; Mountjoy beat Griffiths 6-2

Final: Thorburn beat Mountjoy 9-6

1986
First round: C. Thorburn beat J. Johnson 5-3; T. Griffiths beat A. Higgins 5-4; E. Charlton beat K. Stevens 5-4; A. Knowles beat S. Francisco 5-1; S. Davis beat David Taylor 5-4; W. Thorne beat R. Reardon 5-4; J. White beat T. Meo 5-4; Dennis Taylor beat D. Mountjoy 5-2

Quarter-finals: Thorburn beat Griffiths 5-2; Knowles beat Charlton 5-4; S. Davis beat Thorne 5-4; White beat Dennis Taylor 5-3

Semi-finals: Thorburn beat Knowles 6-4; White beat S. Davis 6-3

Final: Thorburn beat White 9-5

1987
First round: C. Thorburn beat R. Williams 5-1; W. Thorne beat K. Stevens 5-3; S. Francisco beat A. Knowles 5-2; Dennis Taylor beat N. Foulds 5-2; D. Mountjoy beat S. Davis 5-2; T. Meo beat J. White 5-4; A. Higgins beat T. Griffiths 5-4; J. Johnson beat R. Reardon 5-2

Quarter-finals: Thorburn beat Thorne 5-3; Taylor beat S. Francisco 5-3; Meo beat Mountjoy 5-4; Higgins beat Johnson 5-1

Semi-finals: Taylor beat Thorburn 6-5; Higgins beat Meo 6-2

Final: Taylor beat Higgins 9-8

DULUX BRITISH OPEN

First staged 1985
Sponsors Dulux
Venue Assembly Rooms, Derby
Initial prize-money £250,000
Prize-money last season £300,000
TV ITV

1985
Qualifying: T. Chappel beat I. Williamson 6-5; D. Chalmers beat P. Burke 6-5; John Rea beat M. Fisher 6-0; W. King beat P. Medati 6-4; D. Fowler beat C. Everton 6-1; T. Murphy beat D. Sheehan 6-3; R. Foldvari beat S. Duggan 6-4; V. Harris beat L. Dodd 6-1; T. Jones beat G. Foulds 6-0; P. Francisco beat B. Kelly 6-3; D. O'Kane beat G. Cripsey 6-4; S. Newbury beat P. Browne 6-0; M. Bradley beat M. Morra 6-2; A. Kearney beat M. Watterson 6-4; D. French beat E. McLaughlin 6-0; R. Chaperon beat P. Fagan 6-5; B. Harris beat J. Meadowcroft 6-1; S. Longworth beat F. Davis 6-1; B. Mikkelsen beat D. Hughes 6-0; G. Scott beat M. Darrington 6-3; J. Giannaros beat C. Roscoe 6-1; F. Jonik beat J. McLaughlin 6-2; W. Jones beat J. Donnelly 6-1; P. Watchorn beat J. Fitzmaurice 6-1; R. Bales beat I. Black 6-4; M. Gauvreau beat D. Greaves 6-3; M. Gibson beat B. Demarco 6-1; R. Edmonds beat D. Mienie 6-1

First round: D. Reynolds beat Giannaros 6-3; M. Macleod beat Murphy 6-5; E. Hughes beat Watchorn 6-4; Longworth beat C. Wilson 6-3; W. Jones beat J. Johnson 6-5; M. Hallett *wo* Mikkelsen *scr*; C. Thorburn beat G. Rigitano 6-3; A. Higgins beat Bales 6-3; Chaperon beat B. Werbeniuk 6-1; S. Francisco beat Kearney 6-4; T. Meo beat Foldvari 6-0; W. Thorne beat W. Oliver 6-3; B. Harris beat E. Charlton 6-3; J. White beat T. Jones 6-5; A. Knowles beat French 6-2; N. Foulds beat J. Hargreaves 6-1; Newbury beat E. Sinclair 6-3; M. Wildman beat Gibson 6-1; J. Spencer beat Jonik 6-0; V. Harris beat D. Mountjoy 6-5; O'Kane beat J. Campbell 6-4; G. Miles beat Edmonds 6-1; T. Griffiths beat Chalmers 6-0; R. Reardon beat King 6-5; J. Parrott beat John Rea 6-4; Bradley beat David Taylor 6-3; K. Stevens beat Gauvreau 6-3; J. Virgo beat P. Francisco 6-2; Fowler beat R. Williams 6-4; D. Martin beat B. Bennett 6-0; S. Davis beat Chappel 6-5; Dennis Taylor beat Scott 6-2

Second round: Newbury beat Griffiths 5-3; Bradley beat Fowler 5-4; S. Davis beat Virgo 5-2; Knowles beat Longworth 5-2; O'Kane beat V. Harris 5-3;

Thorburn beat Reynolds 5-3; Higgins beat N. Foulds 5-1; Dennis Taylor beat Parrott 5-2; Macleod beat Thorne 5-0; Martin beat Reardon 5-4; Miles beat Spencer 5-3; S. Francisco beat White 5-4; Meo beat Hallett 5-4; E. Hughes beat B. Harris 5-4; Stevens beat Wildman 5-2; Chaperon beat W. Jones 5-2

Third round: Meo beat Knowles 5-2; S. Davis beat Bradley 5-2; O'Kane beat Martin 5-4; S. Francisco beat Chaperon 5-2; Dennis Taylor beat Newbury 5-3; E. Hughes beat Macleod 5-2; Stevens beat Miles 5-2; Higgins beat Thorburn 5-2

Quarter-finals: Stevens beat Dennis Taylor 5-2; S. Davis beat O'Kane 5-1; S. Francisco beat Meo 5-4; Higgins beat E. Hughes 5-2

Semi-finals: Stevens beat S. Davis 9-7; S. Francisco beat Higgins 9-6

Final: S. Francisco beat Stevens 12-9

1986
First round: J. O'Boye beat Jim Bear 5-1; J. Hargreaves *wo* G. Watson *scr*; O. Agrawal beat D. Greaves 5-3; D. Gilbert beat P. Burke 5-1; S. Hendry beat D. Hughes 5-1; G. Wilkinson beat P. Watchorn 5-4; D. Sheehan beat S. Simngam 5-2; G. Jenkins beat B. Demarco 5-1; B. West beat B. Bennett 5-1; G. Cripsey beat M. Darrington 5-4; P. Houlihan *wo* G. Robinson *scr*; A. Kearney beat M. Smith 5-2; R. Bales beat M. Parkin 5-1; T. Drago *wo* D. Mienie *scr*

Second round: T. Jones beat O'Boye 5-2; F. Davis beat W. Kelly 5-4; G. Scott beat D. Chalmers 5-1; Hargreaves beat R. Edmonds 5-3; L. Dodd beat F. Jonik 5-4; W. Jones beat G. Rigitano 5-1; G. Miles beat Agrawal 5-4; R. Chaperon beat V. Harris 5-0; John Rea beat W. King 5-1; D. Fowler beat T. Chappel 5-4; Gilbert beat M. Morra 5-4; P. Browne beat Hendry 5-0; J. Donnelly beat Wilkinson 5-4; S. Newbury beat W. Oliver 5-2; Sheehan *wo* M. Watterson *scr*; Jenkins beat J. Meadowcroft 5-2; I. Black beat M. Gibson 5-0; B. Harris beat E. Sinclair 5-3; P. Medati beat C. Everton 5-1; West beat E. McLaughlin 5-3; P. Fagan beat J. Fitzmaurice 5-4; C. Roscoe beat B. Mikkelsen 5-4; I. Williamson beat Cripsey 5-4; J. Wych beat J. Van Rensberg 5-0; P. Francisco beat G. Foulds 5-2; S. Longworth beat Houlihan 5-3; M. Bradley beat Jack Rea 5-1; S. Duggan beat T. Murphy 5-1; J. McLaughlin beat M. Fisher 5-3; R. Foldvari beat Kearney 5-2; Bales *wo* J. Dunning *scr*; Drago beat M. Gauvreau 5-3

Third round: S. Francisco beat T. Jones 5-2; M. Macleod beat F. Davis 5-4; T. Griffiths beat Scott 5-3; N. Foulds beat Hargreaves 5-4; W. Thorne beat Dodd 5-2; P. Mans beat W. Jones 5-2; K. Stevens beat Miles 5-3; C. Wilson beat Chaperon 5-3; John Rea beat R. Reardon 5-3; J. Virgo beat Fowler 5-1; E. Charlton beat Gilbert 5-2; Browne beat J. Spencer 5-0; T. Meo beat Donnelly 5-3; Newbury beat D. O'Kane 5-3; C. Thorburn beat Sheehan 5-0; M. Wildman beat Jenkins 5-4; S. Davis beat Black 5-2; D. Martin beat B. Harris 5-1; Medati beat David Taylor 5-1; J. Campbell beat West 5-4; Fagan beat D. Mountjoy 5-1; J. Parrott beat Roscoe 5-2; A. Knowles beat Williamson

5-1; Wych beat D. Reynolds 5-3; P. Francisco beat J. White 5-4; Longworth beat E. Hughes 5-4; A. Higgins beat Bradley 5-3; M. Hallett beat Duggan 5-3; J. Johnson beat J. McLaughlin 5-2; B. Werbeniuk beat Foldvari 5-4; Bales beat Dennis Taylor 5-4; R. Williams beat Drago 5-1

Fourth round: Macleod beat S. Francisco 5-1; Griffiths beat N. Foulds 5-3; Thorne beat Mans 5-1; Stevens beat Wilson 5-0; Virgo beat John Rea 5-0; Charlton beat Browne 5-1; Meo beat Newbury 5-0; Thorne beat Wildman 5-1; S. Davis beat Martin 5-1; Campbell beat Medati 5-4; Parrott beat Fagan 5-0; Wych beat Knowles 5-4; P. Francisco beat Longworth 5-2; Higgins beat Hallett 5-1; Werbeniuk beat Johnson 5-3; Williams beat Bales 5-4

Fifth round: Griffiths beat Macleod 5-2; Thorne beat Stevens 5-4; Virgo beat Charlton 5-4; Meo beat Thorburn 5-3; S. Davis beat Campbell 5-0; Wych beat Parrott 5-4; Higgins beat P. Francisco 5-2; Werbeniuk beat Williams 5-3

Quarter-finals: Thorne beat Griffiths 5-4; Virgo beat Meo 5-3; S. Davis beat Wych 5-2; Higgins beat Werbeniuk 5-1

Semi-finals: Thorne beat Virgo 9-4; S. Davis beat Higgins 9-3

Final: S. Davis beat Thorne 12-7

1987
First round: M. Morra beat M. Bennett 5-4; B. Rowswell beat G. Jenkins 5-1; G. Foulds beat D. Greaves 5-3; D. Roe beat M. Watterson 5-3; B. Kelly beat B. Bennett 5-2; P. Gibson beat O. Agrawal 5-0; N. Gilbert beat P. Houlihan 5-4; J. Hargreaves beat M. Parkin 5-4; J. Donnelly *wo* L. Heywood *scr*; C. Roscoe beat D. Mienie 5-2; F. Ellis beat M. Smith 5-2; D. Chalmers *wo* S. Simngam *scr*; P. Watchorn beat J. Dunning 5-2; K. Owers beat F. Jonik 5-4; M. Fisher *wo* C. Everton *scr*; R. Grace beat J. Meadowcroft 5-4; G. Wilkinson beat J. Fitzmaurice 5-0; T. Kearney *wo* Jim Bear *scr*; G. Rigitano beat B. Demarco 5-1; S. James beat M. Darrington 5-3; T. Whitthread beat D. Hughes 5-1; P. Burke *wo* E. McLaughlin *scr*; B. Oliver beat Jack Rea 5-1; D. Sheehan beat J. Wright 5-2

Second round: M. Gauvreau beat R. Bales 5-0; Morra beat J. Van Rensberg 5-1; Rowswell beat D. O'Kane 5-4; G. Foulds beat R. Edmonds 5-3; Roe beat I. Black 5-0; W. King beat Williamson 5-3; B. Harris beat Kelly 5-2; S. Duggan beat Gibson 5-3; D. Fowler beat Dodd 5-1; N. Gilbert beat W. Jones 5-3; J. O'Boye beat M. Bradley 5-1; T. Murphy beat D. Gilbert 5-4; Hargreaves beat John Rea 5-3; T. Jones beat Donnelly 5-2; Roscoe beat S. Newbury 5-3; P. Medati beat Ellis 5-0; M. Wildman beat Chalmers 5-0; G. Cripsey beat Watchorn 5-4; Owers beat F. Davis 5-3; E. Sinclair beat S. Hendry 5-2; R. Chaperon beat Fisher 5-2; Grace beat P. Fagan 5-3; J. McLaughlin beat M. Gibson 5-1; Wilkinson beat Mans 5-2; T. Chappel beat Kearney 5-3; Rigitano beat P. Browne 5-4; R. Foldvari beat B. Mikkelsen 5-3; James beat G. Miles 5-2; J. Spencer beat Whitthread 5-2; G. Scott beat Burke 5-2; T. Drago beat Oliver 5-1; V. Harris beat Sheehan 5-4

Third round: S. Davis beat Gauvreau 5-0; J. Virgo beat Morra 5-3; S. Francisco beat Rowswell 5-0; C. Wilson beat G. Foulds 5-3; N. Foulds beat Roe 5-1; King beat J. Parrott 5-1; W. Thorne beat B. Harris 5-1; Duggan beat S. Longworth 5-2; A. Knowles beat Fowler 5-4; D. Reynolds beat N. Gilbert 5-2; R. Reardon beat O'Boye 5-4; Murphy beat J. Wych 5-1; T. Griffiths beat John Rea 5-2; T. Jones beat M. Macleod 5-4; Dennis Taylor beat Roscoe 5-1; E. Charlton beat Medati 5-4; C. Thorburn beat Wildman 5-3; Cripsey beat B. Werbeniuk 5-2; D. Mountjoy beat Owers 5-1; P. Francisco beat Sinclair 5-3; K. Stevens beat Chaperon 5-4; B. West beat Grace 5-2; J. McLaughlin beat A. Higgins 5-4; David Taylor beat Wilkinson 5-4; J. White beat Chappel 5-1; M. Hallett beat Rigitano 5-1; R. Williams beat Foldvari 5-4; James beat J. Campbell 5-1; Spencer beat T. Meo 5-1; D. Martin beat Scott 5-3; J. Johnson beat Drago 5-0; E. Hughes beat V. Harris 5-1

Fourth round: Virgo beat S. Davis 5-4; Wilson beat S. Francisco 5-4; N. Foulds beat King 5-4; Thorne beat Duggan 5-2; Knowles beat Reynolds 5-0; Murphy beat Reardon 5-4; Griffiths beat T. Jones 5-3; Dennis Taylor beat Charlton 5-1; Thorburn beat Cripsey 5-2; Mountjoy beat P. Francisco 5-3; Stevens beat West 5-4; David Taylor beat J. McLaughlin 5-2; White beat Hallett 5-2; Williams beat James 5-2; Spencer beat Martin 5-2; Johnson beat E. Hughes 5-3

Fifth round: Virgo beat Wilson 5-2; N. Foulds beat Thorne 5-2; Knowles beat Murphy 5-3; Dennis Taylor beat Griffiths 5-4; Thorburn beat Mountjoy 5-4; David Taylor beat Stevens 5-2; White beat Williams 5-0; Spencer beat Johnson 5-3

Quarter-finals: N. Foulds beat Virgo 5-3; Knowles beat Dennis Taylor 5-4; Thorburn beat David Taylor 5-3; White beat Spencer 5-3

Semi-finals: N. Foulds beat Knowles 9-2; White beat Thorburn 9-5

Final: White beat N. Foulds 13-9

In June 1987, Dulux announced that they would not be renewing their sponsorship of the tournament.

TUBORG WORLD CUP

First staged 1979
Sponsors State Express (1979–83), Guinness (1985), Car Care Plan (1986), Tuborg (1987–)
Venue The Hexagon, Reading (1979–83), Bournemouth International Centre (1985–)
Initial prize-money £27,500
Prize-money last season £100,000
TV BBC

1979 (*State Express World Team Classic*)
Group A
England (F. Davis, G. Miles, J. Spencer) beat Rest of World (P. Mans, J. Van

Rensberg, P. Fagan) 8-7; England beat Northern Ireland (Jack Rea, A. Higgins, Dennis Taylor) 8-7; Northern Ireland beat Rest of World 8-7

Group B
Wales (R. Reardon, T. Griffiths, D. Mountjoy) beat Canada (C. Thorburn, K. Stevens, B. Werbeniuk) 9-6; Australia (E. Charlton, G. Owen, P. Morgan) beat Canada 8-7; Wales beat Australia 9-6

Final: Wales beat England 14-3

1980 (*State Express World Team Classic*)
Group A
Wales (R. Reardon, T. Griffiths, D. Mountjoy) beat Canada (C. Thorburn, K. Stevens, B. Werbeniuk) 10-5; Canada beat Rest of World (J. Rempe, E. Sinclair, P. Mans) 9-6; Wales beat Rest of World 13-2

Group B
England (F. Davis, J. Virgo, David Taylor) beat Ireland (A. Higgins, Dennis Taylor, P. Fagan) 11-4; Australia (E. Charlton, I. Anderson, P. Morgan) beat England 8-7; Ireland beat Australia 10-5

Semi-finals: Wales beat Ireland 8-7; Canada beat England 8-5

Final: Wales beat Canada 8-5

1981 (*State Express World Team Classic*)
Preliminary match: Republic of Ireland (E. Hughes, P. Fagan, D. Sheehan) beat Scotland (I. Black, M. Macleod, E. Sinclair) 4-2

Group A
England (S. Davis, J. Spencer, David Taylor) beat Australia (I. Anderson, E. Charlton, P. Morgan) 4-3; Northern Ireland (T. Murphy, Dennis Taylor, A. Higgins) beat Australia 4-1; England beat Northern Ireland 4-3

Group B
Wales (R. Reardon, D. Mountjoy, T. Griffiths) beat Canada (K. Stevens, C. Thorburn, B. Werbeniuk) 4-2; Wales beat Republic of Ireland 4-0; Canada beat Republic of Ireland 4-2

Semi-finals: England beat Canada 4-2; Wales beat Northern Ireland 4-3

Final: England beat Wales 4-3

1982 (*State Express World Team Classic*)
Preliminary match: Scotland (E. Sinclair, J. Donnelly, I. Black) beat Republic of Ireland (E. Hughes, P. Fagan, D. Sheehan) 4-2

Group A
England (A. Knowles, S. Davis, J. White) beat Northern Ireland (A. Higgins,

T. Murphy, Dennis Taylor) 4-3; Scotland beat Northern Ireland 4-1; England beat Scotland 4-1

Group B
Canada (C. Thorburn, B. Werbeniuk, K. Stevens) beat Wales (T. Griffiths, D. Mountjoy, R. Reardon) 4-3; Canada beat Australia (E. Charlton, P. Morgan, I. Anderson) 4-0; Wales beat Australia 4-1

Semi-finals: England beat Wales 4-2; Canada beat Scotland 4-0

Final: Canada beat England 4-2

1983 (*State Express World Team Classic*)
Preliminary match: Scotland (E. Sinclair, M. Macleod, I. Black) beat Republic of Ireland (B. Kelly, E. Hughes, P. Fagan) 4-2

Group A
Wales (D. Mountjoy, R. Reardon, T. Griffiths) beat Canada (C. Thorburn, B. Werbeniuk, K. Stevens) 4-3; Canada beat Australia (E. Charlton, W. King, J. Campbell) 4-2; Wales beat Australia 4-0

Group B
England (S. Davis, A. Knowles, T. Meo) beat Northern Ireland (A. Higgins, T. Murphy, Dennis Taylor) 4-1; Northern Ireland beat Scotland 4-3; England beat Scotland 4-0

Semi-finals: Wales beat Northern Ireland 4-1; England beat Canada 4-2

Final: England beat Wales 4-2

1985 (*Guinness World Cup*)
First round: Wales beat Australia 5-4 (T. Griffiths drew with E. Charlton 1-1; D. Mountjoy beat J. Campbell 2-0; R. Reardon lost to W. King 0-2; Mountjoy drew with Charlton 1-1; Griffiths beat King 1-0); England A beat Scotland 5-4 (S. Davis lost to E. Sinclair 0-2; A. Knowles drew with M. Macleod 1-1; T. Meo beat J. Donnelly 2-0; S. Davis drew with Sinclair 1-1; Knowles beat Macleod 1-0); England B beat Rest of World 5-2 (J. White beat S. Francisco 2-0; W. Thorne drew with J. Rempe 1-1; J. Spencer drew with D. O'Kane 1-1; White beat Francisco 1-0); Ireland beat Canada 5-2 (Dennis Taylor beat K. Stevens 2-0; E. Hughes drew with C. Thorburn 1-1; A. Higgins drew with B. Werbeniuk 1-1; Higgins beat Thorburn 1-0)

Semi-finals: Ireland beat Wales 5-3 (Dennis Taylor drew with Mountjoy 1-1; E. Hughes lost to Griffiths 0-2; Higgins beat Reardon 2-0; Higgins beat Mountjoy 2-0); England A beat England B 5-2 (S. Davis beat Spencer 2-0; Knowles drew with Thorne 1-1; Meo drew with White 1-1; S. Davis beat White 1-0)

Final: Ireland beat England A 9-7 (Dennis Taylor drew with Knowles 1-1; E. Hughes lost to S. Davis 0-2; Higgins drew with Meo 1-1; Dennis Taylor drew with Knowles 1-1; Dennis Taylor drew with S. Davis 1-1; E. Hughes drew with Knowles 1-1; Higgins beat Meo 2-0; Higgins beat S. Davis 2-0)

1986 (*Car Care Plan World Cup*)
First round: Ireland A beat Ireland B 5-0 (A. Higgins beat P. Fagan 2-0; E. Hughes beat T. Murphy 2-0; Dennis Taylor beat P. Browne 1-0); Wales beat Scotland 5-1 (D. Mountjoy beat M. Macleod 2-0; R. Reardon drew with E. Sinclair 1-1; T. Griffiths beat J. Donnelly 2-0); Canada beat Rest of World 5-0 (C. Thorburn beat T. Drago 2-0; K. Stevens beat O. Agrawal 2-0; B. Werbeniuk beat S. Simngam 1-0); England beat Australia 5-2 (A. Knowles drew with J. Campbell 1-1; J. White drew with E. Charlton 1-1; S. Davis beat W. King 2-0; S. Davis beat Campbell 1-0)

Semi-finals: Ireland 'A' beat Wales 5-2 (Higgins beat Mountjoy 2-0; Hughes lost to Reardon 0-2; Dennis Taylor beat Griffiths 2-0; Taylor beat Griffiths 1-0); Canada beat England 5-3 (Thorburn drew with Knowles 1-1; Stevens beat White 2-0; Werbeniuk drew with S. Davis 1-1; Thorburn drew with S. Davis 1-1)

Final: Ireland 'A' beat Canada 9-7 (Dennis Taylor drew with Thorburn 1-1; Hughes lost to Stevens 0-2; Higgins beat Werbeniuk 2-0; Higgins drew with Stevens 1-1; Higgins drew with Thorburn 1-1; Hughes drew with Stevens 1-1; Taylor beat Werbeniuk 2-0; Taylor drew with Thorburn 1-1)

1987
First round: Wales beat Australia 5-1 (R. Reardon drew with E. Charlton 1-1; D. Mountjoy beat W. King 2-0; T. Griffiths beat J. Campbell 2-0); Ireland A beat Ireland B 5-1 (E. Hughes beat P. Browne 2-0; A. Higgins beat P. Fagan 2-0; Dennis Taylor drew with T. Murphy 1-1); Canada beat Rest of World 5-4 (K. Stevens beat S. Francisco 2-0; C. Thorburn drew with T. Drago 1-1; B. Werbeniuk lost to D. O'Kane 0-2; Stevens drew with Drago 1-1; Thorburn beat Francisco 1-0); England beat Scotland 5-1 (J. Johnson drew with S. Hendry 1-1; S. Davis beat M. Gibson 2-0; T. Meo beat M. Macleod 2-0)

Semi-finals: Ireland A beat Wales 5-2 (Taylor lost to Griffiths 0-2; Hughes beat Reardon 2-0; Higgins beat Mountjoy 2-0; Higgins beat Griffiths 1-0); Canada beat England 5-4 (Stevens drew with Johnson 1-1; Thorburn beat Davis 2-0; Werbeniuk drew with Meo 1-1; Stevens lost to Davis 0-2; Thorburn beat Johnson 1-0)

Final: Ireland A beat Canada 9-2 (Hughes drew with Stevens 1-1; Higgins beat Thorburn 2-0; Taylor beat Werbeniuk 2-0; Taylor beat Stevens 2-0; Hughes drew with Stevens 1-1; Taylor beat Thorburn 1-0)

BENSON AND HEDGES IRISH MASTERS

First staged 1978
Sponsors Benson and Hedges
Venue Goffs, Kill, Co Kildare
Initial prize-money £3,000
Prize-money last season £90,000
TV RTE

1978
Final: J. Spencer beat D. Mountjoy 5-3

1979
Final: D. Mountjoy beat R. Reardon 6-5

1980
Final: T. Griffiths beat D. Mountjoy 9-8

1981
First round: Dennis Taylor beat J. Spencer 4-2; S. Davis beat J. Virgo 4-3

Quarter-finals: T. Griffiths beat K. Stevens 4-0; C. Thorburn beat D. Mountjoy 4-0; R. Reardon beat S. Davis 4-2; A. Higgins beat Dennis Taylor 4-2

Semi-finals: Griffiths beat Thorburn 6-5; Reardon beat Higgins 6-5

Final: Griffiths beat Reardon 9-7

1982
First round: Dennis Taylor beat D. Sheehan 5-3; T. Meo beat J. Spencer 5-3; A. Higgins beat J. Wych 5-3; D. Mountjoy beat E. Hughes 5-4

Quarter-finals: T. Griffiths beat Meo 5-3; R. Reardon beat Dennis Taylor 5-4; S. Davis beat Mountjoy 5-2; Higgins beat C. Thorburn 5-4

Semi-finals: Griffiths beat Reardon 6-3; S. Davis beat Higgins 6-2

Final: Griffiths beat S. Davis 9-5

1983
First round: J. White beat Dennis Taylor 5-4; T. Meo beat P. Burke 5-0; D. Mountjoy beat A. Knowles 5-1; E. Charlton beat David Taylor 5-4

Quarter-finals: R. Reardon beat Meo 5-4; A. Higgins beat White 5-2; S. Davis beat Charlton 5-1; T. Griffiths beat Mountjoy 5-4

Semi-finals: Reardon beat Higgins 6-3; S. Davis beat Griffiths 6-2

Final: S. Davis beat Reardon 9-2

1984
First round: T. Griffiths beat B. Werbeniuk 5-2; Dennis Taylor beat E. Hughes 5-1; T. Meo beat J. White 5-4; A. Higgins beat E. Charlton 5-2

Quarter-finals: Dennis Taylor beat C. Thorburn 5-2; Griffiths beat A. Knowles 5-0; Higgins beat R. Reardon 5-2; S. Davis beat Meo 5-4

Semi-finals: Griffiths beat Dennis Taylor 6-5; S. Davis beat Higgins 6-4

Final: S. Davis beat Griffiths 9-1

1985
First round: E. Charlton beat Dennis Taylor 5-4; J. White beat T. Meo 5-1; E. Hughes beat R. Reardon 5-0; A. Higgins beat T. Griffiths 5-2

Quarter-finals: A. Knowles beat Charlton 5-3; White beat C. Thorburn 5-3; S. Davis beat Hughes 5-4; Higgins beat K. Stevens 5-3

Semi-finals: White beat Knowles 6-4; Higgins beat S. Davis 6-2

Final: White beat Higgins 9-5

1986
First round: E. Hughes beat R. Reardon 5-2; W. Thorne beat T. Griffiths 5-2; T. Meo beat A. Higgins 5-4; P. Fagan *wo* K. Stevens *scr*

Quarter-finals: C. Thorburn beat Hughes 5-1; Thorne beat Dennis Taylor 5-2; J. White beat Meo 5-2; Fagan beat A. Knowles 5-4

Semi-finals: Thorne beat Thorburn 6-4; White beat Fagan 6-0

Final: White beat Thorne 9-5

1987
First round: W. Thorne beat K. Stevens 5-1; Dennis Taylor beat E. Hughes 5-4; T. Meo beat A. Knowles 5-2; T. Griffiths beat A. Higgins 5-1

Quarter-finals: Thorne beat J. White 5-4; Taylor beat C. Thorburn 5-1; S. Davis beat Meo 5-2; Griffiths beat J. Johnson 5-0

Semi-finals: Thorne beat Taylor 6-2; Davis beat Griffiths 6-2

Final: Davis beat Thorne 9-1

EMBASSY WORLD PROFESSIONAL CHAMPIONSHIP

First staged 1927
Sponsors Embassy (1976–)
Venue Crucible Theatre, Sheffield (1977–)
Initial prize-money £15,300
Prize-money last season £400,000
TV BBC

1927
First round: M. Inman beat T. Newman 8-5; T. Carpenter beat N. Butler 8-3

Second round: T. A. Dennis beat F. Lawrence 8-7; A. Cope beat A. Mann 8-6; J. Davis beat J. Brady 10-5; Carpenter beat Inman 8-3

Semi-finals: J. Davis beat Cope 16-7; Dennis beat Carpenter 12-10

Final: J. Davis beat Dennis 20-11

1928
First round: T. Newman beat F. Smith 12-6; A. Mann beat A. Cope 14-9

Second round: Newman beat T. A. Dennis 12-5; F. Lawrence beat Mann 12-11

Third round: Lawrence beat Newman 12-7

Final: J. Davis beat Lawrence 16-13

1929
First round: F. Lawrence beat A. Mann 13-12

Semi-finals: J. Davis beat Lawrence 13-10; T. A. Dennis beat K. Prince 14-6

Final: J. Davis beat Dennis 19-14

1930
First round: F. Lawrence beat A. Mann 13-11; N. Butler beat T. Newman 13-11

Semi-finals: J. Davis beat Lawrence 13-2; T. A. Dennis beat Butler 13-11

Final: J. Davis beat Dennis 25-12

1931
Final: J. Davis beat T. A. Dennis 25-21

1932
First round: C. McConachy beat T. A. Dennis 13-11

Final: J. Davis beat McConachy 30-19

1933
First round: W. Donaldson beat W. Leigh 13-11

Semi-finals: J. Davis beat Donaldson 13-1; W. Smith beat T. A. Dennis 16-9

Final: J. Davis beat Smith 25-18

1934
Final: J. Davis beat T. Newman 25-23

1935
First round: W. Smith beat C. Stanbury 13-12

Semi-finals: Smith beat A. Mann 13-4; J. Davis beat T. Newman 15-10

Final: J. Davis beat Smith 25-20

1936
First round: C. O'Donnell beat S. Lee 16-15; H. Lindrum beat H. Terry 20-11; J. Davis beat T. Newman 29-2; W. Smith beat S. Smith 16-15; C. Stanbury beat A. Mann 22-9

Second round: Alec Brown beat Stanbury 16-15; Lindrum beat O'Donnell 19-6 (*retd*); J. Davis beat W. Smith 22-9; S. Newman *wo*

Semi-finals: J. Davis beat Alec Brown 21-10; Lindrum beat S. Newman 29-2

Final: J. Davis beat Lindrum 34-27

1937
First round: W. A. Withers beat F. Davis 17-14

Second round: J. Davis beat Withers 30-1; H. Lindrum beat S. Lee 20-11; W. Smith beat T. Newman 16-15; S. Smith beat Alec Brown 18-13

Semi-finals: Lindrum beat W. Smith 20-11; J. Davis beat S. Smith 18-13

Final: J. Davis beat Lindrum 32-29

1938
First qualifying round: H. Holt beat C. W. Read 21-10

Second qualifying round: F. Davis beat Holt 23-8

First round: F. Davis beat Alec Brown 14-6 (*retd ill*); S. Smith beat C. Stanbury 27-4; J. Davis beat S. Lee 24-7; W. Smith beat T. Newman 16-15

Semi-finals: J. Davis beat W. Smith (*nrs*); S. Smith beat F. Davis (*nrs*)

Final: J. Davis beat S. Smith 37-24

1939
First qualifying round: W. Donaldson beat H. Holt 18-13; H. W. Laws beat S. Newman 19-12

Second qualifying round: Donaldson beat Laws 18-13

First round: S. Smith beat S. Lee 21-10; W. Donaldson beat C. Falkiner 21-10; T. Newman beat A. Mann 19-12; F. Davis beat C. Stanbury 19-12

Second round: J. Davis beat W. Smith 19-12; F. Davis beat T. Newman 20-11; Alec Brown beat H. Lindrum 17-14; S. Smith beat Donaldson 16-15

Semi-finals: J. Davis beat F. Davis 17-14; S. Smith beat Alec Brown 20-11

Final: J. Davis beat S. Smith 43-30

1940
Qualifying round: H. Holt beat C. Stanbury 18-13

First round: W. Donaldson beat Holt 24-7; J. Davis beat Alec Brown 20-11; F. Davis beat S. Lee 20-11; S. Smith beat T. Newman 22-9

Semi-finals: J. Davis beat Donaldson 22-9; F. Davis beat S. Smith 17-14

Final: J. Davis beat F. Davis 37-36

1946
First qualifying round: K. Kennerley beat F. Lawrence 22-9; C. Stanbury beat J. Barrie 18-13; S. Newman beat W. Leigh 16-15

Second qualifying round: Kennerley beat T. Reece 8-2 (*retd*); S. Newman beat Stanbury 17-14

Third qualifying round: S. Newman beat Kennerley 21-10

First round: J. Davis beat W. Donaldson 21-10; S. Newman beat S. Lee 19-12; F. Davis beat Alec Brown 24-7; H. Lindrum beat H. Holt 17-14

Semi-finals: J. Davis beat S. Newman 21-10; Lindrum beat F. Davis 16-12

Final: J. Davis beat Lindrum 78-67

1947
First qualifying round: Albert Brown beat J. Pulman 21-14; W. Leigh beat H. F. Francis 19-16; S. Lee beat J. Lees 19-16; K. Kennerley beat C. Stanbury 23-12; E. Newman *wo* H. Holt *scr*

Second qualifying round: J. Barrie beat F. Lawrence 25-10; Albert Brown beat Newman 28-7; Kennerley beat A. Mann 23-12; Leigh beat Lee 25-10

Third qualifying round: Albert Brown beat Barrie 24-11; Kennerley beat Leigh 21-14

Fourth qualifying round: Albert Brown beat Kennerley 21-14

First round: H. Lindrum beat Albert Brown 39-34; S. Smith beat Alec Brown 43-28; W. Donaldson beat S. Newman 46-25; F. Davis beat C. McConachy 53-20

Semi-finals: Donaldson beat Lindrum 39-32; F. Davis beat Smith 39-32

Final: Donaldson beat F. Davis 82-63

1948
First qualifying round: C. Stanbury beat E. Newman 26-9; W. Leigh beat H. Holt 18-17; J. Barrie beat H. F. Francis 19-16; J. Pulman *wo* S. Lee *scr*

Second qualifying round: Leigh beat Barrie 21-14; Pulman beat Stanbury 19-16

Third qualifying round: Pulman beat Leigh 18-17

First round: F. Davis beat Alec Brown 43-28; C. McConachy beat J. Pulman 42-29; Albert Brown beat S. Smith 36-35; W. Donaldson beat K. Kennerley 46-25

Semi-finals: F. Davis beat McConachy 43-28; Donaldson beat Alec Brown 40-31

Final: F. Davis beat Donaldson 84-61

1949
First qualifying round: C. Stanbury beat H. F. Francis 18-17

Second qualifying round: Stanbury beat Jack Rea 18-17

Third qualifying round: Stanbury beat H. Holt 18-17

First round: W. Donaldson beat Stanbury 58-13; J. Pulman beat Albert Brown 42-29; S. Smith beat Alec Brown 41-30; F. Davis beat K. Kennerley 50-21

Semi-finals: Donaldson beat Pulman 49-22; F. Davis beat Smith 42-29

Final: F. Davis beat Donaldson 80-65

1950
First qualifying round: W. Smith beat W. A. Withers 28-7; H. Holt beat H. W. Laws 26-9; S. Lee beat C. Stanbury 20-15; K. Kennerley beat J. Barrie 21-14

Second qualifying round: Kennerley beat Smith 22-13; Lee beat Holt 16-8 (*retd ill*)

Third qualifying round: Kennerley beat Lee 21-14

First round: Albert Brown beat J. Pulman 37-34; W. Donaldson beat K. Kennerley 42-29; G. Chenier beat P. Mans 37-34; F. Davis beat Alec Brown 44-27

Semi-finals: Donaldson beat Albert Brown 37-34; F. Davis beat Chenier 43-28

Final: Donaldson beat F. Davis 51-46

1951
First qualifying round: J. Barrie beat S. Lee 23-12

Second qualifying round: Barrie beat H. W. Laws 28-7

First round: F. Davis beat Barrie 42-29; H. Lindrum beat Albert Brown 43-28; W. Donaldson beat K. Kennerley 41-30; J. Pulman beat S. Smith 38-33

Semi-finals: Donaldson beat Lindrum 41-30; F. Davis beat Pulman 22-14 (*retd ill*)

Final: F. Davis beat Donaldson 58-39

1952
First round: Alec Brown beat R. Williams 39-22; Jack Rea beat J. Lees 38-32; Albert Brown beat J. Pulman 32-27 (*records incomplete*)

Semi-finals: W. Donaldson beat Albert Brown 31-30

Final: F. Davis beat Donaldson 38-35

1953
First qualifying round: W. Smith beat J. Lees 21-14; K. Kennerley beat R. Williams 25-12

Second qualifying round: Kennerley beat Smith 42-29

First round: Albert Brown beat Alec Brown 35-26; J. Pulman beat Jack Rea 36-25; W. Donaldson beat Kennerley 42-19; F. Davis beat J. Barrie 32-29

Semi-finals: Donaldson beat Brown (*nrs*); F. Davis beat Pulman 36-25

Final: F. Davis beat Donaldson 37-34

1954
First round: J. Pulman beat Jack Rea 31-30

Semi-finals: W. Donaldson beat Alec Brown 36-25; F. Davis beat Pulman 32-29

Final: F. Davis beat Donaldson 39-21

1955
First round: J. Pulman beat R. Williams 22-15; Jack Rea beat H. Stokes (*nrs*)

Semi-finals: F. Davis beat Rea 36-25; Pulman beat Alec Brown (*nrs*)

Final: F. Davis beat Pulman 37-34

1956
Semi-finals: J. Pulman beat Jack Rea 36-25; F. Davis beat R. Williams 35-26

Final: F. Davis beat Pulman 38-35

1957
Semi-finals: J. Pulman beat R. Williams 21-16; Jack Rea beat K. Kennerley 25-12

Final: Pulman beat Rea 39-34

Through lack of public support no Championship was organised between 1957 and 1964. After a truce with the BA and CC a new system was adopted whereby the champion defended his title against a series of single challengers. These matches resulted as follows:

1964
J. Pulman beat F. Davis 19-16; J. Pulman beat R. Williams 40-33

1965
J. Pulman beat F. Davis 37-36; J. Pulman beat R. Williams 25-22 (*matches*); J. Pulman beat F. Van Rensberg 39-12

1966
J. Pulman beat F. Davis 5-2 (*matches*)

1968
J. Pulman beat E. Charlton 39-34

1969 (*Players No. 6*)
First round: J. Spencer beat J. Pulman 25-18; R. Williams beat B. Bennett 25-4; G. Owen beat Jack Rea 25-17; F. Davis beat R. Reardon 25-24

Semi-finals: Spencer beat Williams 37-12; G. Owen beat Davis 37-24

Final: Spencer beat Owen 37-24

1970 (April) (*Players No. 6*)
First round: David Taylor beat B. Bennett 11-8

Quarter-finals: J. Pulman beat David Taylor 31-20; G. Owen beat R. Williams 31-11; R. Reardon beat F. Davis 31-26; J. Spencer beat Jack Rea 31-15

Semi-finals: Pulman beat G. Owen 37-12; Reardon beat Spencer 37-33

Final: Reardon beat Pulman 37-33

1970 (November)
Round robin
J. Spencer beat P. Mans 20-17; beat N. Squire 27-10; beat J. Pulman 23-14
R. Reardon beat Mans 22-15; beat E. Charlton 21-16; beat Spencer 21-16
W. Simpson beat G. Owen 19-18; beat Pulman 21-16; beat Mans 19-18
Charlton beat Squire 27-10; beat Mans 26-11; beat Owen 23-14
Owen beat P. Morgan 26-11; beat Squire 26-11; Morgan beat Simpson 21-16

Semi-finals: Spencer beat Reardon 34-15; Simpson beat Charlton 27-22

Final: Spencer beat Simpson 37-29

1972
First qualifying round: A. Higgins beat R. Gross 15-6; M. Parkin beat G. Thompson 11-10; G. Miles beat B. Bennett 15-6; J. Dunning beat P. Houlihan 11-10

Second qualifying round: Higgins beat Parkin 11-3; Dunning beat Miles 11-5

First round: J. Pulman beat Dunning 19-7; Higgins beat Jack Rea 19-11

Quarter-finals: J. Spencer beat F. Davis 31-21; E. Charlton beat David Taylor 31-25; Higgins beat Pulman 31-23; R. Williams beat R. Reardon 25-23

Semi-finals: Higgins beat Williams 31-30; Spencer beat Charlton 37-32

Final: Higgins beat Spencer 37-32

1973 (*Park Drive*)
First round: P. Houlihan beat Jack Rea 9-2; D. Greaves beat B. Bennett 9-8; G. Miles beat G. Thompson 9-5; P. Mans beat R. Gross 9-2; W. Simpson beat M. Parkin 9-3; C. Thorburn beat Dennis Taylor 9-8; David Taylor beat J. Dunning 9-4; J. Meadowcroft *wo* K. Kennerley *scr*

Second round: F. Davis beat Greaves 16-1; Miles beat J. Pulman 16-10; E. Charlton beat Mans 16-8; G. Owen beat Simpson 16-14; R. Reardon beat Meadowcroft 16-10; R. Williams beat Thorburn 16-15; J. Spencer beat David Taylor 16-5; A. Higgins beat Houlihan 16-3

Quarter-finals: Higgins beat F. Davis 16-14; Spencer beat Williams 16-7; Charlton beat Miles 16-6; Reardon beat G. Owen 16-6

Semi-finals: Charlton beat Higgins 23-9; Reardon beat Spencer 23-22

Final: Reardon beat Charlton 38-32

1974 (*Park Drive*)
Qualifying: J. Dunning beat D. Greaves 8-2; W. Simpson beat Jack Rea 8-3; J. Meadowcroft beat P. Houlihan 8-5; C. Thorburn beat A. McDonald 8-3; J. Pulman beat J. Karnehm 8-0; David Taylor beat R. Gross 8-7; M. Owen beat Dennis Taylor 8-1

First round: B. Bennett beat Simpson 8-2; B. Werbeniuk beat G. Thompson 8-3; Meadowcroft beat K. Kennerley 8-5; M. Owen beat M. Parkin 8-5; P. Mans beat I. Anderson 8-1; Pulman beat S. Lee 8-0; Dunning beat David Taylor 8-6; P. Morgan beat Thorburn 8-4

Second round: Mans beat J. Spencer 15-13; Dunning beat E. Charlton 15-13; M. Owen beat G. Owen 15-8; A. Higgins beat Bennett 15-4; G. Miles beat Morgan 15-7; R. Williams beat Pulman 15-12; F. Davis beat Werbeniuk 15-5; R. Reardon beat Meadowcroft 15-3

Quarter-finals: Williams beat Mans 15-4; Reardon beat M. Owen 15-11; Miles beat Dunning 15-13; F. Davis beat Higgins 15-14

Semi-finals: Miles beat Williams 15-7; Reardon beat F. Davis 15-3

Final: Reardon beat Miles 22-12

1975
Qualifying: P. Tarrant beat B. Bennett 15-8; L. Condo beat M. Parkin 15-8; D. Greaves beat J. Charlton 15-14

First round: W. Simpson beat R. Mares 15-5; J. Pulman beat Tarrant 15-5; David Taylor beat R. King 15-8; I. Anderson beat Condo 15-8; Dennis Taylor beat P. Mans 15-12; G. Owen beat Greaves 15-3; B. Werbeniuk beat J. Meadowcroft 15-9; C. Thorburn beat P. Morgan 15-6

Second round: R. Reardon beat Simpson 15-11; J. Spencer beat Pulman 15-10; A. Higgins beat David Taylor 15-2; R. Williams beat Anderson 15-4; Dennis Taylor beat F. Davis 15-14; G. Owen beat J. Dunning 15-8; E. Charlton beat Werbeniuk 15-11; Thorburn beat G. Miles 15-2

Quarter-finals: Reardon beat Spencer 19-17; Higgins beat Williams 19-12; Dennis Taylor beat G. Owen 19-9; Charlton beat Thorburn 19-12

Semi-finals: Charlton beat Dennis Taylor 19-12; Reardon beat Higgins 19-14

Final: Reardon beat Charlton 31-30

1976
First qualifying round: Jack Rea beat I. Anderson 8-5; D. Greaves beat J. Charlton 8-5; J. Meadowcroft beat D. Wheelwright 8-1; R. Gross beat M. Parkin 8-5; L. Condo beat M. Owen 8-6

Second qualifying round: Jack Rea beat B. Bennett 8-5; David Taylor beat Greaves 8-1; Meadowcroft beat Gross 8-4; W. Thorne beat Condo 8-3

First round: R. Reardon beat J. Dunning 15-7; Dennis Taylor beat G. Owen 15-9; P. Mans beat G. Miles 15-10; Meadowcroft beat R. Williams 15-7; E. Charlton beat J. Pulman 15-9; F. Davis beat B. Werbeniuk 15-12; A. Higgins beat C. Thorburn 15-14; J. Spencer beat David Taylor 15-5

Quarter-finals: Reardon beat Dennis Taylor 15-2; Mans beat Meadowcroft 15-8; Charlton beat F. Davis 15-13; Higgins beat Spencer 15-14

Semi-finals: Reardon beat Mans 20-10; Higgins beat Charlton 20-18

Final: Reardon beat Higgins 27-16

1977
First qualifying round: J. Virgo beat R. Andrewartha 11-1

Second qualifying round: P. Fagan beat J. Meadowcroft 11-9; Virgo beat J. Dunning 11-6; W. Thorne beat B. Bennett 11-4; J. Pulman *wo*; David Taylor beat D. Greaves 11-0; C. Thorburn beat C. Ross 11-0; Dennis Taylor beat J. Karnehm 11-0; D. Mountjoy beat Jack Rea 11-9

First round: R. Reardon beat Fagan 13-7; J. Spencer beat Virgo 13-9; G. Miles beat Thorne 13-4; Pulman beat F. Davis 13-12; E. Charlton beat David Taylor 13-5; Thorburn beat R. Williams 13-6; Dennis Taylor beat P. Mans 13-11; Mountjoy beat A. Higgins 13-12

Quarter-finals: Spencer beat Reardon 13-6; Pulman beat Miles 13-10; Thorburn beat Charlton 13-12; Dennis Taylor beat Mountjoy 13-11

Semi-finals: Spencer beat Pulman 18-16; Thorburn beat Dennis Taylor 18-16

Final: Spencer beat Thorburn 25-21

1978
First qualifying round: M. Parkin beat B. Bennett 9-4; R. Andrewartha beat J. Karnehm 9-0; J. Barrie beat D. Greaves 9-3; P. Houlihan beat C. Ross 9-1

Second qualifying round: D. Mountjoy beat Andrewartha 9-3; P. Fagan beat J. Dunning 9-5; W. Thorne beat R. Williams 9-3; B. Werbeniuk beat M. Parkin 9-2; P. Mans beat Barrie 9-6; David Taylor beat P. Morgan 9-7; Houlihan beat J. Meadowcroft 9-6; F. Davis beat J. Virgo 9-8

First round: Mans beat J. Spencer 13-8; G. Miles beat David Taylor 13-10; Fagan beat A. Higgins 13-12; F. Davis beat Dennis Taylor 13-9; E. Charlton beat Thorne 13-12; C. Thorburn beat Houlihan 13-8; Werbeniuk beat J. Pulman 13-4; R. Reardon beat Mountjoy 13-9

Quarter-finals: Mans beat Miles 13-7; F. Davis beat Fagan 13-10; Charlton beat Thorburn 13-12; Reardon beat Werbeniuk 13-6

Semi-finals: Mans beat F. Davis 18-16; Reardon beat Charlton 18-14

Final: Reardon beat Mans 25-18

1979
First qualifying round: D. Mountjoy beat D. Mienie 9-1; T. Griffiths beat B. Bennett 9-2; P. Houlihan beat J. Barrie 9-5; W. Thorne beat J. Charlton 9-3; J. Virgo beat M. Parkin 9-0; J. Dunning beat Jack Rea 9-5; R. Williams beat D. Greaves 9-2; J. Meadowcroft beat J. Van Rensberg 9-7; R. Andrewartha beat R. Edmonds 9-8; S. Davis beat I. Anderson 9-1; K. Stevens beat R. Amdor 9-1

Second qualifying round: Virgo beat Thorne 9-8; B. Werbeniuk beat Andrewartha 9-2; David Taylor beat Dunning 9-8; Mountjoy beat Houlihan 9-6; S. Davis beat P. Fagan 9-2; Griffiths beat Meadowcroft 9-6; Stevens beat J. Pulman 9-0; G. Miles beat Williams 9-5

First round: E. Charlton beat Mountjoy 13-6; Werbeniuk beat J. Spencer 13-11; Virgo beat C. Thorburn 13-10; F. Davis beat Stevens 13-8; Dennis Taylor beat S. Davis 13-11; A. Higgins beat David Taylor 13-5; Griffiths beat P. Mans 13-8; R. Reardon beat Miles 13-8

Quarter-finals: Charlton beat F. Davis 13-4; Dennis Taylor beat Reardon 13-8; Virgo beat Werbeniuk 13-9; Griffiths beat Higgins 13-12

Semi-finals: Griffiths beat Charlton 19-17; Dennis Taylor beat Virgo 19-12

Final: Griffiths beat Dennis Taylor 24-16

1980
Qualifying groups
1 Jack Rea beat B. Bennett 9-1; W. Thorne beat K. Robitaille 9-4; Thorne beat Rea 9-1
2 S. Davis beat C. Ross 9-3; P. Morgan beat P. Thornely 9-4; Davis beat Morgan 9-0
3 M. Hallett beat K. Kennerley 9-2; K. Stevens beat D. Greaves 9-3; Stevens beat Hallett 9-3
4 J. Johnson beat R. Andrewartha 9-5; P. Houlihan beat Johnson 9-6; T. Meo beat J. Van Rensberg 9-1; Meo beat Houlihan 9-1
5 R. Amdor beat B. Mikkelsen 9-7; R. Williams beat Amdor 9-4; J. Wych beat John Bear 9-5; Wych beat Williams 9-7
6 F. Jonik beat M. Wildman 9-7; C. Wilson beat Jonik 9-6

7   R. Edmonds beat M. Parkin 9-2; S. Hood beat J. Dunning 16-7; Edmonds
    beat Hood 9-6
8   E. Sinclair beat M. Morra 9-5; Sinclair beat D. Mienie 9-7; J. Meadowcroft
    beat Sinclair 9-1

First round: S. Davis beat P. Fagan 10-6; A. Higgins beat Meo 10-9;
D. Mountjoy beat Wilson 10-6; Wych beat J. Pulman 10-5; J. Virgo beat
Meadowcroft 10-2; Stevens beat G. Miles 10-3; David Taylor beat Edmonds
10-3; B. Werbeniuk beat Thorne 10-9

Second round: S. Davis beat T. Griffiths 13-10; Higgins beat P. Mans 13-6;
Stevens beat J. Spencer 13-8; E. Charlton beat Virgo 13-12; C. Thorburn beat
Mountjoy 13-10; Wych beat Dennis Taylor 13-10; R. Reardon beat Werbeniuk
13-6; David Taylor beat F. Davis 13-5

Quarter-finals: David Taylor beat Reardon 13-11; Thorburn beat Wych 13-6;
Stevens beat Charlton 13-7; Higgins beat S. Davis 13-9

Semi-finals: Thorburn beat David Taylor 16-7; Higgins beat Stevens 16-13

Final: Thorburn beat Higgins 18-16

1981
Qualifying groups
1   W. Thorne beat M. Morra 9-5; D. Greaves beat M. Parkin 9-5; Thorne beat
    Greaves 9-3
2   J. White beat B. Mikkelsen 9-4; White beat J. Meadowcroft 9-8
3   R. Edmonds beat M. Wildman 9-3; R. Williams beat S. Hood 9-4; Edmonds
    beat Williams 9-7
4   T. Meo beat J. Johnson 9-8; M. Hallett beat F. Jonik 9-1; Meo beat Hallett
    9-4
5   J. Dunning beat B. Bennett 9-6; Dunning beat P. Fagan 9-7
6   D. Martin beat I. Anderson 9-3; Martin beat J. Pulman 9-2
7   C. Wilson beat R. Andrewartha 9-4; E. Sinclair beat P. Morgan 9-8; Wilson
    beat Sinclair 9-4
8   A. Knowles beat C. Ross 7-0 (*retd*); Knowles beat J. Wych 9-3

First round: G. Miles beat Knowles 10-8; David Taylor beat Wilson 10-6;
D. Mountjoy beat Thorne 10-6; K. Stevens beat Dunning 10-4; Meo beat
J. Virgo 10-6; S. Davis beat White 10-8; B. Werbeniuk beat Martin 10-4;
J. Spencer beat Edmonds 10-9

Second round: C. Thorburn beat Miles 13-2; David Taylor beat F. Davis 13-3;
T. Griffiths beat Meo 13-6; S. Davis beat Alex Higgins 13-8; Mountjoy beat
E. Charlton 13-7; Dennis Taylor beat Stevens 13-11; Werbeniuk beat P. Mans
13-5; R. Reardon beat Spencer 13-11

Quarter-finals: Thorburn beat David Taylor 13-6; S. Davis beat Griffiths 13-9;
Mountjoy beat Dennis Taylor 13-8; Reardon beat Werbeniuk 13-10

Semi-finals: S. Davis beat Thorburn 16-10; Mountjoy beat Reardon 16-10

Final: S. Davis beat Mountjoy 18-12

1982
Qualifying groups
1   John Bear beat F. Jonik 9-4; Bear beat J. Wych 9-4
2   D. Hughes beat C. Everton 9-4; T. Meo beat Hughes 9-4
3   D. Reynolds beat D. Sheehan 9-5; Reynolds beat R. Edmonds 9-6
4   E. Hughes *wo* D. Mienie *scr*; A. Knowles beat Hughes 9-7
5   M. Wildman beat G. Foulds 9-8; J. White beat Wildman 9-4
6   C. Roscoe beat B. Mikkelsen 9-6; W. Thorne beat Roscoe 9-1
7   P. Medati beat J. Phillips 9-3; C. Wilson beat Medati 9-5
8   P. Houlihan beat I. Anderson 9-5; D. Martin beat Houlihan 9-3
9   M. Macleod beat E. McLaughlin 9-8; J. Dunning beat Macleod 9-4
10 M. Watterson beat B. Demarco 9-6; J. Meadowcroft beat Watterson 9-7
11 D. French beat B. Bennett 9-3; P. Fagan beat French 9-6
12 I. Black beat M. Parkin 9-6; R. Williams beat Black 9-2
13 J. Johnson beat V. Harris 9-4; M. Hallett beat Johnson 9-8
14 J. Donnelly beat M. Gibson 9-8; E. Sinclair beat B. Kelly 9-8; Donnelly beat Sinclair 9-8
15 P. Morgan beat D. Greaves 9-2; S. Francisco beat C. Ross 9-0; Francisco beat Morgan 9-1
16 M. Morra beat T. Murphy 9-5; J. Fitzmaurice *wo* J. Pulman *scr*; Fitzmaurice beat Morra 9-7

First round: Knowles beat S. Davis 10-1; G. Miles beat Martin 10-5; B. Werbeniuk beat Bear 10-7; E. Charlton beat Wilson 10-5; S. Francisco beat Dennis Taylor 10-7; Reynolds beat F. Davis 10-7; J. Virgo beat Hallett 10-4; R. Reardon beat Donnelly 10-5; A. Higgins beat Meadowcroft 10-5; D. Mountjoy beat Williams 10-3; Fagan beat David Taylor 10-9; K. Stevens beat Fitzmaurice 10-4; P. Mans beat Meo 10-8; White beat C. Thorburn 10-4

Second round: Knowles beat Miles 13-7; Charlton beat Werbeniuk 13-5; S. Francisco beat Reynolds 13-8; Reardon beat Virgo 13-8; Thorne beat Spencer 13-5; Higgins beat Mountjoy 13-12; Stevens beat Fagan 13-7; White beat Mans 13-6

Quarter-finals: Charlton beat Knowles 13-11; Reardon beat S. Francisco 13-8; Higgins beat Thorne 13-10; White beat Stevens 13-9

Semi-finals: Reardon beat Charlton 16-11; Higgins beat White 16-15

Final: Higgins beat Reardon 18-15

1983
Qualifying groups
1   B. Kelly beat B. Demarco 10-4; S. Francisco beat Kelly 10-5
2   P. Morgan beat P. Burke 10-9; G. Miles beat Morgan 10-6
3   T. Murphy beat P. Houlihan 10-9; J. Virgo beat Murphy 10-8

4   R. Williams beat M. Darrington 10-0; Williams beat F. Davis 10-1
5   M. Wildman beat B. Harris 10-7; Wildman wo J. Wych scr
6   R. Edmonds beat F. Jonik 10-4; D. Reynolds beat Edmonds 10-6
7   M. Fisher beat P. Fagan 10-8; E. McLaughlin beat D. Greaves 10-7; Fisher
    beat McLaughlin 10-9
8   T. Meo beat V. Harris 10-0; G. Foulds beat M. Gibson 10-6; Meo beat
    Foulds 10-4
9   I. Black beat M. Morra 10-9; P. Medati beat John Bear 10-7; Black beat
    Medati 10-4
10 C. Wilson beat C. Everton 10-1; J. Johnson beat P. Watchorn 10-0; Wilson
    beat Johnson 10-8
11 M. Macleod beat M. Owen 10-5; D. Martin beat M. Parkin 10-1; Martin
    beat Macleod 10-7
12 J. Meadowcroft beat B. Bennett 10-3; G. Cripsey beat D. Hughes 10-2;
    Meadowcroft beat Cripsey 10-6
13 J. Donnelly beat D. Sheehan 10-6; J. Campbell beat M. Watterson 10-6;
    Campbell beat Donnelly 10-2
14 L. Dodd wo J. Dunning scr; I. Williamson beat D. French 10-8; Dodd beat
    Williamson 10-9
15 M. Hallett beat R. Andrewartha 10-7; W. King beat I. Anderson 10-6;
    Hallett beat King 10-6
16 E. Hughes beat J. Fitzmaurice 10-7; E. Sinclair beat C. Roscoe 10-2;
    Hughes beat Sinclair 10-8

First round: A. Higgins beat Reynolds 10-4; W. Thorne beat Virgo 10-3;
B. Werbeniuk beat Martin 10-4; David Taylor beat Meadowcroft 10-2;
E. Charlton beat Dodd 10-7; J. Spencer beat Hallett 10-7; Dennis Taylor beat
S. Francisco 10-9; S. Davis beat Williams 10-4; C. Thorburn beat Campbell
10-5; T. Griffiths beat Wildman 10-8; P. Mans beat Black 10-3; K. Stevens beat
Fisher 10-2; D. Mountjoy beat Wilson 10-2; Meo beat J. White 10-8;
A. Knowles beat Miles 10-3; R. Reardon beat E. Hughes 10-7

Second round: Higgins beat Thorne 13-8; Werbeniuk beat David Taylor 13-10;
Charlton beat Spencer 13-11; S. Davis beat Dennis Taylor 13-11; Thorburn beat
Griffiths 13-12; Meo beat Mountjoy 13-11; Knowles beat Reardon 13-12;
Stevens beat Mans 13-3

Quarter-finals: Higgins beat Werbeniuk 13-11; S. Davis beat Charlton 13-5;
Thorburn beat Stevens 13-12; Knowles beat Meo 13-9

Semi-finals: Thorburn beat Knowles 16-15; S. Davis beat Higgins 16-5

Final: S. Davis beat Thorburn 18-6

1984
Qualifying groups
1   J. Parrott beat D. Hughes 10-3; Parrott beat C. Everton 10-2; Parrott beat
    P. Mans 10-0
2   B. Mikkelsen beat P. Medati 10-8; Mikkelsen beat F. Jonik 10-9;
    W. Thorne beat Mikkelsen 10-3

3   M. Morra beat G. Foulds 10-2; T. Murphy beat J. Fitzmaurice 10-8; Morra
    beat Murphy 10-5; Morra beat D. Reynolds 10-7
4   W. Sanderson beat P. Morgan 10-8; P. Mifsud beat E. Hughes 10-5;
    Mifsud beat Sanderson 10-5; Mifsud beat C. Wilson 10-8
5   J. Van Rensberg beat V. Harris 10-7; R. Edmonds beat D. Greaves 10-0;
    Van Rensberg beat Edmonds 10-9; S. Francisco beat Van Rensberg 10-3
6   I. Williamson beat P. Houlihan 10-5; M. Hines beat I. Black 10-5;
    Williamson beat Hines 10-6; G. Miles beat Williamson 10-6
7   M. Gibson beat G. Rigitano 10-7; M. Fisher beat P. Thornley 10-8; Gibson
    beat Fisher 10-7; J. Johnson beat Gibson 10-3
8   E. McLaughlin beat J. Hargreaves 10-5; R. Andrewartha *wo* John Bear
    scr; Andrewartha beat McLaughlin 10-8; Andrewartha beat M. Wildman
    10-9
9   J. Wych beat G. Ganim Jr 10-1; G. Scott beat L. Heywood 10-7; Wych
    beat Scott 10-6; Wych beat P. Fagan 10-3
10 P. Browne beat S. Duggan 10-9; C. Roscoe beat B. Demarco 10-7; Browne
    beat Roscoe 10-4; E. Sinclair beat Browne 10-1
11 M. Gauvreau beat J. Campbell 10-7; G. Cripsey beat M. Parkin 10-4;
    Gauvreau beat Cripsey 10-1; Gauvreau beat M. Macleod 10-6
12 I. Anderson beat G. Watson 10-4; J. Donnelly beat P. Watchorn 10-7;
    Donnelly beat Anderson 10-6; F. Davis beat Donnelly 10-5
13 W. King beat T. Jones 10-9; M. Watterson beat B. Bennett 10-5; King beat
    Watterson 10-8; King beat Dave Martin 10-8
14 J. Caggianello beat M. Darrington 10-7; W. Oliver beat J. Dunning 10-3;
    Oliver beat Caggianello 10-7; R. Williams beat Oliver 10-8
15 N. Foulds beat D. French 10-5; L. Dodd beat J. Giannaros 10-1; Foulds
    beat Dodd 10-4; Foulds beat J. Meadowcroft 10-2
16 B. Harris beat D. Sheehan 10-3; P. Burke beat B. Kelly 10-7; Burke beat
    Harris 10-4; M. Hallett beat Burke 10-5

First round: S. Davis beat King 10-3; J. Spencer beat Miles 10-3; T. Griffiths
beat Mifsud 10-2; B. Werbeniuk beat F. Davis 10-4; N. Foulds beat A. Higgins
10-9; D. Mountjoy beat Hallett 10-4; Dennis Taylor beat Johnson 10-1; Parrott
beat A. Knowles 10-7; C. Thorburn beat Morra 10-3; Thorne beat J. Virgo 10-9;
J. White beat Williams 10-6; E. Charlton beat Andrewartha 10-4; K. Stevens
beat Sinclair 10-1; David Taylor beat Gauvreau 10-5; S. Francisco beat T. Meo
10-5; R. Reardon beat Wych 10-7

Second round: S. Davis beat Spencer 13-5; Griffiths beat Werbeniuk 13-5;
Mountjoy beat N. Foulds 13-6; Dennis Taylor beat Parrott 13-11; Thorburn
beat Thorne 13-11; White beat Charlton 13-7; Stevens beat David Taylor 13-10;
Reardon beat S. Francisco 13-8

Quarter-finals: S. Davis beat Griffiths 13-10; Dennis Taylor beat Mountjoy
13-8; White beat Thorburn 13-8; Stevens beat Reardon 13-2

Semi-finals: S. Davis beat Dennis Taylor 16-9; White beat Stevens 16-14

Final: S. Davis beat White 18-16

1985

Qualifying groups

1 G. Rigitano beat D. Sheehan 10-9; Rigitano beat B. Harris 10-4; Rigitano beat B. Kelly 10-6; Rigitano beat M. Fisher 10-2; N. Foulds beat Rigitano 10-8

2 D. O'Kane *wo* J. McLaughlin *scr*; O'Kane beat V. Harris 10-5; O'Kane beat F. Jonik 10-5; O'Kane beat L. Dodd 10-7; O'Kane beat D. Martin 10-8

3 S. Longworth beat J. Giannaros 10-1; Longworth beat G. Cripsey 10-8; J. Van Rensberg beat Longworth 10-7; M. Gauvreau beat Van Rensberg 10-9; D. Reynolds beat Gauvreau 10-1

4 R. Chaperon beat R. Bales 10-7; Chaperon beat L. Heywood 10-1; Chaperon beat P. Morgan 10-3; F. Davis beat Chaperon 10-9; R. Williams beat F. Davis 10-6

5 D. Hughes beat D. French 10-5; S. Newbury beat Hughes 10-9; Newbury beat P. Burke 10-3; Newbury beat G. Scott 10-2; E. Hughes beat Newbury 10-6

6 M. Hines beat T. Chappel 10-8; Hines beat P. Watchorn 10-4; M. Gibson beat Hines 10-7; P. Fagan beat Gibson 10-8; Fagan beat C. Wilson 10-9

7 D. Fowler beat J. Hargreaves 10-0; Fowler *wo* G. Watson *scr*; Fowler *wo* J. Caggianello *scr*; Fowler beat J. Donnelly 10-0; J. Parrott beat Fowler 10-2

8 R. Foldvari *wo* P. Thornley *scr*; Foldvari beat B. Oliver 10-3; R. Edmonds beat Foldvari 10-3; Edmonds beat M. Wildman 10-7

9 D. Chalmers beat D. Greaves 10-3; Chalmers beat E. McLaughlin 10-9; Chalmers beat I. Black 10-4; M. Hallett beat Chalmers 10-1

10 G. Foulds beat M. Parkin 10-6; Foulds beat C. Everton 10-2; Foulds beat C. Roscoe 10-7; J. Johnson beat Foulds 10-6

11 P. Medati beat B. Bennett 10-4; Medati beat I. Williamson 10-8; Medati beat W. King 10-9; S. Francisco beat Medati 10-7

12 I. Anderson beat A. Kearney 10-8; P. Browne beat Anderson 10-5; M. Morra beat Browne 10-6; J. Campbell beat Morra 10-9

13 W. Jones beat John Rea 10-3; Jones beat J. Dunning 10-6; Jones beat M. Watterson 10-5; Jones beat G. Miles 10-8

14 M. Bradley beat D. Mienie 10-4; Bradley beat B. Mikkelsen 10-9; J. Wych beat Bradley 10-7; J. Virgo beat Wych 10-4

15 P. Francisco beat B. Demarco 10-4; Francisco beat T. Murphy 10-4; Francisco beat J. Meadowcroft 10-5; M. Macleod beat Francisco 10-7

16 T. Jones beat M. Darrington 10-2; Jones beat S. Duggan 10-8; Jones beat J. Fitzmaurice 10-4; Jones beat E. Sinclair 10-2

First round: S. Davis beat N. Foulds 10-8; David Taylor beat O'Kane 10-4; A. Higgins beat Reynolds 10-4; T. Griffiths beat Williams 10-3; R. Reardon beat E. Hughes 10-9; Fagan beat W. Thorne 10-6; Parrott beat J. Spencer 10-3; K. Stevens beat Edmonds 10-8; C. Thorburn beat Hallett 10-8; B. Werbeniuk beat Johnson 10-8; Dennis Taylor beat S. Francisco 10-2; E. Charlton beat Campbell 10-3; J. White beat W. Jones 10-4; T. Meo beat Virgo 10-6; D. Mountjoy beat Macleod 10-5; A. Knowles beat T. Jones 10-8

Second round: S. Davis beat David Taylor 13-4; Griffiths beat Higgins 13-7; Reardon beat Fagan 13-9; Parrott beat Stevens 13-6; Thorburn beat Werbeniuk

13-3; Dennis Taylor beat Charlton 13-6; White beat Meo 13-11; Knowles beat Mountjoy 13-6

Quarter-finals: S. Davis beat Griffiths 13-6; Reardon beat Parrott 13-12; Dennis Taylor beat Thorburn 13-5; Knowles beat White 13-10

Semi-finals: S. Davis beat Reardon 16-5; Dennis Taylor beat Knowles 16-5

Final: Dennis Taylor beat S. Davis 18-17

1986

First qualifying round: D. Gilbert beat R. Bales 10-7; O. Agrawal beat D. Hughes 10-6; A. Kearney beat G. Wilkinson 10-5; B. Oliver beat J. O'Boye 10-8; D. Sheehan beat P. Houlihan 10-7; M. Gibson beat G. Jenkins 10-4; S. Simngam beat B. Bennett 10-0; Jim Bear beat P. Burke 10-8; T. Drago beat G. Cripsey 10-4; M. Smith beat D. Greaves 10-4; B. West *wo* J. Giannaros *scr*; P. Thornley beat D. Mienie 10-3; R. Grace beat M. Parkin 10-8; S. Hendry beat B. Demarco 10-7; P. Watchorn *wo* J. Rempe *scr*; B. Mikkelsen beat J. Hargreaves 10-7; M. Darrington *wo* W. Sanderson *scr*

Second qualifying round: J. Wych beat T. Chappel 10-6; S. Duggan beat M. Fisher 10-3; T. Jones beat V. Harris 10-7; Gilbert beat M. Bradley 10-7; S. Newbury beat Agrawal 10-5; I. Black beat B. Harris 10-8; G. Scott beat Kearney 10-8; D. Fowler beat Oliver 10-8; C. Roscoe beat G. Foulds 10-3; W. King beat Sheehan 10-4; Gibson beat M. Morra 10-9; P. Medati beat Simngam 10-9; R. Chaperon beat F. Jonik 10-8; M. Gauvreau beat Jim Bear 10-5; F. Davis beat D. Chalmers 10-6; P. Francisco beat Drago 10-4; J. Donnelly beat Smith 10-6; West beat J. Dunning 10-3; T. Murphy beat J. McLaughlin 10-7; Thornley beat P. Fagan 10-7; W. Jones beat Grace 10-3; Hendry beat P. Browne 10-9; E. Sinclair beat P. Morgan 10-8; J. Van Rensberg beat I. Williamson 10-9; John Rea beat E. McLaughlin 10-6; S. Longworth beat Watchorn 10-7; G. Miles beat C. Everton 10-3; R. Foldvari beat G. Rigitano 10-6; M. Watterson beat Mikkelsen 10-2; L. Dodd beat J. Fitzmaurice 10-6; Darrington beat J. Meadowcroft 10-6; R. Edmonds beat B. Kelly 10-0

Third qualifying round: Wych beat Duggan 10-5; Gilbert beat T. Jones 10-7; Newbury beat Black 10-2; Fowler beat Scott 10-7; King beat Roscoe 10-5; Medati beat Gibson 10-6; Gauvreau beat Chaperon 10-8; P. Francisco beat F. Davis 10-1; West beat Donnelly 10-5; Murphy beat Thornley 10-3; Hendry beat W. Jones 10-8; Van Rensberg beat Sinclair 10-2; Longworth beat John Rea 10-4; Foldvari beat Miles 10-7; Dodd beat Watterson 10-1; Edmonds beat Darrington 10-5

Fourth qualifying round: M. Hallett beat Wych 10-7; D. Martin beat Gilbert 10-5; J. Spencer beat Newbury 10-7; Fowler beat M. Macleod 10-6; D. Reynolds beat King 10-7; C. Wilson beat Medati 10-6; R. Williams beat Gauvreau 10-3; N. Foulds beat P. Francisco 10-9; B. Werbeniuk beat West 10-8; E. Hughes beat Murphy 10-7; Hendry beat O'Kane 10-9; J. Campbell beat Van Rensberg 10-6; J. Virgo beat Longworth 10-8; J. Parrott beat Foldvari 10-6; P. Mans beat Dodd 10-7; Edmonds beat M. Wildman 10-9

First round: Hallett beat Dennis Taylor 10-6; J. Johnson beat Martin 10-3; A. Higgins beat J. Spencer 10-7; T. Griffiths beat Fowler 10-2; K. Stevens beat Reynolds 10-6; E. Charlton beat Wilson 10-6; S. Francisco beat Williams 10-4; A. Knowles beat N. Foulds 10-9; C. Thorburn beat Werbeniuk 10-5; E. Hughes beat David Taylor 10-7; W. Thorne beat Hendry 10-8; Campbell beat R. Reardon 10-8; J. White beat Virgo 10-7; Parrott beat T. Meo 10-4; D. Mountjoy beat Mans 10-3; S. Davis beat Edmonds 10-4

Second round: Johnson beat Hallett 13-6; Griffiths beat Higgins 13-12; Stevens beat Charlton 13-12; Knowles beat S. Francisco 13-10; Thorburn beat E. Hughes 13-6; Thorne beat Campbell 13-9; White beat Parrott 13-8; S. Davis beat Mountjoy 13-5

Quarter-finals: Johnson beat Griffiths 13-12; Knowles beat Stevens 13-9; Thorburn beat Thorne 13-6; S. Davis beat White 13-5

Final: Johnson beat S. Davis 18-12

1987
First qualifying round: J. Bear beat Jack Rea 10-5; A. Kearney *wo* F. Jonik *scr*; S. James beat M. Watterson 10-2; G. Jenkins beat R. Grace 10-9; D. Greaves beat P. Thornley 10-6; M. Darrington beat B. Demarco 10-6; J. Rempe beat M. Smith 10-9; G. Rigitano beat P. Morgan 4-0; C. Roscoe beat T. Whitthread 10-2; M. Morra beat P. Gibson 10-6; D. Chalmers *wo* E. McLaughlin *scr*; M. Bennett beat J. Hargreaves 10-6; B. Kelly beat B. Bennett 10-0; J. Meadowcroft beat D. Mienie 10-3; G. Foulds beat P. Watchorn 10-6; D. Hughes beat M. Parkin 10-5; B. Oliver beat P. Burke 10-5; J. Dunning beat J. Caggianello 10-7; J. Wright beat P. Houlihan 10-4; B. Rowswell *wo* S. Simngam *scr*; J. Fitzmaurice beat C. Everton 10-2; D. Roe *wo* O. Agrawal *scr*; K. Owers beat M. Fisher 10-5

Second qualifying round: M. Gauvreau beat Bear 10-3; P. Medati beat Kearney 10-8; E. Sinclair beat T. Drago 10-9; R. Edmonds beat James 10-1; T. Murphy beat Jenkins 10-4; G. Miles beat Greaves 10-7; S. Hendry beat Darrington 10-7; Rempe beat John Rea 10-9; Rigitano beat V. Harris 10-6; S. Newbury beat L. Dodd 10-7; S. Duggan beat Roscoe 10-7; T. Chappel beat Morra 10-8; T. Jones beat Chalmers 10-1; J. Van Rensberg beat J. McLaughlin 10-6; M. Bennett beat B. Mikkelsen 10-4; W. Jones beat J. Donnelly 10-3; I. Black beat I. Williamson 10-8; D. O'Kane beat D. Gilbert 10-2; M. Gibson beat Kelly 10-9; G. Cripsey beat Meadowcroft 10-9; D. Fowler beat G. Foulds 10-6; B. Harris beat D. Hughes 10-2; Oliver beat P. Fagan 10-2; G. Scott beat Dunning 10-7; M. Wildman beat Foldvari 10-5; Wright beat Browne 10-6; M. Bradley beat Rowswell 10-6; J. O'Boye beat N. Gilbert 10-5; J. Spencer beat R. Bales 10-2; R. Chaperon beat Fitzmaurice 10-2; W. King beat Roe 10-4; Owers beat F. Davis 10-5

Third qualifying round: Medati beat Gauvreau 10-3; Edmonds beat Sinclair 10-6; Murphy beat Miles 10-7; Hendry beat Rempe 10-4; Newbury beat Rigitano 10-4; Chappel beat Duggan 10-3; T. Jones beat Van Rensberg 10-0; M. Bennett beat W. Jones 10-3; O'Kane beat Black 10-2; Cripsey beat

Jimmy White with wife Maureen and daughter Lauren after winning the Rothmans Grand Prix in 1986.

Steve Davis with the Embassy World Championship Trophy.

M. Gibson 10-4; Fowler beat B. Harris 10-5; Oliver beat Scott 10-5; Wright beat Wildman 10-0; Bradley beat O'Boye 10-7; Spencer beat Chaperon 10-4; King beat Owers 10-4

Fourth qualifying round: E. Hughes beat Medati 10-2; M. Macleod beat Edmonds 10-7; S. Longworth beat Murphy 10-2; Hendry beat D. Martin 10-7; M. Hallett beat Newbury 10-4; J. Campbell beat Chappel 10-6; J. Virgo beat T. Jones 10-9; M. Bennett beat W. Jones 10-3; O'Kane beat P. Francisco 10-5; David Taylor beat Cripsey 10-7; J. Parrott beat Fowler 10-3; D. Reynolds beat Oliver 10-7; Wright beat C. Wilson 10-4; J. Wych beat Bradley 10-7; B. West beat Spencer 10-5; King beat E. Charlton 10-4

First round: J. Johnson beat E. Hughes 10-9; Macleod beat R. Williams 10-5; Longworth beat K. Stevens 10-4; Hendry beat W. Thorne 10-7; Hallett beat A. Knowles 10-6; S. Francisco beat Campbell 10-3; N. Foulds beat Virgo 10-4; Dennis Taylor beat M. Bennett 10-4; O'Kane beat Thorburn 10-5; D. Mountjoy beat David Taylor 10-5; Parrott beat T. Meo 10-8; J. White beat Reynolds 10-8; A. Higgins beat Wright 10-6; T. Griffiths beat Wych 10-4; R. Reardon beat West 10-5; S. Davis beat King 10-7

Second round: Johnson beat Macleod 13-7; Hendry beat Longworth 10-7; Hallett beat S. Francisco 13-9; N. Foulds beat Dennis Taylor 13-10; O'Kane beat Mountjoy 13-5; White beat Parrott 13-11; Griffiths beat Higgins 13-10; S. Davis beat Reardon 13-4

Quarter-finals: Johnson beat Hendry 13-12; N. Foulds beat Hallett 13-9; White beat O'Kane 13-6; S. Davis beat Griffiths 13-5

Semi-finals: Johnson beat N. Foulds 16-9; S. Davis beat White 16-11

Final: S. Davis beat Johnson 18-14

ROTHMANS MATCHROOM LEAGUE

With television companies in this country having wisely decided not to increase their coverage of snooker, Barry Hearn decided to create a non-televised, round-the-country event to enable the public to see 'live' snooker.

He chose a league format and invited Cliff Thorburn to join his seven players in the Rothmans Matchroom League with a first prize of £50,000.

Steve Davis finished top of the table and, should he also take first place in the Rothmans Grand Prix, will receive an additional £35,000 bonus for achieving the Rothmans double. This would take his total Rothmans events earnings for the year to £150,000. It is envisaged that the League will, this season, also have matches played on the continent.

LEAGUE SCORECARD

Match						Attendance
1	Dennis Taylor	4	Terry Griffiths	4		520
2	Steve Davis	7	Willie Thorne	1		1,600
3	Dennis Taylor	7	Tony Meo	1		871
4	Steve Davis	4	Terry Griffiths	4		1,287
5	Terry Griffiths	5	Tony Meo	3		620
6	Jimmy White	5	Dennis Taylor	3		1,070
7	Cliff Thorburn	2	Neal Foulds	6		540
8	Willie Thorne	4	Jimmy White	4		1,800
9	Neal Foulds	4	Terry Griffiths	4		900
10	Steve Davis	7	Tony Meo	1		900
11	Willie Thorne	5	Terry Griffiths	3		550
12	Steve Davis	6	Neal Foulds	2		900
13	Cliff Thorburn	5	Willie Thorne	3		1,120
14	Steve Davis	6	Dennis Taylor	2		2,150
15	Dennis Taylor	3	Neal Foulds	5		550
16	Steve Davis	3	Cliff Thorburn	5		750
17	Willie Thorne	4	Neal Foulds	4		750
18	Jimmy White	1	Tony Meo	7		1,200
19	Jimmy White	6	Terry Griffiths	2		1,100
20	Dennis Taylor	5	Cliff Thorburn	3		750
21	Tony Meo	6	Willie Thorne	2		450
22	Jimmy White	4	Cliff Thorburn	4		1,400
23	Terry Griffiths	6	Cliff Thorburn	2		400
24	Jimmy White	5	Steve Davis	3		1,200
25	Cliff Thorburn	4	Tony Meo	4		560
26	Neal Foulds	6	Jimmy White	2		862
27	Neal Foulds	4	Tony Meo	4		430
28	Dennis Taylor	4	Willie Thorne	4		870

LEAGUE TABLE

Player	Prize-money	P	W	D	L	F	A	Pts
Steve Davis	(£53,600)	7	4	1	2	36	20	13
Neal Foulds	(£3,100)	7	3	3	1	31	25	12
Jimmy White	(£2,700)	7	3	2	2	27	29	11
Terry Griffiths	(£2,800)	7	2	3	2	28	28	9
Dennis Taylor	(£2,800)	7	2	2	3	28	28	8
Tony Meo	(£2,600)	7	2	2	3	26	30	8
Cliff Thorburn	(£2,500)	7	2	2	3	25	31	8
Willie Thorne	(£2,300)	7	1	3	3	23	33	6

Highest break 136 points Terry Griffiths (£2,450 prize-money)

NATIONAL PROFESSIONAL CHAMPIONSHIPS

The WPBSA's prize fund subsidy to national domestic championships of £1,000 per player from 1985 onwards enabled these events to be staged annually and scheduled properly.

There had previously been Australian and Canadian Championships but these had been played in a haphazard way. Eddie Charlton won the Australian title for the first time in 1964 and was beaten only in 1968 until he lost to John Campbell in 1985.

ENGLISH CHAMPIONSHIP

1981 (*John Courage*)
Qualifying: R. Edmonds beat M. Hallett 9-3; J. Johnson beat A. Knowles 9-2; M. Wildman beat B. Bennett 9-3; J. Dunning beat D. Greaves 9-4; J. Meadowcroft beat J. Barrie 9-3

First round: Edmonds beat F. Davis 9-6; T. Meo beat J. Virgo 9-6; G. Miles beat S. Hood 9-1; S. Davis beat Meadowcroft 9-2; J. Spencer beat P. Houlihan 9-1; W. Thorne beat Wildman 9-2; Johnson *wo*; Dunning beat David Taylor 9-8

Quarter-finals: S. Davis beat Spencer 9-7; Meo beat Miles 9-7; Thorne beat Dunning 9-0; Edmonds beat Johnson 9-5

Semi-finals: S. Davis beat Edmonds 9-0; Meo beat Thorne 9-8

Final: S. Davis beat Meo 9-3

1985 (*Tolly Cobbold*)
Qualifying: D. Fowler beat W. Oliver 9-7; M. Bradley beat I. Williamson 9-8; T. Jones beat P. Houlihan 9-1; L. Dodd beat R. Bales 9-5; J. Fitzmaurice beat D. Greaves 9-3; M. Fisher beat D. French 9-8; S. Duggan beat B. Harris 9-8; D. Hughes beat M. Watterson 9-5; D. Chalmers beat J. Meadowcroft 9-3; S. Longworth beat R. Edmonds 9-4; P. Medati beat J. Hargreaves 9-8; G. Foulds beat F. Davis 9-2; G. Cripsey beat B. Bennett 9-0; G. Scott beat V. Harris 9-7

First round: S. Davis beat Fowler 9-3; M. Hallett beat Duggan 9-4; J. Johnson beat Scott 9-1; T. Meo beat Fisher 9-3; J. Virgo beat M. Darrington 9-0; D. Reynolds beat Fitzmaurice 9-2; R. Williams beat T. Jones 9-6; W. Thorne beat Dodd 9-1; Longworth beat M. Wildman 9-3; J. White beat Chalmers 9-5;

Medati beat J. Spencer 9-4; N. Foulds beat D. Hughes 9-3; David Taylor beat Cripsey 9-5; J. Parrott beat G. Foulds 9-4; D. Martin beat G. Miles 9-7; A. Knowles beat Bradley 9-8

Second round: Virgo beat Johnson 9-4; Reynolds beat Thorne 9-6; S. Davis beat Williams 9-2; Meo beat Hallett 9-4; Knowles beat Martin 9-3; David Taylor beat Parrott 9-7; White beat N. Foulds 9-7; Longworth beat Medati 9-7

Quarter-finals: Meo beat Reynolds 9-4; Longworth beat White 9-5; Knowles beat David Taylor 9-2; S. Davis beat Virgo 9-2

Semi-finals: Knowles beat Longworth 9-6; S. Davis beat Meo 9-8

Final: S. Davis beat Knowles 9-2

1986 (*Tolly Cobbold*)
First round: D. Gilbert beat B. West 9-8; P. Houlihan beat J. Hargreaves 9-5

Second round: M. Bradley beat Gilbert 9-5; F. Davis beat D. Hughes 9-6; T. Jones beat B. Harris 9-5; W. Oliver beat L. Dodd 9-5; P. Medati beat D. Greaves 9-4; S. Longworth beat S. Duggan 9-4; G. Cripsey beat J. Meadowcroft 9-1; G. Scott beat B. Bennett 9-1; I. Williamson beat M. Watterson 9-1; R. Edmonds beat M. Smith 9-8; D. Fowler beat M. Darrington 9-3; Houlihan *wo* J. Dunning *scr*; D. Chalmers beat Fisher 9-2; R. Bales beat V. Harris 9-7

Third round: S. Davis beat Bradley 9-3; D. Martin beat F. Davis 9-8; J. Virgo beat T. Jones 9-7; J. Parrott beat Oliver 9-0; W. Thorne beat Medati 9-2; D. Reynolds beat Longworth 9-5; M. Wildman beat Cripsey 9-5; T. Meo beat Scott 9-1; J. White beat Williamson 9-1; R. Williams beat Miles 9-6; N. Foulds beat G. Foulds 9-4; Edmonds beat David Taylor 9-6; J. Johnson beat Fowler 9-7; J. Spencer beat Houlihan 9-5; M. Hallett beat Chalmers 9-1; A. Knowles beat Bales 9-4

Fourth round: S. Davis beat Martin 9-4; Virgo beat Parrott 9-6; Reynolds beat Thorne 9-8; Meo beat Wildman 9-3; White beat Williams 9-5; N. Foulds beat Edmonds 9-4; Johnson beat Spencer 9-7; Hallett beat Knowles 9-5

Quarter-finals: S. Davis beat Virgo 9-2; Meo beat Reynolds 9-4; N. Foulds beat White 9-4; Hallett beat Johnson 9-6

Semi-finals: Meo beat S. Davis 9-7; N. Foulds beat Hallett 9-8

Final: Meo beat Foulds 9-7

1987 (*Tolly Ales*)
First round: M. Fisher beat T. Whitthread 6-3; P. Gibson beat D. Hughes 6-3; J. Wright beat D. Chalmers 6-5; B. Bennett beat N. Gilbert 6-5; D. Roe beat D. Greaves 6-1; K. Owers *wo* P. Houlihan *scr*; S. James beat J. Hargreaves 6-5

Second round: S. Duggan beat Fisher 6-0; M. Bradley beat D. Gilbert 6-3; P. Medati beat Gibson 6-2; M. Wildman *wo* M. Watterson *scr*; B. Harris beat G. Foulds 6-1; J. Spencer beat Wright 6-1; R. Edmonds beat Bennett 6-1; G. Cripsey beat J. Dunning 6-1; L. Dodd beat Smith 6-3; V. Harris beat M. Darrington 6-3; I. Williamson beat Roe 6-4; Owers beat R. Bales 6-5; T. Jones beat B. Oliver 6-1; J. Fitzmaurice beat G. Scott 6-2; James beat F. Davis 6-2; G. Miles *wo* J. Meadowcroft *scr*

Third round: T. Meo beat Duggan 6-3; D. Fowler beat Bradley 6-3; J. Virgo beat Medati 6-1; J. Parrott beat Wildman 6-1; W. Thorne beat B. Harris 6-2; D. Martin beat Spencer 6-5; D. Reynolds beat Edmonds 6-3; J. White beat Cripsey 6-4; Dodd beat A. Knowles 6-2; B. West beat V. Harris 6-3; M. Hallett beat Williamson 6-2; Owers beat N. Foulds 6-3; R. Williams beat Jones 6-4; David Taylor beat Fitzmaurice 6-1; James beat S. Longworth 6-2; J. Johnson beat Miles 6-3

Fourth round: Meo beat Fowler 6-0; Parrott beat Virgo 6-2; Thorne beat Martin 6-3; Reynolds beat White 6-5; Dodd beat West 6-3; Hallett beat Owers 6-2; Williams beat David Taylor 6-2; Johnson beat James 6-3

Quarter-finals: Meo beat Parrott 6-3; Thorne beat Reynolds 6-4; Dodd beat Hallett 6-5; Johnson beat Williams 6-5

Semi-finals: Meo beat Thorne 9-3; Dodd beat Johnson 9-5

Final: Meo beat Dodd 9-5

IRISH CHAMPIONSHIP

1972
Challenge: A. Higgins beat Jack Rea 28-12

1978
Challenge: A. Higgins beat Dennis Taylor 21-7

1979
Challenge: A. Higgins beat P. Fagan 21-13

1980
Challenge: Dennis Taylor beat A. Higgins 21-15

1981
Challenge: Dennis Taylor beat P. Fagan 22-21

1982
First round: E. Hughes beat D. Sheehan 6-1

Quarter-finals: E. Hughes beat Jack Rea 6-0; T. Murphy beat P. Fagan 6-2

Semi-finals: Dennis Taylor beat Murphy 6-0; A. Higgins beat E. Hughes 6-2

Final: Taylor beat Higgins 16-13

1983
First round: Dennis Taylor beat B. Kelly 6-0; P. Fagan beat T. Murphy 6-4;
A. Higgins beat Jack Rea 6-3; E. Hughes beat P. Burke 6-2

Semi-finals: Higgins beat E. Hughes 6-2; Taylor beat Fagan 6-1

Final: Higgins beat Taylor 16-11

1985 (*Strongbow*)
Preliminary: J. McLaughlin beat D. Sheehan 6-3

Qualifying: P. Burke beat A. Kearney 6-4; T. Murphy beat P. Browne 6-3;
B. Kelly beat P. Watchorn 6-2; Jack Rea beat McLaughlin 6-5

Quarter-finals: P. Fagan beat Murphy 6-2; Dennis Taylor beat Jack Rea 6-0;
A. Higgins beat Burke 6-0; E. Hughes beat Kelly 6-2

Semi-finals: Taylor beat Hughes 6-5; Higgins beat Fagan 6-3

Final: Taylor beat Higgins 10-5

1986 (*Strongbow*)
First round: B. Kelly beat Jack Rea 5-0; T. Murphy beat J. O'Boye 5-0;
E. Hughes beat D. Sheehan 5-0; A. Kearney beat P. Fagan 5-0; J. McLaughlin
beat P. Watchorn 5-0; P. Burke beat P. Browne 5-4

Quarter-finals: Dennis Taylor beat Kelly 6-1; Murphy beat Kearney 6-2;
A. Higgins beat McLaughlin 6-2; Hughes beat Burke 6-3

Semi-finals: Taylor beat Murphy 6-3; Higgins beat Hughes 6-2

Final: Taylor beat Higgins 10-7

1987 (*Matchroom*)
First round: D. Sheehan beat J. McLaughlin 5-4; P. Browne beat Jack Rea 5-3;
T. Kearney beat T. Murphy 5-1; J. O'Boye beat B. Kelly 5-0; P. Burke beat
P. Fagan 5-3; E. Hughes beat P. Watchorn 5-2

Quarter-finals: Dennis Taylor beat Sheehan 6-3; Hughes beat Kearney 6-1;
Browne beat Burke 6-2; O'Boye *wo* Higgins *scr*

Semi-finals: Taylor beat Browne 6-1; O'Boye beat Hughes 6-3

Final: Taylor beat O'Boye 9-2

SCOTTISH CHAMPIONSHIP

1980
Challenge: E. Sinclair beat C. Ross 11-6

1981
First round: M. Gibson beat B. Demarco 5-3; J. Donnelly beat E. Sinclair 5-0; E. McLaughlin beat C. Ross 5-3; I. Black beat M. Macleod 5-4

Semi-finals: Gibson beat Donnelly 6-4; Black beat E. McLaughlin 6-3

Final: Black beat Gibson 11-7

1982
First round: M. Macleod beat J. Donnelly 6-5

Quarter-finals: C. Ross beat B. Demarco 6-5; M. Gibson beat E. McLaughlin 6-3; I. Black beat Macleod 6-0; E. Sinclair beat J. Phillips 6-3

Semi-finals: Black beat Ross 6-4; Sinclair beat Gibson 6-2

Final: Sinclair beat Black 11-7

1983
First round: J. Donnelly beat B. Demarco 6-4; I. Black beat E. McLaughlin 6-4; M. Macleod beat M. Gibson 6-5

Semi-finals: E. Sinclair beat Donnelly 6-5; Macleod beat Black 6-2

Final: Macleod beat Sinclair 11-9

1985
First round: M. Macleod beat E. McLaughlin 6-4; M. Gibson beat I. Black 6-2; John Rea beat J. Donnelly 6-2; E. Sinclair beat B. Demarco 6-3

Semi-final: Macleod beat Gibson 6-4; Sinclair beat John Rea 6-2

Final: Macleod beat Sinclair 10-2

1986 (*Canada Dry*)
First round: S. Hendry beat B. Demarco 6-1

Quarter-finals: Hendry beat M. Macleod 6-5; I. Black beat E. McLaughlin 6-4; John Rea beat J. Donnelly 6-1; M. Gibson beat E. Sinclair 6-4

Semi-finals: Hendry beat Black 6-2; Gibson beat John Rea 6-0

Final: Hendry beat Gibson 10-5

1987
First round: S. Hendry beat B. Demarco 6-2; John Rea beat I. Black 6-1;
E. Sinclair beat M. Gibson 6-2; J. Donnelly beat M. Macleod 6-2

Semi-finals: Hendry beat Rea 6-0; Donnelly beat Sinclair 6-4

Final: Hendry beat Donnelly 10-7

WELSH CHAMPIONSHIP

1977 (*William Hill*)
Challenge: R. Reardon beat D. Mountjoy 12-8

1980 (*Woodpecker*)
First round: D. Mountjoy beat T. Griffiths 9-6; R. Reardon beat C. Wilson 9-3

Final: Mountjoy beat Reardon 9-6

1981 (*Woodpecker*)
Qualifying: C. Wilson beat R. Andrewartha 6-5

First round: Wilson beat D. Mountjoy 9-6; R. Reardon beat T. Griffiths 9-6

Final: Reardon beat Wilson 9-6

1982 (*Woodpecker*)
First round: C. Wilson beat M. Owen 6-0; T. Griffiths beat C. Roscoe 6-2;
R. Reardon beat C. Everton 6-1; D. Mountjoy beat R. Andrewartha 6-3

Semi-finals: Griffiths beat Wilson 9-6; Mountjoy beat Reardon 9-7

Final: Mountjoy beat Griffiths 9-8

1983 (*Woodpecker*)
First round: T. Griffiths beat C. Everton 6-1; R. Reardon beat R. Andrewartha
6-2; C. Wilson beat C. Roscoe 6-4; D. Mountjoy beat M. Owen 6-0

Semi-finals: Reardon beat Griffiths 9-4; Mountjoy beat Wilson 9-3

Final: Reardon beat Mountjoy 9-1

1984 (*Strongbow*)
First round: D. Mountjoy beat C. Everton 6-1; T. Griffiths beat
R. Andrewartha 6-1; R. Reardon beat M. Owen 6-1; C. Wilson beat C. Roscoe
6-2

Semi-finals: Mountjoy beat Griffiths 9-5; Wilson beat Reardon 9-4

Final: Mountjoy beat Wilson 9-3

1985 (*BCE*)
First round: S. Newbury beat W. Jones 6-2; T. Chappel beat M. Owen 6-0

Quarter-finals: R. Reardon beat C. Everton 6-2; D. Mountjoy beat Newbury 6-5; C. Wilson beat C. Roscoe 6-3; T. Griffiths beat Chappel 6-0

Semi-finals: Griffiths beat Reardon 9-3; Mountjoy beat Wilson 9-2

Final: Griffiths beat Mountjoy 9-4

1986 (*Zetters*)
First round: T. Chappel *wo* M. Owen *scr*; W. Jones beat C. Everton 6-2

Quarter-finals: T. Griffiths beat Chappel 6-4; C. Wilson beat S. Newbury 6-4; D. Mountjoy beat C. Roscoe 6-4; W. Jones beat Reardon 6-4

Semi-finals: Griffiths beat Wilson 9-1; Mountjoy beat W. Jones 9-7

Final: Griffiths beat Mountjoy 9-3

1987 (*Matchroom*)
First round: W. Jones beat M. Bennett 6-3; C. Roscoe beat C. Everton 6-2

Quarter-finals: T. Griffiths beat Jones 6-2; S. Newbury beat C. Wilson 6-2; T. Chappel beat R. Reardon 6-4; D. Mountjoy beat Roscoe 6-2

Semi-finals: Newbury beat Griffiths 9-6; Mountjoy beat Chappel 9-2

Final: Mountjoy beat Newbury 9-7

AUSTRALIAN CHAMPIONSHIP

1985
First round: G. Wilkinson beat G. Jenkins 6-2; G. Robinson beat J. Charlton* 6-0; L. Condo beat E. Charlton* 6-2

Second round: Wilkinson beat L. Heywood 7-3; R. Foldvari beat Robinson 7-2; J. Giannaros beat Condo 7-2; I. Anderson *wo* G. Ganim *scr*

Quarter-finals: E. Charlton beat Wilkinson 8-2; P. Morgan beat Giannaros 8-4; W. King beat Anderson 8-2; J. Campbell beat Foldvari 8-5

Semi-finals: Charlton beat Morgan 9-3; Campbell beat King 9-6

Final: Campbell beat Charlton 10-7

1986
First round: G. Jenkins beat G. Ganim** 6-2; L. Condo** beat E. Charlton* Jr 6-0; J. Charlton* beat G. Robinson* 6-4

Second round: Condo beat J. Giannaros 6-4; I. Anderson beat J. Charlton 6-2; G. Wilkinson beat L. Heywood 6-0; R. Foldvari beat Jenkins 6-3

Quarter-finals: J. Campbell beat Wilkinson 6-1; Foldvari beat P. Morgan 6-2; W. King beat Condo 6-3; E. Charlton beat Anderson 6-2

Semi-finals: Campbell beat Foldvari 8-3; King beat Charlton 8-6

Final: King beat Campbell 10-3

* Members of the Australian Professional Association but not the WPBSA
** Non-tournament members of the WPBSA

CANADIAN CHAMPIONSHIP

1985
First round: J. Caggianello beat Jim Bear 5-4; R. Chaperon beat P. Thornley 5-1; B. Mikkelsen beat G. Watson 5-3; John Bear beat M. Morra 5-4; J. Wych beat W. Sanderson 5-2

Quarter-finals: Chaperon beat K. Stevens 6-4; F. Jonik beat Mikkelsen 6-4; C. Thorburn beat Caggianello 6-2; Wych beat John Bear 6-3

Semi-finals: Chaperon beat Jonik 6-3; Thorburn beat Wych 6-5

Final: Thorburn beat Chaperon 6-4

1986
First round: G. Watson beat J. Caggianello 6-1; F. Jonik beat G. Rigitano 6-1; R. Chaperon beat J. Bear 6-3; B. Mikkelsen beat W. Sanderson 6-1; P. Thornley beat M. Morra 6-4

Second round: C. Thorburn beat Watson 6-1; Jonik beat Chaperon 6-3; J. Wych beat Mikkelsen 6-3; K. Stevens beat Thornley 6-2

Semi-finals: Thorburn beat Jonik 6-3; Wych beat Stevens 6-2

Final: Thorburn beat Wych 6-2

SOUTH AFRICAN CHAMPIONSHIP

1986
First round: P. Francisco beat V. Blignaut* 6-3; D. Mienie beat M. Hines 6-5; F. Ellis beat R. Amdor* 6-2

Second round: S. Francisco beat G. Johnston* 7-0; P. Francisco beat R. Grace 7-1; J. Van Rensberg beat Mienie 7-1; Ellis beat P. Mans 7-6

Semi-finals: S. Francisco beat P. Francisco 8-3; Ellis beat Van Rensberg 8-2

Final: S. Francisco beat Ellis 9-1

*Members of the South African Professional Association but not the WPBSA

PROFESSIONAL BILLIARDS

THE WORLD PROFESSIONAL BILLIARDS CHAMPIONSHIP

Founded in 1870, the World Professional Billiards Championship is the oldest of all the game's events but since snooker has become by far the most popular of the billiard table games it has declined steadily in public appeal.

The problems started in the 1930s when the four best players in the world, Walter Lindrum, Joe Davis, Tom Newman and Clark McConachy, mastered all aspects of the game so completely that they effectively killed it as a public entertainment. They did such a thorough job that there was only one Championship between 1934 and 1968 that they did not claim – when Rex Williams travelled to New Zealand and beat McConachy, then 73 and suffering from Parkinson's disease.

Williams successfully defended the title three times against various challengers but lost it in June 1980 to Joe's younger brother Fred, who thus became only the second player to have held world titles at both billiards and snooker – the first, of course, was Joe.

In November 1980, the event reverted to a tournament format and a variety of playing systems was tried: time-limit games, points-up games and, for the first time last season, the best of five games of 400-up. This formula gave frequent climaxes, as in frames of snooker, and also eliminated the possibility of very large breaks.

1985 also saw Channel 4 attempt a 'Pot Black'-style billiards event, the Blue Arrow Masters. Viewing figures for this were encouraging and the BBC agreed to televise the final of the 1986 World Professional Championship which was again played over the best of five games of 400-up.

In 1987, from the Albert Hall, Bolton, both the semi-finals and final were televised. Norman Dagley, who had earlier in the season won the UK Championship, added the professional title to his two world amateur victories by beating Robby Foldvari 3-1 in the final.

World Professional Billiards Championship (1870–1920)

1870	(Feb)	W. Cook	J. Roberts Sr	1,200-1,083
	(Apr)	J. Roberts Jr	W. Cook	1,000- 522
	(June)	J. Roberts Jr	A. Bowles	1,000- 759
	(Nov)	J. Bennett	J. Roberts Jr	1,000- 905

1871 (Jan)	J. Roberts Jr	J. Bennett	1,000- 637
(May)	W. Cook	J. Roberts Jr	1,000- 985
(Nov)	W. Cook	J. Bennett	1,000- 942
1872 (Mar)	W. Cook	J. Roberts Jr	1,000- 799
1874 (Feb)	W. Cook	J. Roberts Jr	1,000- 784
1875 (May)	J. Roberts Jr	W. Cook	1,000- 837
(Dec)	J. Roberts Jr	W. Cook	1,000- 865
1877 (May)	J. Roberts Jr	W. Cook	1,000- 779
1880 (Nov)	J. Bennett	W. Cook	1,000- 949
1881 (Jan)	J. Bennett	T. Taylor	1,000- 910
1885 (Apr)	J. Roberts Jr	W. Cook	3,000-2,908
(June)	J. Roberts Jr	J. Bennett	3,000-1,360
1899	C. Dawson	J. North	9,000-4,715
1900	C. Dawson	H. W. Stevenson	9,000-6,775
1901	H. W. Stevenson	C. Dawson	9,000-6,406
	C. Dawson	H. W. Stevenson	9,000-5,796
	H. W. Stevenson (declared champion – no contest)		
1903	C. Dawson	H. W. Stevenson	9,000-8,700
1908	M. Inman (declared champion – no contest)		
1909	M. Inman	A. Williams	9,000-7,662
Under Billiards Control Club Rules			
1909	H. W. Stevenson (declared champion – no contest)		
1910	H. W. Stevenson	M. Inman	13,370-13,212
	(match abandoned)		
	H. W. Stevenson	M. Inman	18,000-16,907
1911	H. W. Stevenson	M. Inman	18,000-16,914
1912	M. Inman	T. Reece	18,000- 9,675
1913	M. Inman	T. Reece	18,000-16,627
1914	M. Inman	T. Reece	18,000-12,826
1919	M. Inman	H. W. Stevenson	16,000- 9,468
1920	W. Smith	C. Falkiner	16,000-14,500

World Professional Billiards Championship (1921–87)

Winner (breaks)	Score (average)	Loser (breaks)	Score (average)
1921			
First round			
C. Falkiner 560	7,334 (35.3)	H. W. Stevenson	5,084 (24.3)
T. Newman 467	8,000 (54.0)	T. Tothill	3,267 (22.0)
Semi-finals			
Newman 627, 531	8,000 (56.7)	Falkiner 587	6,627 (47.3)
T. Reece	*nr*	F. Lawrence	*nr*
Final			
Newman	16,000 (*nr*)	Reece	10,744 (*nr*)
1922			
First round			
T. Reece	8,000 (35.2)	C. McConachy	6,767 (29.9)

Winner (breaks)	Score (average)	Loser (breaks)	Score (average)
Semi-finals			
T. Newman	8,000 (52.6)	J. Davis	5,181 (34.1)
561, 512			
C. Falkiner	8,000 (41.9)	Reece	7,289 (38.2)
391		455	
Final			
Newman	16,000 (56.4)	Falkiner	15,167 (52.7)
1923			
First round			
M. Inman	16,000 (nr)	A. Peall	11,758 (nr)
C. Falkiner	16,000 (nr)	T. Reece	14,952 (nr)
Semi-finals			
T. Newman	16,000 (56.3)	Inman	14,506 (51.1)
850, 705, 500 × 4		701	
W. Smith	16,000 (71.7)	Falkiner	8,695 (29.2)
688		782, 620	
Final			
Smith	16,000 (46.4)	Newman	15,180 (44.0)
451, 446		638, 629, 575	
1924			
First round			
T. Newman	16,000 (71.4)	C. McConachy	8,703 (38.9)
875		349	
Final			
Newman	16,000 (43.5)	T. Reece	14,845 (40.3)
1,021			
1925			
T. Newman	16,000 (68.4)	T. Reece	10,092 (43.1)
957, 672		512	
1926			
T. Newman	16,000 (82.0)	J. Davis	9,505 (49.0)
637, 574, 588		414	
1927			
First round			
M. Inman	8,000 (nr)	T. Reece	5,527 (nr)
459		1,151	
Second round			
J. Davis	8,000 (nr)	Inman	6,895
504, 588			
Challenge round			
T. Newman	16,000 (73.0)	Davis	14,763 (68.0)
787, 1,073, 1,012, 891		2,501, 727	
1928			
First round			
T. Carpenter	8,000 (22.4)	T. Reece	7,283 (20.5)
Second round			
J. Davis	8,000 (66.4)	Carpenter	5,602 (41.8)

Winner (breaks)	Score (average)	Loser (breaks)	Score (average)
Challenge round			
Davis	16,000 (74.4)	T. Newman	14,874 (69.5)
529, 525, 501, 425, 408,		564, 489, 467, 455,	
404, 403, 400		451, 427	
1929			
First round			
T. Newman	8,000 (74.1)	T. Carpenter	5,984 (55.4)
553		453	
Final			
J. Davis	18,000 (100.0)	Newman	17,219 (96.2)
838, 609, 599		723, 691, 672, 647, 576	
1930			
First round			
T. Newman	24,001 (85.1)	M. Inman	10,104 (35.8)
1,567, 1,047			
J. Davis	21,975 (82.0)	C. Falkiner	19,815 (74.0)
Final			
Davis	20,918 (113.1)	Newman	20,117 (109.9)
2,052, 500 × 9		500 × 12	
1932			
J. Davis	25,161 (112.0)	C. McConachy	19,259 (98.0)
1,058, 844, 774		1,432, 916, 889	
1933			
First round			
W. Lindrum	21,470 (*nr*)	T. Newman	20,252 (*nr*)
1,578, 984		877, 805	
J. Davis	20,136 (*nr*)	C. McConachy	16,110 (*nr*)
995		675	
Final			
Lindrum	21,815 (92.0)	Davis	21,121 (89.0)
1,492, 1,272, 1,013		792	
1934			
First round			
W. Lindrum	21,903 (*nr*)	C. McConachy	20,795 (*nr*)
1,065, 807		892, 829	
Final			
Lindrum	23,533 (*nr*)	J. Davis	22,678 (*nr*)
1,474, 1,353		824, 728	
1951			
C. McConachy	6,681 (60.0)	J. Barrie	5,057 (44.8)
481, 438, 425, 397, 376		367, 336	
1968			
R. Williams	5,499 (*nr*)	C. McConachy	5,234 (*nr*)
293		236, 200	
1971			
R. Williams	9,250 (*nr*)	B. Bennett	4,058 (*nr*)
480, 372, 353, 325, 302		132	

Winner (breaks)	Score (average)	Loser (breaks)	Score (average)
1973			
R. Williams	8,360 (50.7)	J. Karnehm	4,336 (26.1)
528, 363, 309		215	
1974			
R. Williams	7,017 (43.6)	E. Charlton	4,916 (30.4)
506, 365, 308, 307		488, 401	
1976			
R. Williams	9,105 (42.1)	E. Charlton	5,149 (23.9)
532, 349, 382, 306		333	
1980 (May)			
Challenge round			
F. Davis	5,978 (39.9)	R. Williams	4,452 (29.9)
403, 225, 234, 239, 275, 583		226, 202, 439, 229	
1980 (Nov)			
Qualifying			
P. Morgan	1,655 (21.5)	J. Dunning	1,107 (12.9)
M. Wildman	1,968 (26.2)	B. Bennett	678 (9.0)
S. Davis	1,809 (16.9)	K. Kennerley	965 (9.1)
Quarter-finals			
J. Barrie	2,186 (53.3)	S. Davis	870 (21.8)
335			
F. Davis	1,907 (43.3)	Morgan	978 (22.2)
309			
R. Edmonds	1,513 (19.4)	J. Karnehm	1,306 (17.0)
Wildman	1,476 (25.9)	R. Williams	1,415 (24.8)
Semi-finals			
F. Davis	1,253 (34.8)	Barrie	1,153 (32.0)
501			
Wildman	1,629 (21.4)	Edmonds	955 (12.6)
204			
Final			
F. Davis	3,037 (30.4)	Wildman	2,064 (20.6)
200, 361			
1982			
First round			
C. Everton	1,500 (23.4)	B. Bennett	556 (8.6)
Quarter-finals			
F. Davis	1,500 (30.6)	Everton	652 (13.6)
R. Williams	1,500 (31.9)	J. Karnehm	569 (11.9)
R. Edmonds	1,500 (16.5)	K. Kennerley	753 (8.2)
M. Wildman	1,500 (21.7)	J. Fitzmaurice	721 (10.5)
Semi-finals			
Williams	1,500 (20.3)	Davis	1,494 (19.9)
Wildman	1,500 (24.2)	Edmonds	765 (12.1)
203			

Winner (breaks)	Score (average)	Loser (breaks)	Score (average)
Final			
Williams	3,000 (26.1)	Wildman	1,785 (15.5)
207, 259, 217			
1983			
Qualifying			
I. Williamson	1,000 (12.5)	D. Martin	710 (8.8)
63, 79, 72, 81		52	
B. Bennett	1,000 (11.2)	G. Cripsey	683 (6.3)
63, 55, 58, 75		50	
First round			
J. Karnehm		M. Darrington	
I 122, 117, 53	752 (15.0)	54, 86, 67	679 (13.3)
II 59, 79	748 (12.1)	63	520 (8.4)
	1,500 (13.4)		1,199 (10.6)
B. Bennett		J. Fitzmaurice	
I 58	751 (10.0)		666 (8.8)
II 70, 80, 81, 50	749 (10.3)	61, 54	730 (10.1)
	1,500 (10.1)		1,396 (9.4)
C. Everton		I. Williamson	
I 153, 72, 84	752 (15.0)	60, 67, 52	591 (11.6)
II 105, 61, 59, 81	748 (17.8)	56, 68	494 (12.0)
	1,500 (16.3)		1,085 (11.8)
E. Charlton		T. Murphy	
I 85, 61, 53	751 (11.7)	61, 54, 51, 112	694 (10.8)
II 55, 102, 92	749 (18.3)	64, 56	411 (10.0)
	1,500 (14.3)		1,105 (10.5)
Quarter-finals			
R. Williams		Bennett	
I 87, 69, 63, 147, 107,			
100 (*unf*)	751 (30.0)		225 (8.7)
II 105 (*full*), 233, 228,			
50 (*unf*)	749 (30.6)		218 (9.5)
	1,500 (31.3)		443 (9.0)
F. Davis		Everton	
I 169, 113, 51, 147,			
83 (*unf*)	751 (37.6)	51	236 (11.2)
II 121 (*full*), 66, 71, 427	749 (39.4)	94, 51	241 (12.7)
	1,500 (38.5)		477 (11.9)
R. Edmonds		Karnehm	
I 60, 75, 135, 61	559 (13.0)	83, 59, 71, 84	
		68, 153	750 (17.4)
II 61, 358, 84, 64,			
138, 92	941 (29.4)	91, 62	325 (9.8)
	1,500 (20.0)		1,075 (14.1)

Winner (breaks)	Score (average)	Loser (breaks)	Score (average)
Charlton		M. Wildman	
I 58, 116, 96, 59	750 (15.6)		408 (8.5)
II 53, 93, 65, 53, 81 (unf)	750 (15.0)	51, 58	370 (7.6)
	1,500 (15.3)		778 (8.0)
Semi-finals			
F. Davis		Charlton	
I 92, 88, 214, 93	750 (25.9)	86, 75	410 (14.1)
II 228, 166, 52, 125	750 (30.0)	80, 102, 76	546 (21.8)
	1,500 (27.8)		956 (17.7)
Williams		Edmonds	
I 56, 54, 194, 84, 161,			
85 (unf)	750 (57.7)	50, 79	288 (22.2)
II 127 (full), 53, 316, 83			
194 (unf)	750 (62.5)	70, 60, 100	383 (31.9)
	1,500 (60.0)		671 (26.8)
Final			
Williams		F. Davis	
I 50, 170, 54, 235,			
132 (unf)	751 (32.7)	102	227 (9.5)
II 212 (full), 64, 192, 120,			
67, 71	749 (46.8)	63, 103, 137	378 (23.6)
	1,500 (38.4)		605 (15.1)
1984			
Preliminary round			
T. Murphy		M. Darrington	
I 76	400 (12.5)		505 (15.8)
II 75	621 (17.7)	66	356 (10.2)
	1,021 (15.0)		861 (12.9)
First round			
P. Morgan		B. Bennett	
I 148, 54	508 (13.0)		306 (8.1)
II 79, 63	513 (17.7)	79, 65	333 (11.5)
	1,021 (15.0)		639 (9.5)
I. Williamson		C. Everton	
I 55, 112, 50	373 (12.4)		189 (6.5)
II 65	373 (14.3)		307 (11.4)
	746 (13.3)		496 (8.9)
J. Karnehm		G. Ganim Jr	
I 56, 62, 127, 52, 61	600 (23.1)	75, 91, 92	383 (14.2)
II 89, 106, 148	670 (23.1)	112 (unf)	350 (12.5)
	1,270 (23.1)		733 (13.3)
Murphy		J. Fitzmaurice	
I 52, 94 (unf)	425 (12.1)	53, 61	497 (14.2)
II 94 (full), 57, 138	625 (15.6)		371 (9.3)
	1,050 (14.2)		868 (11.6)

Winner (breaks)	Score (average)	Loser (breaks)	Score (average)
Quarter-finals			
F. Davis		Murphy	
I 66, 82, 61, 73	550 (21.1)	84, 61, 50	453 (17.4)
II 101, 114, 111, 110, 71	692 (26.6)	89, 81, 58	399 (16.0)
	1,242 (23.9)		852 (16.7)
E. Charlton		Karnehm	
I 130	343 (16.3)	75, 73, 93, 193	623 (28.5)
II 319, 64, 92 (*unf*)	601 (35.4)	62	308 (19.3)
	944 (24.8)		931 (24.5)
Williamson		R. Edmonds	
I 81, 96, 54	407 (22.6)	58, 65, 112, 65	432 (22.7)
II 124, 60, 72, 175	511 (31.9)	85, 57, 127	373 (23.3)
	918 (27.0)		805 (23.0)
M. Wildman		Morgan	
I 168, 97, 178, 107	749 (37.4)	65, 85	299 (14.2)
II 87 (*full*), 58, 50, 62,			
71, 106	598 (15.8)	53, 53, 70, 50	460 (17.6)
	1,347 (28.7)		759 (15.8)
Semi-finals			
Charlton		F. Davis	
I 114, 94, 50, 81, 98,			
121 (*unf*)	795 (29.4)	56, 55	268 (9.2)
II 144 (*full*), 61, 60, 65,			
71, 62, 63	641 (27.9)	62, 135, 143, 124	561 (25.5)
	1,436 (28.7)		829 (16.6)
Wildman		Williamson	
I 226, 61	610 (23.5)	70	468 (17.3)
II 125, 188, 58, 91, 205	891 (35.6)	74, 103	381 (15.2)
	1,501 (29.4)		849 (16.4)
Final			
Wildman		Charlton	
I 111, 121, 241	599 (27.2)	100, 68, 50, 56	508 (23.1)
II 97, 115	446 (14.4)	101, 98, 54 (*unf*)	504 (16.3)
	1,045 (19.7)		1,012 (19.1)
1985			
First round			
P. Francisco 3		M. Darrington 0	
I 75, 125 (*unf*)	400 (22.2)	54	166 (9.2)
II 65	400 (12.6)		249 (7.5)
III 63, 55, 56	400 (16.1)		161 (6.7)
I. Williamson 3		B. Bennett 0	
I 96, 107	400 (17.0)	90	200 (8.6)
II 50, 164	400 (30.9)		89 (6.4)
III 50, 53, 65, 52	400 (15.4)	82	331 (12.7)

Winner (breaks)	Score (average)	Loser (breaks)	Score (average)
J. Karnehm 3		E. Charlton 0	
I 57, 56, 103, 89	400 (22.2)	154, 90	308 (16.2)
II 54, 184	400 (21.1)	77	217 (11.4)
III 98, 85	400 (14.8)	106	354 (12.6)
R. Edmonds 3		A. Higgins 0	
I 55, 68, 63, 111	400 (25.0)	69	188 (11.0)
II 51, 74, 147 (unf)	400 (26.7)	51, 89	221 (14.7)
III 81, 72, 121	400 (25.0)		110 (6.9)
M. Wildman 3		T. Jones 0	
I	400 (20.0)		237 (11.3)
II 188, 53, 55	400 (30.9)		144 (11.0)
III 98, 105, 103	400 (44.4)		125 (12.5)
N. Dagley 3		J. Fitzmaurice 0	
I 60, 63, 75 (unf)	400 (16.7)	60, 96	325 (13.5)
II 83, 94, 59, 67	400 (44.4)	103, 78	284 (28.4)
III 253	400 (33.5)		80 (6.7)
R. Foldvari wo		B. Oliver scr	
F. Davis 3		C. Everton 1	
I 84, 74, 82, 80	400 (16.2)	80	275 (11.4)
II 75, 78, 87	400 (28.6)		206 (13.7)
III 73, 100	293 (20.9)	70, 132 (unf)	400 (30.8)
IV 167, 150	400 (30.8)	54	156 (11.1)
Quarter-finals			
Dagley 3		Karnehm 0	
I 88, 270 (unf)	400 (80.0)		24 (4.8)
II 155, 56, 96, 60	400 (21.1)	102, 79	294 (14.7)
III 90, 104, 182 (unf)	400 (44.4)		59 (6.6)
Foldvari 3		F. Davis 0	
I 98, 80, 50 (unf)	400 (15.4)		130 (4.8)
II 107, 54, 114	400 (33.3)	84, 73, 50	316 (26.3)
III 161, 65, 88	400 (20.0)	71	342 (16.3)
Wildman 3		Francisco 0	
I 162, 102, 84 (unf)	400 (28.6)	55	186 (12.4)
II 184, 126 (unf)	400 (28.6)		106 (7.6)
III 245, 62, 50 (unf)	400 (66.7)		70 (10.0)
Edmonds 3		Williamson 1	
I 117	378 (15.0)	84, 73, 126 (unf)	400 (16.0)
II 159	400 (25.0)	65, 68	246 (15.4)
III 252, 102	400 (28.6)	79	212 (14.1)
IV 56, 54, 118	400 (23.5)	101, 67	248 (14.6)
Semi-finals			
Edmonds 3		Wildman 0	
I 69, 76, 97 (unf)	400 (28.6)	131	313 (22.3)
II 78, 73, 91	400 (22.3)	89	196 (10.3)
III 141, 60 (unf)	400 (22.3)	227	298 (16.6)

Winner (breaks)	Score (average)	Loser (breaks)	Score (average)
Dagley 3		Foldvari 0	
I 53, 52, 164	400 (22.2)	64, 146	352 (19.6)
II 104, 115	400 (25.0)	64, 88, 56	248 (14.6)
III 140	400 (15.4)	58, 50, 60	282 (11.0)
Final			
Edmonds 3		Dagley 1	
I 107, 150, 60	400 (33.3)	58, 201	395 (30.4)
II 159, 77	307 (28.0)	125, 126, 95	400 (40.0)
III 60, 140 (unf)	400 (26.6)	52, 106, 75	315 (19.6)
IV 188	400 (20.0)	60, 119, 52, 110	386 (19.3)
1986			
Qualifying			
R. Close 3		E. Hughes 1	
I 93	319 (12.8)	55, 122, 93 (unf)	400 (16.0)
II 77, 60, 98, 70 (unf)	400 (50.0)		105 (11.7)
III 64, 71	400 (15.4)	52	310 (11.5)
IV 142 (unf)	400 (19.1)	54, 75	338 (16.1)
G. Scott 3		B. Oliver 0	
I 75	400 (7.8)	52	344 (6.9)
II 54, 61	400 (12.9)		164 (5.3)
III	400 (9.3)	60	398 (9.5)
First round			
E. Charlton 3		T. Jones 0	
I 60, 73, 55	400 (10.3)		314 (8.1)
II 144, 59	400 (14.8)		180 (6.7)
III 110, 134 (unf)	400 (25.0)		73 (4.6)
I. Williamson 3		Scott 0	
I 53, 82	400 (14.3)	114, 56	372 (12.8)
II 56, 73, 63, 58	400 (13.8)		288 (10.3)
III 85, 60	400 (12.9)		251 (8.1)
R. Foldvari 3		J. Karnehm 1	
I 59, 65, 84 (unf)	400 (12.5)	68	282 (8.6)
II 154	273 (9.1)	54, 62, 81 (unf)	400 (13.3)
III 106, 69	400 (18.2)	50	268 (12.2)
IV 292	400 (36.4)		116 (10.6)
R. Edmonds 3		J. Fitzmaurice 0	
I 88, 86	400 (19.5)		131 (6.0)
II 129	400 (25.0)		104 (6.9)
III 64, 54	400 (12.1)		295 (8.9)
N. Dagley 3		B. Bennett 0	
I 59	400 (16.0)		148 (5.9)
II 59, 83, 94	400 (17.4)		190 (8.3)
III 95, 105, 154	400 (40.0)		107 (10.7)
Close 3		F. Davis 0	
I 130, 105, 109 (unf)	400 (50.0)		57 (6.3)
II 65, 55, 93, 58	400 (21.1)	63, 102	262 (13.8)
III 68, 94, 64, 66 (unf)	400 (40.0)	79, 88, 102	323 (29.3)

Winner (breaks)	Score (average)	Loser (breaks)	Score (average)
P. Francisco 3		C. Everton 0	
I 56	400 (11.4)		395 (11.3)
II 81, 85, 64	400 (11.5)	101, 70	397 (11.3)
III 52, 53	400 (10.8)	59	349 (9.4)
M. Wildman 3		G. Thompson 0	
I 85, 63, 65	400 (21.0)	52	240 (12.0)
II 63, 61, 131	400 (13.8)		203 (9.0)
III 70, 82	400 (14.8)		317 (11.3)
Quarter-finals			
Edmonds 3		Francisco 0	
I	400 (12.9)	86	291 (9.1)
II 53	400 (15.4)		218 (8.4)
III 112, 55, 56	400 (12.9)	53	347 (10.8)
Dagley 3		Charlton 0	
I 57, 68	400 (16.7)	57	238 (10.0)
II 94, 116	400 (12.9)		130 (4.0)
III 62, 67	400 (13.7)	62	330 (11.3)
Foldvari 3		Close 0	
I 61, 119	400 (19.0)	55	231 (11.0)
II 174	400 (23.6)	94	358 (20.0)
III 133, 135	400 (21.5)	59, 56	241 (12.5)
Wildman 3		Williamson 2	
I 63, 55	400 (9.5)		272 (6.3)
II 121	400 (15.4)	99	355 (13.6)
III 78, 74	259 (16.2)	54, 107	400 (25.1)
IV 62, 96	282 (9.1)	69, 54, 50	400 (13.3)
V 51, 79	400 (12.5)	70	341 (10.3)
Semi-finals			
Dagley 3		Edmonds 1	
I 76	278 (9.3)	66, 97	400 (13.8)
II 55	400 (11.4)	54, 51	353 (9.9)
III 89, 60, 67	400 (16.7)	50	289 (12.0)
IV 74, 62, 64, 68	400 (18.7)	59	214 (9.7)
Foldvari 3		Wildman 1	
I 59, 72	400 (9.8)	75	394 (9.4)
II	191 (8.0)	93, 168 (*unf*)	400 (17.5)
III 65, 53, 67	400 (10.8)	58, 58	301 (7.9)
IV 99, 70, 87, 71 (*unf*)	400 (17.5)		138 (6.0)
Final			
Foldvari 3		Dagley 1	
I 64, 76	322 (11.1)	54, 54, 50, 66	400 (13.8)
II 117, 92, 73 (*unf*)	400 (30.8)	70	200 (15.4)
III 99, 182	400 (28.6)	73	178 (11.9)
IV 193, 73 (*unf*)	400 (30.7)	121	261 (20.0)

Winner (breaks)	Score (average)	Loser (breaks)	Score (average)
1987			
First round			
G. Thompson 2		J. Fitzmaurice 0	
I 53, 55	400 (9.8)	52	305 (7.3)
II 63	400 (8.5)		373 (7.9)
G. Miles *wo*		L. Dielis *scr*	
T. Jones *wo*		R. Ceulemans *scr*	
C. Everton 2		H. Griffiths 1	
I 56	317 (7.4)	61	400 (9.5)
II 61, 95	400 (10.0)	54	380 (9.3)
III 70, 51, 77	400 (18.2)	62	311 (14.1)
Second round			
R. Foldvari 3		E. Hughes 0	
I 73	400 (12.9)		288 (9.0)
II 50	400 (17.4)	54	208 (9.0)
III 109, 58	400 (18.2)	53	308 (14.0)
F. Davis 3		Thompson 0	
I 59, 128, 82, 90	400 (33.3)		99 (8.3)
II 258	400 (22.3)	82, 73, 63	399 (22.0)
III 104, 125 (*unf*)	400 (28.6)	151, 71, 76	364 (26.0)
P. Francisco 3		Miles 0	
I 50, 78, 78 (*unf*)	400 (22.2)		194 (10.8)
II 61, 89, 62, 102	400 (50.0)	63	152 (19.0)
III 58	400 (10.3)		343 (9.0)
R. Edmonds 3		B. Bennett 0	
I 98	400 (15.4)	71	166 (6.1)
II 53, 88, 75	400 (28.6)		177 (12.6)
III 74, 77, 54	400 (14.3)	54	210 (7.3)
N. Dagley 3		R. Close 0	
I 67, 73, 61	400 (18.2)	53, 106, 137	381 (17.3)
II 123, 71, 69, 75 (*unf*)	400 (20.0)	98, 83	228 (11.1)
III 119, 193	400 (36.4)		73 (6.6)
I. Williamson *wo*		Jones *scr*	
E. Charlton 3		J. Karnehm 1	
I	82 (6.3)	105, 87	400 (33.4)
II 51, 66 (*unf*)	400 (16.8)	84	281 (11.7)
III 64, 156	400 (17.4)	75	300 (12.5)
IV 66	400 (15.4)	76	328 (12.6)
M. Wildman 3		Everton 0	
I 130, 114	400 (16.6)	54, 69, 73	320 (12.3)
II 205	400 (23.5)	56	226 (13.3)
III 70, 74	400 (18.2)	61	286 (12.4)

Winner (breaks)	Score (average)	Loser (breaks)	Score (average)
Quarter-finals			
R. Foldvari 3		F. Davis 1	
I 56, 69	400 (9.3)	67	369 (8.2)
II 134, 59, 81 (*unf*)	400 (23.5)	63, 58	235 (13.8)
III 73	323 (10.0)	84, 62	400 (12.5)
IV 97, 100, 71 (*unf*)	400 (16.7)	86, 144	348 (15.1)
R. Edmonds 3		P. Francisco 0	
I 90, 52, 84, 57 (*unf*)	400 (19.0)		300 (14.3)
II 156, 130 (*unf*)	400 (20.0)		221 (11.1)
III 124, 52 (*unf*)	400 (30.8)	72	194 (12.4)
N. Dagley 3		I. Williamson 1	
I 110, 74, 80	400 (28.5)	67	179 (12.8)
II 64, 98	259 (18.5)	162, 54 (*unf*)	400 (28.6)
III 64, 137	400 (16.0)	52, 71	303 (12.1)
IV 50, 74, 108	400 (33.3)	89, 94	334 (25.7)
M. Wildman 3		E. Charlton 1	
I 93, 57, 76	400 (21.1)		179 (9.0)
II 85, 52, 63	378 (12.2)	104, 61	400 (13.3)
III 79, 88, 50	400 (36.4)		160 (13.3)
IV 69, 69, 126 (*unf*)	400 (19.0)	81	145 (6.9)
Semi-finals			
Foldvari 3		Edmonds 1	
I 206, 119	400 (66.7)		86 (12.3)
II 121	266 (12.7)	104, 65, 86, 98 (*unf*)	400 (20.0)
III 80, 66, 75	400 (14.3)	52, 67	315 (10.5)
IV 63	400 (23.5)	64, 178	364 (21.4)
Dagley 3		Wildman 0	
I 164, 53	400 (23.5)		188 (11.1)
II 57, 67, 66	400 (18.2)	95, 73	369 (16.0)
III 120, 183 (*unf*)	400 (44.5)	105	197 (21.9)
Final			
Dagley 3		Foldvari 1	
I 83, 126	313 (28.5)	315	400 (40.0)
II 50, 99, 104, 84	400 (28.6)	207, 62	352 (23.5)
III 88, 60	400 (23.5)		114 (6.7)
IV 146, 129	400 (36.4)	122, 228	365 (30.4)

United Kingdom Professional Billiards Championship (1934–51)

1934

J. Davis	18,745	T. Newman	18,301
537, 504		809, 693, 603, 547	

1935

J. Davis	21,733	T. Newman	19,919
609, 1,264, 548, 564,		848, 677, 749, 732,	
638, 1,002, 545		598	

Winner (breaks)	Score (average)	Loser (breaks)	Score (average)
1936			
First round			
W. Smith	10,373 (60.0)	S. Lee	7,212 (42.0)
Semi-finals			
T. Newman	9,561 (75.0)	S. Smith	7,792 (60.0)
J. Davis	10,965 (93.0)	W. Smith	9,566 (80.0)
Final			
J. Davis	21,710 (125.0)	T. Newman	19,790 (114.0)
1937			
First round			
S. Smith	8,135	S. Lee	4,209
(*match abandoned after nine sessions*)			
Semi-finals			
T. Newman	*wo*	W. Smith	*scr*
J. Davis	12,046	S. Smith	8,516
Final			
J. Davis	22,601 (146.0)	T. Newman	18,321 (118.0)
1,191, 1,179, 1,000,		782, 774, 720, 671,	
997, 793, 592, 587, 580,		670, 603, 593, 588,	
556, 550, 500		547	
1938			
Semi-finals			
T. Newman	8,959	S. Smith	7,227
556, 771, 602, 599		740	
J. Davis	15,238	S. Lee	6,048
1,013, 840, 988, 666			
Final			
J. Davis	20,933	T. Newman	19,542
1939–45 *No contests*			
1946			
J. Barrie	8,972	W. Leigh	6,782
1947			
S. Smith	7,002	J. Barrie	6,428
1948–49 *No contests*			
1950			
First round			
J. Barrie	7,645 (34.8)	S. Lee	5,593 (25.4)
Semi-finals			
J. Barrie	7,009 (46.7)	W. Smith	5,941 (39.6)
K. Kennerley	*wo*		
Final			
J. Barrie	9,046 (48.9)	K. Kennerley	5,069 (27.4)
1951			
F. Davis	8,120	K. Kennerley	6,011

United Kingdom Professional Billiards Championships (1979-83, 1987)

Winner (breaks)	Score (average)	Loser (breaks)	Score (average)
1979 (*Super Crystalate*)			
Quarter-finals			
J. Karnehm	2,041 (35.8)	J. Dunning	760 (13.1)
281, 286			
R. Williams	1,557 (31.8)	R. Edmonds	1,350 (27.0)
259, 309			
J. Barrie	2,292 (46.8)	S. Davis	629 (12.6)
238, 404, 206 (*unf*)			
F. Davis	1,953 (34.9)	B. Bennett	679 (12.1)
Semi-finals			
Williams	1,539 (32.7)	Karnehm	1,182 (24.6)
224, 372			
Barrie	1,548 (43.0)	F. Davis	1,031 (28.6)
227, 444		245	
Final			
Williams	2,952 (44.4)	Barrie	2,116 (32.0)
228, 388, 253		379	
1980			
First round			
S. Davis	1,670 (21.7)	S. Hood	1,029 (13.4)
B. Bennett	1,093 (12.0)	C. Ross	933 (10.1)
Quarter-finals			
J. Barrie	2,001 (32.8)	M. Wildman	815 (13.1)
J. Karnehm	1,990 (28.0)	K. Kennerley	842 (11.9)
322			
R. Edmonds	1,380 (17.7)	Bennett	914 (11.6)
R. Williams	1,871 (33.4)	S. Davis	862 (15.4)
205			
Semi-finals			
Karnehm	1,755 (35.1)	Barrie	1,085 (21.3)
225, 230		229	
Williams	2,159 (41.5)	Edmonds	789 (15.2)
230, 234 (*unf*)			
Final			
Karnehm	2,518 (28.0)	Williams	2,423 (26.6)
205, 208		256, 423	
1981			
Qualifying			
S. Davis	980	B. Bennett	770
R. Edmonds	1,881	G. Miles	473
206			
J. Pulman	1,078	K. Kennerley	879
Quarter-finals			
J. Karnehm	1,307 (22.2)	Edmonds	935 (15.8)
207			
J. Barrie	1,743 (41.5)	Pulman	509 (12.1)
381			

Winner (breaks)	Score (average)	Loser (breaks)	Score (average)
R. Williams	1,575 (50.8)	S. Davis	579 (18.1)
265, 385, 290			
F. Davis	1,304 (29.0)	M. Wildman	805 (17.9)
217			
Semi-finals			
Karnehm	1,338 (23.1)	Barrie	1,074 (18.5)
390			
Williams	2,003 (74.2)	F. Davis	999 (37.0)
217, 505, 231			
Final			
Williams	1,592 (45.5)	Karnehm	1,112 (31.8)
393, 385			
1983			
First round			
B. Bennett	750 (10.4)	D. Greaves	280 (3.7)
C. Everton	750 (28.9)	M. Darrington	177 (6.5)
I. Williamson	750 (14.4)	T. Murphy	625 (11.8)
R. Edmonds	750 (19.7)	J. Fitzmaurice	505 (13.3)
Quarter-finals			
Edmonds	1,500 (30.0)	J. Karnehm	1,194 (23.4)
M. Wildman	1,500 (41.7)	Everton	1,170 (33.4)
285, 217		393	
F. Davis	1,500 (42.9)	Williamson	604 (17.3)
292			
R. Williams	1,500 (46.9)	Bennett	230 (7.0)
246, 461 (*unf*)			
Semi-finals			
Wildman	1,500 (45.5)	Williams	1,272 (38.5)
495		225, 307	
F. Davis	1,500 (36.6)	Edmonds	936 (22.8)
208, 201			
Final			
Wildman	1,500 (21.4)	Davis	1,032 (14.5)
1987			
First round			
C. Everton 2		J. Fitzmaurice 1	
I 116, 72, 61, 65 (*unf*)	400 (50.0)		52 (5.8)
II 53	365 (6.9)	57	400 (7.7)
III 98, 60	400 (22.0)		207 (10.9)
H. Griffiths 2		G. Thompson 1	
I	261 (10.9)		400 (17.4)
II	400 (18.2)		354 (15.4)
III 50, 57	400 (14.3)		335 (11.6)
B. Bennett 2		D. Greaves 0	
I	400 (12.1)	57	148 (4.4)
II	400 (11.1)	52	218 (6.0)

Winner (breaks)	Score (average)	Loser (breaks)	Score (average)
Second round			
M. Wildman *wo*		G. Miles *scr*	
R. Close *wo*		T. Jones *scr*	
E. Hughes *wo*		P. Francisco *scr*	
R. Edmonds 3		M. Darrington 0	
I 51, 63	400 (16.0)		226 (8.7)
II 78, 53, 124	400 (23.5)		138 (8.1)
III 100, 68	400 (15.4)		151 (5.6)
N. Dagley *wo*		J. Karnehm *scr*	
I. Williamson 3		Everton 1	
I 51, 69, 124	400 (30.8)	56	142 (10.1)
II 60, 65, 52, 108 (*unf*)	400 (21.1)	71, 77	245 (12.9)
III 56	184 (11.5)	54, 75, 59, 108 (*unf*)	400 (25.0)
IV 54, 151, 59, 77	400 (21.1)		253 (13.3)
F. Davis 3		Griffiths 0	
I 99, 54	400 (12.9)		287 (9.3)
II 64, 87, 114	400 (20.0)	74, 53, 50	267 (12.7)
III 57, 108	400 (14.8)		271 (10.0)
R. Foldvari 3		Bennett 0	
I 65	400 (12.4)	57, 53	360 (11.3)
II 105, 64	400 (16.7)	53	268 (10.7)
III 54, 129 (*unf*)	400 (19.0)		170 (8.1)
Quarter-finals			
Wildman 3		Close 1	
I 52, 101, 53	400 (20.0)	60	262 (13.1)
II 121	242 (13.4)	97, 81	400 (22.2)
III 173, 91	400 (21.0)	63, 84	271 (14.3)
IV 81, 61	400 (18.2)	51, 52	366 (15.9)
Edmonds 3		Hughes 2	
I 69, 90, 77	400 (16.0)	50	200 (8.0)
II 84	267 (9.2)	62, 56, 90	400 (14.3)
III 113	400 (20.8)		110 (7.9)
IV	277 (12.0)	93, 66, 55 (*unf*)	400 (18.2)
V 69, 106, 95	400 (26.6)	53, 58	204 (12.8)
Dagley 3		Williamson 1	
I 205	205 (18.3)	70, 76, 50, 71, 64 (*unf*)	400 (23.5)
II 57, 89, 68, 97	400 (26.7)	80, 70	202 (13.5)
III 94, 107	400 (21.2)	113, 90	296 (14.8)
IV 134, 106, 56	400 (30.8)	95	156 (12.0)
Foldvari 3		Davis 2	
I 111	400 (13.3)	62	327 (10.5)
II 83, 57	294 (10.0)	56, 171, 53	400 (14.4)
III 63, 149, 89	400 (28.6)	53, 139	302 (20.0)
IV 111	160 (14.6)	155, 121	400 (40.1)
V 70, 84	400 (18.2)	51, 53, 61, 63	341 (14.8)

Winner (breaks)	Score (average)	Loser (breaks)	Score (average)
Semi-finals			
Edmonds 3		Wildman 0	
I 72, 51, 125	400 (16.7)	59	122 (5.1)
II 241, 53	400 (36.4)		132 (11.0)
III 71, 227	400 (33.5)	110, 63	243 (20.0)
Dagley 3		Foldvari 2	
I	322 (16.0)	58, 77, 75	400 (21.5)
II 127, 59, 79	400 (23.5)	59, 58	240 (14.1)
III	112 (5.1)	114, 109, 74	400 (19.0)
IV 70, 61, 192 (*unf*)	400 (22.2)		86 (4.5)
V 249	400 (25.1)	70	290 (18.1)
Final			
Dagley 3		Edmonds 1	
I 56, 83, 60	400 (16.0)	83	344 (13.8)
II 51, 145	286 (17.9)	126, 65, 90	400 (25.0)
III 150, 124, 75 (*unf*)	400 (33.3)	102	339 (28.3)
IV 132, 54 (*unf*)	400 (18.2)	51, 86	352 (15.3)

EUROPEAN BILLIARDS CHAMPIONSHIP

In May 1987, in an attempt to promote the game of English Billiards on the continent, the WPBSA organised an inaugural European Billiards Championship. The prize fund of £15,000 (£7,500 from BCE, £7,500 from the WPBSA) attracted 16 entries but not, for political reasons, either of the two players of the pocketless version of the game who are 'Billiards only' members of the WPBSA.

Norman Dagley won the event to complete the hat-trick of professional titles, having already won both the World and UK.

First round: Robbie Foldvari (Australia) beat Clive Everton (Wales) 4-0; Mike Russell (England) beat Bob Close (England) 4-2; Jack Karnehm (England) beat Howard Griffiths (Wales) 4-1; Michael Ferreira (India) beat Ray Edmonds (England) 4-3; Norman Dagley (England) beat Graham Cripsey (England) 4-0; Ian Williamson (England) beat Eugene Hughes (Republic of Ireland) 4-3; Eddie Charlton (Australia) beat Bernard Bennett (England) 4-0; Mark Wildman (England) beat Geoff Thompson (England) 4-1

Quarter-finals: Foldvari beat Russell 4-1; Karnehm beat Ferreira 4-3; Dagley beat Williamson 4-2; Wildman beat Charlton 4-1

Semi-finals: Foldvari beat Karnehm 4-2; Dagley beat Wildman 4-2

Final: Dagley beat Foldvari 7-5

BILLIARDS PROFESSIONALS

NORMAN DAGLEY (England)

Norman Dagley, after twice losing in the final, won the 1987 Monarflex World Billiards Championship at his third attempt, to complete a unique set of Billiards titles: English Amateur (15 times), World Amateur (twice), UK Professional (1987) and, now, World Professional.

Prompted by the upturn in professional Billiards, Dagley turned professional only in 1984 at the age of 54.

The other Billiards only members of the WPBSA are: Bob Close (England), Michael Ferreira (India), Howard Griffiths (Wales), Jack Karnehm (England), Mike Russell (England) and Geoff Thompson (England).

Norman Dagley celebrates winning the 1987 World Billiards Championship.

THE WOMEN'S GAME

Women have always played Billiards and, more lately, Snooker. Mary Queen of Scots expressed great dissatisfaction when deprived of the use of her billiard table and, to add insult to injury, her head was wrapped in its cloth after her execution.

It was not, however, until one aspect of the Snooker boom – the advent of modern, attractive Snooker centres – that any substantial number of women took to playing the sport. Now there is enough participation and interest for a modest tournament circuit for women players to be developing. The standard of play has improved considerably in the last three or four years and should continue to do so.

There has been a Women's Championship since 1933 but in reality it was only for British players. It was discontinued in 1980 when there was a change in governing body from the Women's Billiards and Snooker Association to the World Ladies' Billiards and Snooker Association.

The Women's World Open Championship, attracting several overseas entries, was first staged in 1976 and three more times until 1983 when, in what proved to be a retrograde step, the game split into professional and amateur ranks. No World Professional Championship was staged, but two World Amateur Championships were. The 1984 event was won by Stacey Hillyard, and Allison Fisher won the following year. The professional circuit, meanwhile, lasted only one season before breaking up in acrimony and disarray.

The two factions then came together, made the game 'Open' and, under a new administration, began developing a circuit of one-day tournaments with modest prize-money. The WLBSA promoted the Womens' World Championship, open to all its members, at 'Breaks', Solihull in 1986. For the 1987 season the WLBSA has secured £10,000 from Warners, who will stage the event at their Puckpool, Isle of Wight, site in October.

Allison Fisher, who will be defending the title, is undoubtedly the most talented woman player the game has seen. Still only 19, she also holds the UK title and has not lost to another woman in competition for two seasons. She has also beaten several leading male amateurs in Open tournaments.

In winning the world title for the loss of only one frame, she set a new championship break record of 84. The only other woman to make a century in competition is Hillyard who, in January 1985, made a break of 114 in the Bournemouth League.

On 23 May 1987, Fisher made a break of 103 in the final of the Billiards and Snooker Control Council Women's tournament, the first century to be recorded in any women's event.

WOMEN'S WORLD CHAMPIONSHIP

1986
Last 16: A. Fisher (England) beat L. Horsbrough (England) 3-0; G. Aplin (England) beat C. Walch (England) 3-1; M. Fisher (England) beat S. Newbury (Wales) 3-0; A. Jones (England) beat S. Martin (Australia) 3-0; S. Hillyard (England) beat J. Dowen (England) 3-1; S. LeMaich (Canada) beat A. Davies (Wales) 3-1; K. Shaw (England) beat S. Sinanan (England) 3-1; M. Tart (England) beat H. Isitt (Wales) 3-0

Quarter-finals: A. Fisher beat Aplin 4-0; Jones beat M. Fisher 4-1; LeMaich beat Hillyard 4-3; Shaw beat Tart 4-0

Semi-finals: A. Fisher beat Jones 4-1; LeMaich beat Shaw 4-3

Final: A. Fisher beat LeMaich 5-0

TUBORG WOMEN'S UK CHAMPIONSHIP

1987
Last 16: A. Fisher (England) beat J. Dowen (England) 3-0; M. Tart (England) beat K. Korr (England) 3-1; S. Hillyard (England) beat T. Duckers (England) 3-2; A.-M. Farren (England) beat A. Radcliffe (England) 3-1; K. Shaw (England) beat G. Jones (England) 3-1; G. Aplin (England) beat J. Mason (England) 3-1; R. Clements (England) beat C. Walch (England) 3-2; M. Fisher (England) beat L. Horsbrough (England) 3-1

Quarter-finals: A. Fisher beat Tart 4-0; Farren beat Hillyard 4-3; Aplin beat Shaw 4-1; M. Fisher beat Clements 4-1

Semi-finals: A. Fisher beat Farren 4-0; M. Fisher beat Aplin 4-0

Final: A. Fisher beat M. Fisher 5-1

THE AMATEUR GAME

THE WORLD AMATEUR SNOOKER CHAMPIONSHIP

The English Amateur Billiards Championship is the oldest domestic amateur title. It was started in 1888 and was followed in 1916 by the English Amateur Snooker Championship. It was not until 1926 that the first World Amateur Billiards Championship, then called the British Empire Championship, was staged, and in 1963, the inaugural World Amateur Snooker Championship was held in Calcutta.

The two events then took place in alternate years until it was decided that from 1985 the snooker would become an annual event. For that first Championship in 1963 there were only five entries from four countries – England, Australia, India and Ceylon (now Sri Lanka). The 1984 Championship in Dublin boasted 41 players representing 22 countries – an indication of just how fast the game is developing all over the world.

Before India's Omprakesh Agrawal captured the title in Dublin, the event had been dominated by British players. Gary Owen (England) won it in 1963 and 1966 and another Englishman, David Taylor, in 1968. Jonathan Barron gave England their fourth title in 1970 and Ray Edmonds made it six in a row when he won both in 1972 and 1974.

Welshman Doug Mountjoy broke the stranglehold by taking the 1976 title and his fellow countryman Cliff Wilson won it in 1978 before England gave the Championship its youngest ever titleholder when Jimmy White won in 1980 at the age of 18. The title went back to Wales with Terry Parsons in 1982 and Parsons again reached the final in 1984 only to lose to Agrawal.

Each country affiliated to the International Billiards and Snooker Federation is entitled to send two competitors who are initially split into round robin groups with the quarter-finals onwards being knockout.

The biggest innovation in amateur snooker came in 1972 when the then world governing body, the Billiards and Snooker Control Council (now effectively the English body), lifted all restrictions on amateurs accepting prize-money or fees for exhibitions. This brought about a new breed of full-time amateur players who capitalise fully on a variety of privately organised tournaments which carry thousands of pounds in prize-money.

However, the money available in the 'amateur' game pales into insignificance when compared to the prosperity at the top of the professional game. Consequently, there is a high turnover of top amateurs who, as soon as they become eligible, join the professional ranks.

World Amateur Snooker Championships

	Wins	For	Agst	Highest break
1963 (*Calcutta*)				
G. Owen (England)	4	23	7	71
F. Harris (Australia)	3	21	17	52
M. J. M. Lafir (Ceylon)	2	19	18	67
T. Monteiro (India)	1	14	19	56
W. Jones (India)	0	7	24	36
1966 (*Karachi*)				
G. Owen (England)	5	30	7	118
J. Spencer (England)	4	26	14	101
W. Barrie (Australia)	3	23	22	73
M. J. M. Lafir (Ceylon)	2	22	20	45
L. U. Demarco (Scotland)	1	14	28	36
H. Karim (Pakistan)	0	6	30	60
1968 (*Sydney*)				
Group A				
David Taylor (England)	4	24	13	96
J. Van Rensberg (S. Africa)	3	22	14	–
H. Andrews (Australia)	2	17	16	–
T. Monteiro (India)	1	17	22	–
L. Napper (N. Zealand)	0	9	24	–
Group B				
M. Williams (Australia)	3	22	14	–
P. Morgan (Ireland)	3	19	14	88
M. J. M. Lafir (Ceylon)	2	19	16	–
S. Shroff (India)	2	20	19	–
R. Flutey (N. Zealand)	0	7	24	–

Play-offs
Semi-finals: Williams beat Van Rensberg 8-7; David Taylor beat Morgan 8-3
Final: David Taylor beat Williams 8-7

	Wins	For	Agst	Highest break
1970 (*Edinburgh*)				
Group A				
S. Hood (England)	5	20	9	50
P. Mifsud (Malta)	4	22	11	61
M. J. M. Lafir (Sri Lanka)	4	20	16	50
J. Phillips (Scotland)	4	19	18	62
D. Sneddon (Scotland)	2	17	17	38
L. Glozier (N. Zealand)	2	10	21	34
J. Clint (N. Ireland)	0	8	24	46
Group B				
J. Barron (England)	5	21	13	51
D. May (Wales)	4	22	18	64
S. Shroff (India)	3	18	14	47
E. Sinclair (Scotland)	3	16	16	49
J. Rogers (Ireland)	3	16	19	65
L. U. Demarco (Scotland)	2	15	19	32
H. Andrews (Australia)	1	13	22	35

Final: Barron beat Hood 11-7

	Wins	For	Agst	Highest break
1972 (*Cardiff*)				
Group A				
J. Van Rensberg (S. Africa)	3	12	6	45
K. Tristram (N. Zealand)	1	8	8	50
G. Thomas (Wales)	1	6	8	32
L. U. Demarco (Scotland)	1	6	10	41
Group B				
M. Francisco (S. Africa)	3	15	5	47
J. Barron (England)	3	15	10	50
A. Borg (Malta)	2	12	11	59
A. Lloyd (Wales)	2	11	14	41
T. Monteiro (India)	0	3	16	46
Group C				
P. Mifsud (Malta)	4	16	5	61
R. Edmonds (England)	3	14	7	101
J. Rogers (Ireland)	2	8	8	36
M. Berni (Wales)	1	7	12	47
B. Bennett (N. Zealand)	0	3	16	30
Group D				
A. Savur (India)	2	10	6	38
M. Williams (Australia)	2	9	7	48
D. Sneddon (Scotland)	2	9	9	34
D. May (Wales)	0	6	12	42
Semi-final groups				
Group A				
Barron	3	12	4	35
Savur	2	10	8	68
Tristram	1	6	8	29
Mifsud	0	6	12	50
Group B				
M. Francisco	2	11	9	70
Edmonds	2	11	9	39
Van Rensberg	1	8	10	51
Williams	1	9	11	78

Semi-finals: Edmonds beat Barron 8-6; M. Francisco beat Savur 8-7(51, 72)
Final: Edmonds beat M. Francisco 11-10

	Wins	For	Agst	Highest break
1974 (*Dublin*)				
Group A				
R. Edmonds (England)	7	31	11	66
M. J. M. Lafir (Sri Lanka)	6	30	19	77
E. Sinclair (Scotland)	6	28	21	67
G. Thomas (Wales)	4	24	22	43
D. Sheehan (Ireland)	4	25	24	43
P. Donnelly (N. Ireland)	3	21	28	42
S. Shroff (India)	3	16	26	44
N. Stockman (N. Zealand)	2	18	29	51
J. Sklazeski (Canada)	1	18	31	79

	Wins	For	Agst	Highest break
Group B				
A. Lloyd (Wales)	8	32	14	104
W. Hill (N. Zealand)	5	26	21	58
P. Burke (Ireland)	4	26	20	71
L. Condo (Australia)	4	26	21	53
A. Borg (Malta)	4	27	23	37
D. Sneddon (Scotland)	4	23	21	54
A. Savur (India)	4	24	23	50
R. Cowley (Isle of Man)	3	16	27	50
N. J. Rahim (Sri Lanka)	0	2	32	25

Quarter-finals: Edmonds beat Condo 4(60)-3; Sinclair beat Hill 4-2; Burke beat Lafir 4-3; Thomas beat Lloyd 4-2
Semi-finals: Edmonds beat Sinclair 8(54)-4(79); Thomas beat Burke 8-2
Final: Edmonds beat Thomas 11-9

1976 (*Johannesburg*)

Group A	Wins	For	Agst	Highest break
D. Mountjoy (Wales)	7	28	9	107
J. Van Rensberg (S. Africa)	5	24	16	72
R. Edmonds (England)	4	20	18	77
N. Stockman (N. Zealand)	4	21	19	45
E. Sinclair (Scotland)	4	21	21	51
P. Burke (Ireland)	2	17	25	48
J. Van Niekerk (S. Africa)	1	17	27	35
P. Reynolds (Isle of Man)	1	14	27	46
Group B				
P. Mifsud (Malta)	6	25	9	47
S. Francisco (S. Africa)	6	27	12	68
T. Griffiths (Wales)	5	23	14	69
C. Ross (England)	4	19	17	58
R. Paquette (Canada)	4	22	22	72
E. Swaffield (N. Ireland)	1	16	26	59
L. Heywood (Australia)	1	13	27	46
L. Watson (Ireland)	1	9	27	45
Group C				
M. Francisco (S. Africa)	6	27	12	62
R. Atkins (Australia)	6	25	12	45
R. Andrewartha (England)	5	25	14	100
J. Clint (N. Ireland)	4	17	18	33
L. U. Demarco (Scotland)	3	21	21	75
B. Mikkelsen (Canada)	3	19	22	60
K. Tristram (N. Zealand)	1	9	27	46
R. Cowley (Isle of Man)	0	11	28	41

Elimination match: Griffiths beat Andrewartha 4(51)-0
Quarter-finals: Mountjoy beat Atkins 5(80)-1; Van Rensberg beat Griffiths 5-3(52); S. Francisco beat M. Francisco 5-1; Mifsud beat Edmonds 5-1
Semi-finals: Mountjoy beat S. Francisco 8(51)-2; Mifsud beat Van Rensberg 8(50)-4
Final: Mountjoy beat Mifsud 11(62, 79)-1

	Wins	For	Agst	Highest break
1978 (*Malta*)				
Group A				
K. Burles (Australia)	6	26	10	69
P. Mifsud (Malta)	6	26	10	62
J. Johnson (England)	5	23	9	101
J. Donnelly (Scotland)	5	20	13	78
D. McVeigh (N. Ireland)	2	15	20	56
P. Reynolds (Isle of Man)	2	10	22	45
V. Cremona (Malta)	2	9	25	–
M. Mohideen (Sri Lanka)	0	8	28	–
Group B				
A. Lloyd (Wales)	6	26	12	65
K. Stevens (Canada)	5	23	16	94
J. Grech (Malta)	4	23	16	63
E. Hughes (Ireland)	4	23	21	56
M. J. M. Lafir (Sri Lanka)	3	19	20	50
D. Meredith (N. Zealand)	3	18	20	81
S. Shroff (India)	2	14	23	39
L. McCann (N. Ireland)	1	10	27	40
Group C				
C. Wilson (Wales)	8	32	10	66
R. Paquette (Canada)	5	24	14	81
D. Kwok (N. Zealand)	5	23	20	49
A. Savur (India)	5	26	22	56
I. Williamson (England)	3	22	24	52
R. Atkins (Australia)	3	21	24	49
R. Miller (Scotland)	3	18	24	48
A. Borg (Malta)	2	15	27	44
C. Cooper (Isle of Man)	2	13	29	33

Elimination match: Grech beat Kwok 4-0
Quarter-finals: Burles beat Paquette 5-4; Stevens beat Mifsud 5-0; Johnson beat Lloyd 5(72)-0; Wilson beat Grech 5-4
Semi-finals: Johnson beat Burles 8(85)-4; Wilson beat Stevens 8(64)-2(81)
Final: Wilson beat Johnson 11(87)-5(66)

	Wins	For	Agst	Highest break
1980 (*Launceston*)				
Group A				
J. White (England)	6	24	9	99
A. Savur (India)	4	20	11	67
E. Hughes (Ireland)	4	21	13	127
J. Grech (Malta)	3	19	18	80
L. Adams (N. Zealand)	3	15	18	54
Loo Yap Long (Singapore)	1	6	23	57
R. Burke (N. Ireland)	0	11	24	50
Group B				
J. Giannaros (Australia)	6	24	11	54
S. Newbury (Wales)	4	20	14	100
R. Paquette (Canada)	4	20	15	90
D. Meredith (N. Zealand)	4	20	16	67

	Wins	For	Agst	*Highest* *break*
G. Parikh (India)	2	17	18	46
S. Clarke (N. Ireland)	1	10	22	44
Lau Weng Yew (Singapore)	0	8	24	36
Group C				
P. Mifsud (Malta)	6	24	3	77
R. Atkins (Australia)	4	19	15	67
J. Bonner (Australia)	4	17	17	53
W. King (Australia)	3	19	15	57
E. McLaughlin (Scotland)	3	16	16	67
J. O'Boye (England)	1	14	21	98
S. Padayachi (Fiji)	0	2	24	40
Group D				
A. Lloyd (Wales)	6	24	4	47
J. Campbell (Australia)	5	22	8	84
D. Sheehan (Ireland)	4	17	14	69
M. Gibson (Scotland)	3	16	20	80
H. Boteju (Sri Lanka)	2	16	20	45
P. Reynolds (Isle of Man)	1	11	23	35
W. Barrie (Australia)	0	7	24	39

Quarter-finals: Savur beat Lloyd 5(54)-3; Atkins beat Giannaros 5(53)-3(82); Mifsud beat Campbell 5(63)-3; White beat Newbury 5(70)-4
Semi-finals: Atkins beat Savur 8-6; White beat Mifsud 8(100)-6(83)
Final: White beat Atkins 11(80, 101)-2(60)

1982 (*Calgary*)
Group A

	Wins	For	Agst	*Highest* *break*
J. Grech (Malta)	6	28	13	68
A. Kearney (Ireland)	6	26	15	57
D. O'Kane (N. Zealand)	6	28	18	68
B. McConnell (Canada)	5	26	19	43
P. Kippie (Scotland)	5	23	16	68
S. Habib (India)	4	22	21	52
V. Saengthong (Thailand)	3	20	28	73
Lui Yew Keong (Singapore)	1	13	30	60
J. A. Wahid (Sri Lanka)	0	6	32	26
Group B				
T. Parsons (Wales)	7	31	7	63
P. Browne (Ireland)	7	31	12	65
G. Kwok Kwan Shing (Hong Kong)	7	28	12	56
G. Parikh (India)	5	27	21	72
A. Thomson (Zimbabwe)	4	17	23	36
G. Kwok (N. Zealand)	3	17	26	62
H. Boteju (Sri Lanka)	2	15	28	31
W. Craig (Isle of Man)	1	14	29	35
T. Dada (Pakistan)	0	10	32	39
Group C				
J. Bear (Canada)	7	30	12	71
M. Bradley (England)	7	30	12	68

	Wins	For	Agst	Highest break
J. Jorgensen (Canada)	6	25	17	46
W. Mills (N. Ireland)	5	26	17	89
J. Giannaros (Australia)	5	25	21	68
P. Reynolds (Isle of Man)	3	23	23	36
Cheung Che-Ming (Hong Kong)	2	17	25	40
E. Amro (Egypt)	1	11	31	40
V. Yassa (Sudan)	0	3	32	22
Group D				
W. Jones (Wales)	6	27	13	70
P. Mifsud (Malta)	6	29	15	80
W. King (Australia)	6	29	17	83
R. Chaperon (Canada)	5	24	18	56
D. Chalmers (England)	5	25	24	57
R. Lane (Scotland)	3	23	23	44
S. Pavis (N. Ireland)	3	19	27	82
Lau Weng Yew (Singapore)	2	15	29	53
S. Sherif (Egypt)	0	7	32	27

Quarter-finals: W. Jones beat Kearney 5-1; Parsons beat Bradley 5(69, 54)-0; Grech beat Browne 5(55)-3; Bear beat Mifsud 5-2
Semi-finals: Parsons beat Jones 8(103, 87)-5(54); Bear beat Grech 8-7
Final: Parsons beat Bear 11(61, 58, 58)-8(57, 69)

1984 (*Dublin*)

	Wins	For	Agst	Highest break
Group A				
A. Micallef (Malta)	9	38	16	75
T. Parsons (Wales)	8	37	11	102
P. Ennis (Ireland)	8	34	28	110
V. Saengthong (Thailand)	7	34	19	86
J. Sigurossonn (Iceland)	6	29	29	70
T. Finstad (Canada)	4	28	28	85
B. Bjorkman (Sweden)	4	26	27	52
A. Thomson (Zimbabwe)	3	24	34	36
D. Feeney (U.S.A.)	3	21	35	42
K. Sirisoma (Sri Lanka)	3	16	33	40
L. Talman (Belgium)	0	11	40	37
Group B				
D. John (Wales)	9	37	10	72
T. Drago (Malta)	8	35	15	132
A. Robidou (Canada)	8	36	20	107
S. Simngam (Thailand)	7	33	20	70
J. Long (Ireland)	6	30	24	62
M. G. Jayaram (India)	5	30	23	84
A. Campbell (Australia)	4	25	29	96
J. McIntyre (N. Ireland)	4	21	30	91
R. Cowley (Isle of Man)	3	20	30	52
M. Sedupathi (Sri Lanka)	1	6	36	37
C. D'Avoine (Mauritius)	0	3	40	38

	Wins	For	Agst	Highest break
Group C				
G. Wilkinson (Australia)	8	30	13	68
J. Wright (England)	7	27	14	68
H. Haenga (N. Zealand)	7	26	14	66
H. Bakahati (Egypt)	6	26	21	73
M. Colquitt (Isle of Man)	5	24	20	57
S. Hendry (Scotland)	5	23	22	118
T. Kollins (U.S.A.)	3	16	27	92
K. Friopjofssonn (Iceland)	3	15	28	28
H. Thwaites (Belgium)	1	3	32	21
Lui Yew Keong (Singapore)	scr			
Group D				
C. Archer (England)	9	32	15	80
O. Agrawal (India)	7	33	16	68
D. Kwok (N. Zealand)	5	27	21	64
G. Kwok Kwan Shing (Hong Kong)	5	26	23	129
H. Morgan (N. Ireland)	5	27	27	78
J. Selby (Wales)	4	24	23	72
L. Yew (Singapore)	3	25	28	55
G. Carnegie (Scotland)	3	22	32	69
M. Hallgren (Sweden)	2	17	32	43
M. Sadek (Egypt)	2	15	31	59

Quarter-finals: Agrawal beat John 5-4; Wright beat A. Micallef 5(69, 70)-1; Archer beat Drago 5-4; Parsons beat Wilkinson 5(66)-2
Semi-finals: Agrawal beat Wright 8(75)-5; Parsons beat Archer 8(58, 78, 52)-3
Final: Agrawal beat Parsons 11(69, 74, 62, 54)-7
1985 (*Blackpool*)

	Wins	For	Agst
Group A			
P. Mifsud (Malta)	8	37	16
R. Marshall (England)	7	33	21
G. Lackenby (Australia)	7	35	23
S. Robertson (N. Zealand)	7	33	24
J. Long (Ireland)	6	31	28
A. Essam (Egypt)	5	28	25
K. Erwin (Ireland)	5	28	27
J. Allan (Scotland)	5	27	29
M. Lemoy (Belgium)	3	22	35
M. Hallgren (Sweden)	2	23	32
I. Adam (Mauritius)	0	3	40
Group B			
J. McNellan (Scotland)	10	40	11
T. Whitthread (England)	8	34	11
T. Saelim (Thailand)	8	37	18
D. Kwok (N. Zealand)	6	28	22
S. Sawant (India)	6	28	22
L. K. Guan (Singapore)	5	25	27
T. Dada (Pakistan)	4	27	27
A. Thomson (Zimbabwe)	3	20	31

	Wins	For	Agst	Highest break
H. Boteju (Sri Lanka)	3	17	32	
P. Reynolds (Isle of Man)	2	18	35	
P. Rivet (Mauritius)	0	2	40	
Group C				
J.Grech (Malta)	9	39	12	
D. John (Wales)	8	37	14	
J. Bonner (Australia)	8	35	20	
G. Kwok Kwan Shing (Hong Kong)	7	35	22	
W. Pu-ob-Orm (Thailand)	6	29	23	
M. Sobala (Canada)	5	29	27	
L. A. Bux (Pakistan)	5	24	28	
H. Bakhaty (Egypt)	3	23	31	
K. Sirisoma (Sri Lanka)	2	14	33	
H. Ramj (Kenya)	1	13	37	
A. Agustsson (Iceland)	1	10	38	
Group D				
M. Bennett (Wales)	11	40	16	
G. Sethi (India)	9	34	15	
A. Robidoux (Canada)	8	34	22	
G. Burns (Ireland)	8	30	23	
J. Wright (England)	6	25	19	
S. Pavis (N. Ireland)	5	28	27	
B. Bjorkman (Sweden)	5	26	30	
M. Colquitt (Isle of Man)	5	25	30	
K. Fridthjofsson (Iceland)	3	14	32	
L. Nazarali (Kenya)	3	15	34	
D. Barron (Zimbabwe)	3	22	35	

Quarter-finals: Marshall beat McNellan 5(50)-1; John beat Bennett 5(44, 37)-2(30); Mifsud beat Whitthread 5(32, 39, 39)-2; Grech beat Sethi 5(42, 59, 50)-2(41, 30)
Semi-finals: John beat Marshall 8(37, 30, 40, 30, 46, 40, 32, 31)-4; Mifsud beat Grech 8(41, 58, 35)-4(56, 82, 40)
Final: Mifsud beat John 11(68, 32, 34, 59, 31, 39)-6(31, 47, 31, 48)
1986 (*New Zealand*)
Group A

G. Burns (Ireland)	9	36	15	
J. Griffiths (Wales)	7	29	20	
B. Lui (Singapore)	6	26	21	
A. Harris (England)	6	31	22	
N. Nopkachorn (Thailand)	6	30	22	
P. Hawkes (Australia)	4	27	23	
M. Lannoye (Belgium)	3	23	26	
B. Bjorkman (Sweden)	2	15	30	
P. De Groot (N. Zealand)	1	19	33	
A. Thomson (Zimbabwe)	1	11	35	

	Wins	For	Agst	Highest break
Group B				
K. Jones (Wales)	7	29	9	
M. Colquitt (Isle of Man)	6	24	12	
M. Haenga (N. Zealand)	4	25	20	
L. Amir Bux (Pakistan)	4	20	20	
G. Sethi (India)	3	23	19	
C. Sewell (N. Ireland)	3	20	19	
M. Raibin (Sri Lanka)	1	10	24	
A. Verny (Mauritius)	0	1	28	
Group C				
G. Grennan (England)	9	36	17	
S. Sawant (India)	6	31	15	
J. Allan (Scotland)	5	28	22	
W. Pu-Ob-Orm (Thailand)	5	26	22	
K. Doherty (Rep. of Ireland)	5	26	27	
R. Johansson (Sweden)	4	23	27	
G. Natale (Canada)	4	22	31	
G. Campbell (N. Ireland)	3	23	31	
F. Chan (Hong Kong)	2	23	33	
H. Bakhaty (Egypt)	2	20	33	
Group D				
P. Mifsud (Malta)	9	36	10	
B. Gollan (Canada)	8	34	8	
G. Miller (Australia)	6	29	17	
S. Leung (Hong Kong)	5	25	19	
L. Weng Yew (Singapore)	5	26	24	
T. Dada (Pakistan)	3	20	28	
R. Young (N. Zealand)	3	16	29	
L. Cameron (Scotland)	2	15	29	
H. Boteju (Sri Lanka)	2	14	34	
Y. Van Velthoven (Belgium)	1	15	32	

Quarter-finals: Grennan beat Griffiths 5(38, 91)-2(39, 88, 39, 48); Jones beat Gollan 5(64)-1; Burns beat Colquitt 5(60)-0; Mifsud beat Sawant 5(66, 81)-2
Semi-finals: Mifsud beat Burns 8(52, 56)-5(57, 60); Jones beat Grennan 8(37, 41, 51, 83, 40)-7(45, 38, 48, 36)
Final: Mifsud beat Jones 11(41, 55, 60, 34, 43, 42)-9(99, 57, 63, 45, 43, 44, 52, 45, 66)

World Amateur Billiards Championships

	Won	Score (average)	Highest break	No of centuries
1926 (*London*)				
J. Earlham (England)	4	8,000 (25.6)	282	18
G. Shailer (Australia)	3	7,394 (16.8)	203	13
M. Smith (Scotland)	2	6,569 (12.7)	130	4
P. Rutledge (S. Africa)	1	5,902 (12.5)	142	2
T. McCluney (N. Ireland)	0	5,617 (11.9)	144	4

	Won	Score (average)	Highest break	No of centuries
1927 (*London*)				
A. Prior (S. Africa)	3	6,000 (16.6)	184	9
H. F. Coles (Wales)	2	5,533 (12.2)	164	2
L. Steeples (England)	1	5,506 (14.8)	236	9
M. Smith (Scotland)	0	4,499 (12.6)	158	1
1929 (*Johannesburg*)				
L. Hayes (Australia)	3	6,000 (15.5)	136	6
A. Prior (S. Africa)	2	5,512 (16.0)	226	7
H. F. Coles (England)	1	5,592 (14.7)	170	7
P. Rutledge (S. Africa)	0	2,882 (10.9)	164	1
1931 (*Sydney*)				
L. Steeples (England)	4	8,000 (37.3)	461	24
S. Lee (England)	3	7,126 (22.1)	433	18
L. Hayes (Australia)	2	6,113 (15.3)	167	6
H. Goldsmith (Australia)	1	4,995 (13.0)	179	4
W. Hackett (N. Zealand)	0	3,549 (7.7)	97	0
1933 (*London*)				
S. Lee (England)	4	12,402 (28.0)	394	31
T. Jones (Wales)	3	9,883 (18.7)	144	8
A. Prior (S. Africa)	2	9,113 (18.3)	235	13
M. Smith (Scotland)	1	8,292 (17.5)	166	5
J. Blackburn (N. Ireland)	0	6,362 (12.5)	94	0
1935 (*London*)				
H. F. Coles (England)	4	13,665 (28.4)	267	33
J. McGhie (Scotland)	3	9,359 (19.4)	207	11
I. Edwards (Wales)	2	9,814 (18.1)	196	11
S. Fenning (Ireland)	1	9,068 (17.4)	161	6
P. Deb (India)	0	7,461 (13.1)	123	5
1936 (*Johannesburg*)				
R. Marshall (Australia)	3	8,526 (22.0)	248	24
A. Prior (S. Africa)	2	7,014 (17.7)	197	11
J. Thompson (England)	1	7,705 (21.2)	245	15
A. Bowlly (S. Africa)	0	4,548 (9.0)	93	0
Three 2˝ hour sessions				
1938 (*Melbourne*)				
R. Marshall (Australia)	6	17,626 (39.0)	427	59
K. Kennerley (England)	5	14,528 (30.1)	472	45
T. Cleary (Australia)	4	8,535 (19.7)	322	17
S. Moses (N. Zealand)	2	6,727 (13.1)	129	4
M. M. Begg (India)	2	6,685 (13.4)	111	2
A. Burke (S. Africa)	1	5,993 (12.0)	119	1
A. Albertson (N. Zealand)	1	5,805 (12.4)	107	1
1951 (*London*)				
R. Marshall (Australia)	6	14,735 (38.1)	423	42
F. Edwards (England)	5	13,459 (26.7)	345	36
T. Cleary (Australia)	4	12,373 (25.5)	330	31
W. Ramage (Scotland)	3	7,638 (19.1)	151	8
W. Pierce (Wales)	2	6,029 (13.6)	225	3

	Won	Score (average)	Highest break	No of centuries
W. Jones (India)	1	7,202 (16.6)	138	10
E. Haslem (N. Ireland)	0	5,896 (14.1)	125	3
1952 *(Calcutta)*				
L. Driffield (England)	5	8,529 (34.5)	278	31
R. Marshall (Australia)	3	9,237 (37.3)	351	27
C. Hirjee (India)	3	7,701 (22.7)	230	14
W. Ramage (Scotland)	3	6,525 (20.8)	211	10
W. Jones (India)	1	6,731 (23.3)	253	6
A. Yunoos (Burma)	0	3,768 (11.0)	79	0
1954 *(Sydney)*				
T. Cleary (Australia)	4	11,496 (33.5)	682	35
R. Marshall (Australia)	3	11,488 (36.0)	407	35
F. Edwards (England)	2	9,053 (24.7)	328	26
W. Jones (India)	1	8,523 (20.5)	209	17
T. G. Rees (S. Africa)	0	6,271 (16.9)	207	6
1958 *(Calcutta)*				
W. Jones (India)	5	16,493	501	56
L. Driffield (England)	4	14,370	499	48
T. Cleary (Australia)	3	13,626	431	52
C. Hirjee (India)	2	12,853	226	38
W. Asciak (Malta)	1	6,329	154	7
M. Hman (Burma)	0	5,633	215	8
1960 *(Edinburgh)*				
J. H. Beetham (England)	7	9,351	277	29
J. Long (Australia)	6	10,634	353	26
W. Jones (India)	5	12,397	589	30
M. Francisco (S. Africa)	4	7,773	148	11
W. Ramage (Scotland)	3	7,938	283	12
W. Asciak (Malta)	2	8,408	194	11
W. Dennison (N. Ireland)	1	6,231	155	4
A. Ramage (Scotland)	0	5,706	101	2
1962 *(Perth)*				
R. Marshall (Australia)	5	12,367 (35.6)	348	57
W. Jones (India)	5	10,805 (26.9)	489	34
T. Cleary (Australia)	4	9,808 (27.0)	315	27
J. H. Beetham (England)	3	7,626 (22.9)	283	18
S. Benajee (India)	3	8,332 (17.2)	219	9
R. A. Karim (Pakistan)	1	5,657 (11.9)	130	3
W. Harcourt (N. Zealand)	0	5,623 (14.3)	123	5
Play-off: Marshall beat Jones 3,623-2,891				
1964 *(Pukekohe)*				
W. Jones (India)	9	16,628 (24.5)	294	49
J. Karnehm (England)	8	12,953 (21.8)	390	28
M. Ferreira (India)	7	13,345 (19.0)	182	29
M. Francisco (S. Africa)	6	12,957 (22.0)	518	38
A. Nolan (England)	5	12,126 (19.9)	259	26
T. Cleary (Australia)	4	10,781 (13.9)	241	19

	Won	Score (average)	Highest break	No of centuries
H. Robinson (N. Zealand)	3	7,643 (10.5)	85	0
T. Yesberg (N. Zealand)	2	7,528 (10.4)	80	0
M. Mavalwala (Pakistan)	1	8,404 (11.3)	174	1
A. E. Redmond (S. Africa)	0	6,914 (9.0)	107	1
1967 (*Colombo*)				
L. Driffield (England)	8	13,556 (30.5)	421	53
M. J. M. Lafir (Ceylon)	7	12,562 (18.4)	218	31
M. Francisco (S. Africa)	6	12,477 (20.4)	301	32
M. Ferreira (India)	5	11,140 (19.5)	507	22
J. Long (Australia)	4	11,068 (17.5)	261	27
T. Cleary (Australia)	3	9,252 (11.6)	322	15
N. J. Rahim (Ceylon)	2	6,895 (8.8)	116	3
M. S. M. Marzuq (Ceylon)	1	7,153 (7.9)	88	0
F. Holz (N. Zealand)	0	5,350 (7.1)	68	0
1969 (*London*)				
J. Karnehm (England)	9	12,902	232	27
M. Ferreira (India)	7	14,115	629	34
M. Francisco (S. Africa)	7	13,760	335	35
M. J. M. Lafir (Ceylon)	7	12,934	296	28
R. Marshall (Australia)	6	13,033	216	33
M. Wildman (England)	6	11,739	274	22
R. Oriel (Wales)	5	13,306	297	30
S. Mohan (India)	5	13,407	219	24
P. Mifsud (Malta)	2	10,410	173	8
A. Twohill (N. Zealand)	1	10,016	146	12
F. Holz (N. Zealand)	0	6,061	65	0
1971 (*Malta*)				
Group A				
M. Francisco (S. Africa)	4	6,450	321	15
M. J. M. Lafir (Ceylon)	3	4,757	233	4
P. Mifsud (Malta)	2	4,142	134	2
D. Sneddon (Scotland)	1	3,160	121	2
L. Napper (N. Zealand)	0	3,798	87	0
Group B				
S. Mohan (India)	4	5,839	188	11
N. Dagley (England)	3	5,454	330	11
M. Ferreira (India)	2	4,423	227	4
C. Everton (Wales)	1	3,893	205	5
W. Asciak (Malta)	0	4,511	188	7
Play-offs:				
Dagley	3	6,041 ·	348	17
M. Francisco	2	3,981	353	11
Mohan	1	3,822	327	11
Lafir	0	2,514	211	5
1973 (*Bombay*)				
M. J. M. Lafir (Sri Lanka)	9	16,956 (34.1)	859	43
S. Mohan (India)	7	17,016 (30.8)	468	53

	Won	Score (average)	Highest break	No of centuries
M. Ferreira (India)	7	15,639 (25.4)	421	41
P. Tarrant (Australia)	6	13,200 (24.4)	373	36
C. Everton (Wales)	5	9,921 (18.2)	240	17
A. Nolan (England)	4	12,709 (20.8)	265	31
P. Mifsud (Malta)	4	12,253 (18.8)	203	23
E. Simons (N. Zealand)	2	8,521 (12.4)	94	0
B. Kirkness (N. Zealand)	1	8,464 (13.5)	195	7
L. U. Demarco (Scotland)	0	7,488 (10.4)	87	0

1975 (*Auckland*)

Group A

	Won	Score (average)	Highest break	No of centuries
N. Dagley (England)	5	9,257	477	24
D. Sneddon (Scotland)	4	6,272	124	4
G. Parikh (India)	3	6,471	197	16
J. Reece (Australia)	2	4,058	125	4
H. Robinson (N. Zealand)	1	4,529	123	2
M. Shaharwardi (Sri Lanka)	0	4,032	121	1

Group B

	Won	Score (average)	Highest break	No of centuries
M. Ferreira (India)	5	9,022	411	26
C. Everton (Wales)	4	6,043	272	13
R. Close (England)	3	5,449	164	10
T. Yesberg (N. Zealand)	2	4,373	131	3
J. Long (Australia)	1	4,598	157	5
B. Bennett (N. Zealand)	0	3,684	95	0

Play-offs

Semi-finals: Dagley beat Everton 1,293(222)-755; Ferreira beat Sneddon 2,470(211)-681
Final: Dagley beat Ferreira 3,385(200, 228, 202, 314)-2,268(281)

1977 (*Melbourne*)

Group A

	Won	Score (average)	Highest break	No of centuries
N. Dagley (England)	5	7,546	272	16
C. Everton (Wales)	4	4,962	170	7
S. Aleem (India)	3	7,028	263	11
G. Ganim Sr (Australia)	2	6,322	231	6
H. Robinson (N. Zealand)	1	4,133	93	0
J. Nugent (Scotland)	0	4,131	68	0

Group B

	Won	Score (average)	Highest break	No of centuries
M. Ferreira (India)	5	12,554	519	33
R. Close (England)	4	7,252	207	15
G. Ganim Jr (Australia)	3	6,424	192	9
T. Yesberg (N. Zealand)	2	4,349	109	1
W. Weerasinghe (Sri Lanka)	1	4,364	97	0
D. Pratt (Scotland)	0	4,316	108	1

Play-offs

Semi-finals: Ferreira beat Everton 2,155-1,310; Close beat Dagley 1,912(234)-1,781(236)
Final: Ferreira beat Close 2,683-2,564(231)

	Won	Score (average)	Highest break	No of centuries
1979 (*Colombo*)				
Group A				
M. Ferreira (India)	7	14,695	467	40
M. J. M. Lafir (Sri Lanka)	5	12,456	370	30
K. Shirley (England)	5	10,656	195	13
W. Barrie (Australia)	4	8,255	128	2
B. Kirkness (N. Zealand)	4	7,283	214	8
H. Nimmo (Scotland)	2	7,022	105	2
M. S. U. Mohideen (Sri Lanka)	1	6,408	76	0
R. Lim Sin Foo (Singapore)	0	6,433	97	0
Group B				
N. Dagley (England)	6	12,539	466	39
P. Mifsud (Malta)	6	12,193	325	31
S. Agrawal (India)	6	11,924	355	30
G. Ganim Jr (Australia)	3	8,486	267	15
C. Everton (Wales)	3	6,905	211	11
W. A. J. Weerasinghe (Sri Lanka)	3	7,883	202	7
B. Bennett (N. Zealand)	1	6,083	101	1
E. Fisher (Canada)	0	4,198	88	0

Play-offs
Semi-finals: Mifsud beat Ferreira 2,489(338, 285)-1,856; Dagley beat Lafir 2,694(266, 444, 289)-1,692(240)
Final: Mifsud beat Dagley 2,943(361)-2,152

1981 (*New Delhi*)				
Group A				
N. Dagley (England)	6	11,982	416	42
S. Agrawal (India)	5	12,967	384	39
G. Ganim Jr (Australia)	4	7,934	178	13
A. K. B. Giles (N. Zealand)	3	6,895	162	5
D. Sneddon (Scotland)	2	7,071	123	6
J. W. H. Boteju (Sri Lanka)	1	6,312	107	1
A. A. Essam (Egypt)	0	3,948	59	–
Group B				
M. Ferreira (India)	6	13,862	630	58
L. A. Bux (Pakistan)	5	8,712	257	21
R. Close (England)	3	7,161	217	15
J. Grech (Malta)	3	7,388	402	9
D. Meredith (N. Zealand)	3	6,507	154	7
H. Roberts-Thomson (Australia)	2	6,535	151	5
S. M. Shahawardi (Sri Lanka)	0	5,111	77	–

Semi-finals: Dagley beat Bux 2,890(229, 277, 218)-1,505(257); Ferreira beat Agrawal 3,272(213, 532, 327, 527, 630)-1,964(233, 253)
Final: Ferreira beat Dagley 2,725(208, 349, 245, 244)-2,631(223, 296, 281)

1983 (*Malta*)				
Group A				
M. Ferreira (India)	6		463	31
R. Foldvari (Australia)	5		302	30
L. A. Bux (Pakistan)	4		177	9

	Won	Score (average)	Highest break	No of centuries
H. Nimmo (Scotland)	3		224	6
D. Meredith (N. Zealand)	2		157	7
H. Griffiths (Wales)	1		112	1
A. Micallef (Malta)	0		122	6
Group B				
S. Agrawal (India)	5		635	42
N. Dagley (England)	5		368	30
J. Grech (Malta)	5		286	31
V. Ellul (Malta)	2		145	2
R. Lim (Singapore)	2		96	–
W. Loughan (N. Ireland)	2		198	5
H. Boteju (Sri Lanka)	0		120	2

Semi-finals: Agrawal beat Foldvari 2,047(240, 503)-1,900(302, 225, 231); Ferreira beat Dagley 1,983(463)-1,919(258)

Final: Ferreira beat Agrawal 3,933(353, 398, 201, 254)-2,744(242, 212)

1985

Group A

R. Marshall (Australia)	7		396*	
M. Ferreira (India)	6		341	
L. A. Bux (Pakistan)	5		229	
R. Robinson (N. Zealand)	4		100	
D. Sneddon (Scotland)	3		190	
T. Ward (England)	2		106	
Lau Weng Yew (Singapore)	1		92	
S. Clarke (N. Ireland)	0		101	

Group B

G. Sethi (India)	7		604	
S. Agrawal (India)	6		599	
R. Close (England)	5		182	
H. Nimmo (Scotland)	3		146	
D. Meredith (N. Zealand)	3		263	
K. Sirisoma (Sri Lanka)	2		118	
F. Humphries	1		131	
A. Micallef (Malta)	1		138	

*unfinished

Semi-finals: Sethi beat Ferreira 2,513(201, 303)-2,379; Marshall beat Agrawal 2,782(300, 204)-1,872

Final: Sethi beat Marshall 3,809(546, 235, 348, 232, 257)-2,453(201)

World Amateur Championship Records

Snooker

T. Drago (Malta)	132	1984

Billiards

T. Cleary (Australia)	682 (2 pots)	1954
M. J. M. Lafir (Sri Lanka)	859 (5 pots)	1973
M. Ferreira (India)	467 (3 pots)	1979

NATIONAL AMATEUR CHAMPIONSHIPS

ENGLAND
Snooker

1916	C. N. Jacques	1939	P. Bendon	1966	J. Spencer
1917	C. N. Jacques	1940	K. Kennerley	1967	M. Owen
1918	T. N. Palmer	1941–45	No contests	1968	David Taylor
1919	S. H. Fry	1946	H. J. Pulman	1969	R. Edmonds
1920	A. R. Wisdom	1947	H. Morris	1970	J. Barron
1921	M. J. Vaughan	1948	S. Battye	1971	J. Barron
1922	J. McGlynn	1949	T. C. Gordon	1972	J. Barron
1923	W. Coupe	1950	A. Nolan	1973	M. Owen
1924	W. Coupe	1951	R. Williams	1974	R. Edmonds
1925	J. McGlynn	1952	C. Downey	1975	S. Hood
1926	W. Nash	1953	T. C. Gordon	1976	C. Ross
1927	O. T. Jackson	1954	G. Thompson	1977	T. Griffiths
1928	P. H. Matthews	1955	M. Parkin	1978	T. Griffiths
1929	L. Steeples	1956	T. C. Gordon	1979	J. White
1930	L. Steeples	1957	R. Gross	1980	J. O'Boye
1931	P. H. Matthews	1958	M. Owen	1981	V. Harris
1932	W. E. Bach	1959	M. Owen	1982	D. Chalmers
1933	E. Bedford	1960	R. Gross	1983	T. Jones
1934	C. H. Beavis	1961	A. Barnett	1984	S. Longworth
1935	C. H. Beavis	1962	R. Gross	1985	T. Whitthread
1936	P. H. Matthews	1963	G. Owen	1986	A. Harris
1937	K. Kennerley	1964	R. Reardon	1987	M. Rowing
1938	P. H. Matthews	1965	P. Houlihan		

Billiards

1888	H. A. O. Lonsdale / A. P. Gaskell	1914	H. C. Virr	1954	A. L. Driffield
1889	A. P. Gaskell / A. P. Gaskell	1915	A. W. T. Good	1955	F. Edwards
		1916	S. H. Fry	1956	F. Edwards
1890	A. P. Gaskell / A. P. Gaskell / W. D. Courtney	1917	J. Graham-Symes	1957	A. L. Driffield
		1918	J. Graham-Symes	1958	A. L. Driffield
		1919	S. H. Fry	1959	A. L. Driffield
1891	W. D. Courtney / A. P. Gaskell	1920	S. H. Fry	1960	J. H. Beetham
		1921	S. H. Fry	1961	J. H. Beetham
1892	A. R. Wisdom / S. S. Christey	1922	J. Graham-Symes	1962	A. L. Driffield
		1923	W. P. McLeod	1963	J. H. Beetham
1893	A. R. Wisdom / S. H. Fry / A. H. Vahid	1924	W. P. McLeod	1964	A. Nolan
		1925	S. H. Fry	1965	N. Dagley
		1926	J. Earlam	1966	N. Dagley
1894	H. Mitchell / W. T. Maughan	1927	L. Steeples	1967	A. L. Driffield
		1928	A. Wardle	1968	M. Wildman
1895	No contests	1929	H. F. E. Coles	1969	J. Karnehm
1896	S. H. Fry	1930	L. Steeples	1970	N. Dagley
1897–98	No contests	1931	S. Lee	1971	N. Dagley
1899	A. R. Wisdom	1932	S. Lee	1972	N. Dagley
1900	S. H. Fry	1933	S. Lee	1973	N. Dagley
1901	S. S. Christey	1934	S. Lee	1974	N. Dagley
1902	A. W. T. Good / A. W. T. Good	1935	H. F. E. Coles	1975	N. Dagley
		1936	J. Thompson	1976	R. Close
1903	A. R. Wisdom / S. S. Christey	1937	K. Kennerley	1977	R. Close
		1938	K. Kennerley	1978	N. Dagley
1904	W. A. Lovejoy	1939	K. Kennerley	1979	N. Dagley
1905	A. W. T. Good	1940	K. Kennerley	1980	N. Dagley
1906	E. C. Breed	1941–45	No contests	1981	N. Dagley
1907	H. C. Virr	1946	M. Showman	1982	N. Dagley
1908	H. C. Virr	1947	J. Thompson	1983	N. Dagley
1909	Major Fleming	1948	J. Thompson	1984	N. Dagley
1910	H. A. O. Lonsdale	1949	F. Edwards	1985	R. Close
1911	H. C. Virr	1950	F. Edwards	1986	K. Shirley
1912	H. C. Virr	1951	F. Edwards	1987	D. Edwards
1913	H. C. Virr	1952	A. L. Driffield		
		1953	A. L. Driffield		

NORTHERN IRELAND
Snooker

1927	G. Barron	1949	J. Bates	1969	D. Anderson
1928	J. Perry	1950	J. Bates	1970	J. Clint
1929	W. Lyttle	1951	J. Stevenson	1971	S. Crothers
1930	J. Luney	1952	J. Stevenson	1972	P. Donnelly
1931	J. McNally	1953	J. Stevenson	1973	J. Clint
1932	Capt. J. Ross	1954	W. Seeds	1974	P. Donnelly
1933	J. French	1955	J. Stevenson	1975	J. Clint
1934	Capt. J. Ross	1956	S. Brooks	1976	E. Swaffield
1935	W. Agnew	1957	M. Gill	1977	D. McVeigh
1936	W. Lowe	1958	W. Agnew	1978	D. McVeigh
1937	J. Chambers	1959	W. Hanna	1979	R. Burke
1938	J. McNally	1960	M. Gill	1980	S. Clarke
1939	J. McNally	1961	D. Anderson	1981	T. Murphy
1940	*No contest*	1962	S. McMahon	1982	S. Pavis
1941	J. McNally	1963	D. Anderson	1983	J. McLaughlin Jr
1942–44	*No contests*	1964	P. Morgan	1984	J. McLaughlin Jr
1945	J. McNally	1965	M. Gill	1985	S. Pavis
1946	J. McNally	1966	S. Crothers	1986	C. Sewell
1947	J. Rea	1967	D. Anderson	1987	S. McClarey
1948	J. Bates	1968	A. Higgins		

Billiards

1925	T. McCluney	1949	J. Bates	1970	S. Crothers
1926	T. McCluney	1950	J. Bates	1971	J. Bates
1927	J. Sloan	1951	E. Haslem	*1972–73*	*No contests*
1928	A. Davison	1952	R. Taylor	1974	P. Donnelly
1929	J. Blackburn	1953	W. Scanlon	1975	P. Donnelly
1930	J. Blackburn	1954	W. Scanlon	1976	P. Donnelly
1931	J. Blackburn	1955	D. Turley	1977	T. Taylor
1932	W. Lowe	1956	J. Stevenson	1978	W. Loughan
1933	W. Mills	1957	W. Scanlon	1979	J. Bates
1934	W. Lowe	1958	W. Hanna	1980	S. Clarke
1935	W. Morrison	1959	W. Hanna	1981	W. Loughan
1936	J. Blackburn	1960	W. Dennison	1982	P. Donnelly
1937	J. Blackburn	1961	R. Hanna	1983	F. Clarke
1938	W. Lowe	1962	N. McQuay	1984	D. Elliott
1939	W. Lowe	1963	W. Hanna	1985	S. Clarke
1940	*No contest*	1964	{ D. Anderson / D. Turley	1986	D. Elliott
1941	E. Haslem			1987	D. Elliott
1942–44	*No contests*	1965	W. Ashe		
1945	E. Haslem	1966	D. Anderson		
1946	J. Holness	1967	W. Loughan		
1947	J. Bates	1968	D. Anderson		
1948	J. Bates	1969	W. Loughan		

REPUBLIC OF IRELAND
Snooker

1931	J. Ayres	1952	W. Brown	1971	D. Sheehan
1932	*No contest*	1953	S. Brooks	1972	J. Rogers
1933	S. Fenning	1954	S. Fenning	1973	F. Murphy
1934	*No contest*	1955	S. Fenning	1974	P. Burke
1935	S. Fenning	1956	W. Brown	1975	F. Nathan
1936	*No contest*	1957	J. Connolly	1976	P. Burke
1937	P. J. O'Connor	1958	G. Gibson	1977	J. Clusker
1938–39	*No contests*	*1959–60*	*No contests*	1978	E. Hughes
1940	P. Merrigan	1961	W. Brown	1979	E. Hughes
1941	*No contest*	1962	J. Weber	1980	D. Sheehan
1942	P. J. O'Connor	1963	J. Rogers	1981	A. Kearney
1943	*No contest*	1964	J. Rogers	1982	P. Browne
1944	S. Fenning	1965	W. Fields	1983	J. Long
1945–46	*No contests*	1966	G. Hanway	1984	P. Ennis
1947	C. Downey	1967	P. Morgan	1985	G. Burns
1948	P. Merrigan	1968	G. Hanway	1986	G. Burns
1949	S. Fenning	1969	D. Dally	1987	K. Doherty
1950–51	*No contests*	1970	D. Sheehan		

Billiards

Year	Winner	Year	Winner	Year	Winner
1931	J. Ayres	1954	M. Nolan	1972	L. Codd
1932	*No contest*	1955	M. Nolan	1973	T. Martin
1933	J. Ayres	1956	M. Nolan	1974	T. Doyle
1934	S. Fenning	1957	M. Nolan	1975	P. Fenelon
1935	S. Fenning	1958	W. Dennison	1976	J. Rogers
1936	S. Fenning	*1959–60*	*No contests*	1977	E. Hughes
1937	T. O'Brien	1961	K. Smyth	1978	E. Hughes
1938–41	*No contests*	1962	K. Smyth	1979	L. Drennan
1942	S. Fenning	1963	J. Bates	1980	P. Burke
1943	*No contest*	1964	J. Bates	1981	P. Burke
1944	S. Fenning	1965	L. Codd	1982	D. Elliott
1945–47	*No contests*	1966	L. Codd	1984	A. Murphy
1948	W. Brown	1967	P. Morgan	1985	A. Roche
1949	S. Fenning	1968	P. Morgan	1986	
1950–51	*No contests*	1969	J. Rogers	1987	L. Drennan
1952	M. Nolan	1970	L. Drennan		
1953	D. Turley	1971	L. Codd		

SCOTLAND
Snooker

Year	Winner	Year	Winner	Year	Winner
1931	G. Brown	1959	J. Phillips	1974	D. Sneddon
1932–45	*No contests*	1960	E. Sinclair	1975	E. Sinclair
1946	J. Levey	1961	J. Phillips	1976	E. Sinclair
1947	J. Levey	1962	A. Kennedy	1977	R. Miller
1948	I. Wexelstein	1963	E. Sinclair	1978	J. Donnelly
1949	W. Ramage	1964	J. Phillips	1979	S. Nivison
1950	W. Ramage	1965	L. U. Demarco	1980	M. Gibson
1951	A. Wilson	1966	L. U. Demarco	1981	R. Lane
1952	D. Emerson	1967	E. Sinclair	1982	P. Kippie
1953	P. Spence	1968	E. Sinclair	1983	G. Carnegie
1954	D. Edmond	1969	A. Kennedy	1984	S. Hendry
1955	L. U. Demarco	1970	D. Sneddon	1985	S. Hendry
1956	W. Barrie	1971	J. Phillips	1986	S. Muir
1957	T. Paul	1972	D. Sneddon	1987	E. Henderson
1958	J. Phillips	1973	E. Sinclair		

Billiards

Year	Winner	Year	Winner	Year	Winner
1913	Capt. Croneen	1947	A. Ramage	1968	A. Kennedy
1914–21	*No contests*	1948	W. Ramage	1969	A. Kennedy
1922	H. L. Fleming	1949	W. Ramage	1970	D. Sneddon
1923	M. Smith	1950	A. Ramage	1971	D. Sneddon
1924	*No contest*	1951	W. Ramage	1972	L. U. Demarco
1925	W. D. Greenlees	1952	J. Murray	1973	D. Sneddon
1926	M. Smith	1953	J. Bates	1974	D. Sneddon
1927	M. Smith	1954	J. Bates	1975	D. Sneddon
1928	M. Smith	1955	W. Ramage	1976	D. Sneddon
1929	J. McGhee	1956	W. Ramage	1977	J. Nugent
1930	M. Smith	1957	W. Ramage	1978	D. Sneddon
1933	A. Ramage	1958	W. Ramage	1979	H. Nimmo
1934	N. Canney	1959	W. Ramage	1980	D. Sneddon
1935	H. King	1960	A. Ramage	1981	D. Sneddon
1936	N. Canney	1961	P. Spence	1982	W. Kelly
1937	J. McGhee	1962	W. Ramage	1983	H. Nimmo
1938	J. McGhee	1963	W. Ramage	1984	D. Sneddon
1939	*No contest*	1964	W. Ramage	1985	
1940	W. McCann	1965	W. Ramage	1986	
1941–45	*No contests*	1966	W. Ramage	1987	W. Kelly
1946	J. Levey	1967	W. Ramage		

WALES
Snooker

Year	Winner	Year	Winner	Year	Winner
1930	T. Jones	1932	T. Jones	1934	T. Jones
1931	T. Jones	1933	T. Jones	1935	T. Jones

1936	T. Jones	1958	A. Kemp	1974	A. Lloyd
1937	G. Howells	1959	J. R. Price	1975	T. Griffiths
1938	B. Gravenor	1960	L. Luker	1976	D. Mountjoy
1939	W. E. James	1961	T. Parsons	1977	C. Wilson
1940–46	No contests	1962	A. J. Ford	1978	A. Lloyd
1947	T. Jones	1963	R. D. Meredith	1979	C. Wilson
1948	R. Smith	1964	M. L. Berni	1980	S. Newbury
1949	A. J. Ford	1965	T. Parsons	1981	C. Roscoe
1950	R. Reardon	1966	L. L. O'Neill	1982	T. Parsons
1951	R. Reardon	1967	L. L. O'Neill	1983	W. Jones
1952	R. Reardon	1968	D. Mountjoy	1984	T. Parsons
1953	R. Reardon	1969	T. Parsons	1985	M. Bennett
1954	R. Reardon	1970	D. T. May	1986	K. Jones
1955	R. Reardon	1971	D. T. May	1987	D. Morgan
1956	C. Wilson	1972	G. Thomas		
1957	R. D. Meredith	1973	A. Lloyd		

Billiards

1920	H. F. E. Coles	1939	B. Gravenor	1963	R. W. Oriel
1921	H. F. E. Coles	1940–45	No contests	1964	R. W. Oriel
1922	H. F. E. Coles	1946	T. G. Rees	1965	R. W. Oriel
1923	H. F. E. Coles	1947	T. C. Morse	1966	R. W. Oriel
1924	H. F. E. Coles	1948	J. Tregoning	1967	R. W. Oriel
1925	Unknown	1949	I. Edwards	1968	D. E. Edwards
1926	Unknown	1950	W. Pierce	1969	R. W. Oriel
1927	Unknown	1951	W. Pierce	1970	R. W. Oriel
1928	G. Moore	1952	J. Tregoning	1971	R. W. Oriel
1929	J. Tregoning	1953	B. Sainsbury	1972	C. Everton
1930	Unknown	1954	R. Smith	1973	C. Everton
1931	L. Prosser	1955	J. Tregoning	1974	R. W. Oriel
1932	T. Jones	1956	A. J. Ford	1975	R. W. Oriel
1933	T. Jones	1957	R. Smith	1976	C. Everton
1934	Unknown	1958	R. W. Oriel	1977	C. Everton
1935	I. Edwards	1959	A. J. Ford	1978	R. W. Oriel
1936	J. Tregoning	1960	C. Everton	1979	R. W. Oriel
1937	B. Gravenor	1961	R. W. Oriel		No further contests
1938	J. Tregoning	1962	R. W. Oriel		

AUSTRALIA
Snooker

1953	W. Simpson	1965	W. Barrie	1977	R. Atkins
1954	W. Simpson	1966	M. Williams	1978	K. Burles
1955	E. Pickett	1967	M. Williams	1979	J. Campbell
1956	R. Marshall	1968	M. Williams	1980	W. King
1957	W. Simpson	1969	M. Williams	1981	W. King
1958	F. Harris	1970	M. Williams	1982	J. Giannaros
1959	K. Burles	1971	M. Williams	1983	G. Lackenby
1960	K. Burles	1972	M. Williams	1984	G. Wilkinson
1961	M. Williams	1973	M. Williams	1985	J. Bonner
1962	W. Barrie	1974	L. Condo	1986	G. Miller
1963	F. Harris	1975	R. Atkins		
1964	W. Barrie	1976	R. Atkins		

Billiards

1913	G. B. Shailer	1929	A. H. Hearndon	1940–45	No contests
1914–19	No contests	1930	S. Ryan	1946	R. Marshall
1920	J. R. Hooper	1931	H. L. Goldsmith	1947	T. Cleary
1921	G. B. Shailer	1932	A. Sakzewski	1948	R. Marshall
1922	G. B. Shailer	1933	L. W. Hayes	1949	R. Marshall
1923	G. B. Shailer	1934	L. W. Hayes	1950	T. Cleary
1924	E. Eccles	1935	L. W. Hayes	1951	R. Marshall
1925	G. B. Shailer	1936	R. Marshall	1952	R. Marshall
1926	L. W. Hayes	1937	R. Marshall	1953	R. Marshall
1927	L. W. Hayes	1938	R. Marshall	1954	R. Marshall
1928	L. W. Hayes	1939	R. Marshall	1955	R. Marshall

1956	J. Long	1967	J. Long	1978	G. Ganim Jr
1957	R. Marshall	1968	J. Long	1979	G. Ganim Jr
1958	T. Cleary	1969	R. Marshall	1980	G. Ganim Jr
1959	R. Marshall	1970	R. Marshall	1981	G. Ganim Jr
1960	J. Long	1971	M. Williams	1982	R. Foldvari
1961	R. Marshall	1972	P. Tarrant	1983	R. Foldvari
1962	R. Marshall	1973	P. Tarrant	1984	F. Humphreys
1963	R. Marshall	1974	J. Reece	1985	R. Marshall
1964	J. Long	1975	J. Long	1986	R. Marshall
1965	T. Cleary	1976	G. Ganim Jr		
1966	T. Cleary	1977	G. Ganim Jr		

CANADA
Snooker

1979	J. Wych	1983	A. Robidoux
1980	Jim Bear	1984	T. Finstad
1981	R. Chaperon	1985	A. Robidoux

Billiards

1979	E. Fisher	1981	R. Chaperon
1980	S. Holden	1982	R. Chaperon

INDIA
Snooker

1939	P. K. Deb	1956	M. J. M. Lafir	1971	T. Monteiro
1940	P. K. Deb	1957	M. J. M. Lafir	1972	S. Shroff
1941	V. R. Freer	1958	W. Jones	1973	S. Shroff
1942	P. K. Deb	1959	M. J. M. Lafir	1974	M. J. M. Lafir
1943–45	No contests	1960	W. Jones	1975	M. J. M. Lafir
1946	T. A. Selvaraj	1961	M. J. M. Lafir	1976	A. Savur
1947	T. Sadler	1962	R. Marshall (Aust)	1977	M. J. M. Lafir
1948	W. Jones	1963	M. J. M. Lafir	1978	A. Savur
1949	T. A. Selvaraj	1964	S. Shroff	1979	A. Savur
1950	F. Edwards (Eng)	1965	S. Shroff	1980	J. White (Eng)
1951	T. A. Selvaraj	1966	T. Monteiro	1981	G. Parikh
1952	W. Jones	1967	S. Shroff	1984	G. Sethi
1953	A. L. Driffield (Eng)	1968	S. Mohan	1985	G. Sethi
1954	W. Jones	1969	S. Shroff		
1955	T. A. Selvaraj	1970	S. Shroff		

Billiards

1935	P. K. Deb	1954	W. Jones	1971	S. Mohan
1936	P. K. Deb	1955	W. Jones	1972	S. Mohan
1937	M. M. Begg	1956	C. Hirjee	1973	S. Mohan
1938	P. K. Deb	1957	W. Jones	1974	M. Ferreira
1939	P. K. Deb	1958	C. Hirjee	1975	G. C. Parikh
1940	S. H. Lyth	1959	T. Cleary (Aust)	1976	M. Ferreira
1941	V. R. Freer	1960	W. Jones	1977	M. J. M. Lafir
1942	V. R. Freer	1961	W. Jones	1978	M. Ferreira
1943–45	No contests	1962	R. Marshall (Aust)	1979	M. Ferreira
1946	C. Hirjee	1963	W. Jones	1980	M. Ferreira
1947	C. Hirjee	1964	W. Jones	1981	G. Sethi
1948	V. R. Freer	1965	W. Jones	1982	M. Ferreira
1949	T. A. Selvaraj	1966	W. Jones	1983	S. Agrawal
1950	W. Jones	1967	A. Savur	1984	G. Sethi
1951	W. Jones	1968	S. Mohan	1985	M. Ferreira
1952	W. Jones	1969	M. Ferreira		
1953	L. Driffield (Eng)	1970	S. Mohan		

MALTA

Snooker

1947	L. Galea	1961	A. Borg	1975	P. Mifsud
1948	T. B. Oliver	1962	A. Borg	1976	P. Mifsud
1949	L. Galea	1963	M. Tonna	1977	A. Borg
1950	W. Asciak	1964	A. Borg	1978	P. Mifsud
1951	W. Asciak	1965	A. Borg	1979	P. Mifsud
1952	A. Borg	1966	A. Borg	1980	J. Grech
1953	A. Borg	1967	A. Borg	1981	J. Grech
1954	W. Asciak	1968	P. Mifsud	1982	P. Mifsud
1955	A. Borg	1969	P. Mifsud	1983	P. Mifsud
1956	W. Asciak	1970	P. Mifsud	1984	T. Drago
1957	W. Asciak	1971	P. Mifsud	1985	P. Mifsud
1958	W. Asciak	1972	P. Mifsud		
1959	A. Borg	1973	A. Borg		
1960	A. Borg	1974	A. Borg		

Billiards

1947	V. Micallef	1960	A. Asciak	1974	P. Mifsud
1948	No contest	1961	A. Borg	1975	P. Mifsud
1949	E. Bartolo	1962	J. Bartolo	1976	P. Mifsud
1950	W. Asciak	1963	J. Bartolo	1977	P. Mifsud
1951	W. Asciak	1964	W. Asciak	1978	J. Grech
1952	W. Asciak	1965	A. Asciak	1979	P. Mifsud
1953	W. Asciak	1966	A. Asciak	1980	J. Grech
1954	W. Asciak	1967	A. Asciak	1981	No contest
1955	W. Asciak	1969	P. Mifsud	1982	V. Ellul
1956	W. Asciak	1970	W. Asciak	1983	J. Grech
1957	A. Asciak	1971	P. Mifsud		
1958	A. Asciak	1972	W. Asciak		
1959	A. Asciak	1973	P. Mifsud		

NEW ZEALAND

Snooker

1945	S. Moses	1960	T. Yesberg	1975	K. Tristram
1946	J. Munro	1961	F. Franks	1976	D. Kwok
1947	W. Thompson	1962	K. Murphy	1977	D. Meredith
1948	L. Stout	1963	W. Harcourt	1978	D. Meredith
1949	L. Stout	1964	T. Yesberg	1979	D. Meredith
1950	L. Stout	1965	L. Napper	1980	D. O'Kane
1951	N. Lewis	1966	L. Napper	1981	D. Kwok
1952	L. Stout	1967	R. Flutey	1982	D. Kwok
1953	L. Stout	1968	L. Napper	1983	D. Kwok
1954	R. Franks	1969	L. Glozier	1984	D. Kwok
1955	L. Stout	1970	K. Tristram	1985	P. de Groot
1956	L. Stout	1971	B. J. Bennett		
1957	W. Harcourt	1972	N. Stockman		
1958	W. Harcourt	1973	W. Hill		
1959	W. Thomas	1974	K. Tristram		

Billiards

1908	J. Ryan	1917	H. Siedeberg	1926	E. V. Roberts
1909	No contest	1918	W. E. Warren	1927	E. V. Roberts
1910	F. Lovelock	1919	H. Siedeberg	1928	A. Bowie
1911	F. Lovelock	1920	W. E. Warren	1929	L. Stout
1912	H. Valentine	1921	H. Siedeberg	1930	W. E. Hackett
1913	H. Valentine	1922	E. V. Roberts	1931	A. Duncan
1914	N. Lynch	1923	E. V. Roberts	1932	C. Mason
1915	W. E. Warren	1924	R. Fredotovich	1933	A. Albertson
1916	H. Siedeberg	1925	C. Mason	1934	H. McLean

1935	L. Holdsworth	1953	A. Twohill	1971	W. Harcourt
1936	S. Moses	1954	A. Twohill	1972	B. Kirkness
1937	S. Moses	1955	A. Twohill	1973	H. C. Robinson
1938	L. Holdsworth	1956	A. Twohill	1974	H. C. Robinson
1939	R. Carrick	1957	A. Twohill	1975	T. Yesberg
1940	S. Moses	1958	A. Albertson	1976	H. C. Robinson
1941	R. Carrick	1959	A. Twohill	1977	B. Kirkness
1942	R. Carrick	1960	W. Harcourt	1978	B. Kirkness
1943	A. Albertson	1961	A. Albertson	1979	R. Adams
1944	S. Moses	1962	W. Harcourt	1980	D. Meredith
1945	J. Shepherd	1963	H. C. Robinson	1981	D. Meredith
1946	R. Carrick	1964	T. Yesberg	1982	D. Meredith
1947	C. Peek	1965	L. Napper	1983	D. Meredith
1948	R. Carrick	1966	A. Twohill	1984	D. Meredith
1949	R. Carrick	1967	A. Twohill	1985	D. Meredith
1950	R. Carrick	1968	A. Twohill	1986	B. Kirkness
1951	R. Carrick	1969	E. Simmons		
1952	L. Stout	1970	L. Napper		

SOUTH AFRICA
Snooker

1937	A. Prior	1958	R. Walker	1974	S. Francisco
1938	A. H. Ashby	1959	M. Francisco	1975	M. Francisco
1939	A. Prior	1960	P. Mans Jr	*1976*	*No contest*
1940–45	*No contests*	1961	J. Van Rensberg	1977	S. Francisco
1946	F. Walker	1962	J. Van Rensberg	1978	J. van Niekerk
1947	*No contest*	1963	J. Van Rensberg	1979	F. Ellis
1948	F. Walker	1964	M. Francisco	1980	F. Ellis
1949	E. Kerr	1965	M. Francisco	1981	P. Francisco
1950	T. G. Rees	1966	M. Francisco	1982	P. Francisco
1951	T. G. Rees	1967	J. Van Rensberg	1983	P. Francisco
1952	T. G. Rees	1968	S. Francisco	1984	N. van Niekerk
1953	J. Van Rensberg	1969	S. Francisco	1985	P. Smallshaw
1954	J. Van Rensberg	1970	J. Van Rensberg	1986	S. Mouton
1955	J. Van Rensberg	1971	M. Francisco		
1956	F. Walker	1972	J. Van Rensberg		
1957	J. Van Rensberg	1973	J. Van Rensberg		

Billiards

1920	Sgt Bruyns	1950	T. G. Rees	1970	M. Francisco
1921	A. Prior	1951	I. Drapin	1971	M. Francisco
1922	A. Prior	1952	T. G. Rees	1972	S. Francisco
1923	*No contest*	1953	T. G. Rees	1973	S. Francisco
1924	A. Prior	1954	F. Walker	1974	M. Francisco
1925	P. Rutledge	1955	F. Walker	1975	S. Francisco
1926	A. Prior	1956	G. Povall	*1976*	*No contest*
1927	A. Percival	1957	F. Walker	1977	M. Francisco
1928	P. Rutledge	1958	F. Walker	1978	C. van Dijk
1929–30	*No contests*	1959	M. Francisco	1979	C. van Dijk
1931	A. Prior	1960	R. Walker	1980	C. van Dijk
1932–36	*No contests*	1961	M. Francisco	1981	P. Spence
1937	A. M. Burke	1962	M. Francisco	1982	P. Francisco
1938	A. Prior	1963	M. Francisco	1983	C. van Dijk
1939	A. Prior	1964	M. Francisco	1984	C. van Dijk
1940–45	*No contests*	1965	M. Francisco	1985	C. van Dijk
1946	P. G. Kempen	1966	M. Francisco	1986	C. van Dijk
1947	*No contest*	1967	J. Van Rensberg		
1948	P. G. Kempen	1968	M. Francisco		
1949	T. G. Rees	1969	M. Francisco		

SRI LANKA
Snooker

1951	M. S. A. Hassan	1953	M. J. M. Lafir	1955	M. J. M. Lafir
1952	M. J. M. Lafir	1954	M. J. M. Lafir	1956	M. J. M. Lafir

1957	M. J. M. Lafir	1967	N. J. Rahim	1977	M. S. U. Mohideen
1958	M. J. M. Lafir	1968	No contest	1978	N. A. Rahim
1959	M. J. M. Lafir	1969	M. J. M. Lafir	1981	J. W. H. Boteju
1960	M. J. M. Lafir	1970	N. J. Rahim	1982	J. A. Wahid
1961	M. J. M. Lafir	1971	No contest	1983	J. W. H. Boteju
1962	M. J. M. Lafir	1972	N. J. Rahim	1984	K. Scrisoma
1963	M. J. M. Izzath	1973	M. J. M. Lafir	1985	J. W. H. Boteju
1964	M. J. M. Lafir	1974	Abandoned		
1965	M. J. M. Lafir	1975	N. A. Rahim		
1966	M. J. M. Lafir	1976	M. S. U. Mohideen		

Billiards

1951	M. J. M. Lafir	1963	M. H. M. Mujahid	1977	W. Weerasinghe
1952	M. J. M. Lafir	1964	M. J. M. Lafir	1978	J. W. H. Boteju
1953	M. J. M. Lafir	1966	M. J. M. Lafir	1979	W. Weerasinghe
1954	A. C. Cambal	1967	J. K. Bakshani	1981	J. W. H. Boteju
1955	T. A. Selvaraj	1969	M. J. M. Lafir	1982	J. W. H. Boteju
1956	T. A. Selvaraj	1970	M. J. M. Lafir	1983	W. Weerasinghe
1957	M. J. M. Lafir	1972	M. J. M. Lafir	1984	J. W. H. Boteju
1959	M. J. M. Lafir	1973	M. J. M. Lafir	1985	K. Scrisoma
1960	M. J. M. Lafir	1974	S. Shaharwardi		
1961	M. J. M. Lafir	1975	M. S. U. Mohideen		
1962	M. J. M. Lafir	1976	W. Weerasinghe		

FIXTURES 1987-88

September 14–16	CARLSBERG CHALLENGE at RTE Studios, Dublin
September 17–20	LANGS SCOTTISH MASTERS at Hospitality Inn, Glasgow Box office: 041 332 3311
September 24– October 4	FIDELITY UNIT TRUSTS INTERNATIONAL at Trentham Gardens, Stoke Box office: 0782 657341
October 17–25	ROTHMANS GRAND PRIX at Hexagon, Reading Box office: 0734 591591
November 13–29	TENNENTS UK OPEN at Guild Hall, Preston Box office: 0772 21721
December 1–13	HOFMEISTER WORLD DOUBLES CHAMPIONSHIP at Derngate, Northampton Box office: 0604 24811
January 1–10	MERCANTILE CREDIT CLASSIC at Norbreck Castle Hotel, Blackpool Box office: 0253 52341
January 24–31	BENSON AND HEDGES MASTERS at Wembley Conference Centre Box office: 01 902 1234
February 21– March 6	BRITISH OPEN at Assembly Rooms, Derby Box office: 0332 369311
March 16–19	WORLD CUP at International Centre, Bournemouth
March 22–27	BENSON AND HEDGES IRISH MASTERS at Goffs, Kill, Co Kildare
April 16–May 2	EMBASSY WORLD CHAMPIONSHIP at Crucible Theatre, Sheffield By post to: Box Office, Crucible Theatre, Norfolk Street, Sheffield S1 1DA